Pro Visual Studio 2005 Team System

Jeff Levinson and David Nelson

apress®

Pro Visual Studio 2005 Team System

Copyright © 2006 by Jeff Levinson and David Nelson

All rights reserved. No part of this work may be reproduced or transmitted in any form or by any means, electronic or mechanical, including photocopying, recording, or by any information storage or retrieval system, without the prior written permission of the copyright owner and the publisher.

ISBN-13 (pbk): 978-1-59059-460-5

ISBN-10 (pbk): 1-59059-460-6

Printed and bound in the United States of America 9 8 7 6 5 4 3 2 1

Trademarked names may appear in this book. Rather than use a trademark symbol with every occurrence of a trademarked name, we use the names only in an editorial fashion and to the benefit of the trademark owner, with no intention of infringement of the trademark.

Lead Editor: Ewan Buckingham
Technical Reviewers: Gautam Goenka, Bata Chadraa, Anutthara Bharadwaj, Munjal Doshi, Winnie Ng,
  Joe Rhode, Siddharth Bhatia, Amy Hagstrom, Yogita Manghnani, Tom Patton, Alan Hebert, Bill Essary,
  Sam Jarawan, John Lawrence, Jimmy Li, Bryan MacFarlane, Erik Gunvaldson, Adam Singer,
  Chuck Russell, Kathryn Edens, Patrick Tseng, Ramesh Rajagopal, John Stallo, Jochen Seemann,
  Michael Fanning, Ed Glas, Eric Lee, Bindia Hallauer, Michael Leworthy, Jason Anderson,
  Michael Koltachev, Boris Vidolov, James Su, Thomas Lewis, Steven Houglum, Bill Gibson,
  Ali Pasha, Dmitriy Nikonov, Prashant Sridharan
Editorial Board: Steve Anglin, Ewan Buckingham, Gary Cornell, Jason Gilmore, Jonathan Gennick,
  Jonathan Hassell, James Huddleston, Chris Mills, Matthew Moodie, Dominic Shakeshaft,
  Jim Sumser, Keir Thomas, Matt Wade
Project Manager: Sofia Marchant
Copy Edit Manager: Nicole LeClerc
Copy Editors: Marilyn Smith, Jennifer Whipple
Assistant Production Director: Kari Brooks-Copony
Production Editor: Katie Stence
Compositor: Dina Quan
Proofreader: Nancy Riddiough
Indexer: Brenda Miller
Artist: Kinetic Publishing Services, LLC
Cover Designer: Kurt Krames
Manufacturing Director: Tom Debolski

Distributed to the book trade worldwide by Springer-Verlag New York, Inc., 233 Spring Street, 6th Floor, New York, NY 10013. Phone 1-800-SPRINGER, fax 201-348-4505, e-mail orders-ny@springer-sbm.com, or visit http://www.springeronline.com.

For information on translations, please contact Apress directly at 2560 Ninth Street, Suite 219, Berkeley, CA 94710. Phone 510-549-5930, fax 510-549-5939, e-mail info@apress.com, or visit http://www.apress.com.

The information in this book is distributed on an "as is" basis, without warranty. Although every precaution has been taken in the preparation of this work, neither the author(s) nor Apress shall have any liability to any person or entity with respect to any loss or damage caused or alleged to be caused directly or indirectly by the information contained in this work.

The source code for this book is available to readers at http://www.apress.com in the Source Code section. You will need to answer questions pertaining to this book in order to successfully download the code.

For Tami, my wonderful new wife, who kept me going through everything. I love you.
and
My cousin, Dr. Alicia Lindheim, who inspired me to go beyond myself with her courage, conviction, and strength. When the phrase, "where there's a will, there's a way" was written, they were talking about her.

— Jeff Levinson

For Sammi, my love, my inspiration, and my beautiful bride of twenty years, and for our tribe Jake, Josiah, Peter, Grace, and Lydia, my hope. I love you all with all my heart.
and
To my Mom and Dad, who gave me faith and belief in the Lord Jesus Christ, a marriage extending half a century, and a commitment to hard work, integrity, and family.

— David Nelson

Contents at a Glance

Foreword xvii
About the Authors xix
Acknowledgments xxi
Introduction xxiii

CHAPTER 1   Introduction to Visual Studio Team System 1

PART 1 ■ ■ ■ Team Foundation

CHAPTER 2   Team Projects 17
CHAPTER 3   Team Foundation Version Control 59
CHAPTER 4   Project Management 103
CHAPTER 5   Team Work Item Tracking 121
CHAPTER 6   Team Reporting 159
CHAPTER 7   Team Foundation Build 197

PART 2 ■ ■ ■ Team Edition for Software Architects

CHAPTER 8   Application Designer 219
CHAPTER 9   System and Logical Datacenter Designers 255
CHAPTER 10   Deployment Designer 285

PART 3 ■ ■ ■ Team Edition for Software Developers

CHAPTER 11   Class Designer 311
CHAPTER 12   Unit Testing and Code Coverage 339
CHAPTER 13   Static Code Analysis 377
CHAPTER 14   Performance Analysis 403

PART 4 ■ ■ ■ Team Edition for Software Testers

CHAPTER 15   Web Testing 433
CHAPTER 16   Load Testing 471
APPENDIX   Command-Line Tools Reference 497

INDEX 501

Contents

Foreword xvii
About the Authors xix
Acknowledgments xxi
Introduction xxiii

CHAPTER 1 Introduction to Visual Studio Team System 1

What Is Visual Studio Team System? 2
What Are the Benefits of Using Visual Studio Team System? 2
Visual Studio Team System Editions 3
    Team Foundation 4
    Team Edition for Software Architects 5
    Team Edition for Software Developers 7
    Team Edition for Software Testers 8
Visual Studio Integration Partners Program 10
The Effort Tracking Application 10
Summary 13

PART 1 ■■■ Team Foundation

CHAPTER 2 Team Projects 17

Starting Your Team Project 17
    Planning a New Team Project 17
    Connecting to the Team Foundation Server 19
    Creating a New Team Project 20
    Viewing Process Guidance 23
    Working with the Team Explorer 24
Introducing VSTS Components 25
    Process Templates 25
    Project Portal 26
    Work Item Tracking 29
    Documents 29
    Reports 30

    Team Builds 30
    Version Control 31
    Areas and Iterations 32
    Project Alerts 32
   Customizing the Project Portal 32
    Adding an Image 34
    Adding Reports 35
    Working with Lists 36
   Customizing a Process Template 36
    Understanding the Process Template Architecture 37
    Modifying a Process Template 41
   Customizing the Process Guidance 43
   Managing Team Foundation Security 45
    Managing Windows AD Security 46
    Managing Global Team Foundation Security 47
    Managing Project Security 52
    Managing WSS Security 55
    Managing SSRS Security 56
   Summary 57

CHAPTER 3: Team Foundation Version Control 59

   Starting with Version Control 59
   Source Control Explorer 61
    File/Folder Properties 62
   Workspaces 66
   Creating Solutions 68
   Pending Changes Window 70
    Source Files 70
    Work Items 71
    Check-in Notes 71
    Policy Warnings 71
   Changesets 72
    History 73
    Comparing Versions 74
   Labeling Versions 76
   Retrieving Versions 78
   Branching 80

Shelvesets 82
Merging Files 83
Configuring Version Control 89
    Configuring Project Settings 90
    Check-in Notes 93
IDE Version Control Configuration 93
    Plugin Selection 94
    Environment 94
    Visual Studio Team Foundation 94
Creating Custom Check-in Policies 95
    Creating the Policy 95
    Registering the Policy 99
Converting from Visual SourceSafe to Team Foundation
    Version Control 100
Command-Line Access 101
Summary 102

CHAPTER 4 Project Management 103

A Week in the Life of a Project Manager (without VSTS) 104
    Day 1, Monday 104
    Day 2, Tuesday 104
    Day 3, Wednesday 104
    Day 4, Thursday 104
    Day 5, Friday 104
Two Days in the Life of a Project Manager (with VSTS) 105
    Day 1, Monday 105
    Day 2, Tuesday 105
Using Microsoft Project 105
    Retrieving, Adding, and Updating Work Items 107
    Adding Attachments and Links 109
    Areas and Iterations 112
    Column Mapping 112
Using Microsoft Excel 115
    Creating Lists in Excel 116
    Configuring Lists in Excel 117
Using Visual Studio 119
Summary 120

CHAPTER 5: Team Work Item Tracking ... 121

Working with Work Items ... 121
- Using the Form View ... 123
- Using the Query View ... 125
- Using the Results (Triage) View ... 129

Understanding Work Item Types ... 130
- Task Work Items ... 131
- Bug Work Items ... 133
- Risk Work Items ... 134
- Change Request Work Items ... 136
- Review Work Items ... 137
- Requirement Work Items ... 138
- Issue Work Items ... 140

Configuring Project Alerts for Work Item Tracking ... 141
Looking Under the Hood ... 142
Customizing Work Item Types ... 144
- Modifying the Assign To List ... 145
- Creating a New Field That References a Global List ... 149
- Creating a New Work Item Type ... 152
- Assigning Field Reference Names ... 156

Summary ... 157

CHAPTER 6: Team Reporting ... 159

Introducing the Business Intelligence Platform ... 159
Understanding the Reporting Life Cycle ... 161
Using Predefined Team Reports ... 162
Customizing Team Reports ... 166
- Extracting the Report Definition ... 168
- Adding the Report Definition to a Project ... 168
- Modifying the Report ... 169
- Saving the Modified Report Definition ... 170
- Deploying and Viewing Your Report ... 171

Introducing the Team Foundation Data Warehouse ... 172
- Understanding the Data Warehouse Architecture ... 173
- Exploring the Data Warehouse Schema ... 174
- Managing the Data Warehouse ... 181
- Adding Elements to the Data Warehouse ... 182

	Data Mining with Microsoft Excel	182
	Bringing Team Foundation Data into Excel	183
	Creating a Report	187
	Creating a New Report	189
	Summary	196

CHAPTER 7 Team Foundation Build 197

Benefits of Automated Builds 197
Using Team Foundation Build 198
    Creating a Build Type 198
    Running the Build and Viewing Build Results 203
    Viewing Build History 208
Customizing the Build Process 211
    Reviewing the Build Type Configuration File 211
    Retrieving the Build Type 212
    Editing the Build File 212
Using the Build Command-Line Tool 213
Setting Up Continuous Integration Testing 214
Summary 215

PART 2 ■■■ Team Edition for Software Architects

CHAPTER 8 Application Designer 219

Overview of the Distributed System Designers 220
    System Definition Model 220
    Benefits of the Distributed Designers 221
Using the Application Designer 223
    Getting Started with the Application Designer 224
    Defining the Database Component 226
    Adding a Web Service Component 227
    Connecting the Application Types 228
    Defining Operations for ASP.NET Web Service Prototypes 232
    Implementing the Application 233
    Adding a Web Application Component 240
    Adding Comments to Application Diagrams 244
    Understanding Connections and Endpoints 245
    Adding a Web Service Endpoint from a WSDL File 247

Understanding Constraints and Settings 249
    Setting Constraints 249
    Searching Settings and Constraints 250
Reverse-Engineering Existing Solutions 251
Troubleshooting Application Diagrams 253
Summary 253

CHAPTER 9 System and Logical Datacenter Designers 255

Using the System Designer 255
    Creating a New System Diagram 256
    Building a System Diagram from an Application Diagram 261
    Nesting Systems 262
    Viewing Web Service Details, Settings, and Constraints 264
    Overriding Settings and Constraints 265
Using the Logical Datacenter Designer 266
    Creating a Logical Datacenter Diagram 267
    Importing Settings from IIS 277
    Building a Logical Datacenter Diagram for the
        Sample Application 281
Summary 283

CHAPTER 10 Deployment Designer 285

Using the Explicit Deployment Method 285
    Creating a Deployment Diagram 287
    Validating a Deployment Implementation 291
    Generating the Deployment Report 295
Using the Implicit Deployment Method 296
    Building the Deployment Diagram 297
    Validating the Diagram 301
    Setting Deployment Properties 303
    Generating the Deployment Report 305
Summary 307

PART 3 Team Edition for Software Developers

CHAPTER 11 Class Designer 311

Design Goals 311
    Understanding Existing Code 311
    Initial Class Design 312
    Reviewing and Refactoring 312
    Relevant Diagrams and Documentation 312
Microsoft, UML, and Visio 313
Using the Class Designer 314
    Exploring a Class 316
    Viewing Properties 317
    Working with Class Designer Tools and Options 319
    Adding Items to the Class Diagram 320
    Working with Interfaces 327
    Showing Object Relationships 330
    Adding Fields and Properties 333
    Adding Comments 335
Looking Under the Hood 336
Summary 337

CHAPTER 12 Unit Testing and Code Coverage 339

Planning Unit Tests 339
Creating Unit Tests 342
Understanding Unit Tests 346
    Exploring a Test Method 346
    Exploring a Test Class 348
Managing Unit Tests 349
    Using the Test View Window 349
    Using the Test Manager Window 351
    Creating Ordered Tests 353

Setting Up Tests 355
    Configuring Test Runs 355
    Completing the Test Methods 358
    Setting Other Configuration Options 359
Running Tests 359
    Viewing the Test Run Information 360
    Viewing Code Coverage Results 362
    Testing for Exceptions 364
Data-Driven Testing 367
    Building a Test Database 367
    Preparing the Production Database 368
    Setting Up the Test 370
Manual Testing 373
    Creating a Manual Test 374
    Running a Manual Test 375
Testing Using MSTest 375
Summary 376

CHAPTER 13 Static Code Analysis 377

Static Code Analysis vs. Code Reviews 377
Using PREfast 378
    Enabling PREfast Checking 378
    Reviewing PREfast Results 379
    Enabling, Disabling, and Suppressing PREfast Warnings 383
    Annotating Code for PREfast Checks 385
Using FxCop 387
    Enabling FxCop 388
    Examining FxCop Results 388
    Suppressing Messages 390
    Configuring FxCop Rules 391
    Running FxCop from the Command Line 392
    Creating Custom FxCop Rules 392
Summary 401

CHAPTER 14 Performance Analysis 403

Performance Profiling Terms 404
Instrumentation 405
Sampling 407
Running a Performance Test 407

Understanding the Performance Report 409
    Summary Tab 409
    Functions Tab 411
    Caller/Callee Tab 414
    Calltree Tab 415
    Allocation 416
    Objects Lifetime 417
Performance Session Options 418
Target Options 420
Profiling Unit Tests 421
Profiling Web/Load Tests 421
Profiling Production Applications 422
    Command-Line Performance Tools 422
    Profiling Windows Applications and Windows Services 423
    Profiling ASP.NET Applications 425
Summary 430

PART 4 ■■■ Team Edition for Software Testers

■CHAPTER 15 Web Testing 433

Recording Web Tests 434
    Test Steps Explained 437
    Test Detail Properties 437
    Test Options 439
Running Recorded Web Tests 440
    Passing or Failing Tests 443
    Data-Driven Web Testing 443
Coded Web Tests 447
    Coded Data-Driven Tests 449
Extraction Rules 453
    Creating Custom Extraction Rules 454
    Extract Method 456
    Implementing Custom Extraction Rules 456
Validation Rules 457
    Creating Custom Validation Rules 459
Web Test Request Plugins 459
Web Test Plugins 459
Testing Web Services 462

Test Results 465
    Test Results Schema 466
    Publishing Test Results 468
Summary 469

CHAPTER 16 Load Testing 471

Controllers and Agents 472
    Administering a Controller 473
    Configuring the Test Run 476
Load Test Wizard 477
    Scenario 477
    Load Pattern 479
    Test Mix 480
    Browser Mix 481
    Network Mix 482
    Counter Sets 483
    Run Settings 484
    Extending Load Test Settings 484
Load Test Window 488
Analyzing Load Test Results 491
    Counters Pane 492
    Graphs/Tables Pane 493
    Points Pane 495
    Summary Pane 495
Publishing Test Results 495
Summary 495

APPENDIX Command-Line Tools Reference 497

Server Command-Line Tools 497
Client Command-Line Tools 498

INDEX 501

Foreword

Microsoft has always provided world-class development tools for developers. From the release of Visual Basic 1 to Visual Studio 2005, Microsoft has provided groundbreaking tools to make developers' lives easier. With the release of Visual Studio 2005, we've done a considerable amount of work to help the individual developer be even more productive—refactoring, the My Namespace, edit-and-continue, and improvements in the .NET Framework are just a few examples.

But with Visual Studio 2005, we've expanded our focus beyond the developer to the entire development process itself. Visual Studio Team System takes a larger view of the developer's world. It acknowledges the project management aspects of development, the architecture, and the testing phase of the development life cycle; in other words, Visual Studio Team System takes into account the entire software development life cycle. This shift away from purely an individual's perspective is designed to ease the burden on development organizations by helping every member of the team gain more insight, and oversight, of the software development life cycle.

This larger view of the development process promotes communication and collaboration among groups that in the past almost never spoke with each other. It helps project managers to communicate with architects, architects with developers, and developers with testers. And it helps everyone to communicate with stakeholders and to collaborate with other interested observers. By providing timely reporting of events, project status, development statistics, and other information, organizations can leverage Visual Studio Team System to streamline the development process.

Software development has shifted from groups of developers working in the same building to groups of developers working around the world. This shift crosses geographical boundaries and allows teams to collaborate with each other in real time. Team System enables the organization that owns the code to actually own the code! Nightly builds can be performed in the target environment instead of being built and tested in an environment that usually doesn't match the eventual deployment environment. It also helps organizations to keep better track of how their outsourced teams are progressing with the project.

There is an overwhelming industry trend toward a more agile approach to software development. At the same time, corporations are pushing for improved quality and reduced cost through repeatable processes. Out of the box, Visual Studio Team System provides two process templates aimed at meeting the vast majority of team project needs. The MSF for Agile template is great for teams that may not have used any "formal" methods in the past, while the MSF for CMMI process template complements the Capability Maturity Model Integration (CMMI) process improvement approach developed at Carnegie Mellon. These processes help developers not only to be productive, but also to create a framework for repeatable development processes. These process improvements ultimately lead to higher quality, lower cost software development.

With all of this, Microsoft has absolutely not forgotten that it is developers who write the code and run the tests. One of the Visual Studio Team System development team's primary goals is to help developers to write high-quality code. We call this helping teams drive better quality, early and often. With the new testing tools for developers and testers, code can be written with a higher quality (it follows standards, passes unit tests, and performs optimally) and that quality can be tested for at every step of the way. Team System makes continuous integration testing, build verification tests, and development standards easy to implement and follow. These processes, instead of being complicated and difficult to follow, are made exceptionally easy with Team System and will help developers write and release more stable code.

What's in store for the future then? At our core, the things we do at Microsoft are all about empowering people to drive business success. With Team System, we've taken the first steps toward helping individuals and teams be more productive in the development process. Our vision is to further expand our Team System offering to help all members of an IT team communicate and collaborate more effectively. Some of the areas that we're focusing on in the immediate future are better tools for working with databases, more advanced and complete testing tools, better integration with Microsoft Office, and better support for managing your organization-wide portfolio of projects. Though some of these new tools may not even be released under the "Visual Studio" brand, you can be assured that we will work diligently across all our product groups to deliver solutions that will help you and your organization be more successful.

We believe that Visual Studio 2005 Team System is a hallmark product for the software industry. To be sure, we're all extraordinarily proud of what we've released. But, even more than that, we're excited to see the overwhelming positive reaction to these first few steps in making our customers' lives easier. On behalf of the entire team in Redmond, North Carolina, India, Copenhagen, and elsewhere, thank you for your support, feedback, and encouragement.

Prashant Sridharan
prashant@microsoft.com
Director, Visual Studio
March 2006

About the Authors

JEFF LEVINSON is a Solution Design and Integration Architect for The Boeing Company. He is the author of *Building Client/Server Applications with VB .NET: An Example-Driven Approach* (Apress 2003) and has written several articles for *Visual Studio Magazine*. He speaks at various Microsoft user groups and was a speaker at Microsoft's DevDays 2004. Jeff holds the following certifications: MCSD, MCAD, MCSD.NET, MCDBA, SCJP, and Security+. He is currently finishing his Masters in Software Engineering at Carnegie Mellon University. He and his wife Tami live in Redmond, Washington. He enjoys golfing, reading, running, and spending time with his wife.

DAVID NELSON is an Enterprise Solutions Architect and Associate Technical Fellow for The Boeing Company, where he has been employed for 20 years. His tenure at Boeing has allowed him to become expert at various technologies, including database solutions, grid computing, service orientation, and most recently, Visual Studio Team System. David is currently responsible for architecture and design of computing solutions across Boeing, with primary focus on the application of emergent technologies. He has taught Windows Server System (SQL Server, SharePoint Server, and Windows Server) classes, and is regularly invited to present at national industry conferences.

David resides in the state of Washington with his wife and five children, where he enjoys riding horses and motorcycles. He is building a tree fort with his sons, planting a garden with his daughters, and restoring a horse trailer for his wife.

Acknowledgments

Writing a book—any book—is difficult at best. For a new product on which there really is no material to use to research on your own, it is even more difficult. The members of the Visual Studio Team System development team have been incredibly gracious and giving of their time to answer questions, go over features, and provide support in general while they were going through their development and release cycles. All of the information in this book comes from the authors fooling around with the product, trying to implement it in an enterprise environment, and from the developers and program managers at Microsoft. Having said that, the authors would like to thank the following people from Microsoft (in no particular order), keeping in mind that many, many more helped us bring this book to you: Gautam Goenka, Bata Chadraa, Anutthara Bharadwaj, Munjal Doshi, Winnie Ng, Joe Rhode, Siddharth Bhatia, Amy Hagstrom, Yogita Manghnani, Tom Patton, Alan Hebert, Bill Essary, Sam Jarawan, John Lawrence, Jimmy Li, Bryan MacFarlane, Erik Gunvaldson, Adam Singer, Chuck Russell, Kathryn Edens, Patrick Tseng, Ramesh Rajagopal, John Stallo, Jochen Seemann, Michael Fanning, Ed Glas, Eric Lee, Bindia Hallauer, Michael Leworthy, Jason Anderson, Michael Koltachev, Boris Vidolov, James Su, Thomas Lewis, Steven Houglum, Bill Gibson, Ali Pasha, Dmitriy Nikonov, and Prashant Sridharan.

We owe a special thanks to Gordon Hogenson. Neither of the authors is a C/C++ expert. Because of this, we turned to someone who is an expert for help with a section in Chapter 13 of this book. He wrote an excellent discussion of PREfast, clearly explaining what you can do with it to write better code. Thanks Gordon!

The authors would like to also thank our editor, Ewan Buckingham, who stuck with us through this whole process, which took considerably longer than usual. Sofia Marchant, as the Project Manager for this book, kept us on track. She took care of getting the materials to the right people at the right time for reviews and pushing people to get information back to us. Thanks Sofia! Without our Copy Editors, Marilyn Smith and Jennifer Whipple, this book would not flow nearly as well or be so readable. Thank you for all of your advice and rewording! Katie Stence kept everything on track for our production edits.

Without the hard work of everyone at Apress, this book would not be in your hands now.

Jeff Levinson and David Nelson

In addition to all of the great people at Microsoft and Apress, this book has had an effect on everyone around both David and myself. It has taken a lot of time and effort, more so because of the constantly shifting nature of working with a new product. Along that line, I would like to thank the following people from my team at Carnegie Mellon University: Angela He, Kiran Hedge, Ed Shepley, Drew Gattis, and Michael Rosett. They put up with me while I was trying to get my school work done, write a book, work, and do a couple of other things. It was a great year working with a supportive team. As usual, I would like to thank my family for their support and shoulders to lean on. I would like to thank all of the great people I work with at Boeing, from developers to managers and my coworkers, for their support of this endeavor over the last two years.

Finally, I would like to thank my coauthor, David. When I first envisioned the idea for this book, I knew there were two issues: 1) There was just too much to write about on my own, and 2) I knew this was going to be a very long road. So I convinced David that we should write the book together. He hung in there with me, even when it seemed like we were getting new builds every month (which we were most of the time), Microsoft kept changing the name of portions of the product, and they kept changing the feature set. His wife was ready to cause me serious harm for monopolizing David's time, and he got to see his kids for only an hour a day or so. Sammi, I'm sorry! But we're done, and in the end, it was a great experience. Thanks David!

Jeff Levinson

I would like to thank everyone who has been excited and encouraging regarding this project. It has been a long road, and we have learned much. Thanks to those who have listened, guided, and supported this effort: The Guys (Brad Carpenter, Tim Pearson, John Rivard, Sam Jarawan, Jeff Whitmore, Gerd Strom, and Johnny Couture) are my rock. Thanks also to Dr. Karl Payne, my mentor, teacher, and friend. The Cassandra Team (Roger Parker, Richard Lonsdale, Gary Westcott, Fred Ervin, and John Zhang) are early adopters of ideas and technology. The ValSim Team (Mike Maple, Kaaren Cramer, Jacques Rousseau, Phil Trautman, and others) push the edge of technology and thought. Team Canada (Steven Guo, Rob Hickling, Stig Westerlund, and others) who take beta tools and make products that work. The Architects (Todd Mickelson, Mick Pegg, Dick Navarro, Brad Belmondo, David Rice, Marty Kitna, and others) have vision, trust, and work to "get'r" done.

And lastly, thanks to Jeff Levinson, my partner in this endeavor. I have learned a great deal over the past 22 months (yeah, it really has been that long; I found the first e-mail). I would never have taken on a project like this book without Jeff's encouragement, expertise, and drive. Since this was his second book, he patiently guided me through some of the finer points of authorship. He would often say, "This isn't a blog; you need to write it like a book." Jeff did the greater portion of work, and I appreciate him letting me join him on this journey. I also want to thank his new bride Tami for letting us work at the house and take time away from the more important wedding plans. He's all yours now! Thanks Jeff, it was a great adventure.

David Nelson

Introduction

Software development is undergoing a huge revolution right now. That is not to say that this is different from any other time in the history of software development—it is always undergoing a revolution of one type or another. This "new" revolution is a shift in development methodologies from teams working in tightly knit groups in geographical proximity to a global development strategy. Software development teams are now faced with communicating with each other from half a world away.

This book talks about how to perform this work *effectively* using the new Microsoft Visual Studio Team System (VSTS) product. This book covers all areas of VSTS, from the basics to tips and tricks to make it easier to use. Because of our work with the development team at Microsoft, we have been able to include several undocumented features and describe some of the thought processes involved in developing various portions of VSTS. In addition, as architects in a Fortune 500 company, we have a unique experience in starting to implement VSTS in an enterprise environment.

This book begins with a chapter that introduces VSTS. Chapter 1 provides a general overview of VSTS, its various components and editions, and who should use it and why. This chapter also introduces the sample application that we use throughout the book. Following the first chapter, the book is organized into four parts.

Part 1, Team Foundation: The Team Foundation Server is the mechanism (set of integrated services and stores) that enables the communication and collaboration aspect of VSTS. The web services provide a loosely coupled interface between the various artifacts (work item tracking, version control, build, and test). The operational stores provide a real-time repository of team activity that feeds the aggregated data warehouse for team reporting and analysis. Part 1 of the book covers this crucial component of VSTS.

- *Chapter 2, Team Projects*: This is your first hands-on introduction to VSTS. Chapter 2 walks you through creating a new team project, introduces you to the Project Portal, and explains how VSTS leverages various software development life cycles and provides integrated process guidance. Chapter 2 also discusses Team Foundation Server security, from both the user's and administrator's perspective.

- *Chapter 3, Team Foundation Version Control*: One of the much anticipated new features of VSTS is Team Foundation Version Control, a new, enterprise-class source code control system. This chapter covers all of the aspects of the VSTS source code control system. It also gives an in-depth look at the new check-in policies and touches on how these policies integrate with the work item tracking system.

- *Chapter 4, Project Management*: Microsoft has expended considerable effort to bring project managers into the software development life cycle. VSTS provides integration between Microsoft Project, Excel, and the work item tracking store. Project managers can extend the default mappings to any field available in Microsoft Project. Team Explorer provides rapid triage of work items. The Project Portal and reporting site provide a wealth of information about the status of the team project. This chapter describes all of these features.

- *Chapter 5, Team Work Item Tracking*: Work item tracking is one of the hottest new features in VSTS. This feature allows a project manager to create a work item (a task, a bug, an issue, and so on), assign it to a team member, and track the status of it from beginning to end. Stakeholders can see how a certain item is progressing as well. Work item tracking is a fully extensible system, so project teams can create their own work item types. Work item attachments can include documents, links to other work items, code, or URLs. This chapter covers work item tracking in detail.

- *Chapter 6, Team Reporting*: SQL Server Reporting Services (SSRS) was introduced as an add-on to SQL Server 2000 several years ago. With the new SQL Server 2005 and the new SSRS, Microsoft has made this tool the core of the VSTS reporting infrastructure. This chapter covers the details—from the out-of-the-box reports (associated with each process template) to the specific features on which the VSTS data warehouse allows you to report.

- *Chapter 7, Team Foundation Build*: In the past, performing automated builds required a great deal of extra work using Microsoft tools. This chapter covers the new Team Foundation Build functionality and shows how you can use it to increase the quality of the final software product.

Part 2, Team Edition for Software Architects: This part of the book is dedicated to the new distributed designers in VSTS. These designers allow you to architect an entire application and then implement portions of the application: projects, configurations, and settings.

- *Chapter 8, Application Designer*: In this chapter, an overview of model-driven development, Software Factories, and Domain-Specific Languages leads into a discussion of the Application Designer. The Application Designer allows you to take the first step in a "contract-first" development process, in which you design the interface before writing the application. Having defined the operations for your services, you can implement real code that stays in sync with the models.

- *Chapter 9, System and Logical Datacenter Designers*: Systems are defined as deployable units of the overall application. The level of abstraction provided by the System Designer allows multiple designs to facilitate deployment onto varying datacenters, customer sites, or geographic locations. The Logical Datacenter Designer allows the creation of models depicting interconnected hosts and provides invaluable implementation details to both the application architect and the developer at design time. Chapter 9 describes how to use both of these designers.

- *Chapter 10, Deployment Designer*: As you will learn in this chapter, the Deployment Designer allows architects and developers to deploy systems into the target logical datacenters. The result is instant validation on configuration, setting, or hosting constraint conflicts.

Part 3, Team Edition for Software Developers: Software developers now get the benefits of a concrete modeling language and strong unit testing tools to help them visualize and implement code with higher quality. To augment this capability, developers can analyze their code for common errors and ensure their code meets organizational coding standards. They can also analyze their code for performance impacts and ways to improve the application's performance. This part of the book describes the VSTS tools for modeling code, unit testing, and code analyses.

- *Chapter 11, Class Designer*: UML can be confusing and complicated. It can take a long time to write and even longer to implement. The implementation is often poorly done because UML is an abstract modeling language. As you'll learn in this chapter, the Class Designer is a concrete modeling language for .NET. The Class Designer can both forward- and reverse-engineer code in a way that makes sense with .NET.

- *Chapter 12, Unit Testing and Code Coverage*: Developers now have the ability to test their own code directly from within Visual Studio. You can perform detailed tests and gather code coverage statistics to ensure your code is of high quality and is thoroughly tested. This chapter explains how these VSTS features work.

- *Chapter 13, Static Code Analysis*: Static code analysis deals with examining code in order to ensure that standards were followed and that any known defects are caught ahead of time. This includes managed *and* unmanaged code (C/C++). In this chapter, you will learn about how the FxCop and PREfast utilities can reduce coding errors and increase maintainability.

- *Chapter 14, Performance Analysis*: Is your application not performing as you expected? Does it need more speed? Analyze your application and improve your users' experience with the new VSTS performance analysis tools. You can either instrument your application for detailed analysis or sample it for long-term performance monitoring. Use these techniques for code under development or production code. Chapter 14 describes how.

Part 4, Team Edition for Software Testers: Testing is becoming an increasing critical area of software development. Customers expect fewer bugs out of the box, and that means development teams need to provide more testing resources. This part of the book discusses the new VSTS testing tools and how to use them to create more reliable applications.

- *Chapter 15, Web Testing*: Many companies are switching to web applications as a way to decrease maintenance costs and allow users to access applications from anywhere. Testing can often be difficult and time-consuming. With the new web testing tools, you can now easily create scripts to test your web application *or* web services. This chapter covers web testing in detail.

- *Chapter 16, Load Testing*: Do you want to know how your application will stand up under high load? Are you wondering when it will fail and what you need to do to prevent it from failing? As you will learn in this final chapter, using the new load testing tools, you can identify points of failure and determine strategies for dealing with high-load situations.

At the end of the book, you will find an appendix that contains a list of all of the command-line tools available for use with VSTS (client and server).

So, now that you know what this book contains, let's get started.

CHAPTER 1

Introduction to Visual Studio Team System

In the modern world of development, developers no longer work alone or in groups of three or four people in a set of side-by-side cubicles. Today's developers typically work in larger teams scattered across the globe. Developers have become a global commodity. Many companies in the United States perform some type of outsourcing in which they hire developers who work in India, China, Canada, Russia, or other parts of the United States. This presents a unique challenge to software project teams.

Development teams may include project managers, developers, architects, testers, support staff, and others. How do the team members communicate? What information should be shared, and whom should it be shared with? Should some people have access to some code but not other code? These questions apply not only to developers located in different parts of the world, but also to teams that work in the same building or the same city.

The number of issues that face development teams today is huge. The preceding questions cover only the communication of information. This list can be expanded to include (but not limited to) the following:

- What is the application architecture?
- What is our methodology and what are the deliverables?
- How is the application going to be deployed?
- How will the various components communicate with each other?
- What am I responsible for and when do I have to have this work done by?
- Has anyone tested this code yet? Did it pass the tests?
- What are the object dependencies?
- How are we doing change management?

The list of relevant questions grows very quickly. Up until now, there was no easy way to answer these questions except with regular status meetings, a large amount of e-mail, or a lot of expensive phone calls. The information is not always up-to-the-minute accurate, and it takes a lot of time to sift through all of it. These are some of the issues that Microsoft set out to solve with the introduction of Visual Studio Team System (VSTS).

What Is Visual Studio Team System?

VSTS is a suite of tools designed to allow members of a development team to communicate not only with one another, but also with stakeholders, in real time. It also contains a set of tools for developing architectural views of a system, generating code from certain views, testing code at all stages (during and after development), and integrating the development experience with project management.

At a high-level view, VSTS is divided into four areas: integration, architecture, development, and testing. Each of these areas contains tools that cater to a different facet of the development team. Some of the tools are available to all groups of users, and some are targeted at a specific group because they pertain to a responsibility associated with only one role.

But this is a superficial view of VSTS. It is also designed, from the ground up, to help an organization implement an effective development methodology, whether it is the Microsoft Solutions Framework (MSF), the Rational Unified Process (RUP), Extreme Programming (XP), or any of a dozen other types of methodologies. The purpose in implementing a structured methodology is the same as the goals of the rest of the VSTS suite of tools: to build better applications for a lower cost, both in the short term and the long term. This concept of integrating methodology into the development process is ingrained in all aspects of VSTS.

What Are the Benefits of Using Visual Studio Team System?

Who would benefit from using VSTS for their projects? In short, the answer is everyone. Specifically, it benefits project managers, architects, developers, testers, infrastructure architects, users, and stakeholders. Here's how:

- *Project managers* can get up-to-date information on which items on the project schedule are being worked and when they are completed through familiar tools like Microsoft Project and Excel.

- *System architects* can design an application as it applies to the network infrastructure and communicate that to the deployment and development team.

- *Infrastructure support* gets a solid understanding of the deployment needs of the application.

- *Technical architects* can design classes, relationships, and hierarchies that automatically generate skeleton code.

- *Developers* can look at the class diagrams to understand what is occurring. Any changes they make to the code will be reflected in the diagrams—no reverse-engineering of the model is necessary. Code can be effectively unit tested.

- *Testers* can use integrated testing tools, which allow for more thorough testing. Tests can also be run automatically via automated build tools.

- *Application stakeholders* can view reports on the progress of the application through Microsoft SharePoint Services.

As you can see, many individuals can benefit from the use of VSTS. These benefits translate directly in a higher return on investment because everything becomes easier and faster for everyone.

Aside from individuals who benefit from using VSTS, organizations and departments will also find tremendous advantages in using this tool. The first and most obvious benefit is that it promotes communication between team members, which is crucial to the success of a project. It allows for problems to be caught early and solved quickly before they become serious issues that affect the schedule. These problems can range from developers not completing work on time to bugs in the code.

VSTS also allows for the analysis of work across multiple projects. It becomes simple for organizations to track their project history and use that information to predict future project schedules. Projects can be reported on by category, developer, deliverable, milestone, and so on. You literally have the power of an online analytical processing (OLAP) database at your fingertips, filled with all of your project information down to the code level and bug-tracking level. To achieve this type of reporting, you've needed to use several different, costly systems. With VSTS, it is all rolled into one integrated system.

All of these benefits come down to one thing: a higher return on investment with one tool than you would get with combinations of tools. When you use one tool for each area of development—such as Borland JBuilder for development, CVS for source control, Rational ClearQuest for issue tracking, Cognos ReportNet for reporting, Ant for building, and JUnit for testing—it becomes exceedingly difficult to keep things simple. On the other hand, you have the following benefits with VSTS:

- VSTS allows all developers to use one tool with which they are familiar. It does not require a developer to learn how to use six different tools to perform the task.

- VSTS integrates all of the needed functionality, including a project management tool and reporting tool, directly into one interface—something that no other integrated development environment (IDE) can do in its out-of-the-box version.

But let's say that you have an in-house testing tool that you would rather use than the tool that comes with VSTS. Because VSTS is an extensible environment, integrating other tools into it requires a minimal amount of work (depending on what you want to integrate). Many tool vendors have been working with Microsoft to create integration points with their tools so that you can swap them with ones that come with VSTS. You are not locked into a wholly Microsoft solution.

All of these points lead to only one conclusion: there is no downside to using VSTS.

Visual Studio Team System Editions

VSTS comes in three different editions and a core component called Team Foundation. This section describes each of these (which correspond to the sections in this book), their tools, and their goals. While this is the out-of-the box functionality available with VSTS, as noted in the previous section, is also highly extensible. Figure 1-1 shows an overview of the VSTS suite.

Figure 1-1. *Visual Studio Team System editions and main components*

Team Foundation

Team Foundation is the server-based component of VSTS. It is the *Team* in Team System. Without Team Foundation, all of the other components of VSTS are essentially stand-alone components that run on the client. Once Team Foundation becomes part of the picture, the various client pieces work together as a cohesive unit. Chapters 2 through 7 cover Team Foundation.

As we mentioned previously, VSTS is designed to provide a framework in which applications can be built. Many companies are working to improve their processes by using the Capability Maturity Model Integrated (CMMI) from Carnegie Mellon's Software Engineering Institute (SEI). With VSTS, Microsoft is releasing the only methodology recognized by SEI as being CMMI level 3 compliant. This methodology is the MSF for CMMI Process Improvement, Version 4.0. The template and instructions on how to use the methodology are all included with VTST. So, what is so significant about this? The U.S. Government uses CMMI levels in determining source selections for contract awards.

Team Foundation Version Control

Team Foundation contains a brand-new version control tool, which is designed for large-scale teams and is backed by SQL Server 2005. For developers, it will be a welcome addition to their toolbox and offer an easy alternative to Visual SourceSafe. Also, unlike Visual SourceSafe, Team

Foundation version control supports document (or code module) security. In addition to supporting developers, it also supports project managers and overall application reporting to the stakeholders.

The final touch for the new version control tool is that it allows you to implement policies to make sure that code meets certain requirements before it is checked in. This helps to ensure that the code goes through a consistent, repeatable process check before check-in.

Project Portal

Another key piece of Team Foundation is the Project Portal. This is a Windows SharePoint Services (WSS) site that serves as a central communication tool for the entire team. Stakeholders can go to this website to review the current status of various tasks on the project, view nightly build and test reports, and communicate with team members.

SharePoint also serves as a project documentation repository (with versioning). This is in contrast to how teams typically set up repositories today—in the file system.

Team Foundation Build

Team Foundation Build is a component that allows a server or workstation to become a build machine. Team Foundation Build automatically gets the latest version from the version control tool, compiles it, deploys it, and runs any automated tests (unit or web tests) against the build. The results of the compilation and testing are stored in the VSTS data warehouse.

Work Item Tracking

Work item tracking is another feature of Team Foundation. Work items can be created in Microsoft Project (directly from the work breakdown structure) or Excel and loaded into Team Foundation as a work item. These work items can be assigned to developers. When team members check their items into the version control, they can associate changes with specific work items. The status of these work items is then reflected on the Project Portal. Work item association can be enforced via policies as well.

Reporting

The final feature of Team Foundation is the reporting component, backed by the new version of SQL Server Reporting Services (SSRS). Out of the box, the reports cover areas such as the number of open bugs, closed bugs, and in-work bugs; work item status; build results; and other information.

As an added bonus, the SSRS features an end-user ad-hoc report builder, so users can create their own reports or customize existing reports. This, combined with the VSTS data warehouse, allows an organization to mine the data for trends in the overall software development life cycle.

Team Edition for Software Architects

Various types of architects may be assigned to a project, and each has different responsibilities. The one thing that all architects have in common is that they must communicate aspects of the architecture to stakeholders in various ways. To facilitate building and then communicating an architecture, Team Edition for Software Architects provides a set of designers, as well as other tools to ease the job of the architect. Chapters 8 through 10 cover the Team Edition for Software Architects.

Designers

The four VSTS designers are Application Designer, System Designer, Logical Datacenter Designer, and Deployment Designer. These designers are a core tenant of Microsoft's focus on Model Driven Architecture (MDA). However, VSTS moves models out of the cumbersome, documentation-only realm and into the practical realm.

The problem with modeling with other tools is that the models are abstract representations of the architecture. They do not mean anything from a tangible perspective. The designers in VSTS have a concrete implementation. When you create a model with VSTS, you also generate the configuration for that model, which is based on physical properties of the object to which you are deploying your application. This allows VSTS to check for inconsistencies in your architecture against the actual physical machines with which you will be working.

Domain-Specific Language

On top of this approach, VSTS leverages the concept of Domain-Specific Languages (DSL). DSL is the language in which the concrete implementation of hardware or software is written. This allows the end users of VSTS to build model objects against which specific implementations can be validated.

Tip Microsoft has released a set of tools specifically for creating domain-specific frameworks. These tools can be found at http://lab.msdn.microsoft.com/teamsystem/workshop/dsltools/default.aspx.

The language is a set of metadata that describes the physical implementation of a given configuration. Microsoft has introduced the System Definition Model (SDM) to provide a schema definition for distributed systems. Because these designers are built in concrete terms, they are easily understandable by their intended audience—data architects, infrastructure architects, or other application architects.

Visio

Team Edition for Software Architects also includes everyone's favorite modeling tool: Visio. This tool is available in all editions of VSTS, but will probably be most used by architects.

Visio for Visual Studio allows for the creation of Unified Modeling Language (UML) diagrams and provides the ability to model different views for different audiences of the application. Visio allows you to create those abstract, notional views, which are helpful in trying to figure out and pinpoint what the architecture will be and then communicate it to everyone else.

Team Edition for Software Developers

Team Edition for Software Developers provides tools that allow developers to quickly understand code structure, generate code from models, write unit tests, and analyze code for errors. The goal of these tools is to reduce the amount of time developers need to actually write code and to ensure that the code that is produced is of a higher quality. Chapters 11 through 14 cover the Team Edition for Software Developers.

Class Designer

To understand and generate code, VSTS provides the Class Designer. This is one of the tools available in all editions of VSTS because it is useful to a wide range of people. Architects can use the tool to create high-level class designs. Developers can generate skeleton classes, for which they can then fill in the details. Testers can use the Class Designer to understand the relationship between classes in order to help them analyze errors. We have included the Class Designer in the Team Edition for Software Developers section of the book because, for the most part, the primary audience is the developer.

The Class Designer also dynamically generates code based on the model, reads changes in code, and incorporates those changes into the model. The key point here is that the model and the code *are never out of sync*. This solves the problem of documentation becoming stale.

Unit Testing

Once the general outline of code is produced, tests can be written for the code. They can also be written after the code is finished. It is entirely up to you, but one thing is certain—with the VSTS unit testing tools, testing will be a lot easier, faster, and more streamlined.

Creating a unit test is as easy as right-clicking a class or a method, selecting Create Unit Tests, and filling in a couple of variables. It could also be more complicated, since unit testing supports data-driven testing, which allows for more complex scenarios without having to continually rewrite the unit tests or write many tests for one method. The unit testing functionality is also part of the Team Edition for Software Testers.

As part of the unit testing functionality, VSTS provides a very cool code coverage tool. This tool not only tells you what percentage of your code was covered versus not covered, but it can also highlight code to show you fully covered lines of code, partially covered lines of code, and code that was not covered at all. We'll elaborate on this in Chapter 12, but to give you an idea of how important this tool is, let's consider an example. Suppose you write a method 100 lines long and you run the unit tests against the code. The results all come back as passing, which is good, but the code covered comes back as 60%, which is bad, because 40 lines of code were never touched. This indicates that while all your tests passed, either you did not test something you should have or there is no way to test that code, and so it is dead code that should be removed.

Code Analysis

Since the inception of .NET 1.0, Microsoft has offered a relatively unsupported tool called FxCop (available for free from http://www.gotdotnet.com). VSTS incorporates this tool into the IDE so that static code analysis on managed code can be performed as part of a compilation, and policies can be written against the results of the analysis. This tool was originally created to ensure that Microsoft developers were following the correct standards when writing the .NET Framework. So, if you follow the coding recommendations of this tool, you will be writing to the same standards as Microsoft (in terms of format, completeness, and the standards of the .NET Framework).

VSTS also incorporates a tool to help developers of unmanaged code. This tool, called PREfast, has been in use within Microsoft for several years as a means for developers to check their C/C++ code for common errors such as buffer overruns. This analysis tool is run simply by checking a box in the project properties. It is customizable to an extent that allows you to implement checks not included in the out-of-the-box product.

Performance Analysis

VSTS also incorporates performance analysis tools, which allow developers to test their code for bottlenecks. In the past, performance testing around a .NET application typically involved monitoring a lot of Windows Performance Monitor logs, which provided less-than-helpful information.

The new performance analysis tools allow you to either instrument or sample your code, depending on the situation, so you can gather details at the individual method level or at the application level. Best of all, you can institute performance monitoring on a production application to pinpoint specific problems that may not have been apparent during development.

Team Edition for Software Testers

Team Edition for Software Testers is devoted to testing all aspects of your code. It includes the unit testing functionality (described in the preceding section about the Team Edition for Software Developers), load testing, manual testing, and web testing, as well as the Test Manager tool. Chapters 15 and 16 cover the Team Edition for Software Testers.

Note While VSTS does not include a Windows Forms testing capability, forms can be tested via the manual tests. In addition, the test facilities are highly extensible, and many third-party tools will probably be available to fill this niche!

Test Manager

Test management is a key component of the testing infrastructure because it allows you to organize your tests. You can run these tests in a noninteractive fashion from the command line or from the Team Foundation Build process. You can organize your tests into lists in order to run tests on like processes. Dependencies can be created between tests via an ordered test list and individual tests, or lists of tests can be slated to run at any given time. The Team Edition for Software Developers includes a subset of the Test Manager tool.

Web Testing

More and more applications are moving to the Web in today's Internet- and intranet-based world. Because of this, Microsoft rewrote the Application Center Test (ACT) web testing tool and included it with VSTS. And when we say they rewrote it, we mean it. It is a completely different tool and far, far more powerful than ACT was. You can interactively record tests and play back tests (which are displayed visually for you as the test is running). The tests can be changed in the IDE, and they can be converted to coded tests, which allow you the freedom to do virtually anything in a test you want via managed code instead of scripting, which had to be done with ACT.

All of the information about a test is recorded. If there is something additional you want to record, a custom extraction rule can be coded to do it. If you want to validate a result in the page and take an action based on the result, you can. The tests can also be run with values supplied from a database. That means that the testing can include dynamic navigation of a website. Think times can be added to each step of the test to simulate real-world browsing of a website.

Manual Testing

Another Team Edition for Software Testers feature is manual testing. This allows you to run tests that are based on a list of steps. The pass/fail status of these tests is recorded, just as any additional test is. Code coverage (if enabled) is captured for these tests as well. The steps for these tests can be written in Microsoft Word or in a plain text file in any format your organization may use.

Load Testing

Finally, the Team Edition for Software Testers provides for load testing. Load testing is designed to see how your application (hardware and software) performs under a real-world load. The options available allow for the testing of almost any situation imaginable. You can set the type of browser that is accessing the site, the type of network connection the browser is using to access the site, the way in which the think times are simulated (set times or a normal distribution, if at all), which tests are actually run as load tests, and their distribution. Ramp up times can also be set, or the tests can be run at a constant user load.

You can run the load tests from the local machine, which will simulate all of the connections. Alternatively, you can test via agents and a controller from many different machines. The controller directs the agents to run the test(s) and records the result in one location. A typical setup for this is a lab where you may have 20 test machines hitting one box with a website. This saves you the time and effort of starting the tests on all of the machines individually. The data that is collected is detailed and useful, and there is a lot of it. Every aspect of the test is recorded from both the software and the hardware perspective, and errors are stored for later analysis. The entire test result is saved to the VSTS data warehouse (if you are working with the Team Foundation piece).

Visual Studio Integration Partners Program

Visual Studio Integration Partners (VSIP) is a Microsoft program that gives developers and companies access to the application program interface (API) documentation, extensibility toolkit, and samples for Visual Studio and VSTS. With the toolkit, VSTS supports extensibility in all areas. This extensibility ranges from customizing the designers to incorporating new types of tests (such as Windows Forms tests). Many of these aspects of VSTS are touched upon briefly in upcoming chapters, and some examples are shown. However, Microsoft prefers that developers and companies who wish to provide extensibility for VSTS join the VSIP program. It is free, so there is no reason not to join it.

■**Note** There are various "levels" of the VSIP program. Free access to the extensibility toolkit is the basic level. Additional levels provide partnerships with Microsoft and access to various groups within Microsoft. It is well worth joining for commercial software development companies.

You can access the VSIP website (and join the program) at http://msdn.microsoft.com/vstudio/partners/default.aspx. There is a wealth of extensibility information located here.

The Effort Tracking Application

Throughout this book, we'll use a simple application as an example. This is a web-based application that records work engagements and stores them in a SQL Server database. The web application connects to a web service, which connects to the database. The deployment of this application is shown in Figure 1-2.

Figure 1-2. *Effort Tracking application logical deployment*

■**Note** The actual physical deployment is such that the website and web service are on the same machine but completely separated so they can be deployed in either configuration. The database itself can be located on the same machine or another machine.

The security is controlled via standard Forms security, where the username and password are stored in the database (obviously not a best practice, but for demonstration purposes only). The database contains four tables, as shown in Figure 1-3.

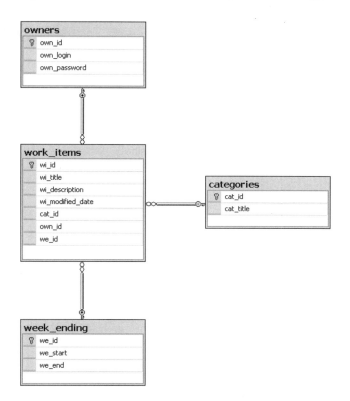

Figure 1-3. *Effort Tracking data model*

The application works as follows:

- User logs on to the system (or registers).
- User is redirected to the Effort Tracking page.
- User selects the week he wants to view.
- User adds a new engagement by clicking Add and entering the title, description, division, and the week ending date, and then clicks OK.
- User can edit or delete a record by clicking the appropriate link. The detail window is displayed, and the user can either confirm the deletion or change and save the record.

The various screens of the application are shown in Figures 1-4, 1-5, and 1-6.

Figure 1-4. *Effort Tracking login/add new user screen*

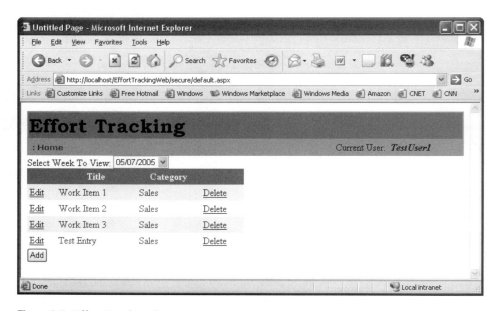

Figure 1-5. *Effort Tracking homepage*

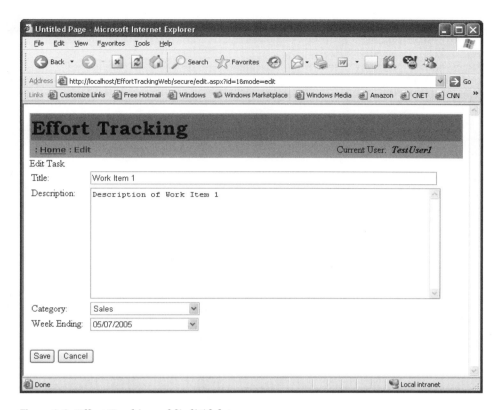

Figure 1-6. *Effort Tracking add/edit/delete page*

The web service comprises the bulk of the code for this application. There are eight methods in the web service, which handle all of the functions of the user interface.

Caution The sample application is designed to be used with the examples included in the various chapters. In many cases, it does not conform to proper development guidelines, especially with regard to security. While we do point out some best practices in this regard, this application should not be used as a model for building any type of secure applications.

Summary

Various problems face development teams today, and these can cause a project to fail. You have seen how VSTS can help organizations and individual projects solve these problems and provide a positive return on investment for everyone.

This chapter has provided a high-level view of VSTS. It described each of the editions of VSTS and an overview of the benefits they offer. Here's a quick summary:

- Team Foundation provides a new version control tool, work item tracking, Team Foundation Build, and core integration and communication features available to all stakeholders in a project.

- Team Edition for Software Architects provides architects the ability to design a system and communicate that design effectively to the stakeholders. It also provides the ability to deploy the design into logical data centers and autogenerate real code.

- Team Edition for Software Developers provides developers with the ability to understand code, generate code, and unit test code quickly and easily. It also provides the ability to analyze code for defects and to ensure conformance to coding standards.

- Team Edition for Software Testers provides testers with the ability to test all aspects of the code. Testing covers web, manual, and load testing. Test management is provided to help organize and describe the testing process.

Chapter 2 introduces the process of creating a team project. You'll explore the methodology templates and process guidance, along with how to customize them. You will also learn how to configure the security for Team Foundation, the Project Portal, and SQL Server.

PART 1

Team Foundation

CHAPTER 2

■■■

Team Projects

In our current positions (our "day jobs," when we're not authoring books), Jeff and I spend a great deal of time performing independent reviews of projects in some form of peril. We are brought in for technical expertise and insight, but the vast majority of time, the key finding is a lack of communication. The classic line from *Cool Hand Luke* (1967) is fitting: "What we have here is a failure to communicate."

The *team project* is all about communication. The resounding message throughout VSTS is that of the team, and this concept comes to life by the instantiation of a team project.

The notion of a team project appears at several levels. The conceptual level is that of the business view or customer view. It is the reason the project exists. What problem are you trying to solve, how is the project being funded, how large is the team, and most important, what will the code name and logo be for the project? The logical level includes the technical view of the team project. What is the underlying architecture, which set of technologies are being used, what process is being followed, and will it fit with our existing infrastructure? Finally, there is the VSTS view of a team project. A VSTS team project is a physical thing.

This chapter will explore all of the features of the team project, how it integrates with VSTS, and how it makes the exchange of information easier for everyone on the team.

Starting Your Team Project

Before you dive into creating a team project, you should take the time to plan what template it will use, its roles and security, and other aspects. We'll begin with some guidance on planning your project, and then get started with a new team project.

Planning a New Team Project

You might have heard of the carpenter's expression "measure twice, cut once." It is meant to remind the novice that acting without planning can be very expensive. Consider also the account of a groundskeeper who lays intricate pathways through his meticulous lawns. After a few months of use, dirt pathways are etched in the grass, because the planned pathways were inconvenient. This second tale is intended to highlight that if your plan is impractical, it will be bypassed for convenience at the expense of elegance. Therefore, the realistic conclusion is that planning is both necessary and dangerous. That statement will send most project managers running for their Gantt charts. But we have seen far too many overplanned projects that never see the light of day. Fortunately, the Team Foundation Server bridges the gap between acting without planning and overplanning the unknown.

Both the Agile and Formal methodologies provide prescriptive guidance with the goal of delivering quality solutions, not just pretty documents. Best of all, you can tailor your process at any stage of the project to provide the ultimate in flexibility. In planning a team project, you need to address seven high-level areas:

Determine the process template to be used: If you are part of a large enterprise, you may already have a process methodology that is prescribed for you. If you are supporting specific industry or government contracts, you may be required to support the Capability Maturity Model Integration (CMMI) process improvement approach. If you use a third-party process that is supported by a template such as Scrum, Rational Unified Process (RUP), or Fujitsu, you should use the third party's provided template. If you have a relatively small project with a short life cycle, the Agile process would be a good place to start. Even after you have chosen your process template, you have a lot of freedom to add or change components, such as work item types, reporting, areas, and iterations.

Define roles and security: Roles and security for a project can be either fine- or coarse-grained, depending on your needs. You may find that only a few security groups cover all the roles on your project, or you may need to build a multilayered structure to meet all your needs. This chapter covers server-level security. Source code security will be discussed in Chapter 3.

Gather team work products: If you have existing artifacts that you want to reuse in other projects, such as best practices, coding standards, or templates, you can include these in the document libraries of the Windows SharePoint Services (WSS) portal. You can also design a standard structure for your work products, leveraging the portal document libraries that can be reused by subsequent projects.

Plan for version control: When you create a new team project, you are prompted either to create an empty source code control repository or to branch off an existing one. If you have unique check-in policies, you will want to create a new source code control repository. You will need to determine which fields you want to capture at check-in time and what type of check-in policies you want to enforce. If your organization already has mandatory policies, you can extend the predefined policies by creating a custom policy plugin. Version control will be covered in detail in Chapter 3.

Determine project work item types: Your team will need to agree on the set of work items to include in the project template. It is best to review the work item types that ship with the existing templates and choose the ones that work best for your project. It is easy to export, modify, and import work item types for a project or to create your own from scratch. Work item customization is covered in Chapter 5.

Determine the project structure: To properly categorize and report on your project, you will need to determine the organizational areas and the project iterations you want to include. This classification structure is made up of parent and child nodes. The project areas may be organizational, feature areas, or technical tiers (such as database, application layer, and client layer). The iterations have to do with the repeating cycles your project will go through. You can also apply security to areas of your project.

Determine project reporting needs: Your organization may already have a discrete set of metrics that each project is measured against. If not, there are a number of predefined reports provided in each of the default process templates. Project reporting is built off of SQL Server Reporting Services (SSRS) and an integrated data warehouse. SSRS provides complete report customization for your project to leverage. Team reporting is discussed in Chapter 6.

Connecting to the Team Foundation Server

Before you can create a new team project, you need to connect to the Team Foundation Server.

Note You must install the Team Explorer add-in to Visual Studio in order to connect to a Team Foundation Server and launch the New Team Project Wizard. There is no command-line tool for creating a new team project.

Follow these steps to connect to the Team Foundation Server:

1. Select View ➤ Team Explorer from the main menu bar, if the Team Explorer is not already visible.

2. Select Tools ➤ Connect to Team Foundation Server from the main menu bar.

3. Click the Servers button, and then click the Add button.

4. Enter the name of the server where the Team Foundation application tier is located, as shown in Figure 2-1, and then click OK.

Figure 2-1. *The Add Team Foundation Server dialog box*

5. Select the Server you just added, and then click OK.

6. Click OK in the Connect to Team Foundation Server dialog box.

Any team projects that have previously been created on the Team Foundation Server are listed here. The Team Explorer will now list your server, along with a My Favorites node (discussed in the "Working with the Team Explorer" section later in this chapter).

Creating a New Team Project

If you are a project lead or administrator, you can create a team project using the New Team Project Wizard and an existing process template.

To create a team project, follow these steps:

1. Right-click the Team Foundation Server node in the Team Explorer and select New Team Project, as shown in Figure 2-2. This will launch the New Team Project Wizard. Optionally, you can select File ➤ New ➤ Team Project.

Figure 2-2. *Selecting to create a team project*

Note We named our application server Kiona and our data server Januik. These names refer to wineries in Washington State. (We name our lab servers after wineries and scotch houses.)

---

2. In the New Team Project dialog box, enter the team project name as EffortTracking, as shown in Figure 2-3, and then click Next.

3. Select a process template. Selecting the process template when you create your team project is the key decision point in the entire procedure. Everything that follows is based on this one decision, as described in this chapter. For this example, choose MSF for CMMI Process Improvement – v4.0, as shown in Figure 2-4. Click Next to continue.

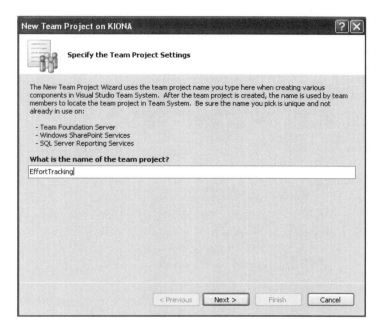

Figure 2-3. *Naming your team project*

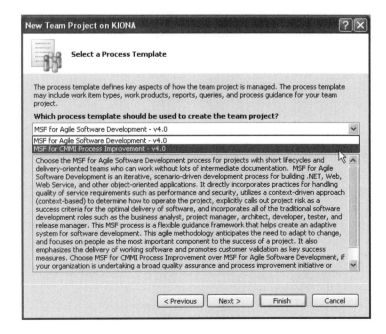

Figure 2-4. *Selecting a process template*

4. On the next wizard page, provide a title for the team project portal site and an optional description.

5. Specify your source control settings. For this example, select to create an empty source control folder, as shown in Figure 2-5.

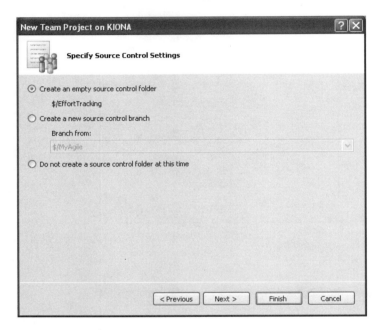

Figure 2-5. *Specifying source control settings*

6. The next wizard page will show your selections. Click Finish.

Note It can take a long time to create a new team project. Behind the scenes, a lot is taking place. You can follow along by watching the status messages.

---

7. After the process is complete, the final wizard page will inform you that your team project was created, as shown in Figure 2-6. You can either view the team project creation log or select Close to finish the wizard. We recommend that you view the creation log, if for no other reason than to appreciate the amount of work performed in the creation of the team project.

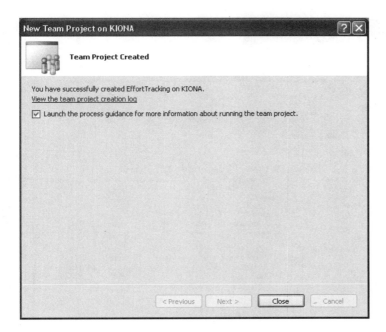

Figure 2-6. *Team project completion message*

If you left the "Launch the process guidance . . ." check box selected at the end of the New Team Project Wizard, the process guidance page will automatically be displayed, as described next.

Viewing Process Guidance

The *process guidance* documents the roles, activities, work products, and reports tailored to a specific software engineering method. The process guidance provided in Team Foundation is a collection of XML, XSL, and HTML files. Essentially, you get an out-of-the-box website describing the work streams, roles, activities, and work products for your chosen process template, as shown in Figure 2-7.

The process guidance is distinctive for each process template and is intended to remain intricately tied to the template. Therefore, if a new component is added to the process template, then the corresponding process guidance will need to be created, as described in the "Customizing the Process Guidance" section later in this chapter.

Spend some time reviewing the seven overview topics provided down the left side of the site. This will give you a good foundation for the Microsoft Solution Framework (MSF) approach, principles, and paradigms. You should then move though the top-level navigation into roles, work items, views, and the Capability Maturity Model Integration (CMMI) in general.

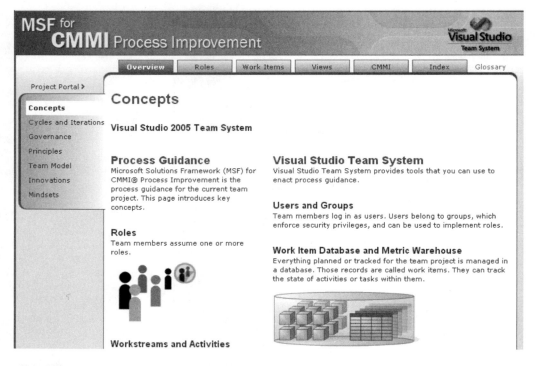

Figure 2-7. *Process guidance for the MSF CMMI Process Improvement – v4 process template*

Working with the Team Explorer

Now that you have created your first team project, EffortTracking is the only project listed in the Team Explorer, with no other information, as shown in Figure 2-8.

Figure 2-8. *Team Explorer components*

The Team Explorer has a My Favorites node located just under the Team Foundation Server name and above the Team Project name. It functions similarly to the Internet Explorer Favorites and has the familiar star symbol. Most of the items contained in the nodes below the

Team Project are eligible to be favorites. To add an item to the My Favorites node, just right-click an item (a report, for example) and select Add to My Favorites, as shown in Figure 2-9.

Figure 2-9. *Adding to the Team Explorer My Favorites node*

Introducing VSTS Components

All of the capabilities of the Team Foundation Server are instantiated by the creation of a new team project. The project instantiation is determined by the process template you select. The preconfigured work items, reports, classifications, version control, portal structure, groups, and permissions available to the project are all determined from the process template. Let's begin with the process template choices.

Process Templates

The two collections being offered in this first release of the Team Foundation Server are MSF for Agile Software Development – v4.0 and MSF for CMMI Process Improvement – v4.0. Third parties are working to incorporate various other methodologies into VSTS process templates. The templates being developed at the time of this writing are RUP (www.osellus.com/solutions/microsoft/rup-vsts_solutions.html), Macroscope (www.fujitsu.com/us/services/consulting/method/macroscope/index_p2.html), and Scrum (www.scrum-master.com/ScrumVSTS).

Both the Agile and CMMI methods are based on the MSF. MSF 4.0 is a full-grown process framework recognized as being compliant with CMMI level 3.

Note The Capability Maturity Model Integration (CMMI) is a method for evaluating and measuring the maturity of the software development process of organizations on a scale of 1 to 5. The CMMI was developed by the Software Engineering Institute (SEI) at Carnegie Mellon University in Pittsburgh (www.sei.cmu.edu) in the mid-1980s as CMM and revised in 2000 as CMMI.

> ## SOFTWARE ENGINEERING METHODOLOGIES
>
> Software engineering methodologies are the frameworks that tell us how we should go about developing our software systems. Also known as the Software Development Life Cycle (SDLC), the most common frameworks or paradigms include the following:
>
> - *Waterfall:* The classic method, which breaks the project into phases for comprehending and constructing information systems. Some of the more popular phases include opportunity, analysis, design, code, test, and implementation. The key understanding is that each prior phase must be completed before moving to the next phase. The Waterfall method has been criticized for being heavy, bureaucratic, and slow.
>
> - *Evolutionary Prototyping:* This method's goal is to build a very robust prototype of the target system and then constantly refine it. The mantra of this process is to refine and rebuild. Evolutionary Prototyping led to Evolutionary Rapid Development.
>
> - *Spiral:* This method includes the phases of the Waterfall approach with the agility of the prototyping model. The larger "big bang" of a complex project is broken into iterations that can be rapidly moved through the phases of the traditional Waterfall type approach and built one upon the other. Boehm's Spiral Model was first postulated in 1986.
>
> - *Agile:* This method had its four values solidified in the spring of 2001. These four values include the value of individuals and interactions over processes and tools, the value of working software over documentation, the value of customer collaboration over contract negotiation, and the value of responding to change over following a plan.

Project Portal

You can access the Project Portal by right-clicking the team project and then choosing Show Project Portal, as shown in Figure 2-10, or by selecting Team ➤ Show Project Portal from the Team menu.

Figure 2-10. *Choosing to show the Project Portal*

The out-of-the-box Project Portal contains a single column of content showing announcements, links, and a single report named Remaining Work, as shown in Figure 2-11. The quick launch bar on the left is arranged by documents, process guidance, and reports. This default layout is highly customizable, as described in the "Customizing the Project Portal" section later in this chapter.

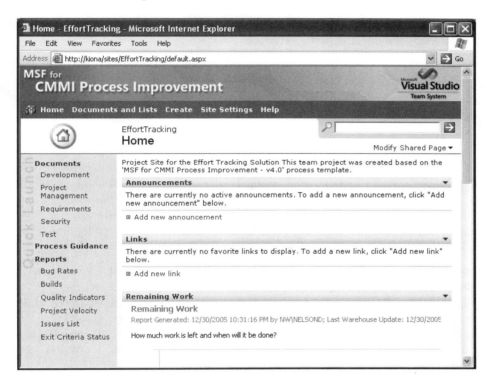

Figure 2-11. *The Project Portal default site*

The Project Portal is a Windows SharePoint Services (WSS) team site based on a custom site definition. Out-of-the-box, VSTS provides two SharePoint custom template files: `MSFAgile.stp` and `MSFFormal.stp`. Custom site definitions provide a complete layout for all the items to be housed inside a team Project Portal.

■**Note** Many companies already have an enterprise SharePoint installation. It is possible to use a remote WSS server (the enterprise service), though it isn't a currently supported configuration. A whitepaper is being written to describe the steps that need to be taken for this to function properly with the Team Foundation Server. Once the Team Foundation Server is pointed at the enterprise WSS server, it is recommended that all future team project portal sites are located on the enterprise server.

The Project Portal includes the following:

Web parts: These are predefined web components designed to address a specific task. Basically, they are nothing more than ASP.NET custom server controls. Visually, they are composed of a frame, title bar, and content. Common web parts on the default Project Portal site include Announcements, Links, Members, and Page Viewer for rendering reports. You can customize your own web parts or download many from third-party sites.

Note Other files associated with web parts are `.dwp` files, which are XML files containing details of the web part (title, description, link to assembly); `.dll`, which are web part assemblies; `.htm` and `.gif`, which are class resource files; and `manifest.xml`, which is a configuration file that describes the structure and contents.

Zones: These are containers on the page in which web parts reside. Zones allow you to create the framework for a common layout within your site. The default Project Portal site is created from a template with only a single zone titled `loc:Left`. You can easily add, delete, and modify zones using a web page design tool such as Microsoft Office FrontPage 2003.

Document libraries: These are the most-used feature of the Project Portal. It is here that documents are stored, managed, and shared. These libraries support versioning—or creating a backup copy of a file whenever you save a file to the library—as well as check-in and check-out, subfolders, and alerts. The Project Portal includes viewers for files that enable you to view documents from programs such as Microsoft Office 2003, even if you don't have the program installed. By default, document libraries include an "explorer view," in which files can be copied, moved, or deleted from the desktop.

Lists: Issue lists, calendar views, group-by views, personal views, and rich text expand the possibilities of the Project Portal lists. You can use formulas and functions in lists to create calculated columns and views. Creating a list is even easier from the one-stop Create page. Lists can be set up to require the list owner's approval before new items appear.

Note For managed lists such as Requirements, Bugs, and Tasks that require state and transition behavior, you will want to use the work item tracking feature of VSTS. This feature is covered in Chapter 5.

Picture libraries: You can store photos and graphics in the picture libraries. View pictures as thumbnails, filmstrips, or in standard file lists. You may want to create a site image library (SIL) to store site-related logos, images, and graphics.

Notification (alerts): the Project Portal uses alerts to notify you through e-mail about additions, deletions, and changes to lists, list items, libraries, and other parts of sites. You can receive alert results immediately, or request daily or weekly alert results summaries.

Work Item Tracking

Work items are the currency of Team Foundation. A work item is a database record used to track the assignment and state of work. Work item types are definitions of specific work items including fields, forms, states, and transitions. Work item queries are predefined views into the work item database.

By default, the MSF for Agile Software Development - v4.0 process template comes with five predefined work item types: Bug, Task, Risk, Scenario, and Quality of Service Requirement. The MSF for CMMI Process Improvement - v4.0 process template includes Scenario and Quality of Service as types of the Requirement work item and an additional three: Review, Change Request, and Issue, as shown in Figure 2-12. Chapter 5 covers work item tracking in detail.

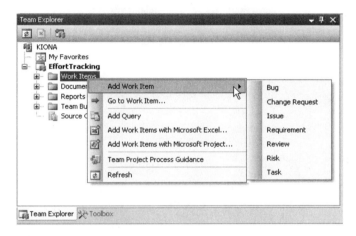

Figure 2-12. *Work item types*

Documents

Documents in the Project Portal are simply links to the underlying document libraries and the items they contain. These are predetermined by the process template selected. However, you can easily add or remove document libraries.

Click Documents and Lists on the Project Portal menu bar to see a list of all your document libraries. From the Team Explorer, you can right-click the Documents node and choose to add a document library. This will display the dialog box shown in Figure 2-13.

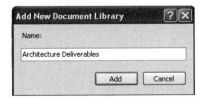

Figure 2-13. *The Add New Document Library dialog box*

Reports

Each process template includes a predefined set of SSRS-based reports. For the MSF for CMMI Process Improvement - v4.0 process template, there are more than 20. The MSF for Agile Software Development - v4.0 process template focuses on around 10 core reports in the process guidance. These reports are a mix of tabular, graphical, and subreport types.

SSRS reports query data from a centralized data warehouse based on SQL Server Analysis Services (SSAS) cubes. You can view these reports directly in the Project Portal or by browsing the Report Manager window, as shown in Figure 2-14. Reports are discussed in detail in Chapter 6.

Figure 2-14. *The Report Manager window*

Team Builds

The goal of Team Foundation Build was to provide a "build lab out of the box." Team Foundation Build provides a very simple way to kick-start this build process. You go through a simple wizard that generates a build script for you. The wizard, shown in Figure 2-15, prompts you to select a solution to build from source control, configurations, locations, and options to run tests. Team Foundation Build is discussed in detail in Chapter 7.

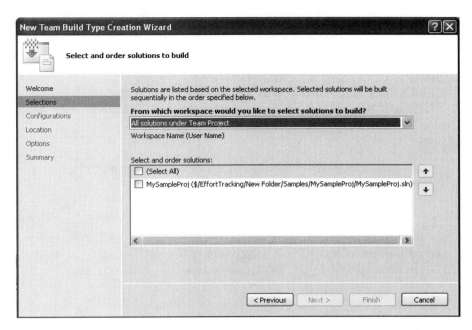

Figure 2-15. *Using the New Team Build Type Creation Wizard*

Version Control

Version Control is the enterprise source code control tool in the Team Foundation Server. Key features include changesets, branching and merging, shelving, and integrated check-in and check-out. Check-in policy provides a mechanism for validating source changes on the client, including things like a Bad Word check-in policy, which won't allow a developer to check in code containing bad words without a warning.

The Source Control Explorer, shown in Figure 2-16, is activated when you double-click the Source Control node in the team project. Chapter 3 covers the Version Control tool in detail.

Figure 2-16. *The Source Control Explorer*

Areas and Iterations

Areas and iterations are hierarchical collection structures to help organize and classify work. *Areas* are simply organizational groupings to help partition the work to be done within a project. Often, the areas are reflective of the major feature set for the project.

Iterations are the spirals that the project has predetermined. MSF for Agile recommends moving from project setup, through a number of feature iterations, to a final build and release.

Project Alerts

You can create project alerts against defined events in the subcomponents of the Team Foundation Server. The four predefined alerts are shown in Table 2-1.

Tip You can add alerts by writing against the notification service directly. For more information, see the guidance provided in the Visual Studio 2005 Software Developers Kit (SDK), available at the Visual Studio Industry Partner (VSIP) Affiliate homepage (`http://affiliate.vsipmembers.com/affiliate/default.aspx`).

Table 2-1. *Project Alerts*

Alert	Description
My work items are changed by others	Alert sent when your work items are changed by others
Anything is checked in	Alert sent when anything is checked in to the project source control
A build status is changed	Alert sent when the status of a project build is changed
A build completes	Alert sent when any build is completed for the project

Note You will probably want the alert on your work items to send e-mail directly to you when your work items are changed. The other three alerts are project-level alerts and are usually sent to an alias made up of the entire team membership.

Customizing the Project Portal

If you are so inclined, you can edit the Project Portal using a website editor. Figure 2-17 shows an example of a customized Project Portal we created for one of our labs using FrontPage.

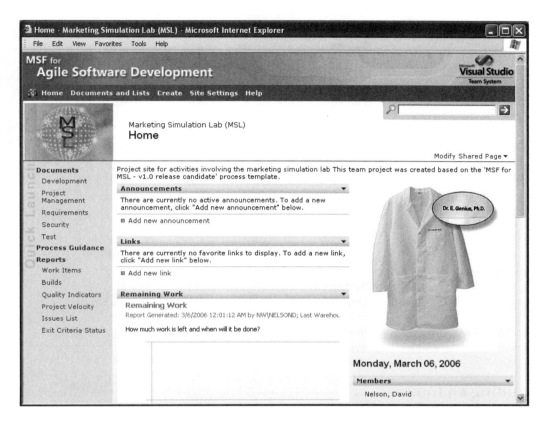

Figure 2-17. *A Project Portal customized in FrontPage*

■**Note** For a high level of customization, you can create your own site template to be used in the creation of the team project site.

The easiest way to customize the Project Portal is to modify its web parts. You can add web parts to the Project Portal by clicking the Modify Shared Page link at the top-left side of the Project Portal. Table 2-2 lists the built-in web parts that are available in WSS. Additionally, there is one web part for viewing each document library in the team project.

Table 2-2. *Default Project Portal Web Parts*

Web Part	Description
Announcements	Typically contains news of interest; allows attachments; can be set to expire
Contacts	Contact list important to the project; can be imported from Outlook
Content Editor Web Part	For adding more complex HTML, images, links, and code within a zone
Events	Complete with start and stop times, descriptions, locations, and recurrence
Form Web Part	Used to connect simple form controls to other web parts
General Discussion	Used to allow newsgroup type discussions of interest
Image Web Part	Container for an image; link to the image by URL or path
Links	List of links to web pages of interest to the team
Members	List of team project site members and their online status
Page Viewer Web Part	Used to display a specified page within a zone; used to render reports from SSRS
Task	General task list that can be assigned and prioritized, with start and stop dates and percentage complete
XML Web Part	Used for XML and XSL transformation of the XML

Adding an Image

To add a new image to your Project Portal, follow these steps:

1. Click Modify Shared Page at the top-left side of the Project Portal, select Add Web Parts, and then click Browse.

2. Select the Image Web Part from the EffortTracking Gallery list, as shown in Figure 2-18, and then click Add.

3. Click the down arrow on the title bar of the new web part and select Modify Shared Web Part.

4. In the Image Web Part Editor, enter the URL of the image you would like rendered, adjust the alignment, and set the border style. Click OK when you are finished.

Figure 2-18. *Adding a web part*

Adding Reports

Reports on the Project Portal are accessed using the Page Viewer web part. The easiest way to add a new report is to copy the link in the existing Remaining Work report, as shown in Figure 2-19.

Figure 2-19. *The Page Viewer web part*

To get to the web part, click the arrow on the Remaining Work title bar in the Project Portal and select Modify Shared Web Part. Copy the path in the Link text box. Add a new Page Viewer web part to the page and modify the report name to match one of the existing reports listed in the Report Manager window. Paste the previously copied path into the Link text box and modify the report name. Use the Test Link link to verify that the report name is correct before clicking Apply.

Working with Lists

Each list on the Project Portal has a corresponding web part for displaying and managing content. You can view the available lists by clicking the Documents and Lists link at the top of the Project Portal.

You can edit lists in a datasheet, which provides an easier mechanism for adding multiple items to the list at one time. For example, to work with the Links list, click the Links title at the top of the Links web part. When the empty Links list appears, select Edit in Datasheet to allow multiple-line entry, as shown in Figure 2-20.

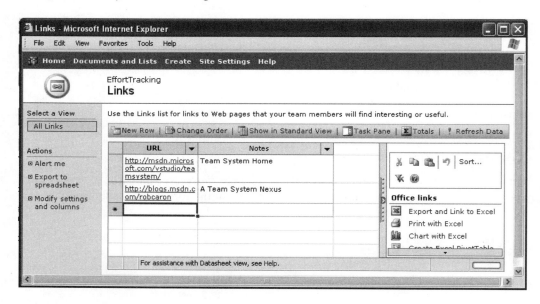

Figure 2-20. *Editing lists in a datasheet*

Customizing a Process Template

The process template is the blueprint for a team project. When you create your own team project, you may find that you need to add or change items, such as security groups, policies, and work item types. Here, we will describe how to modify the process template.

Understanding the Process Template Architecture

A process template includes descriptions of the following components:

- *Portal:* The portal is based on WSS. The portal site is just a predefined SharePoint Team Site. The portal definition includes a custom site template, document libraries, files, and folders.

- *Process Guidance:* Process Guidance is a subsite on the Project Portal. This section describes the website pages, images, and script to support the integration of the process guidance with the rest of VSTS.

- *Work Items*: This section includes work item type definitions (WITD), work item queries (WIQ), and the initial set of prepopulated tasks.

- *Areas and Iterations:* This section describes the hierarchical structures enumerating the phases (iterations), organizational units (areas), and the mappings to Microsoft Project.

- *Reporting:* This section includes the predefined reports for the template against the underlying VSTS data warehouse.

- *Security Groups and Permissions*: This section defines a team project's initial security groups and their permissions. Security is covered in detail in the "Managing Team Foundation Security" section later in this chapter.

- *Source Control:* This section includes Checkin Notes, Checkout Settings, and Security.

The best way to understand the process template architecture is to download one of the two existing templates shipped with the product. To accomplish this, right-click the Team Foundation Server in the Team Explorer and select Team Foundation Server Settings ➤ Process Template Manager. This opens the Process Template Manager window, as shown in Figure 2-21.

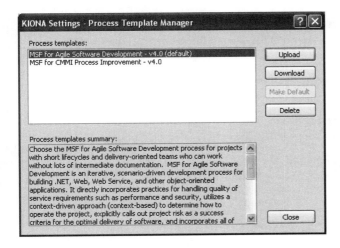

Figure 2-21. *Process Template Manager window*

Select one of the process templates (MSF for CMMI Process Improvement - v4.0 for this example) and click Download. Select an appropriate location on your local machine and click Save. After several minutes, you will receive a confirmation that the process template has been downloaded, as shown in Figure 2-22.

Figure 2-22. *Process template download verification*

Navigate to the folder in which you just saved the process template, and you will see the structure shown in Figure 2-23.

Figure 2-23. *Process template download folder structure*

The `ProcessTemplate.xml` file is the root XML file that describes the entire assemblage for the prescribed template, including the subtasks for each of the process plugins. This file has four main segments:

- `<name>`: This is the name that is displayed in the drop-down list in the New Team Project Wizard.

- `<description>`: This is the description that is displayed in the New Team Project Wizard's Select a Process Template page.

- `<plugins>`: This section lists all the plugins used by the New Team Project Wizard to create the team project. The first release offers the following plugin options:

    - Classification
    - Reporting
    - Portal (wizard page)
    - Groups
    - WorkItemTracking
    - VersionControl (wizard page)

- `<groups>`: This section describes the actions to be performed within the plugin. It has the following nodes:

  - `<group id>` contains the name of the plugin group.

  - `<description>` provides a meaningful narrative.

  - `<completionMessage>` provides a message that is displayed at task completion.

  - `<dependencies>` includes a list of dependent group IDs (names) to identify any other plugin's tasks that must complete prior to launching this plugin's tasks.

  - `<taskList>` points to an XML file of tasks for plugin actions to be performed for the plugin.

Listing 2-1 shows a snippet of the `ProcessTemplate.xml` file containing three of the four key sections.

Listing 2-1. *Portion of ProcessTemplate.xml*

```xml
<?xml version="1.0" encoding="utf-8" ?>
<ProcessTemplate>
 <metadata>
  <name>MSF for CMMI Process Improvement - v4.0</name>
<description>Choose the MSF for CMMI Process Improvement process for
  projects with longer life cycles and that require a record of
  decisions made. Choose MSF for CMMI Process Improvement over MSF
  for Agile Software Development, if your organization is undertaking
  a broad quality assurance and process improvement initiative or
  your team needs the assistance of explicit process guidance rather
  than relying on tacit knowledge and experience.</description>
<plugins>
<plugin name="Microsoft.ProjectCreationWizard.Classification"
    wizardPage="false"/>
   <plugin name="Microsoft.ProjectCreationWizard.Reporting"
    wizardPage="false"/>
   <plugin name="Microsoft.ProjectCreationWizard.Portal"
    wizardPage="true"/>
   <plugin name="Microsoft.ProjectCreationWizard.Groups"
    wizardPage="false"/>
<plugin name="Microsoft.ProjectCreationWizard.WorkItemTracking"
    wizardPage="false"/>
   <plugin name="Microsoft.ProjectCreationWizard.VersionControl"
    wizardPage="true"/>
  </plugins>
 </metadata>
```

Listing 2-2 shows the `<groups>` section. Notice that each of the six plugins has its own `<group>` section.

Listing 2-2. *ProcessTemplate.xml Groups Section*

```
<groups>
 <group id="Classification"
   description="Structure definition for the project."
   completionMessage="Project Structure uploaded.">
  <dependencies>
  </dependencies>
  <taskList filename="Classification\classification.xml"/>
 </group>
 <group id="Groups"
   description="Create Groups and assign Permissions."
   completionMessage="Groups created and Permissions assigned.">
  <dependencies>
   <dependency groupId="Classification" />
  </dependencies>
  <taskList filename="Groups and
  Permissions\GroupsandPermissions.xml" />
 </group>
 <group id="Portal"
   description="Creating project Site"
   completionMessage="Project site created.">
  <dependencies>
   <dependency groupId="Classification"/>
   <dependency groupId="WorkItemTracking"/>
   <dependency groupId="VersionControl" />
  </dependencies>
  <taskList filename="Windows SharePoint Services\WssTasks.xml"/>
 </group>
 <group id="Reporting"
   description="Project reports uploading."
   completionMessage="Project reports uploaded.">
  <dependencies>
   <dependency groupId="Classification"/>
   <dependency groupId="Portal"/>
  </dependencies>
  <taskList filename="Reports\ReportsTasks.xml"/>
 </group>
 <group id="WorkItemTracking"
   description="Workitem definitions uploading."
   completionMessage="Workitem definitions uploaded.">
  <dependencies>
```

```
      <dependency groupId="Classification"/>
      <dependency groupId="Groups"/>
    </dependencies>
    <taskList filename="WorkItem Tracking\WorkItems.xml"/>
  </group>
  <group id="VersionControl"
    description="Creating Version control."
    completionMessage="Version control task completed.">
    <dependencies>
      <dependency groupId="Classification"/>
      <dependency groupId="Groups"/>
      <dependency groupId="WorkItemTracking" />
        <!-- This is just to serialize execution with WIT -->
    </dependencies>
    <taskList filename="Version Control\VersionControl.xml"/>
  </group>
 </groups>
</ProcessTemplate>
```

Modifying a Process Template

Customizing the process template is an incremental, iterative, and often irritating endeavor. To help you, we have composed a ten-step guide, as illustrated in Figure 2-24.

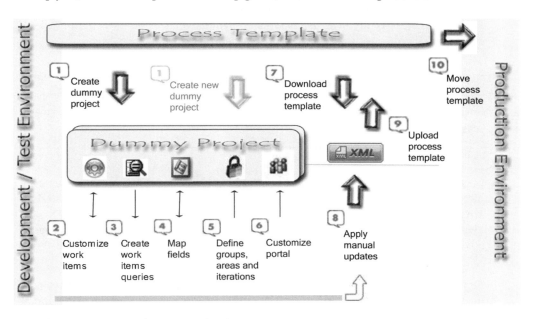

Figure 2-24. *Process template customization steps*

> **■Caution** We strongly recommend that you do not attempt to modify the process template against a production Team Foundation Server. Since the process is both incremental and iterative, you will find the procedure a lot smoother if you practice on a test system. A virtual build of the Team Foundation Server using a differencing disk is preferred for manipulating and testing a process template.

Here are the steps:

1. Select one of the two predefined process templates (MSF for Agile Software Development - v4.0 or MSF for CMMI Process Improvement - v4.0). Choose the one that best resembles your target process. Create a dummy project based on the selected template. This will give you an environment in which to validate your changes as they are being applied.

2. Customize the work items to reflect your process. You most likely will need to create custom work items to support your unique development process. Two utilities exist to enable you to manipulate work item structure: the `witimport` and `witexport` command-line utilities (discussed in Chapter 5). Other tools, such as the Process Template Editor and Work Item Type Designer, allow you to modify work items in a graphical user interface and are available from the GotDotNet community.

3. Create and save custom work item queries. The simplest way to create work item queries is in the Team Explorer. In the dummy project, add queries in the work item section. Test the queries against the dummy project until you are satisfied with them. Save the queries to your local file system as `.wiq` files. You will add these to the `Work Item Tracking\Queries` folder of your process template in step 8.

> **■Note** Saved queries are associated with the Team Foundation Server and project from which they are captured. You will need to remove the references prior to uploading files to the `Queries` folder within the target process template.

4. Map fields in the work items to Microsoft Project fields. The predefined work items have been mapped for you, but if you create a custom work item that will be edited in Microsoft Project, you will need to map to a custom column. You can use the TFS-FieldMapping command-line utility to do the mapping changes. Column mappings are discussed in detail in Chapter 4.

5. Define security groups. You can define and manipulate your security groups on the dummy project to verify they will support your project needs. There is no tool available to synchronize changes, so you will have to note them separately and manually update them in step 8. Similarly, you can map out your areas and iterations within the dummy project to verify the correct organizational groupings and project cycles are captured. Last, define security groups and check-in notes for version control.

6. Customize the WSS portal. You can use the dummy project to test the structure for your WSS portal sites. Create document libraries and compose process template artifacts within the libraries. However, the final modification to the WSS XML template will need to be manual.

7. Download the process template. Now that you are comfortable with the changes to be made to the base process template, you can set the baseline for the modifications. This downloaded template is unchanged from when the dummy project was created; however, you now know explicitly the changes to make. Furthermore, many of the changes have been tested against an instantiated project.

8. This is where all your prior work gets implemented. Change the name and description of your process template in the root `ProcessTemplate.xml` file. Move your custom work item definitions from step 2 into the `TypeDefinitions` folder and modify the `workitemtypes` section of `workitems.xml` to recognize them. Move your custom work item queries from step 3 into the `Queries` folder under the `WorkItem Tracking` folder and modify the `queries` section of `workitems.xml` to recognize them. If needed, duplicate any custom Microsoft Project mappings from step 4 in the `Classification` folder to the `FileMapping.xml`. Reapply any custom security groups defined in step 5 to the `GroupsandPermissions.xml` file in the folder of the same name. Manually describe the document libraries, folders, and individual files from step 6 in the `WssTasks.xml` file under WSS. Make any changes to the version control security or check-in policies in the `VersionControl.xml` file in the `Version Control` folder.

9. Test the work from step 8. Upload the new template (refer to Figure 2-21) within the development environment. If the upload fails, you will need to review the log file and fix the XML. Once the template is successfully uploaded, you will want to start the process again and create a new dummy project to verify your template changes.

10. Once you have tested your new process template and fully exercised the modified components within the new dummy project, you are ready to move the template into the production environment.

Customizing the Process Guidance

The MSF process guidance consists of XML, XSL, and HTML files. You will need the following tools to customize the process guidance files:

- Microsoft Office InfoPath 2003 with Service Pack 1
- An XML or XSL editor
- The MSFWinBuild tool (available from www.gotdotnet.com/workspaces/workspace.aspx?id=c0ce8992-2955-4371-904b-1f93a9efffe6)

Customizing the process guidance consists of four general steps, as illustrated in Figure 2-25.

Figure 2-25. *Process guidance customization steps*

1. Update the process guidance source XML files. The easiest way to start updating the process guidance files is by using Microsoft InfoPath and the supplied template. When you bring up a source XML file in InfoPath, you are presented with a standard framework for the page content, as shown in Figure 2-26. Click the buttons across the top of the form to access the different views: Content, Bullet Menu, Glossary, Help Map, Image, Index, and Menu. Each view allows you to work with various types of content.

Note There are two modes for the process guidance files: edit and run. The editable files are XML and stored in the `Process Guidance\Source\XML` folder. The run files are prerendered HTML and stored in the `Process Guidance\Supporting` folder.

2. Verify your changes in the browser. Working within the `Source` folder, you can open `ProcessGuidance.htm`, and your changes within the XML documents will be rendered.

3. Build pregenerated HTML content. To build the prerendered HTML files, you will need to run the MSFWinBuild tool.

4. Update the XML manifest. Any files that were added or deleted in the modification process need to be noted in the `WssTasks.xml` manifest file. Note that the MSFWinBuild tool will automatically update the `WssTasks.xml` file.

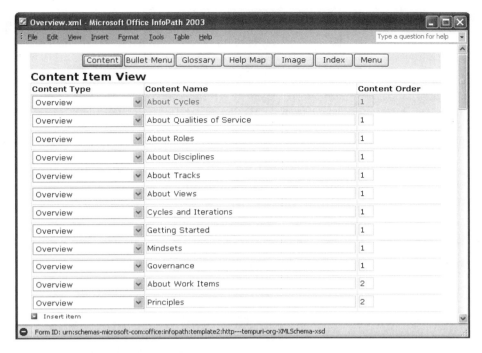

Figure 2-26. *InfoPath view of process guidance overview.xml*

Managing Team Foundation Security

In this section, we'll cover security from the Team Foundation Server perspective; that is, how it relates to server operations. (See Chapter 3 for a discussion of item-level permissions from within the source code system.)

Security for the Team Foundation Server is not fully integrated in this release. You will need to manage at least four areas, as shown in Figure 2-27.

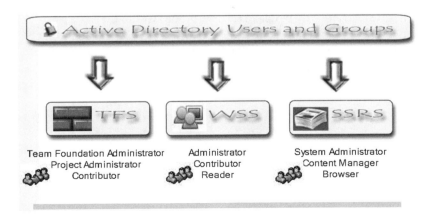

Figure 2-27. *Team Foundation security areas*

These four areas control security as follows:

- *Windows Active Directory (AD) and computer management:* Entire books are written about AD and Windows security. For this brief discussion, we will limit the discussion to AD security groups and Windows machine local groups.

- *Team Foundation Server group settings:* Security is based on users and groups. Users will most likely be Windows users from an AD domain or, for testing purposes, local accounts within Windows Server 2003. The Team Foundation Server supports two levels of groups: one at the global level and one at the project level.

- *WSS user management:* WSS uses a series of built-in site groups to control access to SharePoint sites, lists, and document libraries. The permissions set in SharePoint use existing AD accounts.

- *SSRS role assignment:* SSRS implements a role-based security model to protect reports and reporting resources. Several predefined roles exist, and you can create your own.

The following sections describe how to manage security in each of these areas.

Caution Typically, developers make the mistake of developing while logged on as an Administrator user on their machine. You never want to do this with the Team Foundation Server though. If you use this server as intended and store all of your code and documentation here, then this is the last place you want an intruder to be able to access or unauthorized users to be allowed to make changes. Because of this, it is important that you take some time to think about who gets access to what when you create a new team project.

Managing Windows AD Security

Windows Server 2003 provides a client-based set of remote administration tools in the Windows Server 2003 Administration Tools Pack (`adminpak.msi`). Included in this set is the Active Directory Users and Computers Microsoft Management Console (MMC) snap-in. From here, you can create, modify, or delete security groups within the AD, as shown in Figure 2-28.

You manage local groups on your Team Foundation Server using the Computer Management MMC snap-in. Within Local Computer Management, select Local Users and Groups to add users or groups to your local server.

Figure 2-28. *Active Directory Security Groups*

Managing Global Team Foundation Security

All security for the Team Foundation Server (not a specific project) is accessed by right-clicking the name of the server in the Team Explorer. Only one server can be displayed in Team Explorer at a time, so this will always be the root node of the Team Explorer.

By default, the Team Foundation Server comes with three preinstalled global groups, which are described in Table 2-3.

Table 2-3. *Team Foundation Server Default Global Groups*

Group	Description
Service Accounts	Any service accounts that are used to run various portions of the Team Foundation Server. If you set up the Team Foundation Server by following the installation instructions, the Windows account TFS Service is the only account in this group.
Team Foundation Administrators	Users in this group can perform any operation on the server.
Team Foundation Valid Users	Users in this group can access the server. All users are a part of this group; they do not need to be assigned specifically. When a new project is created, each group in that project is added to this group during project creation.

> **Note** Team Foundation Server Workgroup Edition includes a fourth security group, named Team Foundation Licensed Users. In order to use the Team Foundation Server Workgroup Edition, a user must be added to this group.

Group Permissions

To set group permissions, right-click the server name (Kiona in this example) and select Team Foundation Server Settings, as shown in Figure 2-29. From the submenu, choose Security.

Figure 2-29. *Team Foundation Server security options*

The Global Security dialog box appears, as shown in Figure 2-30. Note that you cannot create new global Team Foundation Server groups through this dialog box. You create new groups via the Global Groups dialog box, as described in the next section.

You can add Windows users and groups to the Global Security dialog box list by selecting the Windows User or Group option and clicking the Add button. You will be taken to the standard Windows Select User or Group dialog box to add users or groups.

You can allow or deny permissions by checking the corresponding check box. The available permissions—all the permissions available at the server level—are described in Table 2-4. Item permissions work the same from Team Foundation Server as they do for Windows. If a user belongs to multiple groups, and one group gives a user permission to perform an action, and the group does not give the permission but does not specifically deny it, then the user has permission to perform the action. If one group gives a permission but another group explicitly denies a permission, the user cannot perform that action. By default, none of the permissions are set to Deny.

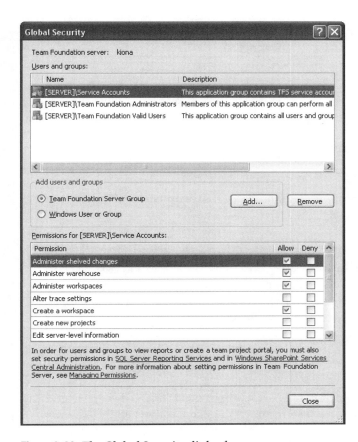

Figure 2-30. *The Global Security dialog box*

Table 2-4. *Team Foundation Server Permissions*

Permission	Description
Administer shelved changes	Can delete shelvesets created by other users
Administer warehouse	Can change warehouse settings (see Chapter 6 for more information)
Administer workspaces	Can create/delete workspaces for other users
Alter trace settings	Can change trace settings for detailed diagnostic information regarding Team Foundation Server Web Services
Create a workspace	Can create a version control workspace
Create new projects	Can create new projects in the Team Foundation Server (must be an Administrator user for SharePoint and SQL reporting)
Edit server-level information	Can edit server-level groups and permissions (create, delete, and rename)

Continued

Table 2-4. *Continued*

Permission	Description
Manage process template	Can modify or add a process template
Trigger events	Can trigger project events (alerts) within the Team Foundation Server (service account)
View server-level information	Can view server-level group membership and user permissions
View system synchronization information	Can trigger synchronization events for the Team Foundation Server (service account)

At the bottom of the Global Security dialog box is a message explaining that permissions for SSRS and WSS must be set separately.

Note Obviously, having to manage Team Foundation Server, SSRS, and WSS security separately is not ideal. The Developer Division Customer Product Lifecycle Experience Team (DDCPX) has released an administration tool to help manage permissions across Team Foundation Server project groups, WSS site groups, and SSRS role assignments. This tool is available from the GotDotNet community.

Group Management

You can manage group membership from the Global Groups dialog box, shown in Figure 2-31. To access this dialog box, right-click the server name in the Team Explorer and select Team Foundation Server Settings ➤ Group Membership. From here, you can add new groups, view group properties, and edit some group properties.

Figure 2-31. *The Global Groups dialog box*

Click the New button to add a new global group. You'll be prompted for the group name and a description, as shown in Figure 2-32.

Figure 2-32. *The Create New Team Foundation Server Group dialog box*

Note You cannot remove the three default security groups. The Remove option is available only for groups that you added.

To view and, in certain cases, edit group properties, select the group in the Global Groups dialog box and click the Properties button. Figure 2-33 shows the Properties box for the Team Foundation Valid Users group.

Figure 2-33. *The Team Foundation Server Group Properties dialog box*

You can see in Figure 2-33 that all of the default groups for the `EffortTracking` project and subsequent projects have been added to the Team Foundation Valid Users group (this occurs during project creation). Selecting Properties for any selected member will display the Team Foundation Server Group Properties dialog box for that member. The Member Of tab lists all of the groups to which the current group or user belongs.

There are several items to note with regard to the Team Foundation Valid Users group:

- The Team Foundation Valid Users group and Service Accounts group cannot be edited through the Global Groups dialog box.
- Team Foundation Valid Users group members are added when new projects are created or new groups are created within those projects.
- Team Foundation Valid Users is the base group for all users and has the lowest level of permissions. This group is not a member of any other group.
- Users are never directly added to the Team Foundation Valid Users group. Only groups are added.

For custom groups, any Team Foundation Server group, Windows group, or Windows user can be added or removed.

Managing Project Security

The security settings for a team project are identical in structure to the security settings for the server. Along with setting group permissions and managing groups, you can also set security for Area Nodes within Areas and Iterations.

Project Group Permissions and Management

To access the group settings for a project, right-click the project name in the Team Explorer and select Team Project Settings ➤ Security or Team Project Settings ➤ Group Membership. The dialog boxes are identical to those you saw for the Team Foundation Server in the previous section. However, the project security settings have different default groups and permissions. At a project level, the groups and permissions are more granular in order to control access to certain functions/items within the project. When a new project is created, four new groups are created by default, as described in Table 2-5.

Table 2-5. *Default Project Groups*

Group	Description
Build Services	Can perform actions related to building and publishing build results. A build manager or developer in charge of running nightly builds would be in this group.
Contributors	Can add, modify, and delete items. All developers need to be members of this group.
Project Administrators	Can perform any action within a specific project. A project manager would most likely be in this group.

Group	Description
Readers	Can view all information about a project, but cannot add, modify, or delete items. Stakeholders would typically belong to this group.
Team Foundation Administrators	Can perform all tasks for the project. This group is added by default to all new projects.
Team Foundation Valid Users	Can view information in a project (by default, members are assigned the same permissions as the Readers group). This group is added by default to all new projects.

Tip In order to deny access to users of other projects who should not be able to view project information, just uncheck the View Project Level Information permission for the Team Foundation Valid Users account. The change is specific to the project only.

The project permissions are at a fairly high level, even for a project, as shown in Table 2-6. The reason for this is that the majority of security for project items is controlled at the source code control level and is not needed at this higher level of permissions. The project permissions cover project security as it relates to performing operations on the server and publishing information to the server. The documentation control (requirements, scope, and so on) is handled through the WSS security, and access to reports is managed through the SSRS security. Both of these types of security are covered in upcoming sections of this chapter.

Table 2-6. *Project Permissions*

Permission	Description
Administer a build	Can delete a completed build or stop a build in progress
Delete this project	Can delete the project for which the user has this permission
Edit build quality	Can change the quality of a build from one value to another (see Chapter 7 for more information about builds)
Edit project-level information	Can edit project-level permissions for users and groups; this includes work item queries and source control write access
Publish test results	Can publish test results to the server and associate the test results with a particular build
Start a build	Can start a new build
View project-level information	Can view project-level permissions for users and groups
Write to build operational store	Can write to the build store (build service account permission)

Areas

Areas are used to categorize items within a project—to segregate items for clarity and security. Because areas allow you to categorize information, you can also control the security of work items in specific areas. (Work items are covered in Chapter 5.) This functionality allows you to set permissions for work items, which is different from setting permissions for accessing documents in WSS or accessing code (or a changeset) associated with a specific work item.

To access the security for areas, right-click the project name in Team Explorer and select Team Project Settings ➤ Areas and Iterations. This will display the Areas and Iterations dialog box, as shown in Figure 2-34. On the Area tab, click the Security button in the lower-right corner. This displays the Area Node Security dialog box (which looks like the Global Security dialog box, shown earlier in Figure 2-30), which lists the permissions described in Table 2-7.

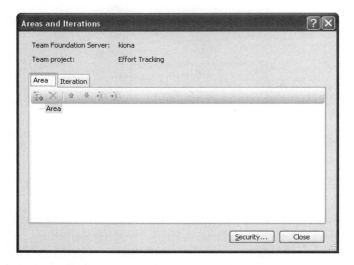

Figure 2-34. *The Areas and Iterations dialog box*

Table 2-7. *Area Permissions*

Permission	Description
Create and order child nodes	Can add new areas and order the areas
Delete this node	Can delete the selected node
Edit this node	Can edit the name of the selected node
Edit work items in this node	Can modify work items that are characterized as a member of the selected node
View this node	Can see the selected node
View work items in this node	Can see the work items associated with the selected node

Managing WSS Security

One of the key tenets of the Project Portal is that it should be a "lightweight access point for casual stakeholders." This means that it should have the ability to communicate project information to anyone with a browser. Your organization may choose to allow access to any authenticated user within your corporation. In order to do that, you will need to be able to manage user access to your project site. If you have the Administrator privileges, you can manage WSS users.

To add a member to the WSS site, open the Project Portal and select the Site Settings link at the top of the page. Within the Administration section, select Manage Users to bring up the Manage Users form. Click Add Users to start the Add Users process, as shown in Figure 2-35.

Figure 2-35. *The Add Users page for WSS*

Table 2-8 shows the default groups for WSS.

Table 2-8. *WSS Default Groups*

Site Group	Description
Administrator	Has full authority over the website
Web Designer	Can create document libraries and lists, and customize website pages
Contributor	Can add content to document libraries and lists
Readers	Has read-only access to the website

Managing SSRS Security

As noted earlier, you can manage SSRS security by assigning roles. Table 2-9 shows the predefined roles.

Table 2-9. *SSRS Default Groups*

Site Group	Description
Content Manager	Has full authority over the report server (can take ownership of an item)
Publisher	Can add content to the server
Report Builder	Can view report definitions
My Reports	Can manage reports separately from the main folder hierarchy
Browser	Has read-only access to navigate folders and view reports

To add a member to the report site, open the Report Manager window by right-clicking Reports in the Team Explorer and selecting Show Report Site. Within the Report Manager window for the project, select the Properties tab, and then select Security. The existing security for the site is displayed, and you can click New Role Assignment to add members to predefined roles, as shown in Figure 2-36.

Add the group or username, and then select the role to be assigned. You can also create a new role for the report site by clicking New Role. Click OK to finish the process. The new role assignments will be displayed. You can then edit or delete the new roles, or create additional new roles.

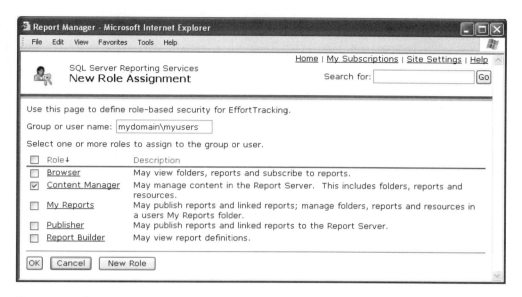

Figure 2-36. *The Report Manager's New Role Assignment window*

Summary

In VSTS, a team project is an instantiation of a development project. Within VSTS, there are templates, guidance, best practices, source control, work items, build machines, a portal for the project, reporting, and more. This chapter has introduced you to the various components of VTST by way of the team project. Many of these components will be covered in more detail in later chapters.

First, we talked about creating a new team project, including the prerequisites. Then we presented an overview of the various components that come with your chosen project process template, which is the blueprint for a team project.

Then we described how to customize your Project Portal, project template, and process guidance. Finally, we took a look at security across three major platforms: Team Foundation Server, WSS, and SRSS.

CHAPTER 3

Team Foundation Version Control

Raise your hand if you worked on a large-scale project and were absolutely frustrated by the limitations in Visual SourceSafe (VSS). Okay, you can put your hand down now. Welcome to the new wave of source code control from Microsoft. The Team Foundation Version Control (TFVC) system takes the best features of various enterprise-class source code control systems, incorporates them, and makes them better and easier to use in the classic Microsoft style. This chapter explores all the facets of the TFVC and how it integrates with Visual Studio and makes developing on large-scale teams easier for you.

> **Note** TFVC is definitely an enterprise-class repository. It is much more powerful than needed for small-scale development teams (three to five people). For small teams, it is still perfectly acceptable to use Visual SourceSafe. The new features add some ease and a little more flexibility for teams, making VSS a perfectly acceptable source code control system.

TFVC is an extensible source code control system that underpins the project management aspects of Visual Studio Team System (VSTS). You will see how it fits in with work-item tracking and policies and makes VSTS a truly integrated solution. Finally, VSTS includes a utility to migrate your code stored in Visual SourceSafe to TFVC.

Starting with Version Control

When you created your first team project (in the example in the previous chapter), you had the option to create a new source control folder, branch from an existing source control folder, or not create a folder at all.

If you elected to create a new source control folder, then a brand new root-level folder was added to the version control repository as shown in Figure 3-1 (the Source Control Explorer is covered in the next section).

Figure 3-1. *Source Control Explorer*

If you elected to branch from an existing source control folder (at least one folder in version control must exist for you to do then) then the existing data in the branch you selected was copied into a new folder in version control (Figure 3-2). You will note that everything in the new project (Demo Project in Figure 3-2) is grayed out. This is because there is no default workspace (discussed later in the "Workspaces" section) for the files, and the latest version has not been retrieved.

Figure 3-2. *A new project starting with branched source code*

If you did not create a new source control folder, you can do so at a later date.

These three options are your first introduction to Team Foundation Version Control. Welcome.

Note As of this writing, Microsoft has released tools that allow previous versions of Visual Studio .NET and Visual Studio 6 to integrate with Team Foundation Version Control. In addition, various tools are being released to incorporate TFVC and work item tracking with Eclipse.

Source Control Explorer

The Source Control Explorer (SCE) is your view into the TFVC. From it you can control all aspects of files under version control. You can add files, delete files, check files out, check files in, branch files, compare files, examine file history, and the list goes on. Figures 3-1 and 3-2 show the SCE. To get to it, you have two options: expand the Team Project node in Team Explorer and double-click the Source Control node or, from the main menu, select View ➤ Other Windows ➤ Source Control Explorer.

As with the Windows Explorer, the folder structure is contained on the left and the files within those folders are shown on the right. Additionally, any information about pending changes is noted along with the files.

The root node in the SCE is the server. The nodes below the server level are the team project nodes. All of the solutions for a team project are located below the Team Project node. Right-clicking any item within the SCE (either in the tree view or the details view) will bring up the options menu described in Table 3-1.

Note Some of the terminology at this point may not be familiar to you. Each of these terms is discussed in detail later in the chapter.

Table 3-1. *Source Control Explorer Options*

Option	Description
View	Opens TFVC's version of the file for viewing. This will use the application registered for use with the file extension to view the file.
Get Latest Version	Retrieves the latest version of the file to your workspace.
Get Specific Version	Allows you to retrieve any particular version of the file.
Check Out For Edit	Allows you to check out a file. Gives you the option to perform a shared check-out, lock the file so only you can edit it, or allow other users to check out the file but not check it in.
Lock	Either locks the file so no one can check it out, or allows people to check it out, but not check it in.
Delete	Deletes a file. When you select a file for deleting directly from the SCE you must also commit that change in order for the file to be deleted.
Rename	Renames a file.
Undo Pending Changes	Cancels any pending changes to the item and any subitems.
Check In Pending Changes	Checks in the pending changes to the item and any subitems.
Shelve Pending Changes	Shelves pending changes.
View History	Displays the history window.

Continued

Table 3-1. *Continued*

Option	Description
Compare	Allows you to compare the TFVC version to the local version of a file, the version in a particular changeset, the version on a specific date, or a labeled version.
Branch	Allows you to create a separate tree of changes to a file independent of the original code base.
Merge	Allows you to merge two files from separate branches.
Move	Allows you to move the file from the current location in the TFVC to another location in the TFVC.
Apply Label	Allows you to label an entire project, a selected folder, or a single file within a project or folder with a specific label.
New Folder*	Creates a new folder in the TFVC project.
Properties	Views the TFVC properties of the file or folder.
Refresh	Refreshes the contents of a folder or the status of a single file.

* New Folder only appears in the menu when you click on a blank area in the details pane (right window), although you can add a new folder from the SCE's toolbar while you are in the tree view pane.

File/Folder Properties

To view the File or Folder properties, right-click the item and select Properties. This displays the Properties dialog box shown in Figure 3-3. This dialog box is the same for all items under version control.

Figure 3-3. *The Item Properties dialog box*

General

The Server Name is the name of the file under version control. The Local Name is the name of the file currently on your hard drive. The same is true for the version numbers. The Latest Version is the version on the server, and the Workspace Version is the version on your hard drive. The Encoding is the file system encoding. VSTS automatically detects this so you should never have to change it. If you do have to change it, there are about 100 different encodings to choose from.

Status

The Status tab shows any pending changes to the item as shown in Figure 3-4.

Figure 3-4. *Status tab*

Figure 3-4 shows that users jxl0575 and alicew are both making changes to the file. It also shows which workspace the items are checked out to. Because both are checked out to the same workspace it indicates that both users are using the same machine (which is true!).

Security

Let us talk about security for a moment. Do you remember how security works (or does not work as the case may be) in Visual SourceSafe? You can set security for the file share and you can allow or not allow a user access to a repository. You can even set whether they had read-only or read-write privileges—but you cannot do anything else.

The VSTS team took this into account when designing TFVC. You can now control security at all levels and to a very granular degree (Figure 3-5).

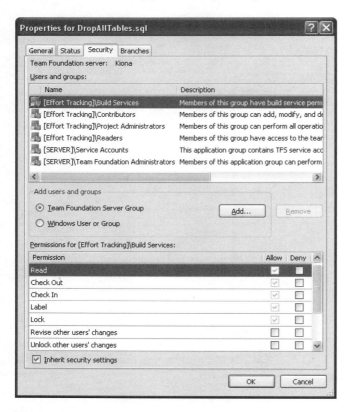

Figure 3-5. *Security tab*

The users and groups list contains all the users (or groups) that have access to the given folder or file in the folder. By default, all project members have some type of access to the items in version control. The server accounts shown in Figure 3-5 (Service Accounts and Team Foundation Administrators) have administrator rights to the items in version control which cannot be removed. You can add additional users or groups to this list.

> **Note** If you add a user or a group that is not at least already a part of the Readers account for the project, they will be unable to access the file (or folder). Aside from this one restriction, adding users and groups and setting permissions is done as normal.

The available permissions for a given file or folder are listed in Table 3-2.

Table 3-2. *Item Permissions*

Permission	Description
Read	Can read an item.
Check out	Can check out an item.
Check in	Can check in an item.
Label	Can label the item
Lock	Can lock an item.
Revise other users' changes	Allows user to change the comments, work item associations, or check-in notes associated with a changeset they did not create.
Unlock other users' changes	Allows a user to unlock another user's locked item.
Undo other users' changes	Lets pending changes be cancelled on an item that another user has checked out.
Administer labels	Allows users to label changes and alter labels.
Manipulate security settings	Indicates the user has permissions to change the security of the item.
Check in other users' changes	Causes items checked out by another user to be checked in.

The four default groups associated with every project have certain permissions by default which cannot be removed, only revoked (in other words, the group either has the right or it is specifically denied). These permissions are listed below:

- *Build Services*: Read, Check out, Check in, Label, Lock
- *Contributors*: Read, Check out, Check in, Label, Lock
- *Project Administrators*: All permissions
- *Readers*: Read

Additional permissions may be assigned to these groups. All in all, security has been greatly improved over VSS and this is a welcome change.

Branches

The Branches tab shows the branches that exist for the selected item as shown in Figure 3-6.

Figure 3-6. *Branches tab*

This dialog box shows that a branch exists for DropAllTables.sql at version 3. It also shows that the branched file is part of the Demo Project. This allows you to trace back to where a branch came from. This dialog box does not show shelved items, as they are not part of any code base (see the "Shelvesets" section later in this chapter for more information).

Workspaces

One of the key things to note is the Workspace setting. A workspace (similar to a collection of working folders as in Visual SourceSafe) is a local "sandbox" where the project code is stored and where you work with it. Any changes you make to the code are made in the local workspace, and when you sync your code with the repository, the changes you made are uploaded to the repository.

Tip You can maintain multiple workspaces on a single system for a single project. One reason to do this is to handle working on multiple branches at once, where you want to avoid shelving items (discussed later in this chapter).

To create additional workspaces (or to set up a new workspace on a system that does not have one) select the Workspace drop-down in the SCE and click Workspaces (or select File ➤ Source Control ➤ Workspaces). This will bring up the Manage Workspaces dialog box shown in Figure 3-7.

Figure 3-7. *Manage Workspaces dialog box*

This dialog box will list all of the workspace names and the systems on which those workspaces are located. Selecting the Edit or Add button will bring up the Add/Edit Workspace dialog box shown in Figure 3-8.

Figure 3-8. *Add/Edit Workspace dialog box*

Here you can add a comment or create additional working folders and map them to repository folders.

> **Tip** As a best practice, the workspace layout should match the repository layout upon which it is based. This makes it easier to navigate both of them.

To set up the working folders, you have a couple of options. The first option is to do a Get Latest on a folder. SCE will prompt you for the local folder, and a working folder entry is automatically made for the workspace. The second option is to do the task manually in the Edit Workspace dialog box.

> **Tip** Another best practice is to map the root team project folder (in this example the $/Effort Tracking folder) to a folder on your hard drive and keep all of the other folders for the project under this directory.

One other thing you can do in the Edit Workspace dialog box is to cloak a folder. Cloaking a folder sets the folder to be "invisible" to the local workspace. For example, if you were to cloak the $/Effort Tracking/EffortTrackingSolutionVB folder, when you did a Get Latest on the root folder, the cloaked folder would not be retrieved. To cloak a folder, select the Status column and select Cloaked.

Creating Solutions

Now that you have a basic overview of the Source Control Explorer and an understanding of workspaces, we will use a simple solution to demonstrate the rest of the features of Team Foundation Version Control. The walkthrough and explanations assume you have created a team project called Effort Tracking and have set up a source control folder (the default setting when creating a new team project). In order to start using TFVC, you are going to create a new database project to hold the Effort Tracking database called, conveniently enough, EffortTrackingDatabase. The database project is a new project type that allows you to store queries, table definitions, change scripts, and data load scripts (and will also generate these scripts for you).

> **Note** One of the key benefits of this change is that it becomes more natural to put these scripts under source code control. In previous versions of Visual Studio, all of this work would have had to be done manually, and grouping the database information with the project was rarely done.

To create the new solution (remember that at this point you have only created a team project not an actual solution) and project, do the following:

1. Select File ➤ New ➤ Project.

2. Select Other Project Types ➤ Visual Studio Solutions ➤ Blank Solution.

3. Call the solution "Effort Tracking Solution," select Add to Source Code Control and click OK. This will display the Add Solution dialog box shown in Figure 3-9.

4. Leave the default settings as they are and select OK.

5. Right-click the created solution and select Add ➤ New Project.

6. Select Other Project Types ➤ Database Project.

7. Enter the name as "EffortTrackingDatabase" and select OK.

Figure 3-9. *Add Solution dialog box*

Tip The Advanced button allows you to override the default workspace mappings.

At this point you will have a Solution Explorer structure that looks like the one in Figure 3-10.

Figure 3-10. *Solution Explorer*

The pluses next to the solution and the project indicate that these items have pending adds but have not yet been stored in the source code repository.

Pending Changes Window

Right-click either node and select View Pending Changes. This will display the Pending Changes dialog box shown in Figure 3-11 where you have a number of options for handling items in your workspace.

Figure 3-11. *Pending Changes dialog box*

The Pending Changes window is where you see the work you have done in preparation for your next check-in. Here you can associate work items with code, check that your changes comply with the check-in policy, add comments, and have reviewers sign off on your code.

The tab buttons down the left side of the window change the view displayed in the Pending Changes window. The selected tab in Figure 3-11 is the Source Files tab which displays this window.

Source Files

The Source Files section allows you to work with the files from your project and provide status on those files. Every file with a check next to it is a change that will be committed. The type of change is noted here and can be one of the following: Add, Edit, Rename, Merge, Branch, Delete, or Undelete (if a file is locked for editing, "locked" will appear in this column in addition to the type of change). In this example, all of the changes are additions. The folder list displays where that item is in the workspace on your local drive. Holding your cursor over the item will show the version number of the item to be added. The Comments field at the top of the pane allows you to add a comment that will be applied to all changes that are committed at the same time.

Tip It is a good practice to work on only one change at a time or one piece of functionality at a time. That way it is easy to add comments to the files you are committing. However, if you work on multiple changes at once, it is worthwhile to do your changes in batches so that you apply a uniform comment to groups of related work.

To check in the files, you simply click the Check In button on the toolbar. For right now, check in the pending changes. Once the changes are successfully checked in, the files will no longer be displayed in the Pending Changes dialog box, and the plus icon next to each file will become a lock (in the Solution Explorer).

Note Before checking the changes in, review the information on the other tabs, because some of the information will not be displayed after all pending changes are checked in.

Later in this chapter the section "Shelvesets" explains the shelving and unshelving options available via the Source Files tab.

You can work with individual files by right-clicking the file in the Solution Explorer and selecting the appropriate option.

Work Items

Work items are essentially assignments tracked by the system. Chapter 4 deals entirely with work items and work item tracking. The work items that show up in the Pending Changes dialog box allow you to associate a given task with the given changeset. Changesets are discussed later in this chapter in the "Changesets" section.

Check-in Notes

For now you will notice that the check-in notes consist of three fields: Code Reviewer, Security Reviewer, and Performance Reviewer. These are configurable fields that can be made mandatory prior to a check-in or left as optional. Right now they are optional but you will see how to change this later in this chapter in the "Configuring Version Control" section.

Policy Warnings

The policy warnings page, at this point, contains no policies. Any policies that have been violated are listed here. You will see how to create and enforce policies later in this chapter in the "Configuring Version Control" and "Creating Custom Check-in Policies" sections.

Changesets

A changeset is a grouping of all metadata related to changes checked in at the same time from the same workspace. The metadata includes files, work items, comments, check-in notes, policy violation overrides, the user, and the date. Changesets are persisted for the life of the source control repository.

Note Visual SourceSafe has no equivalent to a changeset. In VSS, every check-in you make is an independent check-in and there is no way to track which other files are checked in at the same time (although you can run a report on the date and time checked in but this is difficult at best).

Changeset numbers start at one and are incremented by one for each new changeset. The Get Latest Version option (available from various places such as right-clicking on a node in the Solution Explorer) will retrieve the latest version from the latest changeset. To retrieve a specific changeset version the Get option can be used and the appropriate version chosen. The Get option will be described in more detail in the section "Retrieving Versions" later in this chapter.

To see how changesets work, create a new table in the EffortTrackingDatabase project by right-clicking the Create Scripts folder and selecting Add New Item. Then select the Table Script and call it dbo.Categories.sql.

Note While this is certainly not a book on database projects, it should be noted that all objects in a database can be reverse-engineered into a database project. This is one of the great new features of Visual Studio 2005.

Add the SQL statements in Listing 3-1 to the categories script (replacing what is autogenerated in the file).

Listing 3-1. *Create Categories Script v1*

```
CREATE TABLE [dbo].[categories]
(
    [cat_id] [int] IDENTITY(1,1) NOT NULL,
    [cat_title] [varchar](100) NOT NULL,
    CONSTRAINT [PK_categories] PRIMARY KEY CLUSTERED
    (
        [cat_id] ASC
    ) ON [PRIMARY]
) ON [PRIMARY]
```

In the Pending Changes window, add the comment "Added the categories table create script" and check in the pending changes. Now you discover that you have a problem—you did not check to see if the table existed before you tried to create it. A common component of a create script is a check to see if the table is there, so you want to add the check for the table. Add the SQL statement in Listing 3-2 above the create table statement.

Listing 3-2. *Create Categories Script v2*

```
IF  EXISTS (SELECT * FROM dbo.sysobjects
WHERE id = OBJECT_ID(N'[dbo].[categories]')
AND OBJECTPROPERTY(id, N'IsUserTable') = 1)
DROP TABLE [dbo].[categories]
GO
```

Notice that when you make the additions, the file is automatically checked out for you, but not the database project, because the project structure did not change, only a single file within the project. Again, check in the changes but make a comment to the effect that you added a drop existing categories table section.

History

To view the history of changes for a given file, right-click the file in the Solution Explorer and select View History. Alternatively, you can select the file in the Solution Explorer and select File ➤ Source Control ➤ View History from the main menu (you can also view the history from with the SCE). This will show the History window seen in Figure 3-12.

■**Note** There is a 99% chance that the changeset numbers you see on your system will be different than those shown here. Not to worry, though; just remember that the lower the number, the earlier the version.

Changeset	Change	User	Date	Comment
20	edit	jxl0575	3/10/2006 9:02 PM	Added a drop categories section before the create section.
19	add	jxl0575	3/10/2006 9:01 PM	Added the categories table create script

Figure 3-12. *History window*

The initial version is version 19, and the change is noted as an add. Version 20 contains the addition of the drop categories section. To view the changeset information for a given entry, double-click the version in the list. This will bring up the Changeset Details dialog box shown in Figure 3-13.

Figure 3-13. *Changeset Details dialog box*

This shows the changes that were made when each of the files was checked in. Here it notes that the categories script was added (along with the Change Scripts folder) and the database project itself was edited. The view of the files shown in Figure 3-13 is the folder view as opposed to the flat view that is displayed by default (this can be changed by selecting the appropriate icon above the Comment field).

Comparing Versions

From this view you can actually examine the contents of the files or run a compare against different versions. Right-clicking the `dbo.categories.sql` file from the Changeset Details dialog box and selecting View will display the contents of the file in Notepad. Right-click the `dbo.categories.sql` file and select Compare ➤ With Workspace Version (workspace name here). This will bring up the Differences dialog box shown in Figure 3-14.

The legend at the bottom explains the colored text. In this case you inserted a block of text in the latest version. But you will notice that the text appears as deleted. The comparison is always done from the point of view of the document selected in the changeset. In this case, you selected the original version and asked to see what the difference was with the workspace version (which happens to be the latest version). Since the latest version had the exists statement and the earlier version does not, it appears to the differencing engine that the text was deleted. All other comparisons work from the latest version to the previous version (which is the best way to do comparisons).

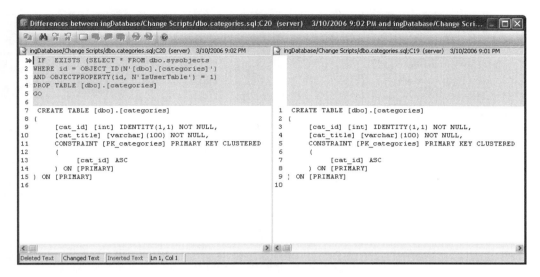

Figure 3-14. *Differences dialog box*

■**Tip** To see how this works, close this window and close the changeset window. In the History window, select both changesets, right-click, and select Compare. You will see the exists clause as green text in the latest version.

The various options going across the top are Copy, Find, Find Next, Find Previous, Toggle Bookmark, Next Bookmark, Previous Bookmark, Clear All Bookmarks, Next Change, and Previous Change.

■**Note** Bookmarks are not persisted between comparisons. Once you close the Differences dialog box, all of your bookmarks are cleared.

You may also compare different versions by selecting both of the versions to compare in the History window, or you can compare any version to the latest version by right-clicking the file in the History window and selecting Compare.

In the "Configuring Version Control" section you will see how to change the tools used to do comparisons and merges in case you want to use your own tools.

Labeling Versions

Applying a label to a set of files or folders gives you a more granular way to mark a specific version. You have seen how a changeset marks everything in the repository as being a part of a particular changeset when you check things in. The label allows you to target specific files and specific versions of files—even files that are not part of the project, such as help files—as being part of a specific version. The labeled files can cross changesets as well. Labels are typically applied for beta release code, release candidates, or tested versions.

Note In Visual SourceSafe you could label a build but you could not easily get the labeled version afterward.

Labels are attached to specific versions of a file and each version can have as many labels as you want. Labeling can be done at the file or folder level since you manually select which files and folders, from which changesets, you would like to add. To label a version, do the following:

1. Right-click the Effort Tracking Solution in the Source Control Explorer and select Apply Label. The Choose Item Version dialog box is displayed (Figure 3-15).

Figure 3-15. *The Choose Item Version dialog box*

2. Click OK and the Apply Label dialog is displayed (Figure 3-16).

Figure 3-16. *Apply Label dialog box*

3. Enter the label "First Label" in the Name box.

4. Click OK and the label is applied.

A label can also be applied via the File ➤ Source Control ➤ Label ➤ Apply Label menu item (Source Control Explorer must be open and a node or item selected).

Now that the version is labeled you can retrieve it at a later date, delete the label, or add additional files to the label. The easiest way to work with labels is via the File ➤ Source Control ➤ Label ➤ Find Label menu item (SCE must be open and active in the IDE). Selecting this brings up the Find Label dialog box (Figure 3-17).

From this dialog box you can search for a specific label by name, project, or owner. Clicking Find displays all of the labels that match your criteria. Once you select a label you can either edit it (which allows you to add or remove items from the label) or delete it. You may also create new labels from this dialog box.

Note When you delete a label, only the label is deleted, not the versions attached to it.

Figure 3-17. *Find Label dialog box*

Retrieving Versions

There are many ways to retrieve versions in TFVC. The Get Latest Version option (available in several locations—SCE, Solution Explorer, File ➤ Source Control, the History window, or the Changeset dialog box) always retrieves the latest checked-in version from the server. The Get Specific version displays the dialog box shown in Figure 3-18.

Figure 3-18. *Get dialog box*

The item(s) selected when you click Get Latest Version are displayed in this dialog box. If a folder is selected, the Get operation is a recursive operation—all files within the folder that match the specified version will be retrieved. The Version Type drop-down lets you choose the version based on the following items:

- *Changeset*: Specifies a specific changeset (see Figure 3-19).
- *Date*: Specifies a date/time.
- *Label*: Specifies a specific label.
- *Latest Version*: Nothing to specify.
- *Workspace Version*: Specifies files that match a user's workspace. This is useful if you need to duplicate another user's workspace.

To locate a specific changeset (or the files in a specific changeset) you can use the Find Changesets dialog box (Figure 3-19).

Figure 3-19. *Find Changesets dialog box*

For this dialog box you can specify two options: the file contained in the changeset, and who created the changeset. You can search all of the changesets or just a specific range—either by number or by the date they were created.

Branching

Now that you have seen the basics of working with the version control tool, it is time to move on to cover more complex scenarios.

Branching is the act of splitting files into separate development paths—it is also known as *forking*. Typically code is branched for one of two reasons: there has been a software release (usually on a commercial product) and it needs to be supported while updated versions are developed; or a developer needs to experiment with a different way of writing code or with new techniques but does not want to contaminate the base code, which may cause production problems. In the latter case, assuming the experimentation works out, the branched code is almost always merged back in with the main code and with any changes made up to that point by the maintenance team. See Figure 3-20.

■**Note** Shelving can be used to accomplish the same thing. Shelving is covered later in this chapter.

Figure 3-20. *Branched code flow*

To branch code using TFVC, use the Source Control Explorer to find the file you want to branch. Right-click the files or folders you want to branch and select Branch. This brings up the Branch dialog box shown in Figure 3-21 (for this example, continue to use the categories sql file).

Figure 3-21. *Branch dialog box*

This dialog box indicates that a single file was selected to be branched. The branched file, by default, has a target name of the filename + "-branch." This will become the name of the file in your local workspace so it does not conflict with the original file. The branch-from version can be based on the changeset, the date, the latest version, the workspace version, or a specific label. The result of a branch is shown in Figure 3-22.

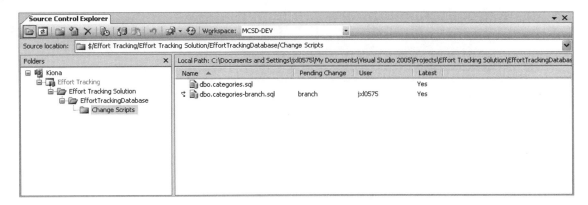

Figure 3-22. *Branch results*

A new file (the branched file) is created and added to the source code control. At this point you can add the branched file to another project and work on it as normal (or add it to the same project if you want).

■**Tip** If you are branching a file or a project but not editing it, you can uncheck the "Create local working copies for the new branch" option (see Figure 3-21). This creates a new branch on the server but does not retrieve the branched version, which can save a lot of time, depending on the number of files involved.

To see how this works, right-click the Change Scripts folder in the Solution Explorer and select Add Existing Item. Select the dbo.categories-branch.sql file and click OK. Add a comment to the top of the branched file (any comment will do—a double dash (--) followed by any text). Check in the change. When you have reached the point that the branched file (or folder) and main file (or folder) are ready to be merged back into each other, right-click the main or the branched file (or folder) in TFVC and select Merge.

VSTS knows the original file that you branched from (this can be seen by right-clicking either file and selecting Properties and then selecting the Branches tab) and displays the Source Control Merge Wizard dialog box (shown in Figure 3-23).

Figure 3-23. *Source Control Merge Wizard*

The source branch is the code that has been changed that you want to merge with the original code. Selecting "All changes up to a specific version" gives you the option of selecting a version in the main version control path to merge with. Selecting "Selected changesets" allows you to select a specific changeset. By default, the merge process tries to perform an automated merge that merges the two versions if the areas of change do not cause any conflict. If a conflict is detected (this scenario is covered in the "Merging Files" section later in this chapter), you will have to resolve the conflicts manually.

At this point you can delete the branched file (note that it will still be a part of that particular changeset so you can always get back to it).

Shelvesets

Frequently, when developers are working on changes, another change will be required that has a higher priority. Usually a developer stops work on the changes he or she is working on and begins working on the new change. The problem with this is that it leaves the code in an unstable state. The shelveset solves that problem for you. The process of shelving a change, or a set of changes, allows you to store pending changes under source control without creating a branch and to revert your workspace to a known, stable version of the code base. The high-priority change can then be performed, and after it is checked in, the editing on the shelved changes can continue. Figure 3-24 shows a typical process flow for how this might work.

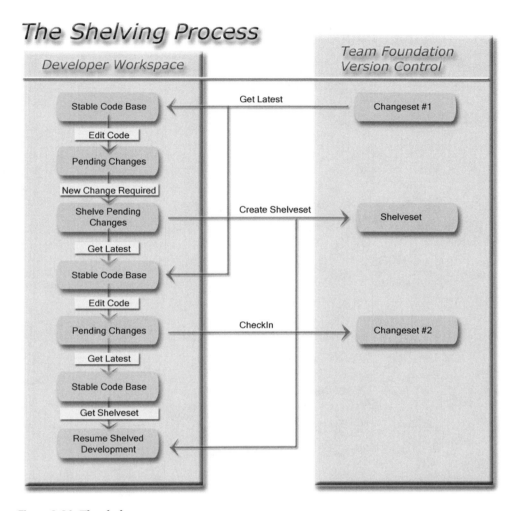

Figure 3-24. *The shelveset process*

Shelvesets exist in TFVC but are unversioned. They can also be deleted, whereas a changeset cannot be deleted. Another common scenario is that you can share your code with other developers without contaminating the code base (for example, if you are experimenting and want to get help with code from another developer).

Merging Files

Merging is the process of taking multiple changes in a file and combining them into the original file. You saw a small example of this in the "Branching" section of this chapter. This situation can arise in branching, shelveset, or multiple check-out scenarios. Figure 3-25 depicts a multiple check-out scenario.

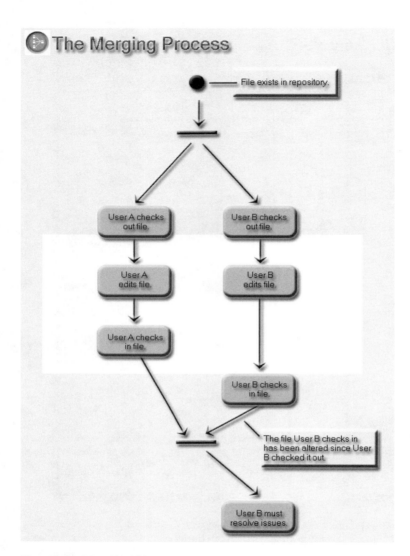

Figure 3-25. *Merging files scenario*

This behavior can typically be avoided on small development teams by just not allowing multiple check-outs (see the "Configuring Version Control" section). It also does not usually occur when code is structured very tightly (i.e., it is highly object-oriented and only one person is working on one particular piece of functionality).

In the scenario in Figure 3-25, the first thing User B would see during check-in is the dialog box shown in Figure 3-26.

■Note If User B looks in the Source Control Explorer, he or she would notice that the latest version (the root-level folder would be grayed out and No would be listed under Latest next to the file) is no longer there.

Figure 3-26. *Resolve Conflicts dialog box*

■Note To see this dialog box, so you can see how it works for you, you can do the following: Have two users set up for a project. Log on as one user and make a change to the file. Log off and then log on as the other user, make a change, and check in the file. Then log off and log on as the original user. Try to check in the changes.

This dialog box describes any conflicts that exist with a given file. It can be shown for several reasons, which include problems with invalid mappings between the repository and the working folder of the workspace. In that case, the dialog box is telling User B that a newer version of the file exists on the server.

■Tip The Auto Merge All option attempts to figure out what to keep from each file without user intervention. In general, it works very well if edits have not been made to the same section of code. If such edits have been made, using the Resolve option to perform a manual merge is the only way to merge files.

Selecting the Resolve option brings up the Resolve Conflict dialog box shown in Figure 3-27.

Figure 3-27. *Resolve Conflict dialog box*

Path shows the location of the local file, which is different from that on the server. Changes indicates how many changes are different in each file and how many are conflicting. Resolution options are described in Table 3-3.

Table 3-3. *Resolution Options*

Option	Description
Merge changes for me	Attempts to merge the files automatically. Same as the Auto Merge option.
Merge changes in merge tool	Allows the developer to manually work through the files to choose the correct lines to merge.
Undo my local changes	Discards the local changes, does not check in the file, retrieves the server version to the local workspace.
Discard server changes	Overwrites the changes on the server with the changes from the local file.

The Compare option allows you to view the differences between the local version and the server version or the original version of the file that was checked out. When you select OK, the Merge Tool shown in Figure 3-28 is displayed.

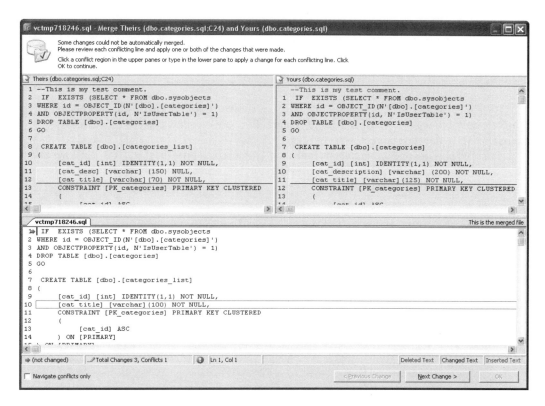

Figure 3-28. *Merge Tool window*

There are a number of important pieces of information available to you in this window. The first piece of information is in the title bar. Theirs (dbo.categories.sql;C24) indicates the file on the server that the local file is attempting to be merged with and the changeset that the file exists in. The two windows at the top of the dialog box are the two different versions of the file. The server version of the file is located on the left and the local version on the right. Changes are noted by the lines in colors (the legend is in the lower right of the window). In Figure 3-28, three lines were changed in the server version, two lines were changed on the local version, and one line was deleted from the local version. The lower window shows you what the final merged file will look like.

So, what is the merge tool telling you? First, looking at the bottom left of the window you can see that there are three changes in total, and one conflict. The blue arrow in the lower window is pointing at the first change in the file.

Tip You can click in any window and the blue arrow will jump to that window. Then you can navigate the changes in each window (using the Next Change and the Previous Change buttons in the lower right).

The exclamation mark tells you there is an unresolved conflict. Checking the "Navigate conflicts only" check box in the lower left corner of the dialog allows you to move between items that VSTS cannot figure out on its own.

The only actual conflict that exists in the file is the boxed area (in the lower window) on line 10. The changes made in one file or another, but not both, are resolved automatically.

Note If Auto Merge was selected, this dialog box would still have been displayed because VSTS cannot figure out how to merge a conflict like this on its own.

To select the actual changes to merge, just click the correct row from either or both files (in the upper windows). Figure 3-29 shows the result of selecting each line from each file.

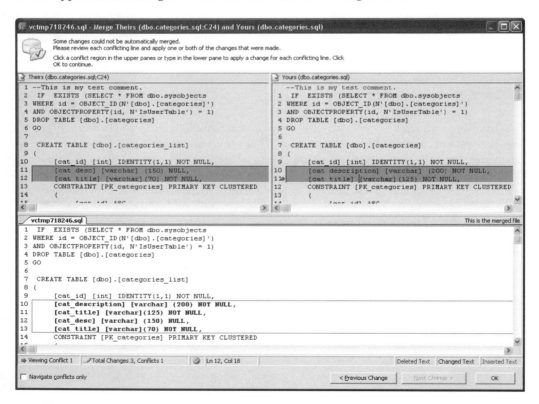

Figure 3-29. *Merge Tool with code lines selected*

The lines of code are added bottom to top. So if the conflict on line 11 from the server file is selected (as shown in Figure 3-29) and then the conflict on line 11 from the local file is selected, the resulting merge file would be as shown, at the bottom of the merge dialog box. Obviously, this is not the desired solution. You can unselect a change from one of the files and click OK. After OK is selected the files are merged and saved in the repository.

Configuring Version Control

Now that you have seen how to use Team Foundation Version Control, you will see how to configure it and what your options are. TFVC is configured on a per-team-project basis (although there are some options that are specific to the IDE and not a team project).

There is one option that is specific to the server and spans all team projects—file types. To see the file types supported by the server, right-click the server name in the Team Explorer and select Team Foundation Server Settings ➤ Source Control File Types. This displays the dialog box in Figure 3-30.

Figure 3-30. *File Types dialog box*

This dialog box allows you to specify a couple of options related to how specific types are supported on a global basis. You can edit any of the values or add new file types. The purpose of this dialog box is to configure file merging and check-out options. If File Merging is enabled, then the file type is supported by multiple check-outs as well. The other information is just classification information and has no effect on the file.

Configuring Project Settings

To configure a team project, right-click the project in Team Explorer and select Team Project Settings ➤ Source Control. There are three different categories of options you can set: Checkout Settings, Checkin Policy, and Checkin Notes (Figure 3-31).

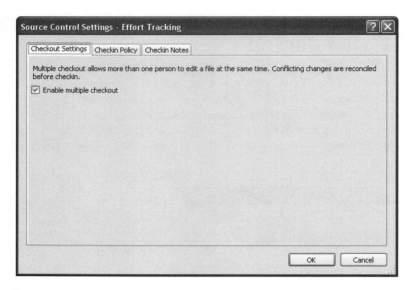

Figure 3-31. *Source Control Settings dialog box*

Checkout Settings

There is only one option for Checkout: enable (or disable) multiple checkout. Multiple checkout is designed for projects where multiple people will be working on the same files at the same time (but hopefully not the same section of a file). Typically, in an object-oriented design, objects are encapsulated and have a small set of tasks to perform so only one developer is working on a given class (with each class in its own file). However, in situations where there are very large classes with specialized functions, more than one developer may need to work on the code at the same time. To facilitate this you can enable multiple checkout. When multiple checkout is disabled, only one person at a time can check the file out. Other developers can perform a Get on the file, but they cannot check it out for editing.

Checkin Policy

Policies allow you to control when a file can get checked in by ensuring that the file, or the build in the developers' workspace, meets certain criteria.

Tip Policies are good if everyone follows them. But there are always ways to get around checks like this, so a rigorous process on top of this is a good idea.

To create a new policy, switch to the Checkin Policy tab and select Add. This brings up the Add Check-in Policy dialog box shown in Figure 3-32.

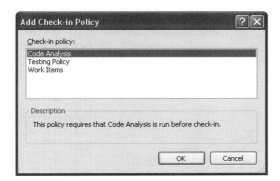

Figure 3-32. *Add Check-in Policy dialog box*

There are three basic policies which you can customize based on the needs of the project. You can also create custom policies.

Caution It is critical to note that any policy can be overridden, but it is a bad practice and should not be done. However, if you do override a policy to check in code, everyone will know about it and you will have to provide an explanation.

Creating custom check-in policies is covered toward the end of the chapter.

Code Analysis

Selecting the code analysis policy brings up the Code Analysis Policy Editor shown in Figure 3-33.

Figure 3-33. *Code Analysis Policy Editor*

Code analysis is discussed in detail in Chapter 13. For now, you should understand that you can enforce conformance to a set of design standards. The standards that come with VSTS out of the box are the standards Microsoft uses in .NET Framework and Visual Studio. You can select all or just a subset of code analysis warnings to enforce.

Note C/C++ code analysis engages a separate code analysis tool for unmanaged code. This is covered in Chapter 13.

Testing Policy

This policy ensures that the code to be checked in has passed a given set of tests. These tests are not tests created on the local machine. They are loaded from a test meta data file (.vsmdi) located in TFVC. This prevents a developer from writing any test that will work in order to get the code checked in. It also ensures that the checked-in code will work as advertised before it is checked in.

When you select this option, you will be able to browse to a specific .vsmdi file and will be given a list of tests that exist for the current project. You can then select the specific lists you want to ensure are run before code is checked in.

Tip You cannot specify individual tests, only specific lists of tests. This is a best practice because it allows a project to ensure that certain basic standards are met (for example, can whatever code you write integrate with the security system, or something along those lines?).

You can also add additional tests to the list(s) without having to change the policy. Keeping a base set of mandatory test lists is a good idea.

Work Items Policy

The work items policy says you must associate a work item with the code you are checking in. Work items are discussed in detail in Chapter 4. For the moment it is enough to understand that you can associate specific pieces of work with specific tasks. For example, if a project manager assigns you a bug to work on, you will check out the code necessary to fix the bug. When the bug is fixed you will check the code back in. By requiring that you associate checked-in items with a work item, the status of bugs and other assignments can be reported and tracked at the project-management level.

Check-in Notes

This setting allows you to specify who must review the changes before they are checked in. The default values are Code Reviewer, Security Reviewer, and Performance Reviewer. These are user-defined values and you can enter your own titles, such as Developer Lead or some other value. None of these reviews are required by default but checking the Required check box will make them required.

Caution As mentioned earlier, there are ways around the check-in settings. In the case of the reviewers, all a developer has to do is type anything into the entry field when they go to check in a file and it will be accepted. This is one of those areas to watch out for.

IDE Version Control Configuration

Certain settings are available in the IDE and support a specific developer's needs when working with version control. To access the IDE configuration, select Tools ➤ Options, and select Source Control from the tree view (Figure 3-34).

Figure 3-34. *Environment Options*

Plugin Selection

This displays the list of available source control providers. For example, a typical installation of VSTS might have Visual Studio Team Foundation Server, Microsoft Visual SourceSafe, and Microsoft Visual SourceSafe (Internet). There are also other plugins available from other vendors. If you have any problems with TFVC (for example, everything is grayed out and you have no menu options for dealing with version control), then it is a good bet that the wrong source control provider has been selected.

Environment

This allows you to specify how the IDE will react to given situations. Figure 3-34 shows the various options you can set.

For dealing with checked-in items, you have the following options when performing a save: check out the file automatically; prompt for check-out; or perform a Save As. For files you are editing: check out automatically (when you start editing); prompt for check-out; prompt for exclusive check-out; or do nothing. If you choose the last option you will not be able to edit the file at all unless you check "Allow checked-in items to be edited."

Visual Studio Team Foundation

These options deal with how your local system will interact with the Team Foundation Server. The first option is whether to use the Team Foundation Proxy Server (TFPS). TFPS was built to facilitate remote access to the Team Foundation Version Control. Often the Internet is less than reliable—there are outages or there are a large number of files involved. TFPS is installed on a server in a remote location. When you use TFPS, the first check for a file is made on the proxy server. If the file is found, it is downloaded from the cache. If it is not found it is downloaded from the central repository. The proxy server ensures that files are kept in a consistent state (i.e., you cannot do a Get Latest, and it retrieves the latest version of the proxy server, which is actually two versions behind the central server). This can help ease the burden of slow connections on remote teams.

■Tip For more information on setting up a Team Foundation Proxy Server, see the Team Foundation Installation Guide.

You also have the option to show deleted items in SCE. This will show the item grayed out and noted as deleted. By default this is off.

Finally, there is a Configure User Tools section. This allows you to specify your own tools (as opposed to the default tools provided for you by VSTS). It allows you to specify your own Merge or Compare tools. For example, Diff Doc is a popular (and free) tool for comparing Microsoft Word documents. Figure 3-35 shows the settings for DiffDoc.exe.

Figure 3-35. *Diff Doc tool settings*

The arguments for various tools can be somewhat confusing and difficult to configure. James Manning at Microsoft has an excellent blog describing how to configure different tools at http://blogs.msdn.com/jmanning/articles/535573.aspx.

Creating Custom Check-in Policies

Custom check-in policies allow you to specify your own constraints, which must be met before items can be checked in. Creating a check-in policy is fairly straightforward. The example presented here was originally written by Jeff Atwood of Vertigo Software (you can check out his blog at http://blogs.vertigosoftware.com/jatwood/default.aspx) and was helped along by James Manning.

Creating the Policy

This example requires that a user enter a comment before checking code in. All in all this is probably the most useful check-in policy ever, as we are notorious for *not* entering comments! Listing 3-3 shows the code for the empty comment check-in policy.

Listing 3-3. *Required Comment Check-in Policy*

```csharp
[C#]
using System;
using System.Windows.Forms;
using Microsoft.TeamFoundation.VersionControl.Client;
[Serializable]
public class CheckForCommentsPolicy : PolicyBase
{
    public override string Description
    {
        get { return "Remind users to add meaningful comments "
                    + "to their checkins"; }
    }

    public override string InstallationInstructions
    {
        get { return "To install this policy, follow the "
                    + "instructions in CheckForCommentsPolicy.cs."; }
    }

    public override string Type
    {
        get { return "Check for Comments Policy"; }
    }

    public override string TypeDescription
    {
        get { return "This policy will prompt the user to decide whether or not "
                        + "they should be allowed to check in."; }
    }

    public override bool Edit(IPolicyEditArgs args)
    {
        // no configuration to save
        return true;
    }

    public override PolicyFailure[] Evaluate()
    {
        string proposedComment = PendingCheckin.PendingChanges.Comment;
        if (String.IsNullOrEmpty(proposedComment))
        {
            return new PolicyFailure[] {
                new PolicyFailure("Please provide some comments "
                        + "about your checkin", this) };
```

```csharp
            }
            else
            {
                return new PolicyFailure[0];
            }
        }

        public override void Activate(PolicyFailure failure)
        {
            MessageBox.Show("Please provide comments for your checkin.",
                            "How to fix your policy failure");
        }

        public override void DisplayHelp(PolicyFailure failure)
        {
            MessageBox.Show("This policy helps you to remember to "
                + "add comments to your checkins.", "Prompt Policy Help");
        }
}
```
[VB]
```vb
Imports System
Imports System.Windows.Forms
Imports Microsoft.TeamFoundation.VersionControl.Client

<Serializable()> _
Public Class CheckForCommentsPolicy
    Inherits PolicyBase

    Public Overrides ReadOnly Property Description() As String
        Get
            Return "Remind users to add meaningful comments " _
                    & "to their checkins"
        End Get
    End Property

    Public Overrides Property InstallationInstructions() As String
        Get
            Return "To install this policy, follow the " _
                    & "instructions in CheckForCommentsPolicyVB.vb."
        End Get
        Set(ByVal value As String)
            MyBase.InstallationInstructions = value
        End Set
    End Property
```

```vb
    Public Overrides ReadOnly Property Type() As String
        Get
            Return "Check for Comments Policy"
        End Get
    End Property

    Public Overrides ReadOnly Property TypeDescription() As String
        Get
            Return "This policy will prompt the user to " _
                & "decide whether or not they should be " _
                & "allowed to check in."
        End Get
    End Property

    Public Overrides Function Edit(ByVal args As IPolicyEditArgs) As Boolean
        ' no configuration to save
        Return True
    End Function

    Public Overrides Function Evaluate() As _
Microsoft.TeamFoundation.VersionControl.Client.PolicyFailure()
        Dim proposedComment As String = PendingCheckin.PendingChanges.Comment
        If String.IsNullOrEmpty(proposedComment) Then
            Dim msg As String = "Please provide some comments " _
                & "about your checkin"
            Dim p As PolicyFailure() = New PolicyFailure(1) {}
            p(0) = New PolicyFailure(msg, Me)
            Return p
        Else
            Return New PolicyFailure(0) {}
        End If
    End Function

    Public Overrides Sub Activate(ByVal failure As PolicyFailure)
        MessageBox.Show("Please provide comments for your checkin.", _
                        "How to fix your policy failure")
    End Sub

    Public Overrides Sub DisplayHelp(ByVal failure As PolicyFailure)
        MessageBox.Show("This policy helps you to remember to " _
            & "add comments to your checkins.", "Prompt Policy Help")
    End Sub

End Class
```

Now, what does all of this mean? Table 3-4 describes each custom policy method.

Table 3-4. *Custom Policy Methods Described*

Method	Description
Description	This provides a description of the policy.
InstallationInstruction	The return value of this method is stored on the Team Foundation Server and is displayed when a user does not have the policy installed. As a best practice, a policy should be installed on the local machine that needs the policy. In version 1 of VSTS, partially trusted code is not allowed to be executed. That means that to install the policy in a remote location requires that full trust is enabled for code running on a remote system, which is not recommended.
Type	This describes the type of policy.
TypeDescription	This gives a more detailed identification of the type.
Edit	This method displays a UI and saves the configuration of your type if your custom check-in policy contains configuration options (such as the Testing Policy).
Evaluate	This validates that what you are checking in passes the policy check.
Activate	This method displays information to the user when they double-click an item on the Policy Failure page to explain why a policy failed (or whatever other information you want to present to the user).
DisplayHelp	This can be used to display a custom help file or link to a web page or to just display a simple message. It is invoked when the user presses the F1 key and the policy is selected on the Policy Failure page.

Registering the Policy

Creating the policy is the first part of the process. Once you create it, you have to install it.

Caution Microsoft recommends that policies be installed on the local machine. If this is not done, you will have to allow full trust of assemblies residing on remote machines, which, in general, is not a secure practice.

To install the policy, copy the assembly to your local machine (preferably, all assemblies that need to be downloaded to a developer's machine should be stored on a secure network share). Make the following entries in the registry:

Key: HKLM\Software\Microsoft\VisualStudio\8.0\TeamFoundation\SourceControl\Checkin Policies or HKCU\Software\Microsoft\VisualStudio\8.0\TeamFoundation\SourceControl\Checkin Policies

Type: Reg_sz

Name: Policy Class (in this example, Check for Comments Policy)

Data: Absolute path to the assembly

Alternatively, you can (and probably should) configure a .reg file, the contents of which are shown in Listing 3-4.

Listing 3-4. *Registration File*

```
Windows Registry Editor Version 5.00

[HKEY_LOCAL_MACHINE\SOFTWARE\Microsoft\VisualStudio\8.0\
    TeamFoundation\SourceControl\Checkin Policies]
"CheckForCommentsPolicy"="[Full Path to File]\\CheckForCommentsPolicy.dll"
```

After you run this file (simply double-click on it and you will be prompted to make the change to the registry), the Check for Comments Policy will be displayed in the list of available policies (Figure 3-36).

Figure 3-36. *Custom check-in policy*

With this example in hand, you should be able to create any type of policies you or your organization feel are necessary.

Converting from Visual SourceSafe to Team Foundation Version Control

Needless to say, this is a welcome conversion tool. In addition to this, you can migrate from Rational ClearQuest. The process of migration is an extensive process that needs to be carefully planned. We have not included this process here, since Microsoft has done a very thorough job of explaining it in the MSDN documentation. We just wanted to let you know that you could do it!

Command-Line Access

Team Foundation Version Control allows you to perform all of the operations you normally would through Visual Studio via the command line. This powerful feature means you can easily incorporate version control actions within batch files.

Tip Microsoft provides excellent documentation on the version control command-line tool (`tf.exe`) in its MSDN documentation. The broad overview of topics covered will give you a solid introduction to using the tool.

The command-line application is `tf.exe`. It resides in the `C:\Program Files\Microsoft Visual Studio 8\Common 7\IDE` folder. You can use this tool to perform individual commands at the command prompt or to process scripted files that contain version control commands. The best use of the command-line tool is with scripted files. When used with a scripted file, the command-line tool can accept any number of arguments that can be referenced in the scripted file by using %1, %2, …, %n where the number refers to the argument number on the command line. To invoke a script file, use the following syntax:

`tf.exe @filename.tfc arguments`

You can also change directories and include comments in the script files. The available commands are grouped into two categories: informational and action. Each of these commands has various options that allow you to control which objects they are applied to. They are fairly self-explanatory and are described in detail in the MSDN documentation.

Informational commands allow data concerning various items under version control to be retrieved.

- *Branches*: Lists the branch history of a file or a folder.
- *Changeset*: Lists information regarding changesets.
- *Difference*: Compares and displays (depending on the mode used) differences between two files or folders.
- *Dir*: Lists files and folders in a given directory.
- *Labels*: Lists all labels in the repository.
- *Permission*: Lists users and groups along with their permissions.
- *Properties*: Lists information about a given file or folder.
- *Shelvesets*: Lists information about shelved changes.
- *Status*: Lists information concerning pending changes.
- *WorkFold*: Creates, modifies, or lists mappings between repository folders and the corresponding work folders.
- *Workspaces*: Lists information about workspaces in the repository.

Action commands, listed below, allow you to perform various actions on those items under source code control.

- Add
- Branch
- Branches
- Checkin
- Checkout
- Configure
- Delete
- Dir
- Get
- History
- Label
- Lock
- Merge
- Merges
- Permission
- Properties
- Rename
- Resolve
- Shelve
- Status
- Undelete
- Undo
- Unlabel
- Unshelve
- View
- Workspace

Summary

At this point you now have extensive knowledge about using the new Team Foundation Version Control. You know how to create repositories, check items in, check them out, alter them, resolve conflicts, and merge them. You have been introduced to the concepts of shelving and branching, which ensure that you never have to worry about a hard-drive crash causing you to lose work (but it is not our fault if you forget to actually add the code to the repository!).

You can also configure check-in policies, which in our opinion is one of the best features of TFVC. And you have the ability to create your own check-in policies that fit your organization's specific needs. The ability to supply your own merge and compare tools to replace the out-of-the-box versions that come with Team Foundation will no doubt be a welcome option to many developers. And you have seen how the Team Foundation Proxy Server helps support distributed teams by caching versions of files on a local network; this should ease the burden when projects are outsourced around the globe.

Chapter 4 gives you the ins and outs of project management and VSTS integration. You will learn how to use Microsoft Project and Excel to create schedules, assign work, and track issues without using Visual Studio or Team Explorer.

CHAPTER 4

Project Management

Neither of the authors has ever been a project manager. We have had the luxury of leading teams from a technical perspective and have left the high-profile leadership to others. Project management is, to say the least, a thankless job at times. We have worked with numerous project managers and have seen the problems they face. These problems range from getting developers to track their time against work items, to explaining to the customer why the project is not going as smoothly as the customer imagines it will go. There are many more problems in between that the project manager has to deal with.

At the base of the project manager's job is creating schedules, recording data, and reporting data. This is where Visual Studio Team System plays a role in simplifying the project manager's role. The tools in VSTS that relate to project management help bring together tasks performed by Microsoft Project (or Excel), work item tracking, and the Project Portal. VSTS allows the project manager to create schedules in Microsoft Project (these schedules include the work items for the team members), add work items from Microsoft Excel (or Project), track changes to work items via the project schedule, and publish updates to the Project Portal. No longer do team members have to report status to the project manager—the project manager can just pull the data.

Note Okay, let us face facts. Team members (and you know who you are) do not report anything to the project manager. It's like pulling teeth. So, in this case, project managers no longer have to pester team members to report what they are working on.

The heart of this system is the work item tracking system and the version control system. They work together to supply the information the project manager needs to provide accurate information in a timely fashion to the appropriate people—the people who ultimately continue to fund the development of a project.

In this chapter you will see how the integration with MS Project works, and how to add work items, update work items, and refresh work items using both Microsoft Project and Microsoft Excel. We discuss work items in great detail in Chapter 5.

A Week in the Life of a Project Manager (without VSTS)

Before showing you how to use VSTS to manage projects, let's take a look at what project managers actually do by looking at the starting week of a new project.

Day 1, Monday

The project manager, whom we'll call John, sets up Microsoft Project with all of the resources available at the time (typically, the system architect and/or the application architect, and possibly a lead developer and tester). John creates the basic outline of the project (system development life cycle phases and high-level deliverables) and assigns some deliverables to the available resources. In real life this usually takes more than a day but in this case John is very fast.

Day 2, Tuesday

John creates Excel spreadsheets for each member of the project team. He transfers the tasks they are responsible for from Microsoft Project to each of the spreadsheets (if John is really technical, he has written or has used a previously created macro to do this automatically). John has to do this at the beginning or end of every week for the following week for each member of the team. This becomes more tedious as more resources are added.

Day 3, Wednesday

Now the project manager has to set up a communication plan with the stakeholders. John has to find out what the stakeholders want to know and when they want to know it. He needs to figure out how to configure a change management system (i.e., create the process for the system and integrate it with the tools—usually Excel spreadsheets and e-mails). This is sometimes exceedingly difficult because different classes of stakeholders want to know different things.

Day 4, Thursday

On the fourth day of the week, the project manager has to set up shares, folders, etc., for the project team to store their files (user requirements, owner specifications, architecture documents, etc.). He then has to publicize and document the structure so the location of all of the deliverables and related documents is known.

Day 5, Friday

The end of the first week. Whew. John is almost done. Now he just needs to find out what everyone did for the week so he can report their status to the stakeholders and find out what is left to do for each deliverable assigned to the various project team members. The only problem is that no one filled in the Excel time sheets and mailed them to John. Now he has to send e-mails and hound team members for their status. Once they send him the Excel spreadsheets (because everyone on the team is really good at doing that) he has to extract all of the numbers and update Microsoft Project with the number of hours left to complete a deliverable, or mark the deliverable as complete.

Two Days in the Life of a Project Manager (with VSTS)

Now, let's see that scenario with Visual Studio Team System's project management integration capabilities.

Day 1, Monday

The project manager creates a new team project using Visual Studio Team System (selecting the appropriate methodology template). He adds all of the resources that he knows about to the new team project. John opens Microsoft Project and adds all of the project resources to the new project file. John creates the basic outline of the project (SDLC phases and high-level deliverables) and assigns some deliverables to the available resources. In real life this usually takes more than a day, but in this case John is very fast. John updates the changes he made in Microsoft Project with the Team Foundation Server.

Day 2, Tuesday

John sends out an e-mail to the stakeholders detailing where the team project portal is and how to access the available reports. John sets the policy that changesets must be associated with work items, and then John spends the rest of the week fishing.

Okay, it is not quite that cushy for a project manager, but you get the idea. Much of the tedious work simply does not need to be done. In the rest of this chapter, you will see how this is actually accomplished.

Note There is a lot more that goes into creating a project schedule than is described here. For the purposes of this chapter, only those items that are directly related to Visual Studio Team System will be discussed. The "schedule" will only consist of the items assigned when the project was created.

Using Microsoft Project

The first thing a project manager will do (after the team project is created) is create a project schedule. The project schedule consists of a series of tasks, which may also include other tasks—in other words, a hierarchical structure of tasks. They consist of start times, due dates, descriptions, and to whom the tasks are assigned.

CHAPTER 4 ■ PROJECT MANAGEMENT

■Note Tasks are a type of work item. These terms are used interchangeably in this chapter.

To begin with, launch Microsoft Project from the Start menu (Start ➤ Programs ➤ Microsoft Office ➤ Microsoft Project). If everything is installed correctly, you will see an additional toolbar in Project (shown in Figure 4-1).

Figure 4-1. *VSTS toolbar in Microsoft Project*

As you can see, before you can create a schedule, you need to select the team project this schedule will be associated with. To do this, select Choose Team Project (also available from the Team menu on the main menu). This brings up the Connect to Team Foundation Server dialog box shown in Figure 4-2.

Figure 4-2. *Connect to Team Foundation Server dialog box*

Select the server where your project resides, then select the Effort Tracking project and click OK.

TIP You can also open a project from Team Explorer by selecting Server ➤ [Project Name] ➤ Project Management ➤ Development Project Plan.mpp which is associated with the project by default.

Once you have done this, the Get Work Items, Publish, and Refresh options become available to you. At this point though you still do not have any work items visible.

Retrieving, Adding, and Updating Work Items

To get the work items from the server, select Get Work Items from the toolbar. This will display the Get Work Items dialog box shown in Figure 4-3.

Figure 4-3. *Get Work Items dialog box*

For this exercise, select the All Tasks saved query and click Find. Note though that you can search on various items depending on what your needs are. At the beginning of a project, the All Tasks query is a good place to start, as these are the only tasks that are currently part of the project. By default, everything returned by the lookup is selected for inclusion in the project schedule. Click OK to import the items into Microsoft Project (Figure 4-4).

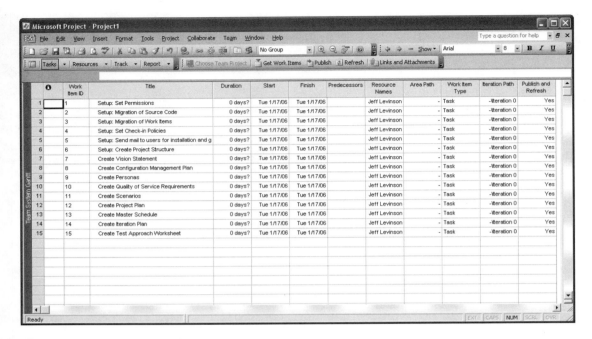

Figure 4-4. *Initial project schedule*

There are a couple of small items to note here:

- The start and end times for all tasks are for the day the project is created and have a duration of zero days.

- No predecessors are set.

- The resource for all items is the individual who created the team project.

- There are no project areas at this point, so no changes can be made there.

- All iterations are iteration 0, even though there are three iterations, since it is assumed these tasks occur at the start of the project.

At this point you can change whatever you want to change as needed. To begin with, you would probably remove any items that were not needed on your project. To delete an item, select it (item 15 is a good choice here) and press the Delete key (or right-click the item and select Delete. After you have completed making changes, you must publish the changes to the server. To publish the changes, just select the Publish button from the toolbar.

Tip You can elect *not* to publish an item by selecting either No or Refresh Only from the Publish and Refresh column. Selecting No indicates that the item will never be published, and selecting Refresh Only indicates that the item will be refreshed, but no changes you make to the item will ever be published.

This updates Team Foundation Server and if you added any items will return the Work Item ID to populate the project schedule.

■Caution In version 1 of VSTS you cannot assign multiple resources to a single task. You have to duplicate the task and set one resource per task. The VSTS development team is actively looking at this issue. If you try to assign multiple resources to a single task, an error message will be displayed when you publish the changes.

The ability to publish only certain items is important. A project manager would probably *not* want to publish the roll-up tasks because those are not tasks that can be "worked," per se.

■Tip To assign work items to multiple resources, you must create the work item several times and assign only one resource to each work item.

Adding Attachments and Links

In addition to adding, retrieving, and updating items, you can also attach files and links to specific work items. To attach files and links, an item must already be published. Select a published item in the list and then select Links & Attachments. This will bring up the View/Edit Work Item Links and Attachments dialog box (Figure 4-5).

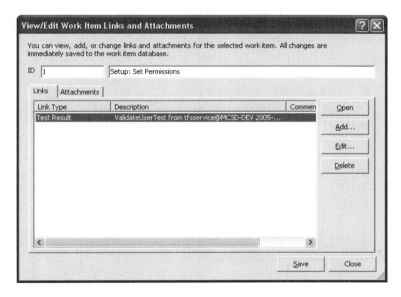

Figure 4-5. *View/Edit Work Item Links and Attachments dialog box*

A link can be one of the following: Changeset, Work Item, Versioned Item, Test Result, or a regular hyperlink. Depending on the type of link you are adding, the options are different. The Add Link dialog box is shown in Figure 4-6.

Figure 4-6. *Add Link dialog box*

The dialog in Figure 4-6 shows the options for a Work Item link type. Clicking the Browse button will display the Get Work Items dialog box shown in Figure 4-3. The Find Changesets dialog box will be displayed if you elect to link to a changeset (Figure 4-7).

Figure 4-7. *Find Changesets dialog box*

■Note While project managers *can* associate work items with changesets, it is generally not something a project manager would often do. Consider it as a tip for what you can do within Microsoft Project.

For the Find Changesets dialog, you browse to a specific file (contained in the source code control system) or enter a specific user's name and click Find. This will return all of the changesets for either that file or that user. The Range options let you filter the result set more granularly. From there you may either view the details of the changeset or select a result to link to.

The Versioned Item option provides the same dialog, only it lets you link to the item in a specific changeset (which you can browse for) or to the latest version of the item.

Selecting the Test Result option lets you browse for a specific test result (Figure 4-8).

Figure 4-8. *Choose Test Result dialog box*

In this dialog box you can select the build number, the type, and a specific test run. From there you can select the specific test to link an item to. In this case, select any test that appears in the list and click OK.

■Tip For the project manager, many of these options are a way of tracking developers' time and ensuring that a given task is completed. Using the Test Result link as an example, if a bug in the system needs to be fixed, a bug work item would be created (work items are discussed in depth in Chapter 5). When fixed, the developer could mark it as completed, and a project manager (or a developer, or a tester) could associate the results that validate the fix with the bug.

All link types allow you to enter a comment against the link.

Once you have selected your links, they will be displayed in the list view in Figure 4-5. Selecting an item in the list and then clicking Open will cause various windows to open, depending on the type of link you select. With the previous example, using a test result link, clicking the Open button displays the result shown in Figure 4-9.

Figure 4-9. *Test Result Details link*

Adding an attachment is fairly straightforward. Click the Attachment tab, click Add, browse to the file you want to attach, and select OK. You can also enter a comment against the file. The one difference here is that links are automatically saved to the server as they are entered; files are not. When you have finished attaching all of the files you want, click the Save button. This will upload the files to the server.

Areas and Iterations

Areas and iterations can be added, deleted, and configured from within Microsoft Project, which displays the same dialogs as described in detail in Chapter 2.

Column Mapping

Finally, a project manager can view column mappings in Microsoft Project. Figure 4-10 shows a column displayed in Microsoft Project and the equivalent column in the VSTS database. You cannot actually make changes to the mapping through this dialog box. In order to make changes you will need to use the TFSFieldMapping command-line tool described next.

Figure 4-10. *Column Mapping dialog box*

■**Note** The work item tracking command-line tools provide the ability to add and remove columns from the TFS database in order to support custom fields. These tools are discussed in Chapter 5.

To use the TFSFieldMapping tool, open the Visual Studio Command Prompt. Before changing mappings, you need to have a copy of the mapping file. To download the mapping file, run the following at the command prompt (or replace the items with appropriate values):

```
Tfsfieldmapping download kiona "Effort Tracking" "c:\mapping.xml"
```

This will download the mapping file for your project. The file is in, as with almost every other file in VSTS, an XML format. This file is shown in Listing 4-1.

Listing 4-1. *TFS Field Mapping File*

```
<?xml version="1.0" encoding="utf-8"?>
<MSProject>
  <Mappings>
    <Mapping WorkItemTrackingFieldReferenceName="System.Id"
      ProjectField="pjTaskText10" ProjectName="Work Item ID"/>
        <Mapping WorkItemTrackingFieldReferenceName="System.Title"
          ProjectField="pjTaskName" />
     <Mapping WorkItemTrackingFieldReferenceName="System.WorkItemType"
       ProjectField="pjTaskText24" />
```

```xml
        <Mapping WorkItemTrackingFieldReferenceName=
          "Microsoft.VSTS.Common.Discipline"
          ProjectField="pjTaskText17" />
        <Mapping WorkItemTrackingFieldReferenceName="System.AssignedTo"
          ProjectField="pjTaskResourceNames" />
        <Mapping WorkItemTrackingFieldReferenceName=
          "Microsoft.VSTS.Scheduling.CompletedWork" ProjectField="pjTaskActualWork"
          ProjectUnits="pjHour"/>
        <Mapping WorkItemTrackingFieldReferenceName=
          "Microsoft.VSTS.Scheduling.RemainingWork"
          ProjectField="pjTaskRemainingWork"
          ProjectUnits="pjHour"/>
        <Mapping WorkItemTrackingFieldReferenceName=
          "Microsoft.VSTS.Scheduling.BaselineWork" ProjectField="pjTaskBaselineWork"
          ProjectUnits="pjHour"/>
        <Mapping WorkItemTrackingFieldReferenceName=
          "Microsoft.VSTS.Scheduling.StartDate" ProjectField="pjTaskStart"
          PublishOnly="true"/>
        <Mapping WorkItemTrackingFieldReferenceName=
          "Microsoft.VSTS.Scheduling.FinishDate" ProjectField="pjTaskFinish"
          PublishOnly="true"/>
        <Mapping WorkItemTrackingFieldReferenceName="System.State"
          ProjectField="pjTaskText13" />
        <Mapping WorkItemTrackingFieldReferenceName="System.Reason"
          ProjectField="pjTaskText14" />
        <Mapping WorkItemTrackingFieldReferenceName="Microsoft.VSTS.Common.Priority"
          ProjectField="pjTaskText19" ProjectName="Work Item Priority" />
        <Mapping WorkItemTrackingFieldReferenceName="System.AreaPath"
          ProjectField="pjTaskOutlineCode9" />
        <Mapping WorkItemTrackingFieldReferenceName="System.IterationPath"
          ProjectField="pjTaskOutlineCode10" />
        <Mapping WorkItemTrackingFieldReferenceName="System.Rev"
          ProjectField="pjTaskText23" />
        <ContextField WorkItemTrackingFieldReferenceName=
          "Microsoft.VSTS.Scheduling.TaskHierarchy"/>
        <LinksField    ProjectField="pjTaskText26" />
        <SyncField     ProjectField="pjTaskText25" />
    </Mappings>
</MSProject>
```

In order to change the mappings, simply update the WorkItemTrackingFieldReference-Name values or the ProjectField values. When you have finished making changes, upload this file back to TFS to complete the mapping update. To do that, use the same command as you did to download the file—just use the word "upload" instead of "download" and you are done.

> **■Tip** The PublishOnly setting is an incredibly useful field. As a project manager, you may not want people to be able to change start and end dates of work items via Microsoft Project or Excel. You may not want them to change other items that you consider important. Adding this attribute allows people to retrieve the value, but not update it.

Using Microsoft Excel

Microsoft Excel is everyone's favorite friend. If some major problem caused Excel to go down all over the world, virtually every business on the planet would grind to a halt rather suddenly. Knowing how useful Excel is to everyone, the VSTS team used the capabilities of Excel to allow team members to enter items into TFS through the Excel interface.

> **■Note** Excel is a part of Microsoft Office; Microsoft Project requires a separate license. In general, only the project manager needs to be using Project, and everyone else can use Excel to make entries if they need to (all entries by the development team can be made from within Visual Studio though).

If you are a project manager reading this, how often have you had to create macros to pull data from MS Project into Excel so developers can log their hours against specific items? If you are a developer reading this, how many times have you gone from project to project, where everyone has a different way of recording hours? The beauty of this solution is that it is all automatic. You can get your work items (if you need to fill this sheet in); you can get everyone's work items (if you are a project manager); you can customize the query to see if work was completed (or just filter this list); or you can perform a hundred other operations to slice and dice the data any way you see fit to gather useful information.

> **■Tip** Another key benefit of Excel, and one of the reasons Microsoft chose to use it as the interface, is its easy ability to create charts from any type of data in VSTS. Even though you have the benefits of SQL Server Reporting Services, using Excel is often much faster—especially if the reports are for the project manager only.

The Excel interface is slightly different from the Project interface. When you first launch a new Excel file, the toolbar shown in Figure 4-11 is displayed.

Figure 4-11. *The Excel Team System toolbar*

Creating Lists in Excel

Before you can do anything with Excel and VSTS, you need to create a new list by selecting New List from the toolbar. This displays the Connect to a Team Foundation Server dialog box (Figure 4-2). Once you connect to a Team Foundation Server you have the option of retrieving the results of a query or inputting new items (Figure 4-12).

Figure 4-12. *The Excel New List dialog box*

For this first example, assume that you select the All Tasks query and click OK. This creates the list in Excel as shown in Figure 4-13.

This list should immediately validate why this is a popular tool for both project managers and other team members alike.

■**Note** Some fields in this list are read-only. For instance, you cannot change the work item type once it has been created.

Publishing items from Excel works the same way as it does in Project—you just click the Publish button. However, you can also configure a list in Excel and choose which columns you want to view as part of the list.

Selecting the Input List option (Figure 4-12) creates a blank list with several default columns. This allows you to enter items without having to first retrieve items from the server.

CHAPTER 4 ■ PROJECT MANAGEMENT   117

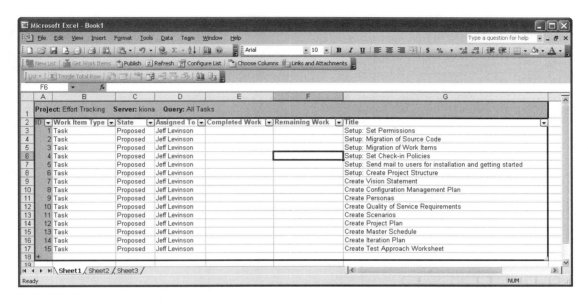

Figure 4-13. *Query results in Microsoft Excel*

Configuring Lists in Excel

To configure the list, select Configure List from the toolbar. This will display the Configure List Properties dialog box shown in Figure 4-14.

Figure 4-14. *Configure List Properties*

This dialog box in itself does not do anything; however, it affects how the list is updated from the server. The default is to Refresh from query. This means that whenever you click Refresh on the toolbar, the same query will be run over again and any new or updated items will be shown in the list. Selecting the "Refresh current work items only" option means that when you click Refresh, only items that are currently in the list will be updated.

> **Note** Clicking Refresh also enables the Get Work Items button, which allows you to add other items not in the current list (see Figure 4-3 and the associated explanation).

The other option to configure lists in Excel is to select the columns you want to display in the list. To do this, select the Choose Columns button. This will display the Choose Columns dialog box shown in Figure 4-15.

Figure 4-15. *Choose Columns dialog box*

This dialog box lets you choose columns associated with any work item type (via the drop-down list at the top of the form) because the list in Excel can display mixed item types. This means that the possible configurations in Excel are virtually endless depending on your need. The available columns are too extensive to list here, but any column you have seen so far, and in the next chapter, is available through this dialog box. To add a column, just select the column on the right and click the right arrow button. Click the left arrow button to remove an item from the selected columns list.

Clicking reset will reset the columns to the default for the given list. Selecting Add Required will add all required items from the Available Columns list (those identified with a "Required" after the column name) to the Selected Columns column.

Links and attachments work the same way as described in the "Adding Attachments and Links" section.

Using Visual Studio

You can of course use Visual Studio to perform project management duties. You can add tasks, assign tasks, and set start and end dates all from within Visual Studio (see Figure 4-16).

Figure 4-16. *Task list in Visual Studio*

The details tab contains the schedule information. Virtually everything else on this work item form (bottom portion of Figure 4-16) maps to a field in Excel or Microsoft Project. In general, this is not a very friendly view for project managers, which Microsoft realizes. This is the reason for the Excel and Microsoft Project integration. However, when a project manager finds himself or herself looking at a task list in Visual Studio (come to think of it, this applies to anyone who works with VSTS), the team member can view everything in the task list in Excel or Microsoft Project. To do this, simply select all of the items you want to export, and select the appropriate icon on the task list toolbar. Enough said about project management from within Visual Studio.

Summary

In this chapter you saw how the integration between Visual Studio Team System and Microsoft Project and Excel will save you countless hours of work and allow you to manage a project's data more easily. A project manager typically manages multiple software projects at once, because no one software project should take up all of their time. At least, that is the theory. The reality is that project managers often spend way too much time figuring out how they are going to record the team's time, and against which items, track the status of items, and report status to the stakeholders.

With the simple but powerful and well thought out integration described in this chapter, much of the grunt work is simply removed. Teams will now have a repeatable, simple way to track their activities and the hours logged against items, the amount of work left, whether estimates are accurate, and so on. It all leads to one thing: through continued use of the tool, teams will become more efficient and spend more time engineering software rather than performing administrative tasks (which no one likes anyway). The next chapter introduces you to the details of the work items.

CHAPTER 5

Team Work Item Tracking

When you're working on a project of any size, you need to manage a number of lists. Even building a tree fort for your kids may involve several lists: the list of local building projects where you could acquire spare lumber, the list of priority features (like trapdoors, escape ropes, and an electronic drawbridge), and the list of friends who actually know how to build things.

At the startup of a software project, there are the customer requirements, startup tasks, and many other lists to manage. As the project evolves, the team begins to compile lists of bugs, issues, and change requests. Team Foundation addresses the concept of list management in a feature area called work item tracking (WIT). WIT originated from the Microsoft internal bug-tracking systems. Per Kevin Kelly's weblog on MSDN (http://blogs.msdn.com/kkellyatms/archive/2004/05/28/144108.aspx):

> *We knew we had to settle on something . . . ideally somewhat unique, and something folks would just get. The essence of our system helps teams manage discrete units of work, assigned to individuals and, when taken as a whole, it represents all activities (another famous term! and taken) managed in a software development project. They're all the work items of a project . . . work item tracking. Teams define the types of work items they want to track . . . and I'll leave details of this for later posts.*

This chapter introduces WIT, which is arguably the core component of Team Foundation. In a sense, work items are the glue that holds Team Foundation together. If we were discussing a banking scenario, the work items would be analogous to account entries. The common definition for VSTS work items is that they are assigned to an individual for someone to act upon.

Working with Work Items

Work Items is the first node in the Team Explorer window under the project name. Right-click the Work Items node to see the options for working with work items, as shown in Figure 5-1. Table 5-1 describes each of these options.

Figure 5-1. *The Work Items context menu*

Note The Work Items context menu will show the four most recent selections made. For example, if you selected Add Work Item ➤ Bug, then Add Bug would appear above Add Work Item the next time you right-clicked the Work Items node.

Table 5-1. *Work Items Explorer Options*

Option	Description
Add Work Item	Opens a form for the work item type selected
Go to Work Item	Opens a form for the work item based on the ID entered
Add Query	Opens the New Query window
Add Work Items with Microsoft Excel	Allows you to populate a Microsoft Excel spreadsheet with work items and publish them to the Team Foundation Server (as described in Chapter 4)
Add Work Items with Microsoft Project	Allows you to populate a Microsoft Project task list with work items and publish them to the Team Foundation Server (as described in Chapter 4)
Team Project Process Guidance	Opens the Process Guidance Work Items section within the Project Portal (as described in Chapter 2)

Optionally, you can create and manage work items from the Team menu, as shown in Figure 5-2.

Figure 5-2. *Team menu options*

Team Foundation provides three views for creating and managing work items:

- The *form view*, as its name suggests, presents each field of the work items in a standardized form layout.

- The *query view* allows you to query the work item database based on selection criteria and provides a list of results.

- The *results* (or *triage*) *view* displays the results of saved queries in a combination of form and list view, which makes it easy to route and assign work items.

The following sections describe these views in more detail.

Using the Form View

The first view most people encounter is the form view of the work item. When you select Add Work Item from the Work Items context menu, you will be presented with this view. Figure 5-3 shows the first task work item in the EffortTracking project.

The standard layout for the work item form is to have the summary information at the top of the form and detail items presented at the bottom on separate tabs. The middle section contains status fields, including State and Reason, which represent basic elements of workflow in this first release of Team Foundation Server.

Two of the key features for work items are the ability to link to other items and to include attachments.

Figure 5-3. *Form view of a work item*

Adding Links

Click the Links tab at the bottom of the form to view the Links pane, which shows the link type, description, and comments. Click the Add button on the right side of the pane to open the Add Link dialog box, shown in Figure 5-4.

Figure 5-4. *The Add Link dialog box*

Here, you can select from four Team Foundation Server elements (Changeset, Work Item, Versioned Item, or Test Result) and the hyperlink to any URL (Web) or UNC (server) location. After you've added the link, you can open the linked item by double-clicking the item in the Links pane or by selecting the Open button for a highlighted link.

Adding Attachments

Click the Attachments tab at the bottom of the form to view the Attachments pane, which shows the name, size, and comments for any attached items. Click the Add button on the right to open the Add Attachment dialog box, as shown in Figure 5-5.

Figure 5-5. *The Add Attachment dialog box*

In this example, we added a picture of the security groups from Active Directory for the Set Permissions task.

Using the Query View

The query view is very similar to the query builder for SQL Server. In fact, the project team refers to the query builder as "sick SQL" and the query language as Work Item Query Language (WIQL).

Using Predefined Queries

A number of predefined project queries are provided, depending on the selected process template. In the MSF for CMMI Process Improvement - v4.0 process template, 16 predefined project queries are available, as shown in Table 5-2. The MSF for Agile Software Development - v4.0 process template has 11 predefined project queries.

Table 5-2. *Predefined Project Queries (MSF for CMMI Process Improvement - v4.0 Template)*

Query Name	Query Parameters
Active Bugs	Team Project=@Project, WorkItemType=Bug, State=Active
All My Team Project Work Items	Assigned To=@Me
All Tasks	Team Project=@Project, WorkItemType=Task
All Work Items	Team Project=@Project

Continued

Table 5-2. *Continued*

Query Name	Query Parameters
Blocked Work Items	Team Project=@Project, Blocked=Yes
Change Requests	Team Project=@Project, WorkItemType=Change Request
Corrective Actions	Team Project=@Project, WorkItemType=Task, Task Type=Corrective Action
Customer Requirements	Team Project=@Project, WorkItemType=Task, Requirement Type=Scenario (or) Requirement Type=Quality of Service
Development Tasks	Team Project=@Project, WorkItemType=Task, Discipline=Development
Issues	Team Project=@Project, WorkItemType=Issue
Mitigation Action Status	Team Project=@Project, WorkItemType=Task, Task Type=Mitigation Action
My Work Items	Team Project=@Project, Assigned To=@Me
Product Requirements	Team Project=@Project, WorkItemType=Task, Requirement Type=Functional (or) Requirement Type=Interface, (or) Requirement Type=Operational, (or) Requirement Type=Security, (or) Requirement Type=Safety
Resolved Bugs	Team Project=@Project, WorkItemType=Bug, State=Resolved
Reviews	Team Project=@Project, WorkItemType=Review
Risks	Team Project=@Project, WorkItemType=Risk

Creating Queries

You can create your own queries and save them in the My Queries folder under Work Items. To create a new query, right-click Work Items and select Add Query, as shown in Figure 5-6.

Figure 5-6. *Choosing to add a query*

Note If you have the appropriate permissions, you can edit and modify the project queries themselves.

You'll see the New Query window, as shown in Figure 5-7. Create your query, and then right-click in the New Query window and select Run Query to see the query results.

Figure 5-7. *The New Query window*

Saving Queries

Another nice feature is the ability to save a private or team query to a file. This allows you to send queries via e-mail and port them between installations of Team Server. To save your new query, select File ➤ Save New Query1 [Query] As to open the Save Query As dialog box, as shown in Figure 5-8.

Figure 5-8. *The Save Query As dialog box*

Here, you can give your query a unique name and then choose from three options:

- Allow your query to be used as a team query by everyone.
- Save it as a private query visible only to you.
- Save it to a local file for e-mail distribution as a `.wiq`.

You can also select the team project in this dialog box, which makes it easy to save a query from one project to another project.

Sending Queries in E-Mail

Occasionally, you will want to exchange work item queries with other projects or other team members via e-mail. To do this, simply save the query as a `.wiq` file on you local machine, as described in the previous section, and send it as a file attachment to your target recipients. The recipients can then save the attachment to their local machine and open it with Visual Studio to run it.

Tip If you have e-mail access on the same computer as Team Foundation, you can right-click the query you want to send and select Send to Mail Recipient.

Using Query Macros

WIQL provides some convenient macros to make the query process more convenient and portable. In the example in Figure 5-7, we used three of the most popular: @Me, @Project, and @Today. The prebuilt query macros are described in Table 5-3.

Table 5-3. *Prebuilt Query Macros*

Query	Description
@Project	Inserts the current project context into the query
@Me	Inserts the Windows integrated account name into the query
@Today	Inserts midnight of the current date of the local machine running the query
@Today-1	Inserts the date of yesterday (@Today minus 24 hours)
@Today-7	Inserts the date of last week (@Today minus 7 days)
@Today-30	Insert the date of the last month (@Today minus 30 days)

You can execute the query and view the results in a list by pressing F5. To adjust the result display, right-click the Results pane and select Column Options, as shown in Figure 5-9. These options allow you to add columns, sort, and adjust the column width.

Figure 5-9. *Choosing to set column options*

Finally, you can click the View Results icon in the task pane of the query window as shown in Figure 5-10, to display the third type of view.

Figure 5-10. *Choosing to view results*

Using the Results (Triage) View

The other view for working with work items is the results view. You can display this view by either running a previously saved query or clicking the View Results icon in the query window (see Figure 5-10). The results view shows the list in the upper half of the window and the full form for the selected work item in the bottom section, as shown in Figure 5-11.

Figure 5-11. *Results (triage) view*

The project manager can use the results view to quickly review the work items that come in over a period of time, assign them to the appropriate resources, and manage the state and transition for each. The developers can use this view to review items assigned to them and rapidly prioritize, transition, or transfer items to other team members.

Understanding Work Item Types

Each work item type consists of fields, forms, rules, and states (work item life cycle), which are defined in Table 5-4.

Table 5-4. *Work Item Type Information*

Item	Description
Fields	Global across an installation of Team Foundation Server. Fields include a name, reference name, type, help text, and applicable constraints.
Forms	Controls the layout of the form that is displayed. The goal is to provide a single form definition (fields, groups, and tabs) that can be used in VSTS and with SharePoint web parts.
Workflow	Describe the valid states, transitions, and reasons for the transitions.

The specific work item types differ depending on the process template used for the team project. The MSF for CMMI Process Improvement - v4.0 process template defines seven work items to assign and track work. The MSF for Agile Software Development - v4.0 process template defines five work items. (We'll refer to these as the CMMI template and the Agile template.) The specific work item types and associated process templates are shown in Table 5-5.

Table 5-5. *Work Items by Process Template*

Work Item	Agile	CMMI
Task	X	X
Bug	X	X
Risk	X	X
Requirement*	--	X
Quality of Service	X	--
Scenario	X	--
Change Request	--	X
Issue*	--	X
Review	--	X

*Both Quality of Service and Scenario are subtypes of Requirement in the CMMI template. Additional requirement subtypes include Function, Interface, Operation, Safety, and Security. Issue is a unique work item type for the CMMI template and an attribute of work items under the Agile template.

The following sections describe each of the work item types.

Task Work Items

A Task work item type is the most generic type and communicates the need to do some work. All of the predefined work items in the provided process templates are of type Task.

Within the team of peers on a project, each member has his own share of tasks. For instance, a project manager uses the Task work item to assign defining personas to the business analyst, assign defining a test approach to the test manager, and assign fixing a bug to a developer. A Task can also be used generally to assign work within the project.

The required Task work item type fields are described in Table 5-6.

Table 5-6. *Required Task Work Item Fields*

Field Name	Description	Default
Title	Brief explanation of task	None; must be supplied
State	Proposed, Active, Resolved, Closed	Proposed
Reason	Basis for existing state	New
Priority	Subjective importance of task (1–3)	3
Triage	Info Recv, More Info, Pending, Triaged	Pending

> **Note** For the Agile template, the default state is Active and the initial priority (rank) is blank.

Figure 5-12 shows the states, transitions, and reasons for the Task work item type. In the normal path for a Task work item, the Task is initiated when there is work to be done. A Task starts in the Proposed state pending agreement, with a reason of New. It is then triaged and placed into the Active state as Accepted (if it is to be implemented in the current iteration) or as Investigate (if analysis of impact is needed). An investigated Task should go back to the Proposed state at the conclusion of the impact analysis. The Task can move to the Resolved state with the Complete or Requires Review/Tests transition reason. Once the Task passes the review or testing, it can be moved from the Resolved state to the Closed state.

Figure 5-12. *States, transitions, and reasons for the Task work item type*

Alternate paths exists for moving Tasks directly to the Closed state if they are Rejected, Deferred, Cut, Cancelled, Overtaken by Events, or simply have no review or test criteria. A task may also revert from the Resolved state to the Active state with a reason of Review/Test Failed.

> **Note** It is important to understand that when a work item is Closed, the Assigned To field is cleared. This is the default transition for a work item, so that you don't see all your completed work items in queries for items assigned to you. This is described in the work item definition XML file. Some teams assign the Closed work item to a fictitious user named Closed, which gets it off the developers' radar but allows for some optional reporting capabilities.

Bug Work Items

The original bug-tracking system, Product Studio, used within Microsoft was the code base for the WIT feature. Therefore, the tracking of bugs is at the core of the WIT system.

The motivation of opening a Bug work item should be to clearly describe the problem in a way that allows the developer to fully understand the weight of the problem. The teams at Microsoft are very familiar with the bug rates and the concept of zero bug bounce (ZBB). ZBB is the point in the project where you have eliminated your bug backlog, and the development team is handling bugs that are coming in real time. This is a major milestone for any project on the way to beta or final release.

Table 5-7 shows the required Bug work item type fields.

Table 5-7. *Required Bug Work Item Fields*

Field Name	Description	Default
Title	Brief explanation of bug	None; must be supplied
State	Proposed, Active, Resolved, Closed	Proposed
Reason	Basis for existing state	New
Priority	Subjective importance of bug (1–3)	3
Severity	Critical, High, Medium, Low	Low
Triage	Info Recv, More Info, Pending, Triaged	Pending
Symptom	Description of the problem	None; must be supplied
Steps to Reproduce	Detail on how to reproduce the bug	None; must be supplied

■**Note** For the Agile template, the default state for a Bug work item is Active and the initial priority is 2.

Figure 5-13 shows the states, transitions, and reasons for the Bug work item. In the normal path, the Bug work item is initiated when someone identifies a potential problem in the product or a build error exists. This Proposed state can require Investigate, or as the bug is triaged, the work item is assigned directly to a developer (as Approved). Both reasons move the Bug into the Active state. The Bug work item is moved to the Resolved state once the problem is Fixed and the bug is linked to the changeset at check-in. Once the Fixed bug is part of the build, it is moved to the Closed state.

Figure 5-13. *States, transitions, and reasons for the Bug work item type*

Alternate paths exist for moving Bug work items to the Closed state if they are Rejected, Deferred, Not a Bug, Determined a Duplicate, or Cannot Reproduce. A Bug work item may also revert from the Resolved to Active state if testing finds the problem was Not Fixed.

Risk Work Items

Risk is defined as the expectation of loss. It is a function of the probability and the consequences of harm. A Risk work item is used to track potential risk impacts to the project. A successful risk management practice is one in which risks are continuously identified and analyzed for relative importance. Risks are mitigated, tracked, and controlled to effectively use program resources.

Risk work items differ from Issue work items in that a risk is a look into the future and requires a continuous review of the probability of its occurrence. An issue has a more immediate, in-the-trenches team dynamic that is addressed in the daily standup meeting or late-night Xbox lounge.

Table 5-8 shows the required Risk work item type fields.

■**Note** For the Agile template, the default state for a Risk work item is Active, the initial Severity is blank, and the initial priority (rank) is blank. It does not include Probability and Blocked fields.

Table 5-8. *Required Risk Work Item Fields*

Field Name	Description	Default
Title	Brief explanation of risk	None; must be supplied
Probability	Chance the risk will occur (1–99)	None; must be supplied
State	Proposed, Active, Resolved, Closed	Proposed
Reason	Basis for existing state	New
Priority	Subjective importance of risk (1–3)	3
Severity	Critical, High, Medium, Low	Low
Blocked	Indicates progress in mitigating the risk is blocked	No

Figure 5-14 shows the states, transitions, and reasons for the Risk work item. In the normal path, risks are potential events or conditions in the future that may have negative impact on the project. A Risk work item is initiated when this potential is identified. In the Proposed state, a risk is analyzed for likelihood and cost of occurrence, mitigation options, triggers, and proposed contingency plan. A Risk work item is moved to the Active state when the conditions warrant, for the Mitigation Triggered reason. Active Risk work items require tasks to perform the mitigation options. Once these tasks have been executed (the Mitigate Action Complete reason), a Risk work item is moved to the Resolved state. Once the mitigation tasks are verified as sufficiently Mitigated, the Risk work item is moved to the Closed state.

Figure 5-14. *States, transitions, and reasons for the Risk work item type*

Alternate paths exists for moving Risk work items to the Closed state if they are Accepted (assume the risk), Rejected (not a risk), Eliminated, or Overtaken by Events (the risk no longer exists). A Risk work item may revert from the Resolved state to the Active state due to the Mitigation Action Unsatisfactory (Rework) reason.

Change Request Work Items

A change request (CR) is a formal request for modifying the behavior of a system due to normal business changes or because there is a bug in the system. A change request expresses a change in the project baseline, including a previously approved project component. A change request can be introduced during any iteration of the project.

Change requests are governed by a thorough control process intended to reduce the impacts of changes on the work of the delivery team, while still allowing modifications after user specifications have been approved. Once a Change Request work item has been approved, it will initiate other work items to carry out the change.

Table 5-9 describes the required fields for a Change Request work item type.

Table 5-9. *Change Request Work Item Required Fields*

Field Name	Description	Default
Title	Brief explanation of CR	None; must be supplied
State	Proposed, Active, Resolved, Closed	Proposed
Reason	Basis for existing state	New
Priority	Subjective importance of CR (1–3)	3
Triage	Info Recv, More Info, Pending, Triaged	Pending

■Note The Agile template does not include a Change Request work item type.

Figure 5-15 shows the states, transitions, and reasons for the Change Request work item. In the normal path, a Change Request work item is in the Proposed state when a change is needed to a work product under configuration management. Change requests are reviewed by a change board for disposition (formal triage). The change board places the request into the Active state as Accepted (if it is to be made in the current iteration) or as Investigate (if impact analysis is needed). After investigation, the Change Request work item should go back to the Proposed state at the conclusion of the analysis. The Change Request work item can move to the Resolved state only as it reaches Code Complete and System Tested and is placed into the daily build process. Once the customer has validated that the proposed changes have successfully been implemented with Validation Test Passed, the Change Request work item can be moved from the Resolved state to the Closed state.

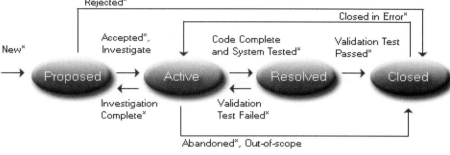

Figure 5-15. *States, transitions, and reasons for the Change Request work item type*

Alternate paths exist for moving Change Request work items to the Closed state if they are Rejected, Abandoned, or determined Out of Scope. A Change Request work item may also revert from the Resolved state to the Active state due to the customer Validation Test Failed reason.

Review Work Items

A program management best practice is to perform periodic reviews during the software development life cycle. The Review work item type provides a mechanism to initiate and track these sessions. Many types of reviews are performed during the life of a project, including code, critical-design, architecture, best practice, security, and deployment reviews.

Table 5-10 shows the required fields for the Review work item type.

Table 5-10. *Review Work Item Required Fields*

Field Name	Description	Default
Title	Brief explanation of review	None; must be supplied
State	Active, Resolved, Closed	Active
Reason	Basis for existing state	New
Purpose	Focus area of the review	None; must be supplied

Note The Agile template does not include a Review work item type.

Figure 5-16 shows the states, transitions, and reasons for the Review work item. In the normal path, Review work items record the outcome of a design or code reviews. A Review work item is in the Active state in order to document the results of the review. The review team will accept the review with either minor or major changes at the end of the session. These changes are assigned to the developer. If a minor change was needed, the developer can move the Review work item to the Resolved state directly. However, if a major change was requested, the developer must move the Review work item back to the Active state (awaiting a second review). Once the changes are verified as Minor Changes Complete, the Review work item is moved from the Resolved state to Closed state. If the design or code review is Accepted (As Is)—without change—it can be moved directly to the Closed state.

Figure 5-16. *States, transitions, and reasons for the Review work item type*

Requirement Work Items

A requirement is a stated or implied expression of a business need. Requirements orient and constrain the products or services to be delivered.

The Requirement work item type captures and tracks what the solution needs to provide to meet the customer's desires. Requirement work items within the CMMI template are divided into Customer and Product requirements. Customer types of requirements include scenario and quality of service (QoS). Product requirements include safety, security, functional, operational, and interface.

Table 5-11 shows the required fields for the Requirement work item type.

Note For the Agile template, the customer-focused requirements of Scenario and Quality of Service (QoS) are separate work item types.

Table 5-11. *Requirement Work Item Required Fields*

Field Name	Description	Default
Title	Brief explanation of requirement	None; must be supplied
Type	Functional, Interface, Operational, QoS, Safety, Scenario, Security	None; must be supplied
Blocked	Progress blocked (Yes, No)	No
State	Proposed, Active, Resolved, Closed	Proposed
Reason	Basis for existing state	New
Priority	Subjective importance of requirement (1–3)	3
Triage	Info Recv, More Info, Pending, Triaged	Pending
Committed	Committed project requirement	No

Figure 5-17 shows the states, transitions, and reasons for the Requirement work item. In the normal path, the Requirement work item tracks "what" the product needs to perform to solve the customer's problem. A Requirement work item starts in the Proposed state at the time it is identified. It is then triaged and placed into the Active state as Accepted (if it is to be implemented in the current iteration) or as Investigate (if impact analysis is needed). After investigation, a Requirement work item should go back to the Proposed state at the conclusion of the study. The requirement can move to the Resolved state only as it reaches Code Complete and System Tests Passed. Once the customer has validated that the requirement has successfully met expectations, it can be moved from the Resolved state to the Closed state.

Figure 5-17. *States, transitions, and reasons for the Requirement work item type*

Alternate paths exist for moving Requirement work items to the Closed state if they are Rejected, Abandoned, Split, or determined Out of Scope. A Requirement work item may also revert from the Resolved to Active state if the customer Validation Test Failed.

Issue Work Items

An issue is an actual event, condition, point of discussion, debate, or dispute that needs to be proactively managed. Unlike a risk, which will not harm the project unless it materializes, an issue is currently harming it or will definitely harm it unless the project is changed.

The Issue work item provides the user with a way to report an issue, track progress toward its resolution, and know who is responsible for resolving the issue.

Table 5-12 shows the required fields for the Issue work item type.

Table 5-12. *Issue Work Item Required Fields*

Field Name	Description	Default
Title	Brief explanation of issue	None; must be supplied
State	Proposed, Active, Resolved, Closed	Proposed
Reason	Basis for existing state	New
Escalate	Raise the criticality of the issue	No
Priority	Subjective importance of the issue (1–3)	3
Triage	Info Recv, More Info, Pending, Triaged	Pending

■**Note** Issues are an attribute of work items under the Agile template.

Figure 5-18 shows the states, transitions, and reasons for the Issue work item. In the normal path, the Issue work item is initiated when someone (normally at the team level) identifies a situation or event that may block work on product. This Proposed state undergoes review and is either moved to the Active state as Accepted (if approved) or as Investigate (if more detail is needed). Active issues require the creation of tasks to perform corrective action. Once these tasks have been executed to remove the blockage (Resolved), an Issue work item is moved to the Resolved state. Once the Issue work item has been Verified and Accepted, it is moved to the Closed state.

Alternate paths exist for moving Issue work items to the Closed state if they are Rejected or Overtaken by Events (and the issue no longer exists). An Issue work item may revert from the Resolved to Active state if it needs more work (Rework), or from the Closed state to the Active state if it was Closed in Error, Reopened, or Reoccurred.

Figure 5-18. *States, transitions, and reasons for the Issue work item type*

Configuring Project Alerts for Work Item Tracking

In VSTS, you can configure project alerts to send e-mail messages based on specific events. This feature leverages the underlying notification service and is customizable and expandable for more granular event notification. For work item tracking, only one project alert is predefined. This alert is to receive notification when your work items are changed by someone else.

To set up this alert, right-click the EffortTracking project and select Project Alerts. A dialog box with several alert options appears. Check the "My work items are changed by others" alert and enter your e-mail address in the Send To column, as shown in Figure 5-19. Optionally, you can have the message sent in either HTML or plain text.

Figure 5-19. *The Project Alerts dialog box*

Once configured, each time a work item assigned to you is changed by another project member, a detailed e-mail message is sent, showing the core work item fields and the changed fields' history.

Looking Under the Hood

Work items must conform to a XML schema referred to as the Work Item Type Definition (WITD) language using a few basic elements. A portion of the WorkItemTypeDefinition.xsd is shown in Figure 5-20.

Figure 5-20. *WorkItemTypeDefinition.xsd fragment*

As an example, we'll look at the Bug work item type definition from the Agile process template. The first element is the WORKITEMTYPE, which differentiates this work item from all others. It includes the unique name and a description.

```
<WORKITEMTYPE name='Bug'>
    <DESCRIPTION>Includes information to track the work to resolve the
    Bug and to verify its resolution.</DESCRIPTION>
```

Next, it identifies the fields associated with the work item to further describe any additional information about the work item. This snippet shows the Id and Title field definitions.

```xml
<FIELDS>
    <FIELD name="Id" refname="System.Id" type="Integer" />
    <FIELD name="Title" refname="System.Title" type="String" >
        <REQUIRED/>
    </Field>
```

In addition, field rules define the constraints on fields and field values as they move through the transition states defined for the work item. Here is an example of the Issue field:

```xml
<FIELD name="Issue" refname="Microsoft.VSTS.Common.Issue"
    type="String" reportable="dimension">
        <REQUIRED/>
        <ALLOWEDVALUES>
            <LISTITEM value="Yes"/>
            <LISTITEM value="No"/>
        </ALLOWEDVALUES>
        <DEFAULT from="value" value="No"/>
</FIELD>
```

> **Note** The `reportable` attribute dictates how the field is used in the data warehouse and reporting cubes. Valid values are measure, dimension, and detail. Reporting is discussed in Chapter 6.

Next is the definition of the workflow and state transitions for the Bug work item type. First is the STATES section, which defines the state valid values and the associated fields for the state with the values they are to receive. The workflow is found in the TRANSITION section, as in this example for the Active to Resolved state of a Bug work item:

```xml
<TRANSITION from="Active" to="Resolved">
    <ACTIONS>
            <ACTION value="Microsoft.VSTS.Actions.Checkin"/>
    </ACTIONS>
    <REASONS>
            <DEFAULTREASON value="Fixed"/>
            <REASON value="Deferred"/>
            <REASON value="Duplicate"/>
            <REASON value="As Designed"/>
            <REASON value="Unable to Reproduce"/>
            <REASON value="Obsolete"/>
    </REASONS>
    <FIELDS>
            <FIELD refname="System.AssignedTo">
                <COPY from="field"
                    field="System.CreatedBy"/>
            </FIELD>
            <FIELD refname="Microsoft.VSTS.Common.ActivatedDate">
            <READONLY/></FIELD>
```

```
                <FIELD refname="Microsoft.VSTS.Common.ActivatedBy">
                <READONLY/></FIELD>
                <FIELD refname="Microsoft.VSTS.Common.ResolvedBy">
                    <COPY from="currentuser"/>
                    <VALIDUSER/>
                     <REQUIRED/>
                </FIELD>
                <FIELD refname="Microsoft.VSTS.Common.ResolvedDate">
                <SERVERDEFAULT from="clock"/></FIELD>
    </FIELDS>
</TRANSITION> >
```

The final element defines the display of the Bug work item in a form.

```
<FORM>
<LAYOUT>
<GROUP>
```

And that is about it. Business rules and behavior for a work item type are also defined in the WITD language as rules associated with fields and scoped by state and transition.

Note For work item tracking, two database tables and two views are of particular interest. The `WorkItemsAre` table contains the current version of the work item, and the `WorkItemsWere` table contains all the old versions, one entry per client update. The `WorkItemsAreUsed` view brings in the namespace column names used in queries, and the `WorkItemsWereUsed` view brings in the namespace column names used in queries. The VSTS team highly recommends that you do not modify any of the underlying tables. The database is discussed in more detail in Chapter 6.

Customizing Work Item Types

You can customize work item types in a variety of ways. Here, we will look at examples of modifying the list displayed by a field, adding a new field that references a global list, and creating a brand-new work item type.

In these examples, you'll use several of the following command-line tools:

- `witimport`: Imports an XML work item type definition to a team project or validates a definition before import.

- `witexport`: Exports an existing work item type from a team project as XML.

- `witfields`: Allows you to view, rename, report, or delete a work item field or reset the `Rebuildcache` flag for all clients.

- `glimport`: Imports an XML global list definition to a team project or validates a definition before import.

- `glexport`: Exports an existing work global list from a team project as XML.

> **Note** In the current version of Team Foundation Server, there is no official way to delete individual work items from a project. You can use the `DeleteTeamProject`, but that will obliterate all work items and the project itself. The reason is that Team Foundation provides a robust auditing function and preserves links between items. There are several discussions in the newsgroups on how to delete from the underlying database tables, but they are all with the caveat "use at own risk" because there are invariably links you will have missed. We hope that the product team will provide a tool or power toy to delete individual work items cleanly.

Modifying the Assign To List

One of the first modifications you may want to make in the work item type definitions is the list of team members who are represented in the Assigned To field. By default, the Assigned To field uses <VALIDUSER> as the source of the display names. <VALIDUSER> corresponds to the Everyone group for Team Foundation Server. In a large enterprise, this list includes Team Foundation Server service accounts, system administrator accounts, and a host of others that may never be assigned to work items.

To customize the list of allowed values in the Assigned To field list, you perform the following steps:

1. Create the global groups for AssignTo using Team Explorer.
2. Export the Task work item type using `witexport.exe`.
3. Rename the work item type `name` field using the XML editor.
4. Modify the XML file for the new type using the XML editor.
5. Import the new Task work item type using `wiimport.exe`.
6. Test the form in Visual Studio using Team Explorer.

The following sections describe each of these steps in detail.

Creating Groups

As mentioned in Chapter 2, you have several options for creating groups with Team Foundation Server. If you maintain your own security groups in Active Directory, you can add those groups to predefined or custom groups in the Team Foundation Server. Optionally, you can add members directly to Team Foundation Server groups at both the server and project level. For this example, you will create a new project group called AssignTo and add members directly to that group.

1. Open Visual Studio. Right-click your team project and select Team Project Settings ➤ Group Membership to open the Project Groups dialog box.
2. Select New to open the Create New Team Foundation Server Group dialog box. Enter **AssignTo** in the Group Name field and a short description, as shown in Figure 5-21. Then click OK.

Figure 5-21. *The Create New Team Foundation Server Group dialog box*

3. Double-click the new AssignTo group to add members. You can select members from Team Foundation Server groups or Windows Users or Groups. Select one of more groups containing a few different members to make this exercise useful.

Exporting a Work Item Type

To export the Task work item type, open a Visual Studio command prompt and enter `witexport /?` to see the list of parameter definitions. To export the Task work item definition from your server, enter the following:

```
witexport /f mytask.xml /t [Team Foundation Server Name] /p [Team Project Name]
 /n Task
```

After a few seconds, you will receive the message "work item type export complete." This will verify that a file called `mytask.xml` has been placed into the current directory.

Renaming the Work Item Type

It is a good idea to rename the work item type so you don't destroy the original copy of the work item while you are making your changes. In a sense, you are doing development on the production server, so you need to be careful. A best practice is to have a separate sandbox server to test your modifications.

To rename the work item type, open the newly created file in Visual Studio (or your favorite XML editor) and change the `name` field from this:

```
<WORKITEMTYPE name="Task">
```

to this:

```
<WORKITEMTYPE name="MyTask">
```

The change is shown in Figure 5-22. Then save the file.

```
mytask.xml*  Start Page                                              ▼ ×
    <?xml version="1.0" encoding="utf-8"?>
  <witd:WITD application="Work item type editor" version="1.0"
      <WORKITEMTYPE name="MyTask">
          <DESCRIPTION>Includes information to track the task throug
          <FIELDS>
              <FIELD name="Title" refname="System.Title" type="String
                  <HELPTEXT>Short description of the task used to differ
                  <REQUIRED />
```

Figure 5-22. *Renaming the work item type*

Modifying the Assigned To Field

Next, you need to find the Assigned To field in the `mytask.xml` file. Do a quick search on Assigned To and you will be taken to the field description section.

```
<FIELD name="Assigned To"
    refname="System.AssignedTo" type="String"
    <VALIDUSER />
</FIELD>
```

Remove the `<VALIDUSER />` tag, which, as noted earlier, corresponds to the Everyone group, and add field list items. Field lists define permissible values for a field and provide list items for users to choose. Field lists can be used for String field types only. There are three types of field lists:

- `ALLOWEDVALUES` provide an exclusive list from which the users must select.
- `SUGGESTEDVALUES` provide an optional list from which the users may select or they may provide their own value.
- `PROHIBITEDVALUES` provide a restricted list from which the users may not provide a matching value.

Two optional attributes related to field lists are `expanditems` and `filteritems`. These are used to manage items that represent a group of discrete values such as a security group. The `expanditems` attribute, if set to `true`, will recursively unpack the individual values from a group. Setting the `filteritems` attribute to `excludegroups` will remove the group names from the expanded list.

In this example, you want to set the field list type to `ALLOWEDVALUES` and provide a list of the project's AssignTo group, and expand the items, as follows:

```
<FIELD name="Assigned To"
    refname="System.AssignedTo" type="String"
    <HELPTEXT>The person assigned to do the work</HELPTEXT>
    <ALLOWEDVALUES expanditems="true" filteritems="excludegroups">
        <LISTITEM value="[project]\AssignTo" />
        <LISTITEM value="PartnerTeam" />
    </ALLOWEDVALUES>
</FIELD>
```

> **Note** The [global] and [project] references are used to allow the XML to be portable across projects. [global] is used to reference a server-scoped Team Foundation Server group. [project] is used to reference a project-scoped group. The system automatically picks up the right server or project when the work item type is uploaded (when a project is created or when the witimport utility is used). Also, you can add placeholder groups, such as Partner Team, for work item assignments.

Finally, to exclude a value from the list, add the following XML for the prohibited values list item:

```
<PROHIBITEDVALUES expanditems="false">
    <LISTITEM value="Bob" />
</PROHIBITEDVALUES>
```

Save the file.

Importing a Work Item Type

Reopen the Visual Studio command prompt (if it's not still open from the export operation). Enter witimport /? to see the list of parameter definitions. To import the new MyTask work item definition to your server, enter the following:

```
witimport /f mytask.xml /t [Team Foundation Server Name] /p [Team Project Name]
```

After a few seconds, you should receive the message "work item type import complete." This will signify the MyTask work item has been uploaded to your server within the specified team project.

Validating a New Work Item Type

For this example, the validation consists of verifying that the expected values show up in the Assigned To list in the form and that the prohibited values are not allowed. To test the form, follow these steps:

1. Open Visual Studio, and the Team Explorer will connect to your Team Foundation Server.

2. Expand your team project, right-click the Work Items node, and Select Add Work Item.

3. Select the new work item type: MyTask. You should see the form view of the MyTask work item with the modified Assigned To field, as shown in Figure 5-23.

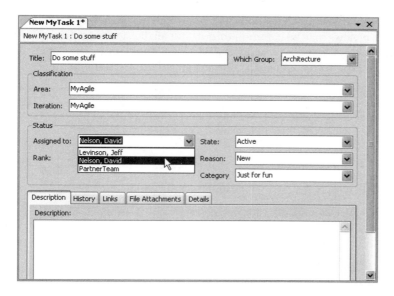

Figure 5-23. *Modified MyTask work item type*

4. Enter **Bob** in the Assigned To field and attempted to save the form. You should see the error message shown in Figure 5-24.

Figure 5-24. *The error message when you enter an invalid value for the modified work item type*

That's it. You have successfully modified your first work item type definition. Now let's see how to customize a work item type by adding a field.

Creating a New Field That References a Global List

Global lists are used to store common lists that will be used throughout the Team Foundation Server. They are server-scoped lists that can be referenced by any team project. Global lists can be used for many purposes.

■Tip You can see an example of populating your global lists from an external source on the Team Foundation weblog at `Populating Lists on Work Items from an External Source`.

Architects frequently participate in various reviews, which may focus on a specific customer concern. These reviews may be common throughout all divisions and projects within the company. To address this, you can modify the Review work item under the CMMI template to include a Focus Area field that references a common global list. Here are the steps:

1. Create the global list for review focus areas using the XML editor.
2. Import the global list to the Team Foundation Server using `glimport.exe`.
3. Verify the global list now exists using `glexport.exe`.
4. Export the review work item type using `witexport.exe`.
5. Rename the work item type name field using the XML editor.
6. Modify the XML file for the new type using the XML editor.
7. Import the new work item type using `witmport.exe`.
8. Test the form in Visual Studio using Team Explorer.

Now we'll go through the process.

Setting Up the Global List

The global list is just an XML file. Open Visual Studio, select File ➤ New File, and then select the XML file template. Insert the following XML, which defines a new global list called Focus Area with six distinct list items.

```xml
<?xml version="1.0" encoding="utf-8"?>
<gl:GLOBALLISTS
    xmlns:gl=
      "http://schemas.microsoft.com/VisualStudio/2005/workitemtracking/globallists">
    <GLOBALLIST name="Focus Area">
        <LISTITEM value="Architecture" />
        <LISTITEM value="Critical Design" />
        <LISTITEM value="Best Practice" />
        <LISTITEM value="Code" />
        <LISTITEM value="Security" />
        <LISTITEM value="Deployment" />
    </GLOBALLIST>
</gl:GLOBALLISTS>
```

Select File menu ➤ Save As and save your global list under the name `MyGL.xml` to your local directory `C:\Temp`.

To import the global list, open a Visual Studio command prompt and type the following:

```
glimport /f c:\temp\mygl.xml /t [Team Foundation Server Name]
```

After a few seconds, the prompt will return.

Since there is no confirmation that the global list has been loaded, run the `glexport` command with the display set to the screen to verify that it exists. Type the following:

`glexport /t [Team Foundation Server Name]`

After a few seconds, you will see the XML representing the global list displayed in the command window.

Adding a Field to the Work Item Type

First, follow the same process as in the previous example to export the work item type. This time, export the Review work item type from the CMMI process template by entering the following at the command prompt:

`witexport /f myreview.xml /t [Team Foundation Server Name] /p [Team Project Name] /n Review`

Next, open the newly created file in Visual Studio and change the name field from `WORKITEMTYPE name="Review">` to `<WORKITEMTYPE name="MyReview">`.

Now you need to define the Focus Area field and specify where to place the item on the form. The easiest way to create a new field is to copy and paste an existing one. Scroll down until you find the name Meeting Type. Copy the field definition, insert a line, and paste the definition back into the XML file. Make the following changes to the field definition:

```
<FIELD name="Focus Area" refname="MyCompany.VSTS.Common.FocusArea" type="String">
<HELPTEXT>The Focus Area of the review meeting</HELPTEXT>
        <ALLOWEDVALUES>
                <GLOBALLIST name="Focus Area" />
        </ALLOWEDVALUES>
</FIELD>
```

The field reference name, `refname`, refers to a namespace constructed according to the recommended guidelines, as explained in the "Assigning Field Reference Names" section later in this chapter.

You will place the new field item below the Reason field on the form. Scroll down farther in the XML file and find the Reason field in the Form Layout section. It is the last field in the Status section. Copy the following Control line for the Reason field definition:

```
<Control Type="FieldControl" FieldName="System.Reason"
    Label="&amp;Reason:" LabelPosition="Left" />
```

Paste it as a new field below the Reason field. Make the following changes for the Focus Area definition:

```
<Control Type="FieldControl" FieldName="MyCompany.VSTS.Common.FocusArea"
    Label="Focus &amp;Area:" LabelPosition="Left" />
```

Then save the file.

With the command prompt still open, enter the following:

witimport /f myreview.xml /t [Team Foundation Server Name] /p [Team Project Name]

After a few seconds, you will receive the message "work item type import complete." This indicates that the MyReview work item has been uploaded to your server within the specified team project.

Open Visual Studio, and Team Explorer will connect to your Team Foundation Server. Expand your team project, right-click the Work Items node, and select Add Work Item. Select the new MyReview work item type.

Select the new Focus Area field, and in the drop-down list, you should see the six review areas listed, as shown in Figure 5-25.

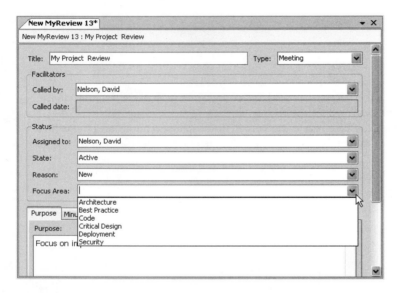

Figure 5-25. *MyReview modified work item type*

Creating a New Work Item Type

You may find that you need a completely custom work item type for your organization, such as one to track engagements—short duration activities in support of a variety of projects, teams, and initiatives. Here is the process for adding a new work item type:

1. Determine a base template type.

2. Design the states and transitions.

3. Export the base template type.

4. Rename the work item type.

5. Modify the work item type definition to add the fields and set the workflow.

6. Import the new work item type.
7. Test the form.

Let's go through the steps to add an Engagement Request type.

Setting Up the Base Template Type

The simplest way to create a brand-new work item type definition is to find an existing one close to what you want to track and modify the definition. For this example, you can use the Issue work item type and a few fields from the Requirement type. The Requirement type is designed for tracking a business need, and the Issue type is designed to investigate and resolve intermittent problems. That fairly completely describes the engagement process.

After you've determined the base work item type, it is best to diagram your states and transitions. You can capture the states and transitions in a specific tool like Visio or just graphically in a tool like Photoshop. Figure 5-26 shows the transition chart for the Engagement Request work item.

Figure 5-26. *State and transition chart for the custom Engagement Request work item type*

Adding the New Work Item Type

Follow the same process as in the previous examples to export the base work item type. If you have a combination, you need to pick just one for the base. You can export both, and then cut and paste items into the base type. For the Engagement Request, export the Issue work item type from the CMMI process template by entering the following from the command prompt:

```
witexport /f engagement.xml /t [Team Foundation Server Name] /p [Team Project Name]
/n Issue
```

Also use `witexport` to export the Requirement work item type for reference.

Open the newly created file in Visual Studio and change `<WORKITEMTYPE name="Issue">` to `<WORKITEMTYPE name="Engagement Request">`.

When you are creating a new work item type, several items need to be addressed. As stated previously, the basic components of the work item type definition are the field, form, and workflow. Each of these must be addressed for the new Engagement Request type.

You need a new field to capture the type of engagement requested. Copy the XML for the Engagement Type field and paste it into your Engagement Request work item type between two existing fields. Bring over the Blocked field and the Committed field from the Requirement type. Also, do a quick search and replace to change the help text from `issue` to `engagement request`. (Be careful not change the field named Issue.)

```xml
<FIELD name="Engagement Type" refname="MyCompany.VSTS.Common.EngagementType"
 type="String" reportable="dimension">
<HELPTEXT>Indicates the type of engagement request</HELPTEXT>
<REQUIRED />
<ALLOWEDVALUES expanditems="true">
        <LISTITEM value="Project" />
        <LISTITEM value="Direction" />
        <LISTITEM value="Standards" />
        <LISTITEM value="Review" />
        <LISTITEM value="QuickFix" />
        <LISTITEM value="Analysis" />
        <LISTITEM value="Consultation" />
</ALLOWEDVALUES>
</FIELD>
<FIELD name="Blocked" refname="Microsoft.VSTS.CMMI.Blocked" type="String">
<HELPTEXT>Indicates that the engagement request is blocked</HELPTEXT>
<ALLOWEDVALUES>
        <LISTITEM value="Yes" />
        <LISTITEM value="No" />
</ALLOWEDVALUES>
<DEFAULT from="value" value="No" />
</FIELD>
<FIELD name="Committed" refname="Microsoft.VSTS.CMMI.Committed" type="String">
<HELPTEXT>Has the engagement been committed?</HELPTEXT>
<REQUIRED />
<ALLOWEDVALUES expanditems="true">
        <LISTITEM value="Yes" />
        <LISTITEM value="No" />
</ALLOWEDVALUES>
<DEFAULT from="value" value="No" />
</FIELD>
```

Next, you need to include the new fields on the form in the desired locations. Scroll down to the Form section and below the Title field on the top line, add the Type field. Change the `Column PercentWidth` for `Title` from 100 to 70 and add a `Column PercentWidth` tag above your Type field with a value of 30. The label should read `Type:`, and the `FieldName` must match the reference name above "MyCompany.VSTS.Common.EngagementType". Add the Committed and Blocked fields to the end of each column in the Status section. Place Committed under the Triage `FieldName` and Blocked under the Escalate `FieldName`.

Finally, set the `DEFAULTREASON` and additional reasons on each `TRANSITION` from one state to another. The following example is the default transition from Proposed to Active for the base Issue work item type. You can modify the workflow to be whatever fits your needs.

```
<TRANSITION from="Proposed" to="Active">
    <REASONS>
        <DEFAULTREASON value="Accepted" />
        <REASON value="Investigate" />
    </REASONS>
```

Save the file.

Now return to the command prompt and enter the following to import the new work item type:

```
witimport /f engagement.xml /t [Team Foundation Server Name] /p [Team Project Name]
```

After a few seconds, you will receive the message "work item type import complete."

You're ready to check that the new work item type works. Open Visual Studio and wait for the Team Explorer to connect to your Team Foundation Server. Expand your team project, right-click the Work Items node, and select Add Work Item. Select the new Engagement Request work item type to view the form, as shown in Figure 5-27.

Figure 5-27. *Engagement Request work item type*

Check that the expected values show up in the Type, Committed, and Blocked fields. Also test any new transitions for your Engagement Request type. Fill out the required fields, and then save the work item in the proposed state. You can now move the work item from state to state and verify that the correct reason codes appear, as shown in Figure 5-28.

Figure 5-28. *Engagement Request state transitions*

Congratulations, you have modified and created work item types. Now that you have mastered long division, we feel it necessary to inform you of a little thing called the calculator. Graphic tools are now available to make work item type modifications a little easier. These are available on the GotDotNet Visual Studio workspace.

Assigning Field Reference Names

A key design goal for Team Foundation Server was to have work item type definitions portable between instantiations. Field reference names satisfy this by using a namespace syntax that is globally unique. Team Foundation Server provides two predefined namespaces: `System` and `Microsoft`. Customers are encouraged to create their own namespaces using the following guidelines:

- The reference name may be up to 70 characters long.

- The reference name must consist of two or more words separated by period. Each word may include English alphanumeric characters, digits, and underscores. The first word can begin only with an English letter (*a–z*) or an underscore.

- The custom reference name must not belong to `System` namespace (cannot begin with `System`).

Note The `System` namespace includes all system fields that are mandatory for Team Foundation system functions. These mandatory system fields are also referred to as *core fields*. Core fields like `System.ID`, `System.AssignedTo`, `System.State`, and `System.Reason` have their own rules that are hard-coded and cannot be changed. These fields are critical to the workflow, and it is extremely important that they behave in the same manner across the Team Foundation Server.

A common naming convention is to follow the Microsoft namespace and replace Microsoft with your company name, as in the following examples:

- `MyCompany.VSTS.Agile.FieldName`
- `MyCompany.VSTS.Common.FieldName`
- `MyCompany.VSTS.MyProcess.FieldName`

Summary

This chapter covered VSTS's work item tracking feature. We discussed the three different views for managing and creating work items: form, query, and result views. Then we looked at each default work item type provided with the MSF for CMMI Process Improvement - v4.0 process template.

We then took a quick peek under the hood and began to customize a default work item type. You learned how to create your own global lists, and also how to author a unique work item type using several base types. You should now have a good feel for the structure of the work item type. Feel free to explore your own modifications and creations.

CHAPTER 6

Team Reporting

The Team Foundation Server includes a data warehouse based on SQL Server 2005 Relational Database and Analysis Services. In this data warehouse, operational data from work item tracking, version control, team builds, and test results is gathered and rendered into multidimensional cubes. This data warehouse is used by Team Foundation and SQL Server 2005 Reporting Services (SSRS) for out-of-the-box reporting functionality. The schema for these databases is tailored to the methodologies used on the Team Foundation Server. SSRS is integrated with Team Foundation to provide easy access to reports and to offer a convenient mechanism for custom extensions.

In this chapter, you will learn how to produce project reports, including predefined reports, customized reports, and entirely new reports. But first, we'll start with an introduction to the SQL Server 2005 Business Intelligence platform.

Introducing the Business Intelligence Platform

Business Intelligence (BI) is a broad term for the services and process that turn a repository of obscure data into valuable business information. Business Intelligence is predicated on the notion of a central data warehouse that pulls disparate data from a wide variety of sources. Customarily, these extract, transform, and loads (ETL) of data are scheduled to occur on a regular basis and process the data into the online analytical processing (OLAP) cubes for reporting.

SQL Server 2005 has been termed "The BI Release." Included in this latest release are vastly upgraded versions of SQL Server Integration Services, SQL Server Analysis Services, and SQL Server Reporting Services, as illustrated in Figure 6-1.

Figure 6-1. *SQL Server Business Intelligence platform*

These services perform the following functions:

SQL Server Integration Services (SSIS): This is the ETL tool provided with SQL Server 2005. SSIS is a rewrite of the Data Transformation Service (DTS) that shipped with SQL Server 2000. SSIS is a very powerful tool that provides many discrete events exposed at all levels of the transforms, as well as a complete workflow engine.

■**Note** The Team Foundation Server does not use SSIS to migrate data between data stores. The Team Foundation Server uses custom adapters on the application tier to facilitate the data movement. SSIS will most likely be used by administrators to perform backup and maintenance functions.

SQL Server Analysis Services (SSAS): This is all about providing real-time business intelligence to the knowledge worker. The ability to combine the most recent information with historical information has been a difficult problem. Customarily, the most current data resides in the OLTP systems, while the historical data is normally stored in the enterprise data warehouse. This release of SSAS introduces the Unified Dimensional Model (UDM), which brings a balance in strength between the relational and OLAP constructs.

SQL Server Reporting Services (SSRS): This is positioned as an enterprise reporting platform and is provided as a core service of the SQL Server 2005 Business Intelligence suite. SSRS has a web services infrastructure and is easy to embed into other applications. SSRS is integrated with existing Microsoft Office applications, from SharePoint to Excel.

As we've mentioned earlier VSTS reporting is based on SSRS. Before we dive into the specifics of generating reports, let's take a look at the reporting life cycle.

Understanding the Reporting Life Cycle

The SSRS reporting life cycle includes authoring, management, and delivery, as illustrated in Figure 6-2.

Figure 6-2. *The reporting life cycle*

Reports can be authored in Visual Studio 2005 or by end users with the Report Builder graphical user interface. Table 6-1 shows a comparison of the features of these authoring tools. Creating reports is discussed in detail in the "Customizing Team Reports" and "Creating New Reports" sections later in this chapter. The report is an XML file based on the Report Definition Language, which has an `.rdl` filename extension.

Table 6-1. *Report Authoring Tools Feature Comparison*

Report Designer	Report Builder
Targeted at developers	Targeted at business users
Integrated into Visual Studio	Click-once application
Managed reports	Ad hoc reports
Native queries	Autogenerates queries
Free-form reports	Reports built on templates
Works with reports built in Report Builder	Cannot import Report Designer reports

■**Note** All of the reports shipped with the Team Foundation Server are built with Report Designer. Since Report Builder cannot import Report Designer reports, modifications must be done using Report Designer. Additionally, there are some difficulties using Report Builder against the Team Foundation Server cube structure.

Managing reports involves administering the reports, data sources, and permissions on the report server. Authored reports can be published to the report server from within Visual Studio, Report Builder, or by using the rs command-line utility (you must have appropriate permission granted on the server). You can also upload reports from within Report Manager on the server itself. Report Manager also provides the ability to organize content, define permissions, and manage properties for reports and data sources.

Delivering reports consists of publishing and managing them on the report server. The publication model can be either a pull or push to the consumer. To pull a report, you can browse to the Report Manager website and navigate to the desired report. If the My Reports feature is enabled, the server users can manage a My Reports page and create custom linked reports tailored for them. SSRS supports rendering of reports into various formats, including HTML, XML, PDF, TIFF, CSV, and Microsoft Excel. Finally, SSRS supports a subscription model in which consumers can subscribe to reports and receive e-mail notification on a scheduled basis.

Using Predefined Team Reports

The predefined reports supplied with your selected process template are listed on the SQL Server Reporting Services site. To access this site, open the Team Explorer window within Visual Studio 2005, right-click the Reports node and select Show Report Site, as shown in Figure 6-3.

Figure 6-3. *Choosing to go to the report site*

Figure 6-4 shows the SQL Server Reporting Services site for the EffortTracking project, which uses the MSF for CMMI Process Improvement - v4.0 process template. The predefined reports available with this process template are listed in Table 6-2.

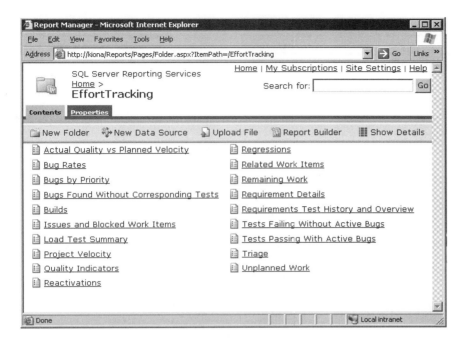

Figure 6-4. *EffortTracking Report Manager*

Note In the current version of Team Foundation Server, the number of default reports provided is a bit confusing. Currently, the MSF for CMMI Process Improvement - v4.0 process template contains 19 reports in the default list view on the report server, 23 reports in the detail view, and 25 reports in total as `.rdl` files included with the process template. The MSF for Agile Software Development - v4.0 process template includes 16 reports in the default list view on the report server, 20 reports in the detail view, and 22 `.rdl` files.

Table 6-2. *MSF for CMMI Process Improvement*

Report	Description	Type
Actual Quality vs. Planned Velocity[1]	Bugs found per requirements resolved	Graph
Bug Rates[1]	Progress in finding, fixing, and closing bugs	Graph
Bugs by Priority[1]	Number of bugs active, found, and fixed by priority	Graph
Bugs Found Without Corresponding Tests	List of bugs found that have no associated tests	Tabular
Builds[1]	Build summary with test result details	Tabular

Continued

Table 6-2. *Continued*

Report	Description	Type
Issues and Blocked Work Items[1]	Issues by type with blocked work items	Graph
Load Test Detail	Subreport for Load Test Summary	Tabular
Load Test Summary	Load tests run by Build with Detail	Tabular
Project Velocity[1]	Direct comparison of resolve and close rates	Graph
Quality Indicators[1]	Number of tests by result vs. active bugs, code churn, and coverage	Graph
Reactivations[1]	Number of reactivated work items related to total work items	Graph
Regressions[1]	List of tests currently failing that had previously passed	Tabular
Related Work Items[1]	List of work items by iteration with linked work items	Tabular
Remaining Work[1]	Active, Resolved, and Closed work items by day	Graph
Requirements Detail[2]	Requirements with work item task/test result detail	Tabular
Requirements Test History and Overview[1]	Progress of testing against requirements over the duration of the project iteration	Graph
Tests Failing Without Active Bugs[1]	List of failing tests without active bugs to fix	Tabular
Tests Passing with Active Bugs[1]	List of passing tests with active bugs still against them	Tabular
Triage[1]	Proposed work items by type over time	Graph
Unplanned Work[1]	Amount of work added since start of iteration vs. planned	Graph
Work Items with Tasks	Subreport for Requirements Detail	Tabular
Work Items with Test Results	Subreport for Requirements Detail	Tabular
Work Items[3]	List of work items by iteration	Tabular

[1] *The report is detailed in the CMMI process guidance.*
[2] *The report is detailed in the process guidance, where it is called Scenario Detail.*
[3] *Work Items by Owner and Work Item by State are listed in the process guidance, but there is but no* `.rdl` *for them in the template.*

Table 6-3 lists the predefined reports that are available with MSF for Agile Software Development - v4.0 process template.

Table 6-3. *MSF for Agile Software Development - v4.0 Process Template Default Reports*

Report	Description	Type
Actual Quality vs. Planned Velocity[1]	Average number bugs per scenario for each iteration	Graph
Bug Rates[1]	Progress on finding, fixing, and closing bugs	Graph
Bugs by Priority[1]	Number of bugs active, found, and fixed by priority	Graph
Bugs Found without Corresponding Tests	List of bugs found that have no tests associated	Tabular
Builds	Build summary with test result details	Tabular
Load Test Detail	Subreport for Load Test Summary	Tabular
Load Test Summary	Load tests run by Build with Detail	Tabular
Project Velocity[1]	Direct comparison of resolve and close rates	Graph
Quality Indicators[1]	Number of tests by result vs. active bugs, code churn, and coverage	Graph
Reactivations[1]	Number of reactivated work items related to total work items	Graph
Regressions	List of tests currently failing that had previously passed	Tabular
Related Work Items	List of work items by iteration with linked work items	Tabular
Remaining Work[1]	Progress on scenario, including work item subreports	Graph
Scenario Detail	Scenario with work item task/test result detail	Tabular
Tests Failing Without Active Bugs	List of failing tests without active bugs to fix	Tabular
Tests Failing with Active Bugs	List of failing tests with active bugs still against them	Tabular
Unplanned Work[1]	Amount of work added since start of iteration vs. planned	Graph
Work Items with Tasks	Subreport list of work items for the Scenario Detail report	Tabular
Work Items with Test Results	Subreport test cases showing outcome, category, and machine for Scenario Detail report	Tabular
Work Items	List of work items by iteration	Tabular

[1] *The report is detailed in the Agile process guidance.*

Customizing Team Reports

Reports contained within the Team Foundation default process templates are simply SSRS custom reports. You can modify these reports to suit your needs using the Report Designer.

To use the Report Designer, you need to install Business Intelligence Development Studio (BIDS), which ships as a client component with SQL Server 2005, as shown in Figure 6-5.

Figure 6-5. *Business Intelligence Development Studio is a SQL Server Setup option.*

BIDS is simply the Visual Studio shell with additional packages for SSAS, SSIS, and SSRS. If you already have VSTS, installing BIDS adds those project types to your suite in the same manner as adding the Team Explorer, as shown in Figure 6-6.

Once you have BIDS installed, you are ready to customize a report. Figure 6-7 illustrates the basic process for customizing a project report.

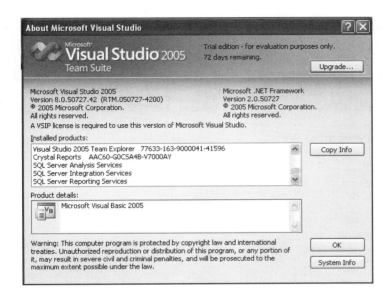

Figure 6-6. *Visual Studio installed products*

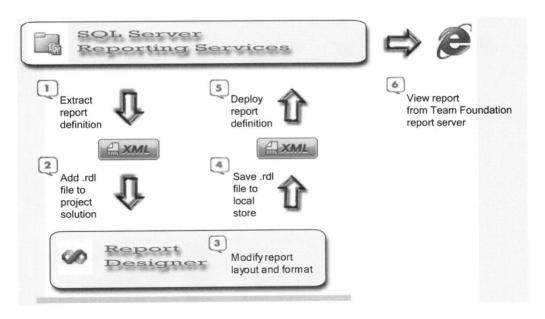

Figure 6-7. *Team report customization steps*

Here, we will work through a simple example of customizing the Work Items report. We will change the layout of the fields and modify the display elements on the report.

Extracting the Report Definition

To get started, you need access to the .rdl file for the existing report you want to customize. If you downloaded the MSF for CMMI Process Improvement - v4.0 process template through the Process Template Manager, as described in Chapter 2 (right-click the Team Foundation Server in the Team Explorer, select Team Foundation Server Settings ➤ Process Template Manager, select the process template, and click Download), you will have the entire report definition set resident on your local machine.

Alternatively, you can extract each one individually. Here's how to extract the .rdl file for the Work Items report:

1. Browse to your reporting services site (http://[server]/reports), select the EffortTracking project, select Show Details, and then select Work Items.

2. The Work Item report will be rendered in view mode. Select the Properties tab and click Edit under the Report Definition section.

3. In the File Download dialog box, select Save.

4. In the Save As dialog box, select a location on your local machine and click Save. An XML version of the report (.rdl) has now been saved.

Adding the Report Definition to a Project

Next, you need to add the .rdl file to a Project solution. Follow these steps:

1. Start Visual Studio 2005 (or BIDS) and select File ➤ New ➤ Project.

2. Select Business Intelligence Projects in the Project Types list, and then select Report Server Project from the Visual Studio installed templates list.

3. Give the project the name My Report and click OK.

4. With the new My Report solution showing in the Solution Explorer, right-click the Reports folder and select Add Existing Item.

5. Browse to the location of your local file Work Items.rdl and click Add. The Work Items report is now listed in your solution.

6. Double-click Work Items.rdl, and you will be brought into the Report Designer, as shown in Figure 6-8.

Figure 6-8. *Report Designer Layout tab*

The Report Designer includes three tabbed surfaces for working with reports:

- The Data tab is where you generate the queries for the report.
- The Layout tab is where you lay out and format the report.
- The Preview tab shows a rendered view of the report.

Note Reports in the Team Foundation Server use two predefined data sources stored on the report server at the root level: `TfsOlapReportDs` for the OLAP database and `TfsReportDS` for the relational database. You will want to create both of these data source references in your project to allow the process template-based reports to function properly.

Modifying the Report

For this example, we will make three changes to the report: move a field to another position, remove some information that is displayed, and add an image.

Moving a Field

Currently, the Title field is in the last column in the row. We will move it to appear next to the ID field.

1. Click inside the table near the word *Title*. This will expose the underlying table.
2. Click the blank header bar directly above the word *Title* to select the entire column.
3. Select Edit Cut to remove the Title field from the end of the row.
4. Press the left arrow key to move the cursor until the Assigned To field is highlighted, and then select Edit Paste. The Title field is now in the second position of the report row.

Removing Information

The default report includes the ID of the user who generated the report in the status text box. We will now remove that bit of information.

1. Select the text box that starts with =*"Report Generated:"*, right-click and select fx Expression.

2. Edit the expression and remove the following text:

   `" by " + User!UserID +`

3. Click OK to save.

Adding an Image

Finally, we will add an image to give the report some color.

1. Click the open space above the Priority column and then drag the Image object from the Report Items list.

2. The Image Wizard will start. Select Next.

3. Keep the default embedded for the image source and click Next.

4. Choose New Image and navigate to a small image you have stored locally. Click Next, and then click Finish. Your image is now embedded in the report definition.

Your layout should look something like that shown in Figure 6-9.

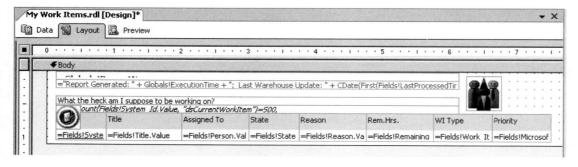

Figure 6-9. *Report Designer custom layout*

Saving the Modified Report Definition

After you've made your changes, you need to save your modified .rdl file.

1. Select File ➤ Save Work Items.rdl As. Click the Create New Folder icon.

2. Type `Version One` for the folder name, and then click OK.

3. In the Save File As dialog box, change the filename to My Work Items.rdl, and then click Save.

Tip Sometimes it takes several iterations before your report functions as intended. By saving the modified file in a separate folder each time, you can always go back to the previous versions.

Deploying and Viewing Your Report

You can deploy your new report to the Team Foundation report server directly from within Visual Studio. First, you must set the deployment properties for your My Report project.

1. Right-click My Report in the Solution Explorer and select Properties. The My Report Property Pages dialog box will be displayed, as shown in Figure 6-10.

Figure 6-10. *My Report Property Page*

2. Verify that OverwriteDataSources is set to False. Enter / for the Target DataSourceFolder. Enter /EffortTracking for the TargetReportFolder. For TargetServerURL, enter your report server's URL. Click Apply to save the changes, and then click OK to close the dialog box.

3. On the main menu, select Build ➤ Deploy My Report.

4. Watch the output window for messages. You should see the message "Deploy: 1 succeeded."

5. Save and close the My Report project.

Note Alternatively, you can browse to your reporting services site (http://[server]/reports), select the EffortTracking project, and then select Upload File from the Contents menu bar. Click the Browse button next to the File to Upload text box, locate your saved My Work Items.rdl file, and then click OK.

6. Open your browser and navigate to your report server site (http://[server]/reports).
7. Select the EffortTracking project, and then choose My Work Items from the Contents list. Your custom report will be rendered, as shown in Figure 6-11.

Figure 6-11. *Rendered customized report*

Note If you get an error binding the data sources to the report, select Properties ➤ Data Sources and manually reconnect them. This is sometimes due to the case or spelling used for the data source; the data source names need to be exact.

Introducing the Team Foundation Data Warehouse

The Team Foundation Server contains a relational data warehouse and an OLAP database, both named TFSWarehouse in their respective environments. Relational databases are by definition two-dimensional, based on rows and columns, and rooted in mathematical set theory. OLAP databases introduce the concept of dimensions, which provide multidimensional views of the data.

Understanding the Data Warehouse Architecture

The relational data warehouse is populated from the main operational data stores within Team Foundation. This architecture is shown in Figure 6-12.

Figure 6-12. *Data warehouse architecture*

Operational Data Stores

Four operational data stores are provided with the Team Foundation Server:

- Work Item Tracking includes both the work item tracking store (TfsWorkItemTracking) and the work item tracking attachments store (TfsWorkItemTrackingAttachments).

- Version Control holds a single data store (TfsVersionControl) containing all the tables to operate the versioning subsystem.

- Team Build contains one data store (TfsBuild), which combines the build and test data stores.

- Integration services include both the activity logging data store (TfsActivityLogging) and the integration store (TfsIntegration).

Warehouse Adapters

Each operational data store has its own version of the warehouse adapter. Because each data store is customizable, it must be able to convey underlying changes to be incorporated into the data warehouse.

The warehouse adapter is a managed assembly that extracts data from the operational data store, transforms the data to a common warehouse format, and then writes that data into the relational warehouse. Each managed assembly implements the IWarehouseAdapter interface to allow the Team Foundation Warehouse Service to activate it, along with the IDataStore interface for writing to the warehouse. The adapters can be found in C:\Program Files\Microsoft Visual Studio 2005 Team Foundation Server\Web Services\Warehouse\bin\Plugins on the Team Foundation Data Tier server.

Star Schema

The most common construct for describing a data warehouse is the star schema. This schema portrays the multidimensional arrangements for relational tables used in data analysis and reporting.

When designing a star schema, all data items are divided into one of two groups: numeric items used in aggregations (measures) and nonnumeric items used as context (descriptors). Fact tables contain the grouping of measures, and dimension tables contain groupings of descriptors. Each star schema contains only one fact table, which represents the subject area to be analyzed and reported on. Descriptors are then grouped around logical entity areas, such as person, date, and builds, and these become dimensions in the star schema.

Only one type of relationship exists in a star schema: a one-to-many relationship from the dimension to the fact. The star schema gets its name by the common arrangement of the fact table in the middle and the dimension tables surrounding the fact table like points on a star.

The Team Foundation reporting warehouse is a traditional data warehouse consisting of a relational database roughly organized around a star schema and an OLAP database built over the top. Figure 6-13 shows one of the subject areas, Code Churn, from TFSWarehouse.

Exploring the Data Warehouse Schema

The data warehouse schema is the template for the layout of the tables in TFSWarehouse. The initial schema can be found at \Program Files\Microsoft Visual Studio 2005 Team Foundation Server\Tools\warehouseschema.xml on the Team Foundation Data Tier Server. An updated copy is stored in the ConfigXML setting in the _WarehouseConfig table of TFSWarehouse. The three main areas in the template are Facts, Dimensions, and FactLinks. Each represents a significant component in the data warehouse and OLAP cube, as described in the previous section.

■**Note** Setupwarehouse.exe uses the version of warehouseschema.xml under the Tools folder during setup to build the warehouse. It is copied to the _WarehouseConfig table during the setup process. Ongoing schema changes update the version in the _WarehouseConfig table.

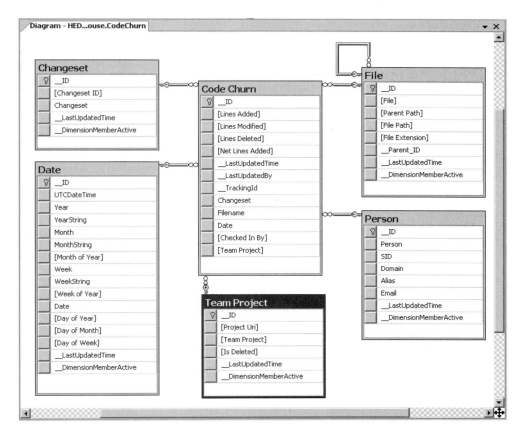

Figure 6-13. *Code Churn star schema*

Data Warehouse Facts

The fact table holds the primary (measurable) data for analysis. Facts are represented by `Fact`, `Fields`, and `DimensionUses`, as shown in Listing 6-1.

Listing 6-1. *Warehouse Template Facts Section*

```
<Facts>
  <Fact>
    <Name>Code Churn</Name>
    <FriendlyName>Code Churn</FriendlyName>
    <PerspectiveName>Code Churn</PerspectiveName>
    <IncludeCountMeasure>true</IncludeCountMeasure>
    <Fields>
      <Field>
        <Name>Lines Added</Name>
        <FriendlyName>Lines Added</FriendlyName>
        <Type>int</Type>
```

```
        <Length>0</Length>
        <Visible>true</Visible>
        <AggregationFunction>Sum</AggregationFunction>
        <RelationalOnly>false</RelationalOnly>
        <CalculatedMembers />
      </Field>
    <Measures />
    <DimensionUses>
      <DimensionUse>
        <UseName>Changeset</UseName>
        <FriendlyUseName>Changeset</FriendlyUseName>
        <DimensionName>Changeset</DimensionName>
        <RelationalOnly>false</RelationalOnly>
      </DimensionUse>
    </Fact>
  </Facts>
```

The first few lines of the template define the fact name, perspective name, and whether or not to include a count. The perspective name refers to predefined subsets of cube metadata, similar to SQL Server views. Each field of the fact table is then enumerated. If `RelationalOnly` has a value of `true`, then the field will appear in the relational data warehouse but not in the analysis services cube. `DimensionUses` defines the dimension tables used by the `Fact`. If `IncludeCountMeasure` contains a value of `true`, then a measure will be created containing an integer value for count. If `Visible` has a value of `true`, then it is available to cube browsing tools.

Table 6-4 lists the fact tables that ship with the Team Foundation Server.

Table 6-4. *Fact Tables for the Team Foundation Server*

Number	Fact Table	Fields
1	Code Churn	Lines Added, Lines Modified, Lines Deleted, Net Lines Added
2	Work Item Changeset	Work Item, Changeset
3	Work Item History	Logical Tracking ID, Record Count, Revision Count, State Change Count
4	Current Work Item	Logical Tracking ID
5	Build Changeset	No fields are specified
6	Build Project	Compile Errors, Compile Warnings, Static Analysis Errors, Static Analysis Warnings
7	Build Details	Logical Tracking ID, Build Duration
8	Load Test Counter	Value
9	Build Coverage	Lines Covered, Lines Not Covered, Lines Partially Covered, Blocks Covered, Blocks Not Covered

Number	Fact Table	Fields
10	Run Coverage	Lines Covered, Lines Not Covered, Lines Partially Covered, Blocks Covered, Blocks Not Covered
11	Load Test Page Summary	Sequence, Test, Response Time, Page Count
12	Test Result	Result Record Count, Result Count, Result Transition Count
13	Load Test summary	Start Time, Actual Duration, Load Test Duration, Load Test Warmup Time
14	Load Test Details	Sequence, Test, Total Tests, Failed Tests, Average Duration
15	Load Test Transaction	Sequence, Test, Transactions, Response Time, Elapsed Time

Data Warehouse Dimensions

Dimensions are the descriptive data or categorical variables. The primary key of the dimension will be stored with the associated fact table. Dimensions are represented by `Dimension`, `Fields`, `KeyFieldName`, and `OrderByField`, as shown in Listing 6-2.

Listing 6-2. *Warehouse Template Dimensions Section*

```
<Dimensions>
  <Dimension>
    <Name>Changeset</Name>
    <FriendlyName>Changeset</FriendlyName>
    <Fields>
      <Field>
        <Name>Changeset ID</Name>
        <FriendlyName>Changeset ID</FriendlyName>
        <Type>int</Type>
        <Length>0</Length>
        <Visible>true</Visible>
        <RelationalOnly>false</RelationalOnly>
        <CalculatedMembers />
      </Field>
    <KeyFieldName>Changeset ID</KeyFieldName>
    <OrderByField>Changeset ID</OrderByField>
    <Levels />
  </Dimension>
```

Table 6-5 lists the dimension tables that ship with the Team Foundation Server.

Table 6-5. *Dimension Tables for the Team Foundation Server*

Number	Dimension Table	Fields
1	Area	Area, Area Uri, Parent Area Uri, Area Path, Forwarding ID, Project Uri
2	Assembly	Assembly
3	Build	Build Artifact Moniker, Build, Build Type, Drop Location, Build Start Time
4	Build Flavor	Build Flavor
5	Build Quality	Build Quality
6	Build Status	Build Status
7	Changeset	Changeset ID, Changeset
8	Date	UTCDateTime, Year, YearString, Month, MonthString, Month of Year, Week, WeekString, Week of Year, Date, Day of Year, Day of Month, Day of Week
9	File	File, Parent Path, File Path, File Extension
10	Iteration	Iteration, Iteration Uri, Parent Iteration Uri, Iteration Path, Forwarding ID, Project Uri
11	Load Test Counter Dimension	Counter ID, Counter Object, Counter, Counter Instance, Counter Result, Higher Is Better
12	Load Test Page Summary Dimension	URL
13	Load Test Scenario	Load Test Scenario
14	Load Test Transaction Dimension	Transaction
15	Machine	Machine
16	Outcome	Outcome, Outcome Passing
17	Person	Person, SID, Domain, Alias, Email
18	Platform	Platform
19	Result	Result ID, Result, Test, Test Type, Test Description, Parent Result, Result Root, Error Message, Load Test Agent List, End Time
20	Run	Run ID, Run, Run Description, Remote Run
21	Run Result	Run Result, Run Result Message
22	Team Project	Project Uri, Team Project
23	Test Category	Category ID, Test Category, Category Full Name, Parent Category
24	Today	Index, UTCDateTime, Year, YearString, Month, MonthString, Month of Year, Week, WeekString, Week of Year, Date, Day of Year, Day of Month, Day of Week
25	Tool Artifact Display URL	Tool Type, Tool Artifact, Display URL
26	WorkItem	Work Item, Previous State

Figure 6-14 shows the dimension tables used by facts for the Team Foundation Server data warehouse.

Dimensions	Code Churn	Work Item Changeset	Work Item History	Current Work Item	Build Changeset	Build Project	Build Details	Build Project	Build Details	Load Test Counter	Build Coverage	Run Coverage	Load Test Page Summary	Test Result	Load Test summary	Load Test Details	Load Test Transaction
1 Area																	
2 Assembly																	
3 Build																	
4 Build Flavor																	
5 Build Quality																	
6 Build Status																	
7 Changeset																	
8 Date																	
9 File																	
10 Iteration																	
11 Load Test Counter Dimension																	
12 Load Test Page Summary Dimension																	
13 Load Test Scenario																	
14 Load Test Transaction Dimension																	
15 Machine																	
16 Outcome																	
17 Person																	
18 Platform																	
19 Result																	
20 Run																	
21 Run Result																	
22 Team Project																	
23 Test Category																	
24 Today																	
25 Tool Artifact Display Url																	
26 Work Item																	

Figure 6-14. *Dimension tables used by facts*

■**Note** Every fact in the data warehouse contains a dimensional relationship with the team project dimension. This ensures that all fact data in the warehouse can be sliced by project.

Data Warehouse FactLinks

`FactLinks` are a view joining two related fact tables in the data warehouse. The result is that all fields from both fact tables are available for reporting. `FactLinks` are represented by the `LinkName`, `SourceFactName`, and `LinkedFactName`, as shown in Listing 6-3.

Listing 6-3. *Warehouse Template FactLinks Section*

```
<FactLinks>
  <FactLink>
    <LinkName>Work Item with Result</LinkName>
    <FriendlyLinkName>Work Item with Result</FriendlyLinkName>
    <SourceFactName>Work Item History</SourceFactName>
    <LinkedFactName>Test Result</LinkedFactName>
  </FactLink>
</FactLinks>
```

Table 6-6 lists the dimension tables for `FactLinks` that ship with the Team Foundation Server.

Table 6-6. *Dimension Tables for FactLinks*

Number	Dimension Table	Fact Tables
1	vWork Items with Result	Work Item History, Test Result
2	vRelated Current Work Items	Current Work Item, Current Work Item
3	vRelated Work Items	Work Item History, Work Item History

The Tool Artifact Display Url Table

A special table named `Tool Artifact Display Url` in the data warehouse holds the URL paths for each of the tool artifacts, as shown in Figure 6-15. The tools correspond to the operational stores: Build (including Test), Version Control, and Work Item Tracking. The artifacts include entries like work items, test results, and versioned items. VSTS uses these display URLs to allow active hyperlinks on various artifacts.

Figure 6-15. *The Tool Artifact Display Url table*

Managing the Data Warehouse

The Controller web service exposes eight operations to help manage the TFSWarehouse, as shown in Figure 6-16. To access this service, log on to the application tier and browse to http://localhost:8080/Warehouse/v1.0/warehousecontroller.asmx.

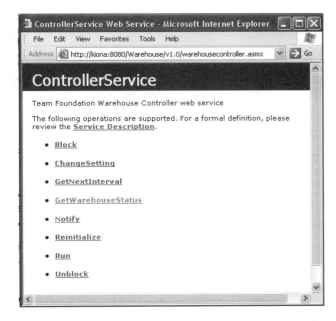

Figure 6-16. *Team Foundation Warehouse Controller web service*

These operations work as follows:

- *Block:* Turns off warehouse processing until Unblock is called.

- *ChangeSetting:* Allows you to change settings stored in the warehouse database table _WarehouseConfig via the web service (settings include RunIntervalSeconds and DailyFullProcessingHour).

- *GetNextInterval:* Returns RunIntervalSeconds from the _WarehouseConfig table.

- *GetWarehouseStatus:* Gets the current status from the warehouse. The service will respond with ProcessingAdapters (schema modifications), ProcessingOlap (schema modifications), ProcessingAdapters (pulling data), ProcessingOlap (processing the cube), or Idle (waiting).

- *Notify:* Makes a Run call. Used by the Project Creation Wizard to bring the warehouse online quicker after project creation.

- *Reinitialize*: Reinitializes the warehouse by reloading the adapters and initializing state. The warehouse must be in a blocked and idle state.

- *Run:* Sets two distinct activities in motion. Each of the operational store plugins will gather data from its associated data store and write to the data warehouse. Next, it will process the cube in transactional mode so it is still available.

- *Unblock:* Turns warehouse processing back on after a Block call.

Adding Elements to the Data Warehouse

The Work Item Type Definition (WITD) language (described in Chapter 5) field definition contains an option named `reportable`, which can be set to `dimension`, `measure`, or `detail`. You can use these as follows:

- Use `reportable="dimension"` for attributes that you want to slice the data (type, area, and so on). A column is added to the fact table and a measure added to measure group.

- Use `reportable="measure"` for numeric values that you want to aggregate (hours, counts, and so on). A column is added to the dimension table and the dimension `ATTRIBUTE` is added to the `Work Item` dimension.

- Use `reportable="detail"` to add a column to the fact table without adding anything to the cube.

Note After the process template is updated using `witimport` or the Process Template Manager, the new `reportable` fields will be put in the data warehouse the next time the adapters are executed.

Data Mining with Microsoft Excel

Microsoft Excel is an excellent client to manipulate data stored in the Team Foundation Server data warehouse. As an example, we'll go through the steps for bringing some data into Excel and then creating a simple report.

Note This functionally is fully support in Microsoft Excel 2003 and enhanced in Microsoft Excel 2007 (currently in beta).

Bringing Team Foundation Data into Excel

Follow these steps to bring Team Foundation data into an Excel pivot table:

1. Open Microsoft Office Excel 2003.
2. From the main menu, select Data ➤ Pivot Table and Pivot Chart Report.
3. On the first page of the wizard, select External Data Source, as shown in Figure 6-17, and click Next

Figure 6-17. *Excel PivotTable and PivotChart Wizard Step 1*

4. On the second page of the wizard, shown in Figure 6-18, click Get Data.

Figure 6-18. *Excel PivotTable and PivotChart Wizard Step 2*

Note If Microsoft Query is not installed, you will be prompted to install it.

5. In the Choose Data Source dialog box, select the OLAP Cubes tab, and then select <New Data Source>, as shown in Figure 6-19. Click OK.

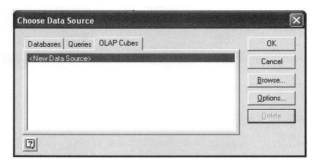

Figure 6-19. *The Choose Data Source dialog box*

6. In the Create New Data Source dialog box, give your data source a name and select Microsoft OLE DB Provider for Analysis Services 9.0 (you can get this by installing the SQL Server 2005 workstation components), as shown in Figure 6-20. Then click Connect.

Figure 6-20. *The Create New Data Source dialog box*

7. In the Multidimensional Connection 9.0 dialog box, make sure Analysis Server is selected. Provide the name of your data tier server and your login credentials, as shown in Figure 6-21. Then click Next.

Figure 6-21. *The Multidimensional Connection dialog box*

8. Select the OLAP database (TfsWarehouse), as shown in Figure 6-22, and then click Finish.

Figure 6-22. *Selecting the TFSWarehouse database*

9. Select the Current Work Item cube, as shown in Figure 6-23, and then click OK.

Figure 6-23. *The Create New Data Source dialog box with the Current Work Item cube selected*

■**Note** With SQL Standard Edition, only one perspective (cube), called Team System, is used.

10. Make sure your new data source is selected in the Choose Data Source dialog box, and then click OK.
11. The data fields will now have been retrieved, as shown in Figure 6-24. Click Next.

■**Note** If you get an error messages stating "Initialization of the data source failed," you will need to register the `msolap90 dll`.

Figure 6-24. *Excel PivotTable and PivotChart Wizard Step 2 after retrieving data*

12. Select the default location on the existing worksheet, as shown in Figure 6-25, and then click Finish.

Figure 6-25. *Excel PivotTable and PivotChart Wizard Step 3*

At this point, you have an empty pivot table bound to the Current Work Item Fact cube, as shown in Figure 6-26.

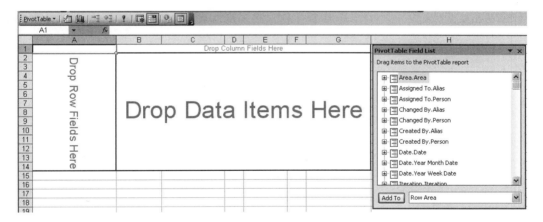

Figure 6-26. *Empty pivot table in Excel*

Creating a Report

There are four measures at the end of the Pivot Table Field List: Current Work Item Count, Remaining Work, Completed Work, and Baseline Work. You'll use Current Work Item Count, which gives you the total counts for any slice, for most queries.

For example, if you want to create a list of your Work Items by Type report, use the Current Work Item Count measure, filter to `Team.Project=EffortTracking`, and slice by Type. `TransitionCount` is used to show the state transition activity.

To see how this works, follow these steps:

1. Select the Current Work Item Count measure and add it to the data area. This will now show a count of the total number of work items without any classification.

2. Select Assigned To.Person and add it to the Row Area. If there are multiple people, you can use the drop-down arrow, deselect (Show All), and select only yourself.

3. Select TeamProject.TeamProject, select the Page Area, and click Add To.

4. Select Work Item.Work Item Type and add it to the Row Area. The Work Items are now sliced by Type.

5. Add Work Item.State to the Row Area.

The simple Excel report from the Team Foundation data warehouse is shown in Figure 6-27.

	A	B	C	D
1	Team Project.Team Project	EffortTracking		
2				
3	Current Work Item Count			
4	Person	Work Item Type	State	Total
5	Nelson, David	Requirement	Proposed	1
6		Requirement Total		1
7		Task	Active	3
8			Proposed	12
9		Task Total		15
10	Nelson, David Total			16
11	Grand Total			16

Figure 6-27. *Custom pivot table in Excel*

To view the same information in a chart format, right-click within your pivot table and select PivotChart. You can change the chart types, title, and labels. Figure 6-28 shows an example of a modified chart.

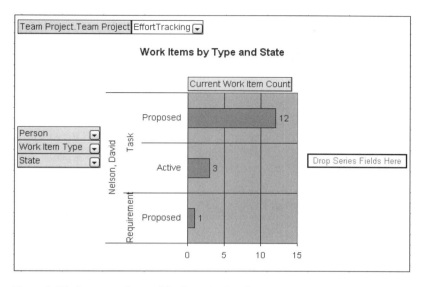

Figure 6-28. *Custom pivot table chart in Excel*

Creating a New Report

Creating a new report from scratch is not difficult using a Visual Studio Business Intelligence Project template, which was introduced earlier in the section about customizing reports. Although you do not have a base report to use as a starting point, you do have the help of the Report Server Project Wizard. An overview of the process is shown in Figure 6-29.

Figure 6-29. *Creating a new report*

As an example, we'll create a simple report. It will be based on a query that shows the distinction between the cumulative count and transition (State Change) count. The cumulative count (sliced by state and date) will show totals for the period (week). The transition count (sliced by state and date) will reveal activations, resolutions, and closures within the period (week).

Follow these steps:

1. Start Visual Studio 2005 (or BIDS) and select File ➤ New ➤ Project. Select Business Intelligence Projects in the Project Types list, and then select Report Server Project Wizard from the Visual Studio installed templates list. Give the project the name MyNewTFSReport, as shown in Figure 6-30, and then click OK.

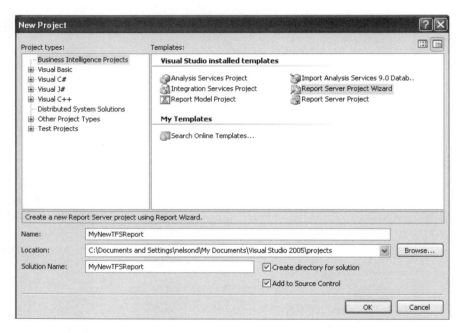

Figure 6-30. *Starting a new Report Server Project Wizard project*

2. This will launch the Report Wizard and display the splash screen. Click Next to continue.

3. On the Select the Data Source page of the wizard, select the "New data source" radio button and give the source a name (myTFSsource). Click the down arrow for the Type and select Microsoft SQL Server Analysis Services. Click the Edit button to define the data source connection. In the Server Name text box, type the name of your database tier server for Team Foundation. Click the down arrow next to the "Select or enter a database name" combo box and select the TFSWarehouse, as shown in Figure 6-31. Click Test Connection to check the connection, and then click OK. Click OK in the Connection Properties dialog box.

Figure 6-31. *The Connection Properties dialog box*

4. You will now see the connection string populated in the Select the Data Source page. Click Next.

5. On the Design the Query page, click Query Builder to launch the Multidimensional Expressions (MDX) query builder. (MDX allows you to query multidimensional sources such as TFSWarehouse cubes and return cell sets of the cube's data.)

6. Now you need to select the cube for the query. Click the ellipsis button in the top-left pane to open the Cube Selection window. For this example, select Work Item History, as shown in Figure 6-32, and then click OK.

Figure 6-32. *The Cube Selection window*

7. Within the Work Item History cube, expand the Assigned To dimension. Right-click Person and select Add to Query. Click to expand Person, then expand Member, then expand All. Scroll down to find your name, right-click it, and select Add to Filter.

8. Repeat this process to expand the Work Item dimension, and add System_State and System_Reason to the query. Add Team Project as a filter item, and filter on `EffortTracking` if you have more than one team project. Expand the Date dimension, expand Year Week Date, and add Week to the query.

9. To add the measures to your query, expand Measures, and then expand Work Item History. Right-click Cumulative Count and select Add to Query. Do the same for State Change Count. Your query design should now look like the one shown in Figure 6-33.

Note If you prefer, you can drag-and-drop items onto the design surface instead of using the right-click and add method.

Figure 6-33. *The query in the Query Builder*

10. Click OK in the Query Builder, and you will see your MDX query displayed in the Design the Query page of the wizard, as shown in Figure 6-34. Click Next to continue.

Tip If you would like to see the MDX query while using the designer, you can click the design mode icon in the Query Builder to toggle back and forth between the design and the MDX query.

Figure 6-34. *The query built with the Query Builder*

11. You will be prompted for the report type. Select the default Tabular report type and click Next.

12. The Design the Table page shows the six available fields. Select Person in the Available fields and click the Page button to move it to the Page level fields. Select Week and click the Group button to move it to the Group level. Move the remaining four fields to the Details level. Your page should look like the one shown in Figure 6-35. Click Next.

Select the Stepped layout and check both Include Subtotals and Enable Drilldown, as shown in Figure 6-36. This will allow you to expand the rows for more detail and provide subtotals on the rows when the detail is collapsed. Click Next.

Figure 6-35. *Designing the tabular report*

Figure 6-36. *Designing the tabular layout*

14. Select the Forest style sheet on the Choose the Table Style page, and then click Next.

15. Select the deployment location for your report: the Team Foundation report server and the team project name for the Deployment folder.

16. Name the report **MyTFSReport**. Then review the summary information, select Preview report, and click Finish.

17. Once the report is rendered in a preview, you can toggle to the layout view and change the title or other layout features. Your final report is shown in Figure 6-37.

Figure 6-37. *Preview of a custom report*

18. To deploy your custom report, right-click `MyTFSReport.rdl` in the Solution Explorer and select Deploy.

Summary

This chapter opened with a brief introduction to the SQL Server 2005 Business Intelligence platform and an overview of SSRS and the reporting life cycle. Then we covered the predefined reports shipped with both the MSF for Agile Software Development - v4.0 and MSF for CMMI Process Improvement - v4.0 process templates. We walked through the process of customizing a report from the CMMI template using the Report Designer integrated within Visual Studio.

We then took a look at the Team Foundation data warehouse and how it works. Next, we worked through an example of data mining with Microsoft Excel against the data warehouse. Finally, we created a report from scratch.

CHAPTER 7

Team Foundation Build

This chapter describes how to perform automated builds using VSTS. Automated builds are a key part of ensuring a high-quality, low-cost system. That is not to say that using nightly, automated builds will result in a low-cost system, but that it will result in a lower cost when compared to an equivalent system that does not perform these builds. That statement in itself should be highly suspect to you right now, because performing builds in and of itself does nothing to reduce cost. With that in mind, it might be a good idea to understand what occurs with these types of builds. So, first we'll explain the automated build process and its benefits, and then we'll look at using Team Foundation Build.

Benefits of Automated Builds

The process of nightly builds typically follows this path:

- Get the latest version of code from the source code repository.
- Perform a build.
- Deploy the build (this may or may not be necessary depending on the type of application).
- Run *all* of the unit tests associated with the code.
- Publish the test results to the Team Foundation Server.

This type of test is called a build verification test (BVT). Believe it or not, this is a concept that has been adopted very slowly. Tools such as Ant, NAnt, JUnit, and NUnit have made this process much easier to implement. There were always barriers for developers though. These revolved around the source code repository itself. Have you ever tried to write code that would automatically pull the latest version of code or a specific version of code from Visual Source-Safe (or CVS for that matter)? If you have, you know that that is a software development project in and of itself.

So how does this help reduce cost and increase quality? First, by performing nightly builds, you know exactly when the code breaks. Compare this to running builds once a week. When did the code break? Who broke it? Where is it broken? By doing this nightly, you avoid these issues.

Second, running the unit testing provides a measure of the quality of the build. It allows for regression testing to be performed every night. Breaks are discovered immediately and corrected immediately. This means that as you work closer toward release, you can be confident that your code works. The other advantage of this approach is that the software can always be demonstrated to the stakeholders because it always works.

This is not to say that you should not worry about the testing using this process, because you still need to perform function and system testing. However, performing BVTs adds a level of confidence in working with your code. It also increases the confidence that your stakeholders have in you and your team because they can see that things are working. And finally, it decreases the number of bugs and the amount of work to fix those bugs that are found as you approach the release date.

■**Tip** If you are using a test-driven development methodology, or even just good coding change management practices, developers should be performing builds and running tests *before* checking their code in anyway. If this process is followed, it is unlikely that the BVTs will report errors, but they may help find errors that were overlooked because of a break in the processes. And any errors found before functional or system testing are that much easier and cheaper to correct.

Using Team Foundation Build

You can use Team Foundation Build simply to perform regular builds to make sure that the project can be built. However, to truly take advantage of Team Foundation Build's capabilities, you should establish procedures that promote using it. This means that there should be rules that say that developers will *not* check in code that a) does not build, b) does not have unit tests, and c) does not pass its unit tests. Following these three, sometimes not-so-simple rules, will increase the quality of your code greatly and allow you to gain more benefit from performing these nightly tests.

■**Note** Chapter 3 discusses setting up check-in policies. One of the available policies is the Testing Policy, which ensures that code passes certain tests before it is checked in. There are no policies to enforce code passing a BVT.

Creating a Build Type

To set up Team Foundation Build, you configure a Team Foundation build type. A *build type* is a set of instructions, or steps, that guide the process of creating and testing an application. These instructions are stored as a build type on the Team Foundation Server.

Caution Even though you can create build types without having Team Foundation Build installed, you do need Team Foundation Build (a separate installation) in order to be able to run the builds. For this demonstration, Team Foundation Build is installed on the same machine as the development machine (`mcsd-dev`).

To create a build type, follow these steps:

1. Select the Team Explorer pane and expand the Team Foundation Builds node.

2. Right-click the Team Foundation Builds node and select New Team Foundation Build Type. This starts the New Team Build Type Creation Wizard.

3. On the wizard's Welcome page, enter a title and optionally a description, as shown in Figure 7-1. The description should describe in detail what this particular build does, as there may be many different build types for various parts of the system, especially when you're working on a large system with many different projects or solutions. After you've entered the information, click Next to continue.

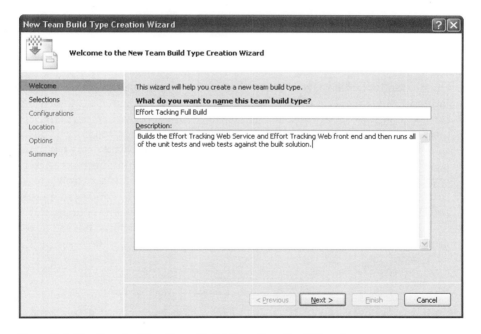

Figure 7-1. *Starting the New Team Build Type Creation Wizard*

4. On the Selections page, select which solutions you want to build. The workspace options allow you to select workspaces defined in version control. Once you have made this selection, the solutions listed are those located within the selected workspace. For this example, select the `EffortTrackingSolution`, as shown in Figure 7-2, and then click Next.

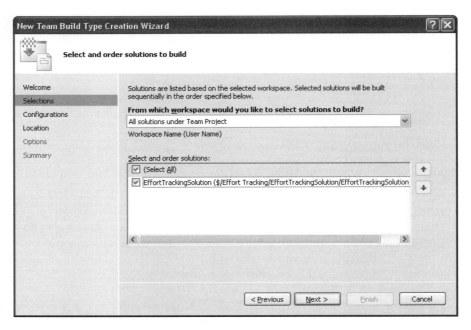

Figure 7-2. *Selections page of the New Team Build Type Creation Wizard*

5. On the Configurations page, you can choose to test your release against various configurations, which must also be defined in the solution's Configuration Manager. As you can see in Figure 7-3, you can elect to build a release or debug version of the solution, and you can target any of the available platforms. This is a great feature if you are building a solution that is targeted for a 32-bit and 64-bit release using the same code base, for example. Select Mixed Platforms if your solution contains more than one type of platform (such as Web, Windows, and so on). This will build each project according to that projects' specific settings. You can also enter your own configuration name in the Configuration combo box, if your solution supports a custom configuration. In addition, you can enter your own platform in the Platform combo box to target in the build. For this demonstration, leave the default configuration of Release/Any CPU and click Next.

Caution If you enter (or select) a Configuration/Platform combination that is not already defined in the solution, that particular build will be skipped.

---

6. On the Location page, select where the build and tests will be performed and where the completed build will be placed after everything has been done, as shown in Figure 7-4. For this example, select the local machine on which you are running VSTS, which must have Team Foundation Build installed on it, and specify a local directory (if it does not exist, it will be created). The drop location can be anywhere.

CHAPTER 7 ■ TEAM FOUNDATION BUILD

Figure 7-3. *Configurations page of the New Team Build Type Creation Wizard*

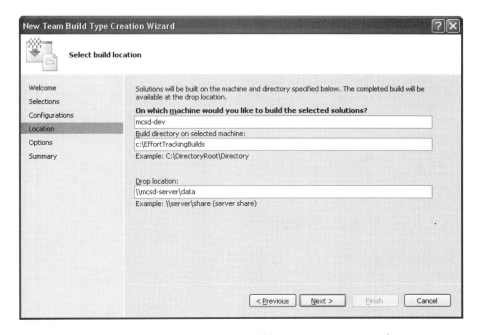

Figure 7-4. *Location page of the New Team Build Type Creation Wizard*

Caution For this release, if you intend to run any of the unit tests, you must specify a build machine that has the Team Edition for Software Developers or Testers installed. For web tests to run, the build machine must have the Team Edition for Software Testers installed. Additionally, the location that you specify for the build must have enough available space to hold all of the source files for the solution and the compiled solution. This is because Team Foundation Build does a "Get Latest" from the version control, and then builds the solution in the specified location.

7. On the Options page, specify the tests and analysis that you want to run as part of the build. Notice that you can select only test lists; you cannot select individual tests (including ordered tests). The list of tests is controlled by which testing metadata file you select from the drop-down list. Each solution can have more than one metadata file and therefore more than one list of tests. For this example, select the Run Test check box and the Read Tests check box, as shown in Figure 7-5. Also select the Perform Code Analysis According to Project Settings check box at the bottom of the page. This will cause FxCop (or PREfast for a C/C++ application) to run as part of the build process, *if* you selected this option to be run as part of the preferences for the specific projects involved in the solution. Click Next to continue.

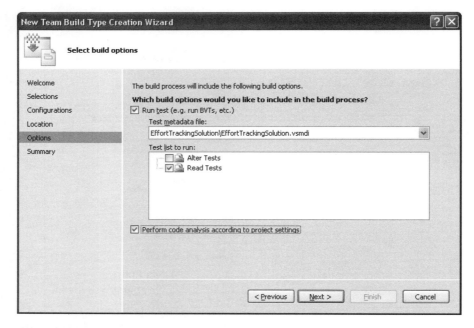

Figure 7-5. *Options page of the New Team Build Type Creation Wizard*

8. The Summary page provides a list of all of the choices you have made in the wizard, as shown in Figure 7-6. Click Finish to complete the wizard.

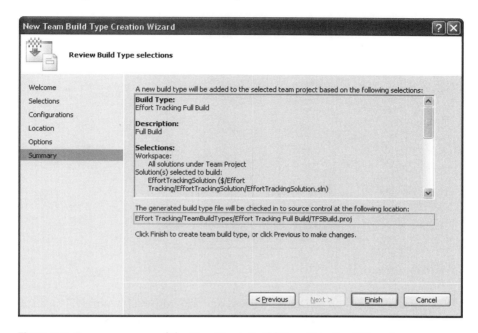

Figure 7-6. *Summary page of the New Team Build Type Creation Wizard*

Team Foundation Build will then display the XML configuration file used to store the settings, which can be edited by hand at any time, as described in the "Customizing the Build Process" section later in this chapter. In addition, the build type that you just created will appear under the Team Foundation Builds node in the Team Explorer.

If you need to delete a build type, open the Source Control Explorer and drill down to the build type folder ((`Server`)\(`Solution`)\TeamBuildTypes\(`BuildType`)). Right-click the build type that you want to delete (the folder) and select Get Latest. Then right-click the build type folder and select Delete. Finally, commit the deletion in the Pending Changes dialog box.

Running the Build and Viewing Build Results

Once you've set up the build type, running the build is simple. Right-click the build type under the Team Foundation Builds node and select Build Team Project Effort Tracking. This displays the Build dialog box, which allows you to make any last-minute changes to the build machine or directory, as shown in Figure 7-7. Click the Build button to run the build.

Figure 7-7. *Build dialog box*

At this point, the solution will start building, and a Build Detail Report will be displayed to let you know the status of the build and where in the process it is, as shown in Figure 7-8.

Figure 7-8. *Summary section of the Build Detail Report*

Tip You can be alerted when a build is performed. To set this up, refer to discussion of project alerts in Chapter 2.

The same report that shows the status of the build progress also shows the results when the build is completed. The results are broken into five areas:

- Summary
- Build steps
- Result details (for each configuration type)
- Associated changesets
- Associated work items

Build Summary

The summary lists basic information about the build (see Figure 7-7). Clicking the build name link will open the folder where the build was output to (specified in the build configuration location section). Opening the build log will provide you with detailed information of everything that occurred as part of the build.

Build Steps

The build steps section shows all the steps that Team Foundation Build took as it was performing the build test and copying the file to the drop location, as shown in Figure 7-9. The details for each of these steps can be found in the build log.

Figure 7-9. *Build steps section of the Build Detail Report*

Result Details

If there were any errors or warnings, they will be summarized in the result details section, as shown in Figure 7-10.

Figure 7-10. *Result details section of the Build Detail Report*

Clicking the `Release.txt` link will open the `release.txt` file and display the details of the errors and warnings. In the case of this particular test, the database projects caused the warnings, because the `.dbp` file could not be built by the build engine, as it is not a supported type. So these warnings are perfectly acceptable.

■**Note** Because database projects cannot be built, you may want to store them in another solution. Of course, then you will need to have multiple instances of Visual Studio open in order to work with your database information and project information at the same time. Alternatively, you could just keep in mind that you will always have as many warnings as you have database projects in your solution. If you see more warnings, it is time to investigate.

The next line details the test results. In this case, all of the tests passed. Under Test Run, the test results link is displayed. Clicking this link allows you to download the test results to your workstation in order to examine the details. These details are presented in the same way that a test run on your local machine is presented.

Finally, the code coverage results are listed here in total and by each assembly. In this case, only the web service assembly was tested. The blocks that were not covered are those that deal with altering data that you did not include in the tests run during the build.

Associated Changesets

All changesets which contribute to a build are showcased in the form of associated changesets. Hence, it becomes easy to figure out which changesets were checked in for each build.

Figure 7-11 shows the associated changesets for the first build that was run against the Effort Tracking solution.

Figure 7-11. *Associated changesets section of the Build Detail Report*

Clicking the changeset ID will display a dialog box indicating what changes were made in the changeset (files that were changed). This is the same dialog box displayed when viewing a changeset from the Source Control Explorer.

Tip Obviously, based on Figure 7-11, you want to make sure that you provide comments describing each changeset (when you check in code), so that you know what changes the changeset covered. (It is also obvious that the authors do not do follow that advice regularly enough.)

Associated Work Items

The associated work items section contains a list of all work items that are associated with the build. For instance, developers fixing work items will associate that work item with the changeset in which the issue is fixed. All of the work items that were associated with the changesets that were included in the build are displayed here, as shown in Figure 7-12.

Figure 7-12. *Associated work items section of the Build Detail Report*

In this particular case, only one work item was associated with the build. In this way, stakeholders can determine when work items were fixed, or even worked on, and what their status is simply by looking at a build output. You can view the details of the work item by clicking the work item ID link.

Viewing Build History

To view build history, right-click the build type in the Team Explorer and select Open to display the Team Build Browser, as shown in Figure 7-13. This window lists all of the builds that have been done (or are in progress) for the selected build type. By default, the builds are listed from newest on the top to oldest on the bottom, with each build's name, status, quality, and when it was completed.

Figure 7-13. *Team Build Browser*

To see the details of a specific build, right-click it and select Open or double-click the build. This also gives you the option to edit its build quality.

Build Quality

The *build quality* is a value that describes the general condition of the build and what stage of quality checks it has passed. Build quality is determined by whoever is reviewing the build and is not set automatically.

Note A person must have Edit Build Quality permissions in order to change the build quality. See Chapter 2 for details about permissions.

As you can see in Figure 7-13, the options for the build quality are as follows:

- Initial Test Passed
- Lab Test Passed
- Ready for Deployment
- Ready for Initial Test
- Ready for Release
- Rejected
- Released
- UAT Passed (Unit Acceptance Test)
- Under Investigation
- Unexamined (default)

You can edit this list by selecting the final option in the drop-down list, <Edit>. This allows you to add your own statuses to the build quality, which can help you to keep track of the purpose of that build.

Build Details

Every completed build has its results published to the Team Foundation Server. The results on the server provide slightly different information than the results reported on the client. A build report is shown in Figure 7-14.

Build Name	Build Quality	% Tests Passed	% Code Coverage	% Code Churn
⊟ Effort Tacking Full Build_20051111.1	Unexamined	100 %	0%	65.7501 %

Test Run Results: 1 test run(s) completed, 5/ 5 test(s) passed.

Test Run Name	Total Tests	Passed	Failed	Other Result
⊞ tfsservice@MCSD-DEV 2005-11-11 15:28:36_Any CPU_Release	5	5	0	0

⊞ Code Coverage Results: 0 % lines covered, 0 % lines not covered, 0 % lines partially covered.

⊟ Code Churn Details: 7492 Total Line of Code, 69 Line(s) Churned, 4908 Line(s) Added, 18 Line(s) Deleted

Relative Code Churn Measure	Value
Line(s) Churned/Total Line of Code	0.00921
Line(s) Added/Total Line of Code	0.6551
Line(s) Deleted/Total Line of Code	0.0024

Build Name	Build Quality	% Tests Passed	% Code Coverage	% Code Churn
⊟ Effort Tacking Full Build_20051111.2	Unexamined	100 %	0%	0 %

⊞ Test Run Results: 1 test run(s) completed, 5/ 5 test(s) passed.

⊞ Code Coverage Results: 0 % lines covered, 0 % lines not covered, 0 % lines partially covered.

⊟ Code Churn Details: 7492 Total Line of Code, 1 Line(s) Churned, 0 Line(s) Added, 0 Line(s) Deleted

Relative Code Churn Measure	Value
Line(s) Churned/Total Line of Code	0.00013
Line(s) Added/Total Line of Code	0
Line(s) Deleted/Total Line of Code	0

Figure 7-14. *Published build results*

All of the builds are listed on the report, and you can drill down into the results. The results shown in Figure 7-14 map to the results shown earlier in Figures 7-8 through 7-12. Note that in addition to the information shown on the client, the published results show the code churn as well. These results are generated by an analysis performed by the Team Foundation Server. The information here can provide your team with a good idea of how much work the team is doing and if that is translating into more passed tests, more failed tests, and so on.

■Note Team Foundation Build outputs all of the resulting binaries, the test results, and the build type information. This information is stored in the location on the machine on which Team Foundation Build ran (specified in the build configuration). On the build machine, the binaries are in (`configured location`)\ `teamprojectname`\(`buildTypeName`)\Binaries, the source code is in `BuildTypeName`\Sources, and the test results are in `BuildTypeName`\TestResults. In the drop location, the folder structure is (`build name`)\Release(`GeneralConfigurationName`)\TestResults. Included in the root of this structure are the `BuildLog.txt`, `ErrorsWarningLog.txt`, and `Release.txt` files. All of this information is available by clicking various links in the build results report.

Customizing the Build Process

Team Foundation Build is fully customizable using a number of different features. To change the build process, you can either create your own TFSBuild project (.proj) file or edit the generated project file. As with all of the tools in Visual Studio 2005, when you edit the XML in the file, you'll have the benefit of almost full IntelliSense (although Team Foundation Build properties are not listed in the IntelliSense drop-down list).

Reviewing the Build Type Configuration File

Because there are so many options, it is almost always easier to start off with a generated build type template. Listing 7-1 shows the build configuration file generated by the New Team Build Type Creation Wizard (minus the XML comments and with line numbers for reference only).

Listing 7-1. *Build Type Configuration File*

```
1  <?xml version="1.0" encoding="utf-8"?>
2  <Project DefaultTargets=
       "DesktopBuild" xmlns="http://schemas.microsoft.com/developer/msbuild/2003">
3  <!-- Do not edit this -->
4  <Import Project=
       "$(MSBuildExtensionsPath)\Microsoft\VisualStudio\v8.0\
       TeamBuild\Microsoft.TeamFoundation.Build.targets" />
5  <ProjectExtensions>
6  <Description>Builds the Effort Tracking Web Service and Effort Tracking
       Web front end and then runs all of the unit tests and web tests against the
       built solution.</Description>
7  <BuildMachine>mcsd-dev</BuildMachine>
8  </ProjectExtensions>
9  <PropertyGroup>
10     <TeamProject>Effort Tracking</TeamProject>
11     <BuildDirectoryPath>c:\EffortTrackingBuilds</BuildDirectoryPath>
12     <DropLocation>\\mcsd-server\data</DropLocation>
13     <RunTest>true</RunTest>
14     <WorkItemFieldValues>Priority=1;Severity=1</WorkItemFieldValues>
15     <RunCodeAnalysis>Default</RunCodeAnalysis>
16     <UpdateAssociatedWorkItems>true</UpdateAssociatedWorkItems>
17  </PropertyGroup>
18  <ItemGroup>
19     <SolutionToBuild Include=
       "$(SolutionRoot)\EffortTrackingSolution\EffortTrackingSolution.sln" />
20  </ItemGroup>
21  <ItemGroup>
22     <ConfigurationToBuild Include="Release|Any CPU">
23         <FlavorToBuild>Release</FlavorToBuild>
24         <PlatformToBuild>Any CPU</PlatformToBuild>
25     </ConfigurationToBuild>
26  </ItemGroup>
```

```
27 <ItemGroup>
28     <MetaDataFile Include=
       "$(SolutionRoot)\EffortTrackingSolution\EffortTrackingSolution.vsmdi">
29         <TestList>Read Tests</TestList>
30     </MetaDataFile>
31 </ItemGroup>
32 </Project>
```

As you can see, the format is very straightforward. Updating it may seem a little complicated at first, but as soon as you understand the procedure, you'll be able to do almost anything you want to (in terms of a build) with this tool. Here are the basics:

- You can reference any node as a variable that you create (or that already exists) in the `PropertyGroup` node by using the $(*variableName*) convention.

- A `Target` is the node that runs when TFSBuild builds the project.

- You can incorporate custom code that performs some operation in a custom task. This compiled assembly can then be used during the build process by including the assembly in a `UsingTask` node.

Keeping these three concepts in mind will allow you to customize a lot of tasks for use with TFSBuild.

Retrieving the Build Type

In order to actually edit this file manually, you need to do the following:

1. Open Source Control Explorer, expand your team project (in this case, the Effort Tracking solution), and then expand the TeamBuildTypes node.

2. Select `TFSBuild.proj`, right-click the file, and select Get Latest.

3. Choose the location to download the file to, and then click OK.

4. Right-click the `TFSBuild.proj` file and select Check Out for Edit.

At this point, you can edit the build file.

Editing the Build File

The build file will be located in the output folder (selected in step 3 in the previous section): (*Location*)\TeamBuildTypes\(*BuildType Name*)\TFSBuild.proj. It is best to edit this in Visual Studio, as you will get the benefit of IntelliSense support.

You can do a lot of customization by editing the project file or creating custom tasks. Microsoft is releasing several labs that describe all of the steps you can take during a project build. Look for this information on the MSDN site or search for Team Foundation Build in the Visual Studio Help.

■**Tip** Implementing your own custom task is fairly straightforward. To do that, create a project and reference `Microsoft.Build.Utilities.dll` and `Microsoft.Build.Framework.dll`. Create a class that inherits from the `Task` class (located in the `Microsoft.Build.Utilities` namespace) and override the `Execute` method.

Using the Build Command-Line Tool

Team Foundation Build comes with a command-line tool, which can be used in conjunction with the Windows Scheduler to schedule nightly builds and publish the results. The command-line tool is called `tfsbuild.exe` and is located in the `C:\Program Files\Microsoft Visual Studio 8\Common7\IDE` folder. With `tfsbuild.exe` you can start a build, delete a build, or stop a build that is in progress. The abilities to delete and stop builds are available only from the command line.

To start a build, use the following syntax:

`tfsbuild.exe start <Team Foundation Server> <Team Project Name> <Build Type Name> [/m:<Build Machine>] [/d:<Build Directory>]`

If no build machine is specified, the build machine in the build type will be used. Similarly, if no build directory is specified, the build directory in the build type will be used. Here is an example of starting a build from the command line:

`tfsbuild.exe start kiona "Effort Tracking" "Effort Tracking Full Build"`

Notice that all entries with a space in them must be enclosed in quotation marks.

`tfsbuild.exe` will supply you with the current build number when it begins the build process. The output from a `tfsbuild.exe` operation is shown in Figure 7-15.

Figure 7-15. *Using the tfsbuild.exe command-line tool*

> **Caution** The server name must be a name from the list of servers known by the local machine. In this case, `kiona` was the specified server name. However, there are numerous occasions when you may not be working on your local network and instead need to enter an IP address to reach the server. If you do this, you must supply the IP address as the server name.

To stop a build, use this syntax:

```
tfsbuild.exe stop <Team Foundation Server> <Team Project Name> <Build Number> [/noprompt]
```

As just mentioned, `tfsbuild.exe` indicates the build number when it starts a build. You can specify multiple build numbers by separating each number with a comma (but no spaces) between the build numbers. The `/noprompt` option suppresses the confirmation question for the stop and delete options. You must specify `noprompt` when doing any type of automated process using either the `stop` or `delete` command. Here is an example of stopping a build:

```
tfsbuild.exe stop kiona "Effort Tracking" "Effort Tracking Full Build_20051228.3" /noprompt
```

To delete a build, use this syntax:

```
tfsbuild.exe delete <Team Foundation Server> <Team Project Name> <Build Number(s)> [/noprompt]
```

Here's an example of deleting a build:

```
tfsbuild.exe delete kiona "Effort Tracking" "Effort Tracking Full Build_20051228.1" /noprompt
```

Setting Up Continuous Integration Testing

Continuous integration testing is a process by which every single change that is made is compiled against a project before the change gets checked in. This is similar to running BVTs, except it catches problems sooner.

Continuous integration testing requires that developers compile their code and run the unit tests against the compiled code before checking anything in. In order to do this, Team Foundation Build includes the ability to run build types with the MSBuild command-line tool. MSBuild is a desktop command line build tool. It can be used without Team Foundation Server and is designed to provide you flexibility in building your code and running tests against it. If you do not have Team Explorer installed, then you will not have access to `tfsbuild.exe`, but you will have access to MSBuild.

MSBuild also has the ability to process a build type in order to perform a build. Before you can run MSBuild against a build type, you need to retrieve the build type from the server. To do this, follow the steps outlined in the "Retrieving the Build Type" section earlier in this chapter. Once you have the file loaded to the local machine, you can run MSBuild simply by passing in the name of the type and setting the solution root. Open a Visual Studio command prompt, navigate to the folder containing the TFSBuild.proj file ((*Location*)\TeamBuildTypes\ (*BuildType Name*)), and enter the following:

msbuild /p:SolutionRoot="(*path to solution root*)" tfsbuild.proj

Summary

In this chapter, you have learned how to create build types, which can be used to build a project, run specified tests against a project, and publish those results to a project SharePoint site. You have also seen how to view the results of the build and learned what the results indicate in terms of code churn, what was tested, code coverage, and whether any errors occurred. Finally, you learned how the build process can be customized and how to run nightly builds using the command-line tools to build a project and schedule a project.

The bottom line is that using the built-in build tools provides a project team immediate feedback as to whether anything is broken and how much code has been tested from one build to another. This provides customers with good feedback as to the progress of the development team and will give them confidence in the development team.

PART 2

Team Edition for Software Architects

CHAPTER 8

Application Designer

The Application Designer is one of four distributed system designers supplied with Team Edition for Software Architects. In this chapter, we will look at how to use the Application Designer to model the services of your system and the applications that consume these services. We are focusing on services here because they are fundamental in the current application model Microsoft promotes as *connected systems*.

The connected systems approach moves to interface-based service contracts, or *contract-first*, as opposed to the traditional code-first approach. Contract-first focuses first on the interface leveraging the Web Service Definition Language (WSDL). This first release of the Application Designer focuses on the contracts from a remote procedure call (RPC) perspective, supporting methods (operations) and parameters, as opposed to a message-centric approach of schema types and elements. Furthermore, you will be defining .NET Framework types, not XML Schema Definition (XSD) types. This full contract-first experience will be provided in a following release of the product.

In this chapter, we will approach service design from two different perspectives. First, we will build a sample application design from scratch. The Application Designer provides a clean design surface for "whiteboarding" your application. The Visual Studio Toolbox comes preconfigured with application building blocks, including Windows applications, web services, web applications, and Office applications. Once you've described your web service endpoints and modeled the application, the Application Designer allows you to generate the skeleton projects for all or part of the system. This includes all of the code needed to implement and consume the defined service contracts. Second, we will generate an application design from our sample book application. When an application diagram is added to an existing solution, it is reverse-engineered, and the application diagram is created for you.

But before we get started using the Application Designer, let's take a broad look at the distributed system designers.

Overview of the Distributed System Designers

Team Edition for Software Architects ships with four distributed system designers:

- *Application Designer (AD):* Represents applications that expose services and communicate through endpoints.

- *Logical Datacenter Designer (LDD):* Represents the logical structure of some portion of the datacenter.

- *System Designer (SD):* Represents the composition of applications defined in the Application Designer for the purpose of composing connected systems.

- *Deployment Designer (DD):* Used to create a deployment configuration for a system.

The design goal for the distributed system design suite is that third parties will document and model aspects of their distributed system for a more complete definition of an application. These extended application or logical server prototypes could then be incorporated in defining connected systems. Figure 8-1 illustrates the artifacts associated with each designer.

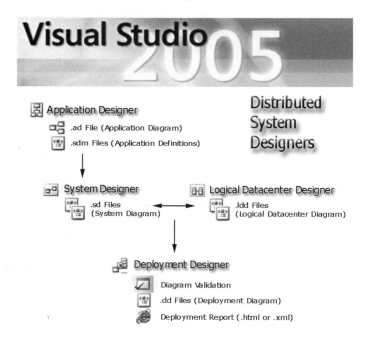

Figure 8-1. *Visual Studio 2005 designers*

System Definition Model

The System Definition Model (SDM) is simply a schema definition for describing distributed systems. SDM views the world as being composed of systems. It is important to distinguish between the notion of atomic and composite systems. Atomic systems are made up of resources such as configuration files, assemblies, and dynamic link libraries (DLLs), and are referred to as *applications*. Composite systems are made up of other systems or applications and referred to as *application systems*. The schema being shipped with VSTS is located at http://schemas.microsoft.com/SystemDefinitionModel/2005/1/DesignData/VisualStudio.

Table 8-1 shows the file extension within the solution and the type of SDM information stored.

Table 8-1. *SDM File Types and Data*

Extension	File	Description
.ad	Application Designer	Presentation and preimplementation endpoint information
.sdm	Project	Information about the project implemented
.sdm	External Components	Information about external entities (databases)
.ldd	Logical Datacenter Designer	Presentation, endpoint, zone, and host information
.sd	System Designer	Presentation and system information
.dd	Deployment Designer	Presentation and system deployment information

As you build your sample designs and deployments in the next few chapters, make sure you take the time to open the generated files in the XML editor and review the structure and information contained in each.

Benefits of the Distributed Designers

The distributed designers were conceived to support both the infrastructure architect (in charge of the network and datacenter designs) and the solution architect (in charge of designing and deploying connected systems). In a small shop, one person may perform both roles, but in more complex enterprise scenarios, many architects may need to communicate their designs and deployments to a host of project constituents.

The distributed system designers provide benefits in three ways:

- They are a rich set of domain-specific designers that target the service-orientation space. If you are building connected systems, the distributed designers are a first step at making Model Driven Architecture (MDA) a reality.

- They are an example of what can be done by targeting the Domain-Specific Language (DSL) framework toward a specific domain (service-oriented architecture in this specific instance). If you want to dive deeper, you can build your own DSL using the same modeling framework on which the distributed system designers are built.

- They begin to address the life cycle issues plaguing software development. Providing a common framework for distinct viewpoints (the application and datacenter) and the ability to deploy one viewpoint onto another is a positive step in reducing ambiguity and reducing cost.

MODEL-DRIVEN DEVELOPMENT

Rick LaPlante, General Manager for VSTS, explains that the design goals of VSTS are two-fold: integration and ease of use. The value proposition for the tools suite is predictable collaboration. Rick stated, "The distributed system designers allow you to enable validation of system configurations against models of target environments to increase the predictability of deployment." It really is a shift of focus from the developer to the entire breadth of development. Modeling will no longer be relegated to the "ivory tower," but will be a normal part of the development life cycle. To facilitate this, VSTS has adopted four main ideas:

- Models are to be "first-class" citizens. They should be thought of not as documentation, but as source code with their own set of implementers (compilers).

- Models are to represent a set of abstractions in a well-defined domain.

- Models are to abstract and aggregate information from a number of artifacts, thereby providing analyses such as consistency and validation checks.

- Models are to be implemented by a process similar to compilation. The generated output is not intended to be edited by hand.

During Jochen Seemann's "Future Directions in Modeling Tools" presentation at the 2005 Professional Developer Conference (PDC), he remarked that for the model-driven development approach, "Don't think about round-trips; think trip-less," and said that it was "bringing modeling to the masses."

Visual languages are a common tool we use in our everyday lives. Maps may be the most common visual language to help get us from point A to point B. Blueprints are useful for putting together a piece of furniture or your million-dollar dream home. A common saying goes, "A picture is worth a thousand words." Unfortunately, one of the biggest problems in the software industry is that we cannot agree on what the thousand words are saying. This is where model-driven development takes center stage.

Back in the 1980s, computer-aided software engineering (CASE) offered the promise of modeling applications at an abstract level, and then "automagically" generating the code to be used to operate the system. While this code generation was the promise of CASE tools, it was also the greatest drawback. These early modeling tools could not be easily kept in sync with the development tools. New revisions to the underlying tools were late to be integrated into the CASE engine. This lag caused the development to get out of sync with the models, and there was no going back. VSTS takes on this challenge by making models first-class development artifacts and an intricate part of the development process. By "making modeling mainstream," Microsoft hopes to change the economics of software development and ensure software systems meet the needs of the business. This approach to model-driven development is part of an initiative called Software Factories.

Software Factories

The 1990s ushered in the world of object-oriented programming to the mainstream and the first work on the Unified Modeling Language (UML). UML comes out of the effort to unify the object modeling world headed by Grady Booch, Ivar Jacobson, and James Rumbaugh. This work was taken industry-wide through the Object Management Group (OMG), and in 1997, the first proposal, UML 1.0, was published. Somewhere in the trudge from UML 1.0 to UML 2.0, a division arose around the appropriateness of applying UML to "all" domains. This led to a spirited debate between Grady Booch (IBM) and the Software Factories team at

Microsoft. The debate centers around the goal of UML. It was developed to provide a common notation for the practice of object-oriented analysis and design. Should it then be the de facto standard beyond its original scope into the realm of model-driven development and Software Factories?

Some of the same people who were driving CASE tools and early UML a decade ago are leading the work being done on Software Factories and Domain-Specific Languages (DSLs) at Microsoft and other corporations.

The concept of Software Factories lives at two levels today. First it is a vision for the future. So a few years out, the Software Factories concept is an ideal for bringing significant automation to the software development process. Today, building software is still very much a craft. We tend to design applications as if they were the first of their kind. We need to automate the parts that are the same every time and concentrate on the key differentials. Steve Cook, an architect for Microsoft's DSL Toolkit team and coauthor of Software Factories, made some interesting observations in one of his talks related to Software Factories: "There is no generic software factory (think about this!)," and "A generic factory that produces bicycles one day and laptop computers the next?"

Second, Software Factories are an initiative grounded in VSTS to provide the framework (tools, SDKs, APIs, and so on) to enable Visual Studio to be purposed into a tool for a specific type of development. One of the key components in this initiative is the concept of DSLs.

Domain-Specific Languages

DSLs are small, highly focused languages for solving some discrete problem space within a specific domain. The DSL framework is Microsoft's modeling platform.

DSLs enable the mapping of the business processes (capabilities) to the technology services (interfaces and implementation). Models are the preferred way of communicating complex ideas and constructs between groups holding diverse viewpoints. An example is a blueprint (architecture model) to map the homeowner's needs and the builder's implementation. Consider how it would affect the construction of your new home if you did away with the blueprint and handed the builder a 1,000-page document describing the home of your dreams.

The distributed designers provided with Team Edition for Software Architects are simply an implementation of a DSL language targeted at visual design and validation of connected systems.

Using the Application Designer

As an example of using the Application Designer, you will create a simple application design consisting of a web application, a web service, and a sample SQL database. The final implemented design is shown in Figure 8-2.

Note The application diagram shows the applications defined within a single Visual Studio solution; therefore, you can have only one .ad file per solution. If you attempt to add a second .ad file to your solution, you will get an error.

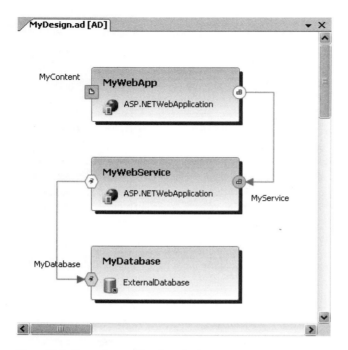

Figure 8-2. *Sample application design*

Getting Started with the Application Designer

To start the diagram, follow these steps:

1. Start a new project. A separate project type has been added to the New Project dialog box to make it easier to find the distributed system designers. They are now located under Distributed System Solutions. There, you will find the Distributed System and Logical Datacenter templates. For this example, select Distributed System, as shown in Figure 8-3.

2. Enter the name `MyDesign`.

3. Click OK. You will be brought into the Application Designer.

You now have a blank work surface, a default application diagram (.ad), and the Application Designer Toolbox. You are reminded from the blank design surface to "Drag from the Toolbox to define applications." This message is like the sign at the end of the ski lift warning, "Keep your tips up." Although such signs may be safely ignored by experts, more than a few novice skiers have learned the hard way.

The Application Designer Toolbox contains eleven predefined prototypes (.adprototype) to be used while designing your application model. These include eight application prototypes and three endpoint prototypes. We will look at each in detail in the following sections. Table 8-2 describes the Toolbox objects.

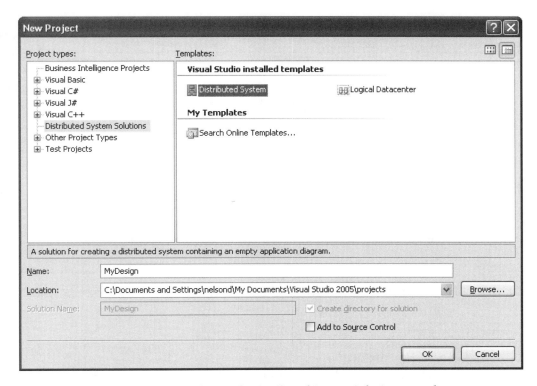

Figure 8-3. *The New Project dialog box with Distributed System Solutions templates*

Table 8-2. *The Application Designer Toolbox Objects*

Item	Description
Pointer	Pointer tool used for selection (one available in each category)
Connection	Connection tool to link two application prototype endpoints
Comment	A comment text box
WebServiceEndpoint	Represents a connection point for a web service (provider)
WebContentEndpoint	Represents a connection point to web content (provider)
GenericEndpoint	Represents a connection point to services of an unspecified type (provider)
WindowsApplication	A Windows application
ASP.NETWebService	An ASP.NET web service application that includes a web service endpoint
ASP.NETWebApplication	An ASP.NET web application that includes a web content endpoint
OfficeApplication	Represents a Microsoft Office application supporting Excel, Word, and Outlook templates
ExternalWebService	A reference to a single web service defined by a single Web Services Description Language (.wsdl) file

Continued

Table 8-2. *Continued*

Item	Description
ExternalDatabase	A reference to a database
BizTalkWebService	A reference to a BizTalk web service
GenericApplication	A user-defined application that supports user-defined settings and constraints; exists for documentation purposes and supports generic endpoints

Defining the Database Component

Using the drag-and-drop method, you will now design and implement a simple sample solution. To start with, you will define the back-end database component. (You can begin on any part of the application design you like, but for this example, we'll start with the database.)

Note To follow this example, you will need to create a database named MyDatabase on your local system.

1. Click the ExternalDatabase component in the Application Designer Toolbox and drag it onto the design surface (near the bottom of the page). It should look like Figure 8-4. By default, the ExternalDatabase application prototype consists of a single provider endpoint. Notice that the database prototype has a shadow effect on the border, which designates an implementation has occurred. Also notice that the solution now has a new file named Database1.sdm.

Figure 8-4. *ExternalDatabase component on the diagram*

2. To examine the generated XML for your new database, right-click the Database1.sdm file and choose to open it with the XML editor. You cannot have the XML editor and the Application Designer open at the same time. You will be prompted to close and save the diagram prior to opening the .sdm file. Listing 8-1 shows a snippet of the .sdm file verifying that Database1 has a state of "Implemented" but still "NeedsGeneration".

Listing 8-1. *Generated Database1.sdm File Portion*

```
<Endpoint Name="Database1" Definition="Database1.DatabaseProviderEndpoint1"
       MinOccurs="1" MaxOccurs="1" Reference="false">
    <DesignData>
        <VisualStudio xmlns=
```

```
                "http://schemas.microsoft.com/SystemDefinitionModel/2005/1/
            DesignData/VisualStudio">
                <ModelElement Type=
                "Microsoft.VisualStudio.EnterpriseTools.Application.
                 Modeling.PlugIns.DeployedDBProviderPort">
                    <Property Name="State" Value="Implemented" />
                    <Property Name="NeedsGeneration" Value="true" />
                </ModelElement>
            </VisualStudio>
        </DesignData>
    </Endpoint>
```

3. Close the XML editor and reopen `MyDesign.ad`. On your diagram, click the `Database1` provider endpoint, which is represented by the plug abstract type icon:

4. Press F4 to open the Properties window. Change the name element from `Database1` to `MyDatabase`. Notice that the name for the external database changes as well, as shown in Figure 8-5.

Figure 8-5. *External database renamed to MyDatabase*

Adding a Web Service Component

Now that the back-end database has been defined, it is time to add a web service to perform the data access function for the application.

1. Click the ASP.NETWebService application prototype in the Application Designer Toolbox and drag it onto the design surface (just above the database component).

2. Double-click the default name (`WebApplication1`) to open the name property box. Change the name to `MyWebService`. Optionally, you can select the web service, press F4 to open the Properties window, and change the name under the Design section.

3. On the `MyWebService` application type, click the web service provider endpoint, represented by this icon:

4. Change the name to MyService. Your diagram now has two application types, as shown in Figure 8-6.

Figure 8-6. *Web service added to the application diagram*

Notice that MyWebService is not implemented by default. It does not have a shadow effect on its border, and no MyWebService.sdm file has been created. If you right-click the MyWebService application type, you will see an option to implement the application. You will do this after you complete the initial design.

Connecting the Application Types

You now need to connect the web service to the database. When you begin a connection directly from an application, the application that starts the connection must be the consumer application. To begin from the provider application, just start the connection from the provider endpoint instead of the application itself. If you begin a connection from the wrong component, you'll see the universal "No" sign, as shown in Figure 8-7.

Figure 8-7. *Incompatible endpoints*

1. Right-click MyWebService on the design surface and select Connect.

2. In the Create Connection dialog box, click the down arrow of the Application box in the Connect To section and select the name of your back-end database component, MyDatabase, as shown in Figure 8-8. Click the down arrow in the Endpoint selection box and select the name of the endpoint associated with the database you selected. This will be the same name as the database, by default. Click OK.

Figure 8-8. *The Create Connection dialog box*

Note When using the Create Connection dialog box, by default, you are presented with only endpoints that are compatible with the component with which you are working. In this simple example, we have only two components so far. In a complex solution with many components, this feature helps aid in maintaining the overall integrity of the design.

3. In the Choose Data Source dialog box, enter the data source and data provider. For this example, select Microsoft SQL Server and the .NET Data Provider for SQL Server, respectively.

4. In the Connection Properties dialog box, enter the database server name, the security context, and the database name. (You can simply enter a period for the server name to indicate your local SQL Server installation, or enter .\sqlexpress for default installations of SQL Express edition.) Click Test Connection to verify that the configuration information for the data source is correct, as shown in Figure 8-9.

Figure 8-9. *Testing your connection from the Connection Properties dialog box*

Note Optionally, if you are just whiteboarding an application design, you can cancel out of the Connection Properties dialog box, and then complete the details for the connection later.

---

5. Click OK. Your diagram should now look similar to Figure 8-10.

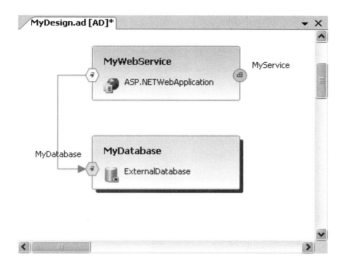

Figure 8-10. *Adding the connection*

6. To verify the connection properties, right-click the database consumer endpoint of `MyWebService` and select Properties. You will see that the connection information has been captured, as shown in Figure 8-11. This Connection String property will be generated in the `Web.config` file of the `MyDatabase` application when it is implemented.

Figure 8-11. *MyDatabase properties with connection information*

Defining Operations for ASP.NET Web Service Prototypes

One of the key features of the Application Designer is the ability to define the operations and parameters for web services that are exposed on the diagram. This is part of the contract-first design, where you first design the service contracts for communicating between different application types. If you have an existing .wsdl file, you can consume the operations from the existing exposed service, as explained in the "Adding a Web Service Endpoint from a WSDL File" section later in this chapter.

Using the Web Service Details window, you can add the operations, parameters, types, and details. For this sample application, you will be notionally creating a local weather-reporting web service.

1. Right-click MyService and select Define Operations to open the Web Service Details window, as shown in Figure 8-12.

Figure 8-12. *The Web Service Details window*

2. Click <add operation> and type the name GetLocalWeather. Give it a type of string and add some comments in the Summary field.

3. Click the plus sign next to your new GetLocalWeather service to reveal the <add parameter> section.

4. Click <add parameter> and type the name ZipCode. Give it a type of integer and accept the default modifier. Place your cursor in the Summary field and click the ellipsis (. . .) on the right. This will bring up detail metadata for your service. Enter some comments in the Summary field and click OK.

5. Follow the same process to add a second service that gets the city name from the database based on the zip code provided. The MyService details are shown in Figure 8-13.

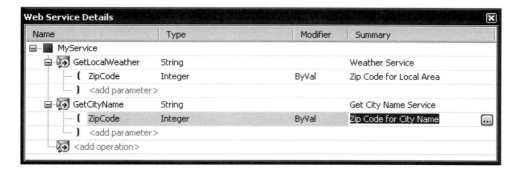

Figure 8-13. *The Web Service Details window with two services*

Implementing the Application

At this point in the design process, you can generate actual framework code for the application. First-time generation of code is referred to as *implementation*. Application definitions can be implemented incrementally or all at once. When an application is implemented, the Application Designer automatically generates the corresponding project, code files, and configuration files. Because the application diagram is synchronized with the code and configuration files, the diagram is immediately updated if the files are modified. Similarly, changes to the diagram are reflected in the code and configuration files. Upon implementation, the application prototypes will be identified by the presence of the shadow effect around the object shape.

■**Tip** Deferred implementation allows you to create what-if designs of your application without the overhead of actual implementation. The Application Designer supports a deferred implementation approach, allowing an architect to create and validate a design before committing the design to code. This whiteboarding approach allows the architect to brainstorm on the design surface and choose the point of generation.

Selecting the Language

First, you will want to select the implementation language to generate. Visual Basic is the default, but you can choose from multiple languages.

A common feature request of the VSTS team early on was the ability to have a global setting where you could change the language choice and have it stick for all prototypes. While this feature does not exist in version 1, if you do not want select a different default language, you can create a custom prototype. To demonstrate this, you will use `MyWebService` as an example.

1. Click `MyWebService` in the application diagram and press F4 to display the Properties window. In the Implementation section, select the language to generate—Visual C# in this example, as shown in Figure 8-14.

Figure 8-14. *Choosing a language for implementation*

2. In the Application Designer, right-click `MyWebService` and select Add to Toolbox. In the Name field, type in a descriptive name, such as `MyWebServiceC#`, as shown in Figure 8-15. Then click OK.

Figure 8-15. *The Add to Toolbox dialog box*

3. The Save File dialog box shows the existing designer prototypes on your system and allows you to save your custom C# version of the `AspNetWebService`. Click Save, and `MyWebServiceC#` is added to your Toolbox.

4. Add a new tab to the Toolbox called **My Prototypes** and drag all custom prototypes in there, as shown in Figure 8-16. This allows you to keep custom items separate from Visual Studio's built-in items.

Figure 8-16. *Adding a new tab to the Toolbox for your custom items*

Generating Framework Code

Now that your language of choice has been selected, you can implement the application.

1. Right-click the `MyWebService` application and choose Implement Application. Alternatively, you can select Diagram ➤ Implement Application from the main menu. This will launch the Confirm Application Implementation dialog box, where you will be notified of the projects about to be generated, as shown in Figure 8-17.

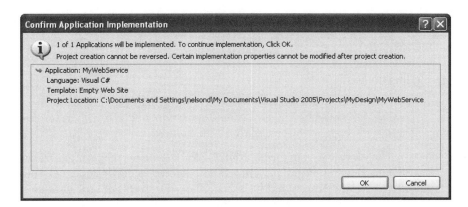

Figure 8-17. *The Confirm Application Implementation dialog box*

2. Select OK and wait for your application framework code to be propagated inside the solution. You may receive a warning that the connection string is being written into the configuration files unencrypted, as shown in Figure 8-18.

Figure 8-18. *The Security Warning dialog box*

The result of implementing your design is that a new web service project has been added to the solution. This new project includes language-specific source and configuration files, as shown in Figure 8-19.

Figure 8-19. *The Solution Explorer window for MyDesign*

Again, notice that an implemented component is represented in the Application Designer by a shadow border outlining the component on the diagram surface. Your `MyWebService` has now been implemented.

Adding to the Implemented Code

As an example, say you want to add another method to bring back the state name from the database. (We realize this would be done in a single operation, but bear with us for this example.) You'll also add some code to the `GetLocalWeather` method.

1. Double-click `MyService.cs` in the Solution Explorer to display the generated code. Notice that the operations and parameters you defined in the designer have been implemented in code. You should see two methods for the `MyWebService` in code: `GetLocalWeather` and `GetCityName`. Also notice how the code and design are kept in sync. Remember that models in Visual Studio are "first-class" citizens and not just documentation.

2. Copy the code for the `GetCityName` method and paste it below as `GetStateName`. Change the method name and descriptive metadata, as shown in Listing 8-2.

   Listing 8-2. *Added GetStateName Method*

   ```
   /// <summary>
   /// Get State Name Service
   /// </summary>
   /// <param name="ZipCode">Zip Code for State Name</param>
   [System.Web.Services.WebMethod(Description = ""),
    System.Web.Services.Protocols.SoapDocumentMethod(Binding = "MyService")]
   public string GetStateName(int ZipCode)
   {
     throw new System.NotImplementedException();
   }
   ```

3. Save the code file.

4. Switch back to the Application Designer by selecting `MyDesign.ad` from the Window menu.

5. Right-click the `MyService` endpoint and select Define Operations. The Web Service Details window now reflects the additional `GetStateName` method, as shown in Figure 8-20.

Name	Type	Modifier	Summary
MyService			
GetLocalWeather	string		Weather Service
GetCityName	string		Get City Name Service
GetStateName	string		Get State Name Service
<add operation>			

Figure 8-20. *The Web Service Details window with updates*

6. Switch back to `MyService.cs`. Since it is still winter in the greater Seattle metropolitan area, replace the `throw new System.NotImplementedException()` template code for the `GetLocalWeather` operation so that it looks like Listing 8-3.

   Listing 8-3. *Additional Code for the GetLocalWeather Method*

   ```
   [System.Web.Services.WebMethod(Description = ""),
    System.Web.Services.Protocols.SoapDocumentMethod(Binding = "MyService")]
   public string GetLocalWeather(int ZipCode)
   {
       return "Rain Today, Rain Tomorrow - always damp and dreary";
   }
   ```

Testing the Web Service

Now you're ready to test the web service.

1. Press Ctrl+F5 and start the application without debugging. The directory listing will display for MyWebService.

2. Click MyService.asmx to open the web service .asmx page, as shown in Figure 8-21.

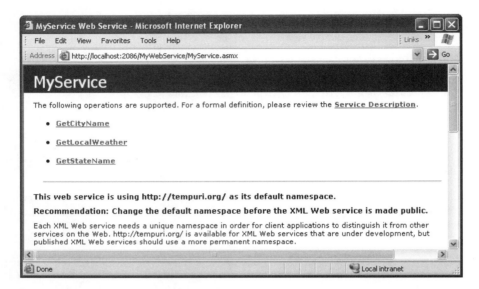

Figure 8-21. *The MyService web service page*

3. Click GetLocalWeather to bring up the test parameter page. You can enter any valid integer here for the zip code parameter, since our sample ignores the zip code. Click Invoke, and the dismal yet accurate local weather forecast will be returned, as shown in Figure 8-22.

Figure 8-22. *MyWebService response for GetLocalWeather*

Hooking Up the Database

For a more realistic example, we will hook up the database portion to return the city name when you pass in the zip code.

1. Create a table in your MyDatabase database named CityZip. The CREATE TABLE statement is shown in Listing 8-4.

   Listing 8-4. *CityZip CREATE TABLE Statement*
   ```
   USE [MyDatabase]
   GO
   /****** Object:  Table [dbo].[CityZip] ******/
   SET ANSI_NULLS ON
   GO
   SET QUOTED_IDENTIFIER ON
   GO
   CREATE TABLE [dbo].[CityZip](
           [zipcode] [int] NULL,
           [city] [nvarchar](50) COLLATE SQL_Latin1_General_CP1_CI_AS NULL
   ) ON [PRIMARY]
   ```

2. With this simple two-column table, you need to insert only one row to get things started. You can add any others for your local town.

   ```
   Insert into CityZip (zipcode, city) Values (98024, 'Seattle')
   ```

3. Replace the throw new System.NotImplementedException() template code for the GetCityName service with the code for accessing the database from the web service, as shown in Listing 8-5.

   Listing 8-5. *Get City Database Lookup*
   ```
       {
          SqlConnection cn = new  SqlConnection(
              ConfigurationManager.ConnectionStrings["MyDatabase"].ToString());
          SqlCommand cmd = new SqlCommand("SELECT city FROM cityzip "
              + "WHERE zipcode = @zipcode", cn);
           SqlDataReader dr;
           string mystring = "";

           cmd.CommandType = CommandType.Text;
           cmd.Parameters.AddWithValue("@zipcode", ZipCode);

            cn.Open();
            dr = cmd.ExecuteReader(CommandBehavior.CloseConnection);
             while (dr.Read())
                {
                   mystring = dr["city"].ToString();
                }
             return mystring;
          }
   ```

> **Note** You must add *using* `System.Data`, *using* `System.Data.SqlClient`, and *using* `System.Configuration` in the `using` section. Also, you need to make sure the connection string name matches the one in your `Web.config` file.

4. Press F5 and start the application (you may need to do some debugging). The directory listing will display for `MyWebService`.

5. Click `MyService.asmx`. This time, select `GetCityName` for the test parameter page. Enter a valid database value for the zip code parameter and click Invoke. The simple database result is returned, as shown in Figure 8-23.

Figure 8-23. *MyService response for GetCityName*

Adding a Web Application Component

Now that your web service is working with the database, you still need to add a front-end to the application. For simplicity, let's add a web application to the application diagram.

Adding and Implementing the Web Application

You'll add the web application, and then follow the same pattern for the web application implementation as you did for the web service implementation.

1. Return to your `MyDesign` application diagram.

> **Note** If your application diagram is grayed out, you may still be running in debug mode. Select Debug ➤ Stop Debugging.

2. Click the ASP.NETWebApplication prototype in the Toolbox and drag it just above `MyWebService`.

3. Rename `WebApplication1` to `MyWebApp` and the provider `WebContent1` endpoint to `MyContent`.

4. To connect the web application to the web service, right-click `MyWebApp` and select Connect. In the Connect To section, select `MyWebService` for the application and `MyService` for the endpoint and click OK. The completed diagram is shown in Figure 8-24.

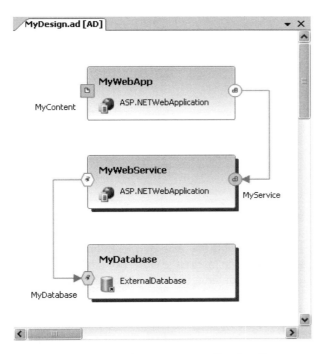

Figure 8-24. *Completed MyDesign application diagram*

5. Select Visual C# as the language for implementation by using the Properties window for `MyWebApp`.

6. Implement the application (by right-clicking `MyWebApp` and selecting Implement Application or choosing that option from the Diagram menu). The result of implementing your design is that a new web application project has been added to the solution, as shown in Figure 8-25.

Figure 8-25. *The Solution Explorer with MyWebApp included*

Creating a User Interface

To create a simple user interface (UI) for the mock local weather application, you will need to edit Default.aspx. To facilitate creating the mock web page, you will start with a table layout. You will drop various UI elements within the table to create an operational web page. You will need a text box to enter the zip code, a button to invoke the code, two labels to display the city name and weather, respectively, and perhaps an image to dress things up. Figure 8-26 shows the mock UI.

Figure 8-26. *Table layout for mock UI*

1. Double-click `Default.aspx` to view the source code.

2. Click the Design tab to create the UI.

3. Click Layout ➤ Insert Table. Enter **5** in the Rows field and **2** in the Columns field. Click OK to view your table.

4. Drag a standard button to row 1, column 1 and change the text from Button to **Get Weather** (this will call the service).

5. Drag a standard text box to row 2, column 2 and add the text **Enter Zip Code** to row 2, column 1 (this will accept the user-supplied zip code).

6. Drag a standard label to row 3, column 2 and add the text **Current Weather for Greater** to row 3, column 1 (this will hold the lookup city name).

7. Drag a second standard label to row 5, column 2 (this will hold the local weather forecast).

8. You need to add a few lines of code to finish a working UI. Double-click the Get Weather button to open the `Default.aspx.cs` code-behind. Copy the code in Listing 8-6 and paste it as the `Button1_Click` event.

Listing 8-6. *Sample Button Code-Behind*

```
{
//Get the zip code requested
     int myzip = Convert.ToInt32(TextBox1.Text);
//Get the Local Data
MyWebApp.WebServiceProxies.MyService s = new
     MyWebApp.WebServiceProxies.MyService();
          Label1.Text= s.GetCityName(myzip);
          Label2.Text = s.GetLocalWeather(myzip);
}
```

9. You can tweak the layout and add an image or two.

10. Press F5 to build the application.

11. Enter a valid zip code and click the button. Your solution should look something like the web page shown in Figure 8-27.

Figure 8-27. *Sample Default.aspx web page invoked*

Adding Comments to Application Diagrams

In addition to creating items with semantic meaning, you can also add comments to your design by dragging the comment shape onto the design surface and adding text. Figure 8-28 shows an example of a comment added to an application diagram.

Tip As a good practice, comment your diagrams heavily where the design purpose is not obvious.

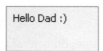

Figure 8-28. *A comment added to a diagram*

Understanding Connections and Endpoints

In the Application Designer, endpoints on applications define services they provide or specify the requirement to use services.

Endpoint Notation

Figure 8-29 shows some examples of endpoints. A provider endpoint (shaded circle attached to the `CommonService` in Figure 8-29) is used to represent services provided by the application. A consumer endpoint (open circle attached to `SampleApp1` and `SampleApp2` in Figure 8-29) is used to represent the use of services offered by other applications. Put simply, a provider endpoint is represented by a shaded object, and a consumer endpoint is represented by an unshaded object.

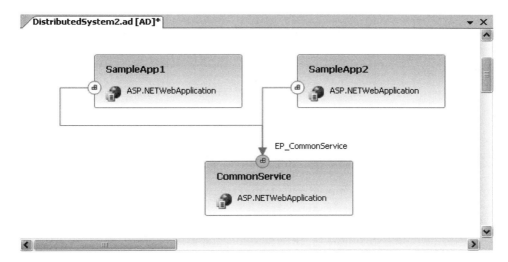

Figure 8-29. *Connection endpoints*

Figure 8-29 illustrates a simple connection between two separate web applications (the consumer of the data services) and the common service (the provider of data services). The connection shown is an ASP.NETWebService provider endpoint connecting to two distinct ASP.NETWebService consumer endpoints.

As a rule, you can connect a provider endpoint to multiple consumer endpoints, but you can connect a consumer endpoint to only a single provider endpoint. (Additional rules and guidelines are covered in the next section).

Table 8-3 shows the notations and the abstract types they represent.

Table 8-3. *Abstract Types and Graphical Representations*

Representation	Abstract Type
	Web service endpoint
	Web content endpoint
	Database endpoint
	Generic endpoint

Rules and Guidelines for Connections

The following are some rules and guidelines for diagramming connections:

- Provider endpoints can connect only to consumer endpoints and vice versa.
- In general, you can connect a provider endpoint to multiple consumer endpoints.
- You can connect a consumer endpoint to only a single provider endpoint.
- You can connect only endpoints that have the same abstract type.
- You cannot directly draw connections between applications using the Connection tool.
- Choosing the Connect command opens a Connection dialog box.
- You can begin a connection from a provider endpoint using the Connection tool or the Connect command.
- If compatible provider and consumer endpoints exist, you can begin connections from either endpoint using the Connection tool or Connect command.

Adding a Web Service Endpoint from a WSDL File

You can add a web service endpoint to your web service from an existing WSDL. To demonstrate, you'll add one to your `MyDesign.ad` application diagram.

1. Right-click the `MyWebService` and select Create Web Service Endpoints from WSDL.

2. In the Add Web Reference dialog box, select Web Services on the local machine. You should find the book's sample application `Service`, as shown in Figure 8-30.

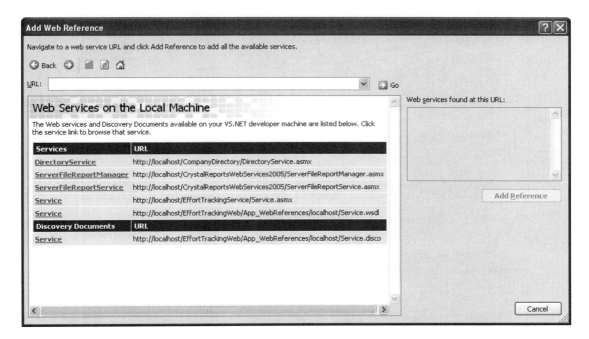

Figure 8-30. *The Add Web Reference dialog box*

3. Select the `Service` link in the Add Web Reference dialog box. You will see "1 Service Found" in the right side display area, as shown in Figure 8-31.

4. Click Add Reference to add this `Service` endpoint to your application diagram.

5. Select the new `Service` endpoint, and then open the Web Service Detail window by selecting Diagram ▶ Define Operations. Here, you can review the operations associated with your imported service, as shown in Figure 8-32.

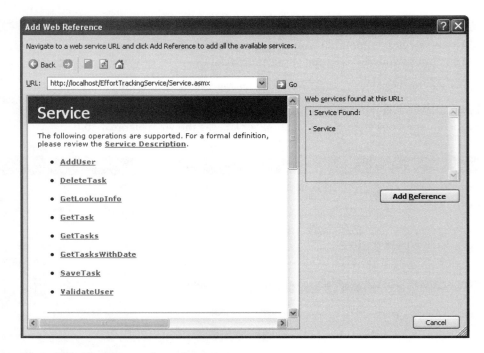

Figure 8-31. *Finding a web service*

Figure 8-32. *The Web Service Details window showing the added service from the WSDL file*

Understanding Constraints and Settings

The distributed system designers allow you to set constraints and settings for your designs. To view the Settings and Constraints window, shown in Figure 8-33, right-click any application type in the Application Designer and select Settings and Constraints.

Figure 8-33. *The Settings and Constraints window*

A *constraint* is a requirement that a configuration value be set in a certain way. Constraints can be created in one layer against settings in another layer. For example, constraints can be set from the application layer against settings on the application hosting layer and vice versa. The application layer is modeled in the Application Designer. The application hosting layer is modeled in the Logical Datacenter Designer. However, constraints can also be created in the same layer. For example, in the Logical Datacenter Designer, zone constraints can be authored against the logical servers the zones contain, as well as the applications hosted on the logical servers within the zones. Zones and zone constraints are discussed in detail in Chapter 9.

Settings are configurable elements of your application environment that control the way your application behaves. For example, for an IIS web server under the SmtpSection, you can set the specific delivery methods allowable for inbound SMTP messages.

Setting Constraints

Constraints are requirements targeted at configuration values. For example, several of the application prototypes allow you to set the constraint on the operating system type, service pack, and build number on which to run. Constraints fall into three categories:

- *Implicit constraints:* Constraints that are nonnegotiable and well defined, authored by the application prototype providers themselves. For example, a Windows Forms application cannot be hosted on a client operating system without the .NET Framework installed.

- *Predefined constraints:* Constraints that are provided by the designer to group common settings to make it more efficient for you to locate groups of settings. The operating system predefined constraint is a good example of a group of settings providing a group of settings to the designers.

- *User-defined constraints:* Constraints that you can author to provide any required constraints that fall outside those provided in the predefined groups.

Searching Settings and Constraints

You can search settings and constraints for a specific item by right-clicking anywhere in the Settings and Constraints window's left pane and selecting Search. For example, if you required IIS 6.0 for the hosting of your web service or web application, you could search for the MajorVersionNumber setting and select Find All, as shown in Figure 8-34.

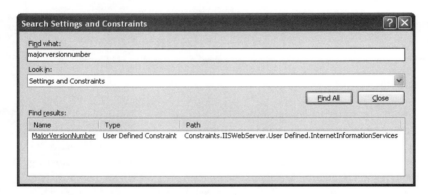

Figure 8-34. *The Search Settings and Constraints dialog box*

Selecting the highlighted constraint in the Find Results list takes you to the constraint. For this example, you would go to the MajorVersionNumber constraint for the InternetInformationService, as shown in Figure 8-35. Here, you could change the Value setting to 6, to require IIS 6.0.

CHAPTER 8 ■ APPLICATION DESIGNER 251

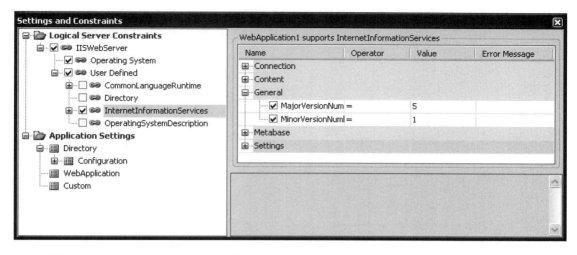

Figure 8-35. *Settings and Constraints detail*

You will explore more details of settings and constraints in the following two chapters.

Reverse-Engineering Existing Solutions

You can also reverse-engineer your Application Designer diagram from an existing solution. In this section, you will reverse-engineer an application diagram from the book's sample Effort Tracking application.

1. Open Visual Studio 2005. Select File ➤ Open Project/Solution, and open the sample solution, `EffortTrackingSolution.sln`.

2. Right-click the `EffortTracking` solution and select Add ➤ New Distributed System Diagram.

3. The Add New Item window displays the solution items available for the distributed system diagrams. Highlight Application Diagram, change the name to `EffortTracking`, and click Add. The result is the implemented application design, as shown in Figure 8-36. You need to make only a few modifications to the default diagram to make it useful.

4. Move `EffortTrackingWeb` directly above `EffortTrackingService`. Right-Click `EffortTrackingWeb` and select Add ➤ New `WebContentEndpoint` and rename to `ETWebContent`. Now drag an ExternalDatabase application prototype just under `EffortTrackingService`. Rename `Database1` to `EffortTracking`.

5. You now need to connect the database to the web service. Starting with the `EffortTrackingService` database consumer endpoint, use the Connection tool to drag the consumer endpoint of the service to the provider endpoint of the `EffortTracking` database, as shown in Figure 8-37. The final version of the `EffortTracking` application diagram is now complete.

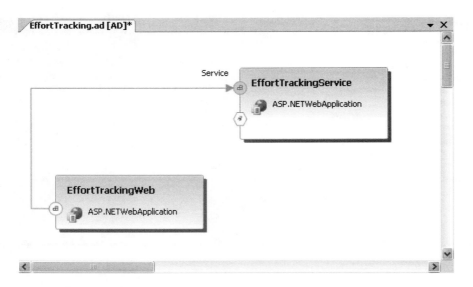

Figure 8-36. *Default application diagram from the EffortTracking solution*

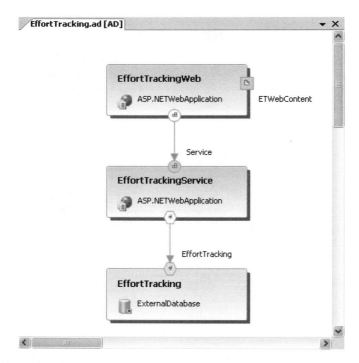

Figure 8-37. *Revised EffortTracking application diagram*

With the sample application for the book now reverse-engineered in the Application Designer, take some time to explore the properties, settings, and constraints.

Troubleshooting Application Diagrams

When working in distributed system designers, performing certain actions often affect the current diagram as well as other distributed system diagrams. The following are three types of errors related to diagrams:

- *Alert states:* A red dashed outline, red error (X), or yellow warning (!) on the diagram indicates an anomaly.

- *Locking:* A shaded diagram (read-only) indicates a check-out, compile, parse, or missing file issue.

- *Synchronization:* Once implemented, a diagram must be kept in sync with the .sdm document. Out-of-sync diagrams will trigger an alert state.

For more information about troubleshooting application diagrams, see the MSDN online help.

Summary

In this chapter, you learned how to design and implement a simple connected system from scratch using the Application Designer. This included defining the application prototypes, connecting them via exposed endpoints, and defining the operations on the web service. You then implemented your design, creating both a web application and web service connected to your local database. Finally, you imported an existing WSDL endpoint. This chapter also introduced constraints and settings. Finally, you learned how to reverse-engineer an entire application in the Application Designer.

In the following chapter, you will use the Logical Datacenter Designer to create an environment in which to deploy your sample application.

CHAPTER 9

System and Logical Datacenter Designers

The System Designer is used to arrange and configure systems from the applications defined in the Application Designer. In the context of the System Designer, a *system* is defined as a single unit of deployment. Since systems can be composed of other systems, very large and complex designs can be accommodated. This should satisfy the "wall-chart" architects (those who spend their time creating application diagrams that fill an entire wall or more). The level of abstraction provided by the System Designer allows multiple designs to facilitate deployment onto varying datacenters, customer sites, or geographic locations.

The Logical Datacenter Designer allows you to "create" a logical structure of interrelated servers describing your physical environment. These designs are used in the Deployment Designer to validate the deployment of systems into the logical infrastructure. A future goal of this designer is to allow the physical instantiation of the logical design into physical and/or virtual datacenters.

In this chapter, you will learn how to use both of these designers.

Using the System Designer

The system diagram depends on the application diagram to provide the basis for a deployable system. (See Figure 8-1 in the previous chapter for an overview of the distributed system designers and how they are related.) So, before you get started with the System Designer, it is best to have a repository of applications (at least one existing application diagram created with the Application Designer) from which to work. One advantage of selecting your applications from the Application Designer as the basis for your system design is that your connections between applications are carried forward. However, as you will discover in the first example in this chapter, you can start from scratch.

SYSTEMS, APPLICATIONS, AND THE SYSTEM DEFINITION MODEL

From a System Designer perspective, the terms *system* and *application* can be a bit confusing. In the industry, these words are often interchangeable. We talk about a sales application or a marketing system. Often, the deciding factor in choosing the term *system* or *application* is how it sounds with the three-letter acronym (TLA). However, there are some differences in how these terms are actually defined.

WhatIs.com defines application as "A shorter form of application program. An application program is a program designed to perform a *specific* function directly for the user or, in some cases, for another application program. Applications use the services of the computer's operating system and other supporting applications."

WhatIs.com defines system as "A *collection* of elements or components that are organized for a common purpose. The word sometimes describes the organization or plan itself (and is similar in meaning to *method*, as in 'I have my own little system') and sometimes describes the parts in the system (as in 'computer system')."

From these definitions, we get a general idea that the application is the specific thing and the system is the collection of those specific things.

At the heart of the System Definition Model (SDM) is the notion of a system. Fundamentally, the system is an independently deployable configuration of resources. Two types of systems are supported within the SDM: atomic and composite. Atomic systems are composed of the specific things, such as assemblies, configuration files, and SQL scripts. Composite systems are composed of applications and/or other systems.

With this fundamental understanding, we see that the Application Designer supports application prototypes (encapsulations of the underlying resources for the base type). These *specific* types can be implemented and synchronized with the actual code. The System Designer provides for the *collection* of applications and other systems for the purpose of deployment validation. This supports repurposing for different environments and nesting for complex scenarios.

Creating a New System Diagram

Most likely, you will create the system diagram directly from the application diagram, which is covered in the "Building a System Diagram from an Application Diagram" section later in the chapter. In this example, you will start with a new project and use copy and paste to get the application information into the new design. You might do this when you want to copy in a section of a larger application to start your system diagram. This example will demonstrate the issues involved with adding an implemented application directly from another diagram. For this example, you will copy the MyDesign application diagram you created in Chapter 8.

1. Start a new project. In the New Project dialog box, select Distributed System Solutions, and then select Distributed System. Enter the name MySystem, as shown in Figure 9-1, and click OK. At this point, you have an empty solution, as shown in Figure 9-2.

Note If you create a new Distributed System Solutions project type, there is no option to start with a system design. The default selection is Distributed System, which provides you with a blank application diagram from which to construct your system diagram.

Figure 9-1. *Creating a new Distributed System project*

Figure 9-2. *The empty MySystem solution*

2. Open the `MyDesign` solution you created in the previous chapter and double-click `MyDesign.ad` to display the application diagram. Right-click the design surface and choose Select All. From the main menu, select Edit ➤ Copy (or press Ctrl+C).

3. Close the `MyDesign` solution and reopen the `MySystem` solution. Double-click `MySystem.ad`, and then paste the copied application diagram using Edit ➤ Paste (or press Ctrl+V). Your resulting diagram should look like Figure 9-3.

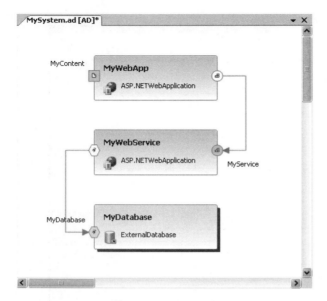

Figure 9-3. *MySystem application diagram copied from MyDesign*

Notice that even though MyDesign was an implemented application in the MyDesign solution, an unimplemented version of the application diagram is provided. This is a great advantage of using the copy-and-paste method. If you had added MyDesign.ad to this solution instead of using copy and paste, the application design operation signatures would be incorrect, and you would see red boxes around each of the applications, as shown in Figure 9-4. This indicates a .synchronization alert, as discussed at the end of Chapter 8.

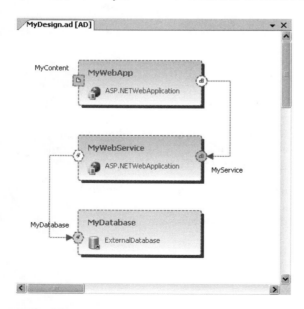

Figure 9-4. *Application Designer synchronization error alert*

> **Note** An application diagram always needs to exist for a system diagram to be present. If you delete the default application diagram, and then try to add a new system diagram, another application diagram will be created for you. Also, if you delete the application diagram from which a system is built, when you reopen the system diagram, Visual Studio will try to re-create the application diagram.

Starting a System Design Diagram

Now that you have a copy of an application design, you can start to create your system diagram. There are several methods for creating a system diagram:

- From within the Solution Explorer, right-click Solution Items and select Add ➤ New Distributed System Diagram. In the Add New Item dialog box, select System Diagram.
- Select Diagram ➤ Design Application System from the main menu.
- Select any or all of the applications on the design surface, right-click, and select Design Application System.

For this example, you will start with a blank system diagram and create a deployable system, exposing the web service with the associated database.

1. In the Solution Explorer, right-click Solution Items and select Add ➤ New Distributed System Diagram. In the Add New Item dialog box, select System Diagram. Provide the name MySystem, and then click Add. The System View window now contains the applications that were copied into the MySystem application designer, as shown in Figure 9-5.

Figure 9-5. *The System View window*

2. You can now just drag-and-drop applications from the System View window onto the designer to create your deployable systems. For this example, drag MyWebService and MyDatabase into the system diagram.

3. Using the Connection tool in the System Designer Toolbox, connect the database endpoints and add a comment that says **MySystem for the Northwest Region**. Your diagram should look like Figure 9-6.

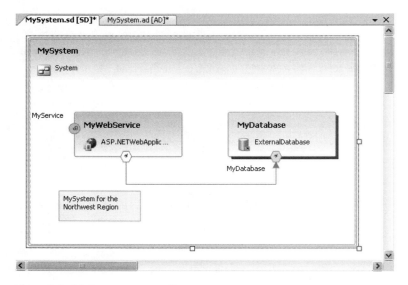

Figure 9-6. *MySystem system diagram*

The System Designer Toolbox contains only three predefined objects to be used while designing your system model. The reason that there are so few tools is that the system diagram is really a container for deployment scenarios of an application diagram. The Toolbox objects are described in Table 9-1.

Table 9-1. *The System Designer Toolbox Objects*

Item	Description
Pointer	Pointer tool used for selection (drag-and-drop)
Connection	Connection tool to link two system endpoints
Comment	A comment text box

Creating a Proxy Endpoint for Applications

Your new system will ultimately need to be connected with other systems or might be nested within a larger system context. To keep the database endpoints properly encapsulated, you need to expose only the web service endpoint. This exposure of an application endpoint to a system boundary is termed *delegation*. Once the endpoint has been delegated, a proxy endpoint is created within the system diagram.

1. Right-click the `MyService` provider endpoint and select Add Proxy Endpoint.

2. Rename the proxy endpoint to distinguish it from the application endpoint. Name it `MyServiceProxy`, as shown in Figure 9-7.

CHAPTER 9 ■ SYSTEM AND LOGICAL DATACENTER DESIGNERS 261

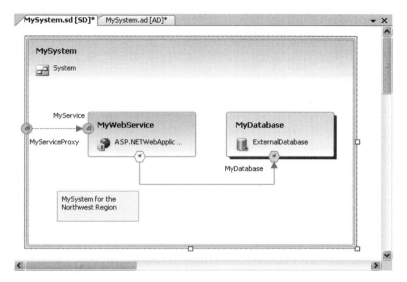

Figure 9-7. *MySystem diagram proxy endpoint*

■**Tip** The Application Designer is always sitting right behind the System Designer. To quickly view the detail in the Application Designer, right-click the application you are interested in and select Go to Definition.

Building a System Diagram from an Application Diagram

In this section, you will create a second system directly from an application diagram, and then connect the two systems via the proxy endpoints.

1. In the `MySystem` solution, double-click `MySystem.ad`. Click the Pointer in the Toolbox and drag a selection box around the `MyWebApp` application.

2. Right-click the `MyWebApp` application and select Design Application System. This will bring up the Design Application System dialog box, where you can enter a name for your new system diagram. For this diagram, enter `MyExposed`, as shown in Figure 9-8, and then click OK.

Figure 9-8. *The Design Application System dialog box*

3. The MyExposed system diagram consists of one application, MyWebApp. Right-click the MyContent endpoint and select Add Proxy Endpoint. This will expose the system to HTTP requests of the website.

4. Right-click the consumer endpoint (MyService) and select Add Proxy Endpoint to expose the service request. The resulting diagram is shown in Figure 9-9.

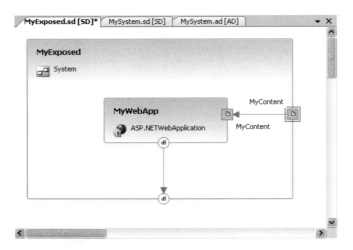

Figure 9-9. *MyExposed system diagram*

Nesting Systems

For a large or complex enterprise scenario, you may need to combine or nest systems. With several systems identified and proxy endpoints exposed, you can create a more complex system diagram. As a simple example, you will create a new complex system that is composed of both the MySystem and the MyExposed systems.

1. In the Solution Explorer, right-click Solution Items and select Add ➤ New Distributed System Diagram. In the Add New Item dialog box, select System Diagram, name it MyComplex, and click Add. The System View window now includes the systems you have defined in the previous exercises, as well as the application you defined in Chapter 8, as shown in Figure 9-10.

2. With a blank system design template open, you can drag-and-drop any combination of applications and systems on the design surface. For this example, drag MySystem and MyExposed onto the design surface.

3. Connect the systems by right-clicking the MyServiceProxy endpoint of MySystem and selecting Connect. In the Create Connection dialog box, select MyExposed as the system and MyService as the endpoint in the Connect To section.

CHAPTER 9 ■ SYSTEM AND LOGICAL DATACENTER DESIGNERS

Figure 9-10. *The MyComplex system*

4. Extend the `MyContent` endpoint (by adding a proxy endpoint) to expose the endpoint to other systems. Your complex system design should look like Figure 9-11.

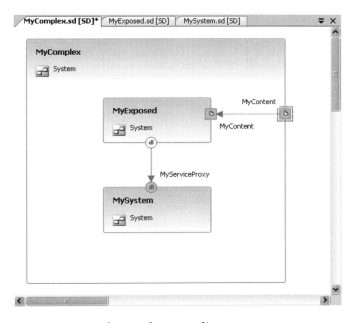

Figure 9-11. *Sample nested systems diagram*

■**Tip** With a multilevel system diagram, you can easily traverse the hierarchy by right-clicking a subsystem and selecting Open in System Designer. You can continue to open subsystems until you get down to the actual application. Once at the application level, you can still select Go to Definition to view the actual application diagram.

Viewing Web Service Details, Settings, and Constraints

The System Designer allows you to view the operation, settings, and constraints of the endpoints and applications exposed on the system design surface. A key item to note is that you can only view these elements. Unlike with the Application Designer, where you can define operations and configure settings and constraints, this is primarily a view into the underlying metadata. We say "primarily" because you do have the option to override certain settings, as described in the next section.

For example, right-click the `MyServiceProxy` endpoint within the `MyComplex` system diagram and select View Operations. You will see a list of operations defined in the Application Designer, as shown in Figure 9-12.

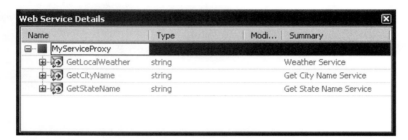

Figure 9-12. *The Web Service Details window for MyServiceProxy*

Close the Web Service Details window. Right-click the `MyServiceProxy` endpoint again and select Settings and Constraints. You will see the Settings and Constraints window, as shown in Figure 9-13.

Figure 9-13. *The Setting and Constraints window for MyServiceProxy*

Overriding Settings and Constraints

A key feature of the distributed designers is the ability to override the settings in a system design that have been provided by an underlying application design. This provides for reusable configurations and tailored deployments of systems. However, before you can override settings in the System Designer, they must first be specified as overridable within the Application Designer. Let's try this out.

1. In the `MySystem` solution, double-click `MySystem.ad`. Within the Application Designer, right-click the `MyService` endpoint and select Settings and Constraints.

2. Choose Application Endpoint Settings and verify that they are set to overridable, as shown in Figure 9-14.

Figure 9-14. *Setting and constraints can be set as Overridable.*

3. Open `MySystem.sd` and view the settings and constraints for the `MyService` web service provider endpoint. Notice that the Binding Namespace is set to the template-coded `http://tempuri.org`. As a best practice, you should change the binding namespace from this default value on web service endpoints.

4. To comply with the best practice suggestion, change the Value field for the Binding Namespace to `http://mysystem.org`, as shown in Figure 9-15.

5. Close the Settings and Constraints window and save your `MySystem` solution. You will use it when you work with the Deployment Designer in the next chapter.

Figure 9-15. *Overriding the Binding Namespace setting*

If you ever want to go back to the original value provided by the application design, you can check the Use Default box in the Settings and Constraints window, and the value will be reset to the original value.

Using the Logical Datacenter Designer

Unless your job description includes infrastructure architecture, you are probably wondering why you would need the Logical Datacenter Designer. In a large organization, the design of the datacenter will most likely be done by lonely individuals, in locked rooms, with high levels of security clearance. For the smaller organizations, this might be you. Regardless, the design of the application and the design of the supporting infrastructure need to be worked in tandem.

A disconnection between the development teams and infrastructure support has been all too apparent in our experience of designing and deploying enterprise systems. For many years now, customer organizations have been forced to build and maintain separate lab environments of production-quality hardware to test applications prior to deploying them in the enterprise datacenter.

Five years ago, we presented the diagram shown in Figure 9-16 to the vice president of information systems of a large corporation to graphically depict the need for architects, developers, and infrastructure groups to work together to provide integrated solutions.

During the presentation, we stressed, "Our key motivation is getting the solution to the customers before the opportunity for benefit has slipped away." Today, as then, we work to engage the architecture, infrastructure, and development communities to advance this framework. Fortunately, a key design goal for VSTS addressed what we already knew needed to be accomplished: "Facilitate collaboration among all members of a software team (including architects, developers, testers, and operations managers)." This focus on bringing the full team together was the key reason we jumped in so early in the release cycle of VSTS.

CHAPTER 9 ■ SYSTEM AND LOGICAL DATACENTER DESIGNERS   267

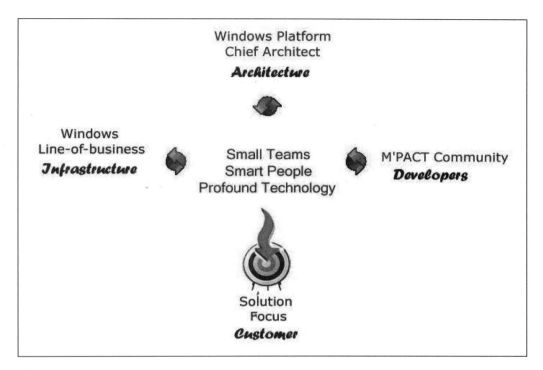

Figure 9-16. *Collaborative team environment*

In this section, you will look at how to use the Logical Datacenter Designer to define and configure logical servers that will be part of the logical datacenter structure. From the overuse of "logical" in the previous sentence, you can see one of the shortcomings of the Logical Datacenter Designer. There is no physical implementation in this release. This fact gave rise to a blogging stream titled "Why the VSTS Logical Datacenter Designer (er, Deployment Designer) Sucks." A reply is posted at http://blogs.msdn.com/a_pasha/articles/409396.aspx.

Creating a Logical Datacenter Diagram

Your logical datacenter design can be created from scratch or may be provided to you by an infrastructure architect in your organization. For this example, you will use Visual Studio 2005 to add a new logical datacenter diagram to the solution you created in Chapter 8.

1. Right-click your MyDesign solution and select Add ➤ New Distributed System Diagram.

2. Select Logical Datacenter Diagram and provide the name MyDesign.ldd, as shown in Figure 9-17, and then click Add. You will be brought in to the Logical Datacenter Designer with a blank work surface and a default logical datacenter diagram (.ldd).

Figure 9-17. *Creating a new logical datacenter diagram*

The Logical Datacenter Designer Toolbox comes preconfigured with eleven predefined prototypes (.lddprototype): five logical server prototypes and six endpoint prototypes to be used while designing your logical datacenter. These generic logical server types include a Windows client, Internet Information Server (IIS) web server, database server, generic server, and zone. The Toolbox objects are described in Table 9-2.

Table 9-2. *The Logical Datacenter Designer Toolbox Objects*

Item	Description
Pointer	Pointer tool used for selection
WebSiteEndpoint	Manages server-side communication with a logical IIS web server
HTTPClientEndpoint	Manages client-side communication with a logical IIS web server
DatabaseClientEndpoint	Manages client-side communication with a logical database server
GenericServerEndpoint	Describes server-side communication with a logical generic server
GenericClientEndpoint	Describes client-side communication with a logical generic server
ZoneEndpoint	Manages communication on the edge of a zone
WindowsClient	Corresponds to a Windows client or server that hosts a Windows application
IISWebServer	Corresponds to an IIS server that hosts web services or ASP.NET web applications
DatabaseServer	Corresponds to a database server
GenericServer	Corresponds to a user-defined server or component
Zone	Logical boundary, such as a firewall, that is separated from other portions of the datacenter; zones can be nested

Item	Description
Pointer	Pointer tool used for selection (again!)
Connection	Connection tool to link two endpoints
Comment	A comment text box

You can extend the Logical Datacenter Designer prototypes, just as you can extend the Application Designer prototypes (as explained in Chapter 8). For example, if you have a hardening policy on your IIS servers, you might want to configure those settings on an IIS server prototype and then save it as Corporate Hardened IIS Server. Similarly, if you have created a certain zone definition that you plan to reuse or share, it would be a good idea to create a prototype of that zone.

To extend a prototype, select the design element (logical server or endpoint) and choose Diagram ➤ Add to Toolbox. To share your prototype with others, you can provide them with a copy of your .lddprototype file, which they can add to their default prototype folder. In the future, Microsoft will be providing additional datacenter prototypes (such as SQL Server), which you can add to your designer.

Adding Zones

To create a logical datacenter diagram, you should begin by adding zones. Zones are an important concept within the Logical Datacenter Designer. They are used to define communication boundaries, physical boundaries (different sites), or security boundaries (internal servers or perimeter servers).

To understand zones, you just need to think about games you played as kid. Games such as capture the flag and dodge ball have the notion of zones. Most of them involve lines that cannot be crossed or policies such as "safety zones," where you cannot be hit or tagged. This is the most secure area during the game and is similar to a datacenter zone. The wide-open spaces are the risky areas, where you might be taken out at any time. In our analogy, this is like the public Internet. In the network world, these zone boundaries are defined by firewalls, routers, ports, and virtual local area networks.

Let's get started by adding some zones to the new diagram.

1. Click the Zone prototype in the Logical Datacenter Designer Toolbox and drag it onto the design surface. Optionally, you can right-click the design surface and select Add New ➤ Zone.

2. By default, the zone is named `zone 1`. Double-click the name and change it to `DMZ` (for demilitarized zone). Change `ZoneEndpoint1` to something a bit shorter, like `DMZ_ZEP`.

▉**Note** The term *demilitarized zone* (DMZ) is taken from the military meaning: "An area from which military forces, operations, and installations are prohibited." Corporations have adopted the DMZ concept of "the area between two enemies" and applied it to networking to mean "A middle ground between an organization's trusted internal network and an untrusted, external network such as the Internet. This is also referred to as a *perimeter network*.

3. Add a second zone and rename it to CIZ (for corporate intranet zone), as shown in Figure 9-18. You can simply copy your DMZ zone and paste it back onto the design surface. Change the zone and endpoint names to CIZ and CIZ_ZEP, respectively.

Figure 9-18. Zone definitions in the Logical Datacenter Designer

Setting Zone Constraints

As you've learned, constraints are used to enforce requirements in one layer of the distributed systems model (such as the Application Designer) against those in another layer (such as the Logical Datacenter Designer). You can think of these constraints as house rules. Some households have a rule that requires you to take your shoes off at the door, and there is even a little sign posted in the entryway:

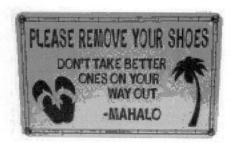

If you forget or ignore the sign, "agents" of the house will remind you of your error. In a similar way, the constraints defined in the distributed designers are enforced across the platform to ensure that corporate policy is integrated into the design tools.

Settings are configuration elements in the environment that control the behavior of the application or server. If you think of constraints as the allow or disallow rules, settings would be the conditions. If we allow you go to the high school dance (constraint), you must be home by 11:00 p.m. (setting).

For example, a common networking practice is to restrict the type of servers allowed within the DMZ. Let's set a zone constraint to do this.

1. Right-click within the DMZ zone and select Settings and Constraints.

2. Under Zone Containment Constraints, deselect the WindowsClient and Zone check boxes, as shown in Figure 9-19. This will restrict Windows clients to within the protected CIZ zone, as well as other zones hosted within this zone (nested zones).

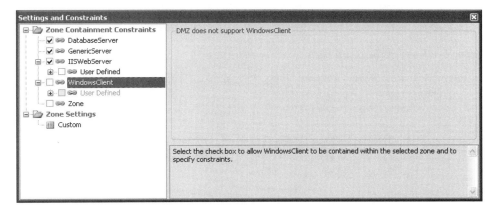

Figure 9-19. *Settings and Constraints for zones*

Note The settings and constraints information that is entered via the Settings and Constraints window maps to data that is generated in the corresponding .sdm file. Editing a setting or a constraint directly affects the generated SDM.

---

3. Verify the constraint by trying to drag a WindowsClient or Zone object from the Toolbox into the DMZ zone on the design surface. Notice also that you can still drag both of these within the CIZ zone.

4. Verify the changes were written into the SDM (.ldd file) for the logical datacenter design. You need to save and close any open designers. Then right-click MyDesign.ldd and select Open With. In the Open With dialog box, select the XML editor. This will open the .ldd file in the XML editor within Visual Studio.

5. Press Ctrl+F to bring up the Find and Replace dialog box. Type **logical servers and zones** in the Find What text box, as shown in Figure 9-20. Click the Find Next button, and you should see the XML fragment shown in Listing 9-1, which is part of the SDM for the DMZ.

Figure 9-20. *Finding the server constraint*

Listing 9-1. *Server Constraint Section of the .ldd File*

```
<ConstraintGroup Name="AllowedTypes" RaiseError="true">
    <Description>
        <Entry Name="Description" Substitute="InstanceName">Zone {0} can only
            contain the following types of logical servers and zones:
            DatabaseServer, GenericServer, IISWebServer.
        </Entry>
    </Description>
```

Notice that the two logical server prototypes (WindowsClient and Zone) are missing from the list of allowed types for zone (0) in the MyDesign.ldd XML file. Close the XML editor.

Placing Servers Inside Zones

Now that the zones have been defined on your design surface, you can start adding servers within the zones. The first server you will add is an IIS server in the DMZ to provide an access point to external clients. Next, you will add another IIS server and database server to host the web service and back-end database, respectively, in the CIZ.

1. Double-click MyDesign.ldd to open. Right-click within the DMZ zone and select Add ➤ IISWebServer. Rename the web server by double-clicking the name and changing it to Exposed_IIS.

2. Add a second IISWebServer to the CIZ zone and name it Safe_IIS.

3. Add a DatabaseServer to the CIZ zone and name it Safe_DB.

Tip If you place a server in the wrong zone or outside a zone on the design surface, you can easily relocate it by right-clicking the lost server and selecting Move to Zone.

4. The incoming zone endpoint within the DMZ zone should already be labeled DMZ_ZEP, and the CIZ zone's endpoint should labeled CIZ_ZEP. If the endpoint label is not showing on the diagram, right-click the endpoint and select Show Label. Rename the endpoints on the logical servers themselves to give them meaningful names. In this case, the chosen convention is to use the server name with the suffix of _EP, as shown in Figure 9-21.

Figure 9-21. *Logical Datacenter Designer with zones and servers identified*

Setting Specific Zone Constraints

You can define a policy for a zone that applies to all the items within that zone. Let's say that you want to make sure that all IIS servers in the CIZ are running the current production version of the Common Language Runtime (CLR), and no beta versions of the CLR are allowed to be present in that zone.

1. Select the CIZ zone. Right-click and select Settings and Constraints to open the Settings and Constraints window.

2. Select User Defined and CommonLanguageRuntime from the list on the left.

3. On the right, select Version and enter the correct version number in the Value field. You can also enter descriptive error text in the Error Message field, as shown in Figure 9-22.

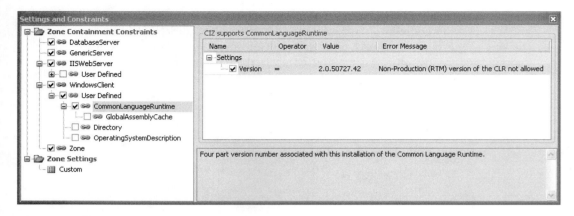

Figure 9-22. *Setting constraints on a zone*

Since this constraint on the CLR version is set at the zone level, any IIS server added to the zone will be required to meet the version-level restriction. If you take the time to open the .ldd file in the XML editor, you will notice a version constraint added to the CIZ zone regarding the CommonLanguageRuntime.

Connecting Servers to Zones

Communication across zones is managed by the zone endpoints. The communication through the zone can be inbound, outbound, or bidirectional. The arrow displayed within the zone endpoint represents the communication flow. You can then define communication pathways between logical servers and zones by connecting and controlling these pathways via their endpoints. You also can control the type of communication using constraints on endpoints.

1. Beginning in the DMZ, connect the inbound DMZ zone endpoint to the IIS server provider endpoint. To do this, right-click Exposed_IIS_EP and select Delegate. Select DMZ as the zone and DMZ_ZEP for the endpoint, as shown in Figure 9-23.

2. Connect the exposed IIS server client endpoint to the outbound DMZ zone endpoint. This time, try using the Connection tool from the Toolbox. Select the Connection tool, click the Exposed_IIS client endpoint, and drag the connection to the outbound DMZ zone endpoint.

3. Continue with the Connection tool and connect that same outbound DMZ zone endpoint to the inbound zone endpoint on the CIZ zone.

4. Connect that inbound zone endpoint on the CIZ zone to the provider endpoint on the Safe_IIS. Your diagram now shows a compete flow from the outside to your safe IIS server.

5. To finish the diagram, right-click Safe_IIS and select Connect. Choose the Safe_DB as the zone and Safe_DB_EP as the endpoint, and then click OK. Your diagram should look like Figure 9-24.

CHAPTER 9 ■ SYSTEM AND LOGICAL DATACENTER DESIGNERS

Figure 9-23. *The Delegate to Endpoint dialog box*

Figure 9-24. *Completed connections in MyDesign.ldd*

You can set the flow behavior on a zone endpoint through its Properties window, as shown in Figure 9-25. Select the zone endpoint you want to configure and press F4 to display the Properties window. In the Behavior section, set the Communication Flow property to Inbound, Outbound, or Bidirectional, based on your scenario.

Figure 9-25. *Setting the communication flow behavior*

Specifying Settings and Constraints for Servers

The Settings and Constraints window is not only useful for working within zones, but also for specifying settings and constraints on individual servers. The settings can include configuration information such as the .NET runtime version, operating system, and service packs. They can also include constraints such as ASP.NET security, membership, or session state.

For this example, we will assume that storing session state on the IIS server in the DMZ is not allowed.

1. Select the `Exposed_IIS` server in the `DMZ` zone. Right-click and select Settings and Constraints.

2. In the Settings and Constraints window, select the check box next to ASP.NET Session State to reveal the configurable constraints. In the Session State Mode list, select Off, as shown in Figure 9-26. This disables session state for an entire site. This selection will be propagated to the associated setting in the `Web.config` file. Also set the Http Cookie Mode to AutoDetect. (You will encounter these settings again in the Deployment Designer, covered in Chapter 10.)

CHAPTER 9 ■ SYSTEM AND LOGICAL DATACENTER DESIGNERS

Figure 9-26. *Disabling session state on the IIS web server*

As explained in Chapter 8, three types of constraints are supported in the distributed designers. Here is how each type might be used with your logical datacenter design:

- Implicit constraints are "baked" into the SDM. An example of an implicit constraint is the available endpoints for a database server prototype. These constraints cannot be edited by users, but they can be authored using the SDM SDK.

- Predefined constraints logically group together settings of a particular type, such as ASP.NET membership or website configuration. These dialog boxes have editing rules built into them to allow specific combinations of settings to define the constraint.

- User-defined constraints allow a user to have full control over desired values and ranges for any setting available on the logical server. These constraints are created by manually defining one or more settings.

Constraints placed on endpoints restrict the type of communication allowed to be carried through the endpoint. For example, a zone endpoint can be constrained to permit only HTTP traffic over a specific port. Establishing such a constraint will affect connections within the Logical Datacenter Designer, as well as restrictions on implementations in the Deployment Designer.

Importing Settings from IIS

You can manage many settings and constraints within the Logical Datacenter Designer, but it can be a daunting task to manually configure all of these for each logical server. Fortunately, there is a wizard that allows you to import your settings from an existing IIS web server.

To demonstrate how this works, you will import the settings and constraints from an IIS server. You can use your local machine if you have IIS installed.

1. Right-click the Safe_IIS server prototype on the diagram and select Settings and Constraints.

2. In the Settings and Constraints window, explore the InternetInformationServices node. Notice that most of the values contain no value ([null]) by default, as shown in Figure 9-27. If you browse the ApplicationPools and WebSites nodes, you will see similar results. Some default values may exist, but they may not accurately represent the web servers in your environment. Close the Settings and Constraints window.

Figure 9-27. *The Setting and Constraints window for the default IIS web server*

3. Right-click the Safe_IIS server prototype on the diagram and select Import Settings to start the Import IIS Settings Wizard. Click Next.

4. As shown in Figure 9-28, the Import IIS Settings Wizard presents three check boxes on the next page:

   - The first option imports all of the websites that reside on the server and creates a new endpoint representing each site on the IIS web server prototype. If you don't select this option, the proceeding page will provide the option to import individual sites to either new or existing endpoints.

   - If the second box is checked, the global configuration settings for the web server will be imported. These settings map to the InternetInformationServices node in the Settings and Configuration window.

   - The third check box determines if application pools will be imported.

For this example, enter your server name and administrator credentials (administrator credentials are required in order to access certain metabase keys and values), accept the defaults for the check boxes, and click Next.

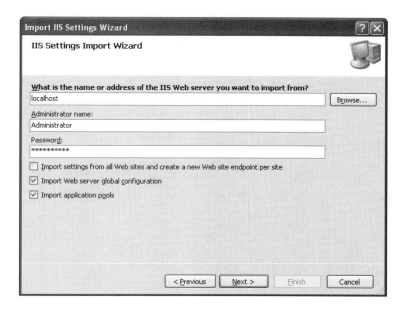

Figure 9-28. *Import IIS Settings Wizard set to import from the local machine*

5. The wizard prompts you to select the websites and endpoint bindings. Click the down arrow in the Endpoint section and select Safe_ISS_EP, as shown in Figure 9-29. Then click Next.

Figure 9-29. *Import IIS Settings Wizard websites and bindings*

6. The confirmation page lists what will be imported, as shown in Figure 9-30. Click Next one more time to perform the import, and then click Finish to exit the wizard.

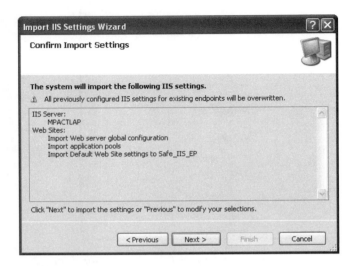

Figure 9-30. *Import IIS Settings Wizard confirmation*

7. Open the Settings and Constraints window again for the Safe_IIS server prototype. Notice that the InternetInformationServices node has been renamed to the server name from which the settings were imported. Select this node, and you will see that the global configuration settings for the web server have been populated with the IIS metabase settings. You can also see that the Connection properties now reflect the imported settings, as shown in Figure 9-31.

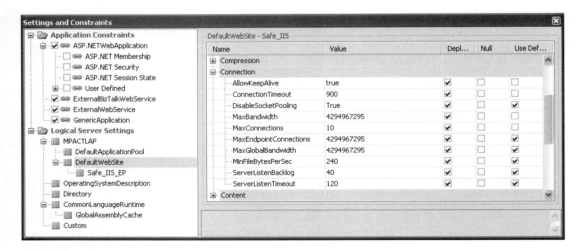

Figure 9-31. *Settings and constraints imported from the local IIS server*

Building a Logical Datacenter Diagram for the Sample Application

In this section, you will build a simple logical datacenter diagram to support the sample application you reverse-engineered using the Application Designer in Chapter 8.

1. Open Visual Studio 2005. Select File ➤ Open Project ➤ Solution and open the sample solution, EffortTrackingSolution.sln.

2. Right-click the EffortTracking solution and select Add ➤ New Distributed System Diagram. Select Logical Datacenter Diagram and change the default name from LogicalDatacenter1.ldd to EffortTracking.ldd. Click the Add button to open the Logical Datacenter Designer.

3. You need a web server to host the web application and the web service. Drag an IISWebServer logical server from the Toolbox onto the design surface, as shown in Figure 9-32. Rename the default provider WebSiteEndpoint1 to ET_Site_EP.

Note With Visual Studio 2005, you can run a virtual web server, which means that you do not need to have IIS. However, throughout the book, IIS is used to host the sample application in order to illustrate certain points and eliminate some of the confusion.

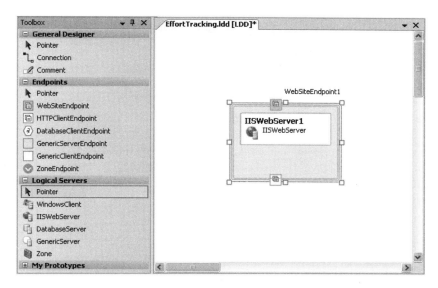

Figure 9-32. *IIS web server added to the logical datacenter diagram*

4. Add a second website endpoint by right-clicking `IISWebServer1` and selecting Add New ➤ WebSiteEndpoint. Rename it `ET_Service_EP`.

5. Rename the server itself to `EffortTrackingWebServer`.

6. You need a back-end database server to host `EffortTracking`. Drag the DatabaseServer logical server from the Toolbox onto the design surface below the IISWebServer server. Rename the database provider endpoint from `DatabaseServerEndpoint1` to `ET_DB_EP`. Rename `DatabaseServer1` to `EffortTrackingDatabase`.

7. Since the web service connects to the database using ADO.NET, you need to provide the connection. Right-click inside `EffortTrackingWebServer` and select Connect. In the Connect To section, select `EffortTrackingDatabase` for the logical server and `ET_DB_EP` for the endpoint, as shown in Figure 9-33. Click OK. Notice that the connection appears between the IIS server and the database.

Figure 9-33. *Creating the connection to the database*

8. To represent the connection between the website (client) and web service (provider), connect the existing `HTTPClientEndpoint` with the `ET_Service_EP`. Using the Connection tool, start with either endpoint and drag to connect. This finishes the logical datacenter design, as shown in Figure 9-34.

Figure 9-34. *Logical datacenter design for the Effort Tracking application infrastructure*

Summary

In this chapter, you looked at the System Designer and Logical Datacenter Designer. The System Designer is the critical link between your application design and the logical datacenter. You learned how to design and build system diagrams and how to nest systems. You also learned how to view and override settings provided by the Application Designer.

Next, you explored the Logical Datacenter Designer. You saw how to separate your logical datacenter into zones and how to interconnect servers, zones, and endpoints. You worked with settings and constraints on both zones and servers to provide configuration information or constrain the scope within the zone or server. You then learned how to import settings from existing servers. Finally, you built a logical datacenter diagram to support the sample application. In a future version of Visual Studio, you will be able to deploy your logical datacenter onto physical devices or into virtual datacenters.

The final step in the process is to "bind" the applications you created in the Application Designer and grouped in the System Designer to the Logical Datacenter Designer diagram you just completed. This binding process is performed by the Deployment Designer, as explained in the following chapter.

CHAPTER 10

Deployment Designer

The final member of the distributed designer suite is the Deployment Designer. Once you have your applications defined and grouped into deployable systems, and have defined one or more logical datacenters, you are ready to validate the deployment into a target datacenter.

The Deployment Designer allows the architect/developer to evaluate the appropriateness of a particular system for a specified logical datacenter. This evaluation occurs between the system diagram (.sd) and the logical datacenter diagram (.ldd), which were discussed in Chapter 9.

VSTS provides two methods for arriving at your deployment diagram: explicit and implicit. The explicit, or formal, method is to first define a system diagram from which to invoke the deployment. The implicit, or quick-and-dirty, method is to invoke the deployment directly from the application diagram and force a default system diagram to be generated.

In this chapter, we will cover the formal method first with our sample design from Chapters 8 and 9. Then we will use the implicit method to start the deployment design from the application diagram of the book's sample Effort Tracking application.

Using the Explicit Deployment Method

Using the explicit deployment method, you start from an existing system diagram that you have defined. Let's begin by reviewing the MyComplex system diagram that you created in Chapter 9.

Open the MySystem solution within Visual Studio 2005 and double-click MyComplex.sd. This complex system is composed of two subsystems and one application diagram, and they are all opened in the System Designer, as shown in Figure 10-1. Notice that the application diagram is sitting in the background and cannot be closed separately from the System Designer.

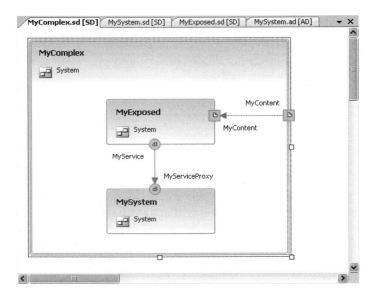

Figure 10-1. *MyComplex in the System Designer*

All the information (metadata) in this diagram is expressed in the underlying System Definition Model (SDM) file. Take some time to review the XML in the MyComplex.sd file, as shown in Figure 10-2. You will need to close the open diagrams and open the MyComplex.sd file using the XML editor. Within the file, you will recognize the association with your other diagrams, the detailed properties for each model element, and the incorporation of versioning.

```xml
<?xml version="1.0" encoding="utf-8"?>
<!--System Definition Model (SDM) based file generated by Visual Studio.-->
<!--Manual editing of this file is not recommended and can result in errors.-->
<SystemDefinitionModel xmlns:xsi="http://www.w3.org/2001/XMLSchema-instance" xmlns:xsd="http://www.w3.org/2001/XMLSchema"
  <Import Alias="System" Name="System" Version="1.0.50729.0" />
  <Import Alias="MicrosoftDistributedApplication" Name="Microsoft.DistributedApplication" Version="1.0.50729.0" />
  <Import Alias="MyExposed" Name="MyExposed" Version="1.0.0.0" Culture="en-US" />
  <Import Alias="MySystem" Name="MySystem" Version="1.0.0.0" Culture="en-US" />
  <Import Alias="MicrosoftWeb" Name="Microsoft.Web" Version="1.0.50729.0" />
  <Import Alias="MyWebApp" Name="MyWebApp" Version="1.0.0.0" Culture="en-US" />
  <Import Alias="MicrosoftWebApplication" Name="Microsoft.WebApplication" Version="1.0.50729.0" />
  <DesignData>
    <VisualStudio xmlns="http://schemas.microsoft.com/SystemDefinitionModel/2005/1/DesignData/VisualStudio">
      <ModelElement Id="dd1c9a8b92bf4a7f90ec3ff0007f3e3b" Type="Microsoft.VisualStudio.EnterpriseTools.Application.Modeli
        <Property Name="DocumentType" Value="ApplicationCompoundComponent" />
        <Property Name="Version" Value="1" />
```

Figure 10-2. *MyComplex.sd in the XML editor*

> **Note** SDM files are identified based on five key attributes: the name, version, culture, platform, and public key token. Only the name attribute is required.

Creating a Deployment Diagram

In this example, you will create a deployment diagram using `MyComplex.sd`. When you choose to define your deployment, you also need to supply a logical datacenter design for deployment validation. You will use the `MyDesign.ldd` file from the `MyDesign` solution you created in Chapter 8.

Starting a Deployment Diagram

Follow these steps to begin your deployment diagram:

1. Open the `MyComplex` system diagram by double-clicking the `MyComplex.sd` file in the Solution Explorer.

2. In the System Designer, right-click the design surface and select Define Deployment, as shown in Figure 10-3.

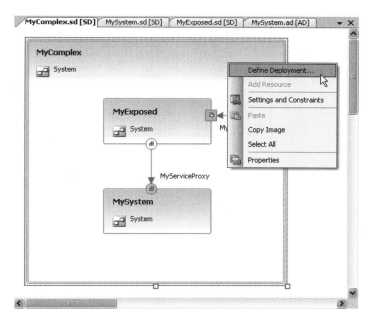

Figure 10-3. *Choosing to start a deployment diagram*

3. In the Define Deployment dialog box, choose `MyDesign.ldd`, as shown in Figure 10-4. (Since you do not have the logical datacenter diagram already attached to your solution, browse to the `MyDesign` solution and select `MyDesign.ldd` from there.) Then click OK.

Figure 10-4. *The Define Deployment dialog box*

A new deployment definition named `MyComplex1.dd` is created in the `MySystem` solution and opened in the Deployment Designer, as shown in Figure 10-5.

Figure 10-5. *The default deployment design*

Also, the logical datacenter diagram, MyDesign.ldd, has been added to your solution, as shown in Figure 10-6.

Figure 10-6. *The Solution Explorer window showing the new MyComplex1.dd and MyDesign.ldd files*

The Toolbox for the Deployment Designer contains only two items: a Pointer tool for making selections and Comment tool for adding comments.

A more interesting aspect of the Deployment Designer is the System View window. It contains the application artifacts from the Application Designer inside your MyComplex system, as shown in Figure 10-7.

Figure 10-7. *The System View window*

Binding the Applications to Logical Servers

Using the System View window, you can drag the applications onto the reproduced logical datacenter diagram. Alternatively, you can right-click an application in the System View window and select Bind Application. This will bring up a dialog box that shows the suitable hosts in your target datacenter. Using either method, the Deployment Designer will not allow you to bind applications to unsuitable hosts. However, you can choose to override this default behavior.

1. In the System View window, right-click the MyDatabase application and select Bind Application. (If the System View window isn't visible, select View ➤ Other Windows ➤ System View). In the Bind MyDatabase to Logical Server dialog box, your only choice will be Safe_DB, as shown in Figure 10-8. Select it and click OK.

Figure 10-8. *The Bind MyDatabase to Logical Server dialog box*

2. Drag MyWebApp onto the Exposed_IIS server.

3. Drag MyWebService over to the design surface. Notice that the only acceptable location is the Safe_IIS server.

The System View window will indicate the binding of the application to the host by placing an arrow to the left of the application and showing <Bound> after the application name, as shown in Figure 10-9.

Figure 10-9. *The System View window with bound application prototypes*

At this point, all your applications are bound to the target datacenter hosts, as shown in Figure 10-10.

Figure 10-10. *The deployment diagram with applications bound to logical servers*

Validating a Deployment Implementation

After you've created your deployment diagram, it's time to validate the proposed deployment definition. When you choose to validate the diagram, the Deployment Designer validates the settings and constraints specified in the .sd file for the system against those specified in the .ldd file for the target datacenter. The Error List window will display any errors, warnings, or messages associated with the validation of the system against the logical datacenter, along with a little white x in a red circle (error mark) inside each offending application, server, or zone. Let's see this in action.

1. Right-click the deployment diagram and select Validate Diagram, as shown in Figure 10-11. Alternatively, you can select Diagram ➤ Validate Diagram from the main menu or click the Validate Diagram icon in the toolbar.

2. The Error List window, shown in Figure 10-12, indicates that four validation warnings occurred. You should see error marks next to the MyWebService application, the MyWebApp application, and the Exposed_IIS logical server. Look over the descriptions of each warning. You will address each one of these in order. Your Errors List may differ depending on settings imported from your IIS Server.

Figure 10-11. *Choosing to validate a diagram*

Figure 10-12. *The Error List window displaying validation warnings*

   3. Double-click the first warning in the Error List window. The Settings and Constraints window will open to the configuration setting causing the conflict, as shown in Figure 10-13. Also, the underlying application, system, or logical datacenter diagram will be brought into focus. Here, the MyExposed system diagram is brought forward.

Figure 10-13. *Settings and Constraints window for the MyService endpoint*

4. You overrode the default Binding Namespace setting on the MyService endpoint in the creation of the MySystem system diagram (in Chapter 9); however, the client (consuming endpoint) within the MyExposed system still expects the default. Select the MyComplex.sd system diagram, and you'll see that the mismatch is clearly depicted, as shown in Figure 10-14. Right-click the MyServiceProxy endpoint and select Settings and Constraints. Notice the Binding Namespace setting of http://MySystem.org. With the Settings and Constraints window still open, click the MyService endpoint. You'll see that the Binding Namespace setting is http://tempuri.org. Now you can override the client (MyService) setting within the MyExposed system to match.

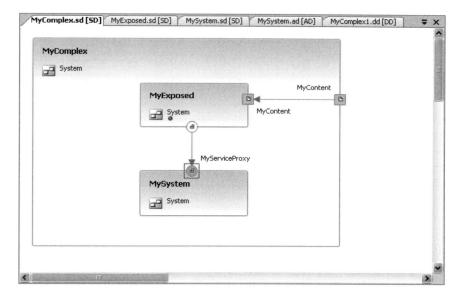

Figure 10-14. *MyComplex system diagram showing error marks*

5. Click the first validation error in the Error List window again to bring up the Settings and Constraints window within the MyExposed system context. Change tempuri to MySystem for the Binding Namespace setting, and then close the Settings and Constraints window.

6. Select the MyComplex1.dd deployment diagram and revalidate it. Notice that the first error has now been resolved, and three warnings remain.

7. Select the next warning in the Error List window to bring up the Settings and Constraints window within the MySystem system design. In this case, the authentication setting for the MyWebService application does not match the configuration settings for the IIS web server. (Your particular IIS setting may not cause this error.) In this simple example, address this issue by setting the mode from Windows to Forms, as shown in Figure 10-15. Then close the Settings and Constraints window.

Figure 10-15. *Setting the web service authentication mode*

8. Select the MyComplex1.dd deployment diagram and revalidate it. The second error has now been resolved.

9. The final two warnings regard the constraints you set within the demilitarized zone (DMZ) for the Exposed_IIS server regarding session state (in Chapter 9). You turned off session state for the logical server, but the MyWebApp application has the session state set to InProc. To fix the problem, double-click either of the last two warnings in the Error List window to open the Settings and Constraints window for the MyExposed system. Set the Cookieless value to AutoDetect and the Mode value to Off, as shown in Figure 10-16. Then close the Settings and Constraints window.

Figure 10-16. *Session state settings for MyWebApp*

10. Select the MyComplex1.dd deployment diagram and revalidate. You'll see that all of the warnings have been resolved, as shown in Figure 10-17.

CHAPTER 10 ■ DEPLOYMENT DESIGNER 295

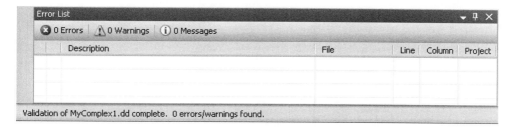

Figure 10-17. *All errors and warnings resolved*

Generating the Deployment Report

After you've created and validated your deployment design, you will want to generate a Deployment Report, which can help you to create installation scripts. Before you generate the report, you should set the deployment properties in the Deployment Designer. We'll discuss this in more detail in the "Setting Deployment Properties" section later in this chapter. For this example, you will leave the default properties and simply generate the Deployment Report.

   1. Right-click the design surface for the MyComplex1 deployment diagram and select Generate Deployment Report, as shown in Figure 10-18.

Figure 10-18. *Choosing to generate a Deployment Report*

   2. The MyComplex1.html report appears within your solution. Right-click the report and select View in Browser.

   3. Notice the wealth of information provided for you in the Deployment Report. Take some time to browse the content and search on some of the areas we have just resolved. For example, search for MySystem.org, and you will see details on the settings for the MyService endpoint, as shown in Figure 10-19. You can also click the "back to parent" link to navigate up to the application to which that endpoint belongs (MyWebApp).

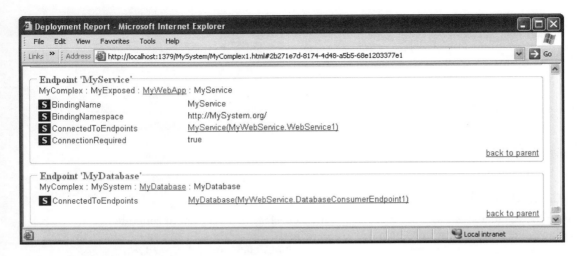

Figure 10-19. *Deployment Report sample section*

We will explore the Deployment Report in more detail after we define the deployment for the book's sample application in the next section.

Using the Implicit Deployment Method

Another way to start a deployment definition is directly from the application diagram, rather than from a system diagram, as in the previous example. This is referred to as the implicit method of deployment. In this section, we'll demonstrate this method and also take a closer look at the Deployment Report.

Note The early builds of the distributed designers called the implicit method a "trial deployment." This early terminology has been dropped, but there are still cautionary notes about running your final deployments from the generated default system. The main issue is that a default system is a direct image of the application diagram, and as such, the configuration cannot be modified independently. For additional information about using the default system, see the TechNote at http://msdn.microsoft.com/vstudio/teamsystem/reference/technotes/apps_designer/default_sys.aspx.

Building the Deployment Diagram

In this section, you will build a deployment diagram for our book's sample Effort Tracking application. You will begin from the `EffortTracking.ad` application diagram you created in Chapter 8.

Starting the Deployment Diagram

Follow these steps to start the deployment diagram from the Application Designer:

1. Open Visual Studio 2005. Select File ➤ Open Project/Solution and open the sample solution, `EffortTrackingSolution.sln`.

2. Double-click the application diagram (`EffortTracking.ad`) to open it in the Application Designer, as shown in Figure 10-20.

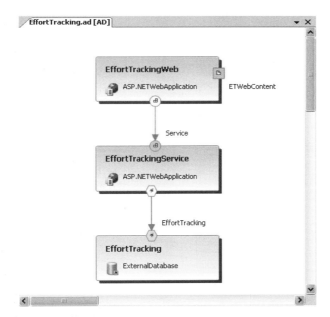

Figure 10-20. *The application diagram for the Effort Tracking application*

3. Select Diagram ➤ Define Deployment from the main menu. In the Define Deployment dialog box, select to use `EffortTracking` as the logical datacenter diagram (created in Chapter 9), as shown in Figure 10-21. Then click OK.

Figure 10-21. *Choosing EffortTracking as the logical datacenter diagram*

Since there was no system definition for the Effort Tracking application created prior to deployment, a default system is created for you. A new Default System folder is added to you solution, and the DefaultSystem1.dd has been placed in this new location, as shown in Figure 10-22.

Figure 10-22. *The Solution Explorer for the EffortTracking sample*

On the design surface, you have a fresh deployment design, which employs the selected logical datacenter diagram, as shown in Figure 10-23.

CHAPTER 10 ■ DEPLOYMENT DESIGNER

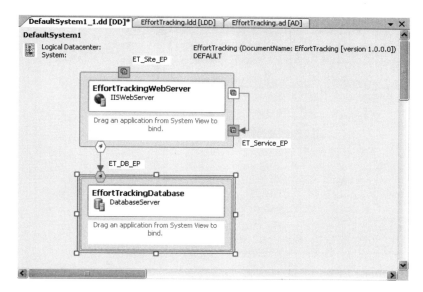

Figure 10-23. *Default EffortTracking deployment diagram*

The System View window contains the Default System and three components of your application design, as shown in Figure 10-24.

Figure 10-24. *The System View window for the EffortTracking sample*

Binding the Applications to Logical Servers

For our sample book application, both the web service and web application will be hosted on a single logical IIS server (EffortTrackingWebServer), and the database will be hosted on the database server (EffortTrackingDatabase).

   1. Drag EffortTrackingService from the System View window onto EffortTrackingWeb➥ Server, and the Bindings Detail dialog box will open. The database endpoint should have been resolved to DatabaseClientEndpoint1. However, since you have exposed two provider endpoints on the IIS server, you need to select ET_Service_EP to bind to the Service endpoint of the EffortTrackingService, as shown in Figure 10-25. Select OK, and you will see the EffortTrackingService bound in the System View window.

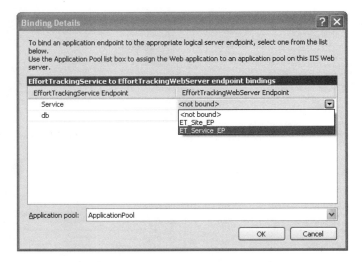

Figure 10-25. *The Binding Details dialog box for EffortTrackingService*

2. Drag `EffortTrackingWeb` onto the same IIS server (`EffortTrackingWebServer`). Set the binding for the `Service` to the `HTTPClientEndpoint1` and the `ETWebContent` endpoint to `ET_Site_EP`, as shown in Figure 10-26.

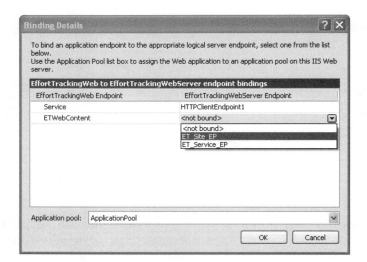

Figure 10-26. *The Binding Details dialog box for EffortTrackingWeb*

3. Drag `EffortTracking` onto `EffortTrackingDatabase`. Since there is only one exposed endpoint, no binding details are requested. You can right-click `EffortTracking` and select Binding Details to verify that the mapping is correct. You should see the `EffortTrackingDatabase` endpoint from the application design bound to the `ET_DB_EP` of the logical datacenter design.

Your sample application is now bound to your target datacenter, as shown in Figure 10-27.

Figure 10-27. *Deployment diagram with application bindings*

Validating the Diagram

Now that you've completed all the bindings between the application components and the logical datacenter, it is time to validate the diagram.

1. Select Diagram ➤ Validate Diagram. The Error List window shows two warnings, indicating that there is a mismatch between the EffortTrackingService, EffortTrackingWeb, and the IIS server in which they are being deployed, as shown in Figure 10-28.

Figure 10-28. *The Error List window for the EffortTracking validation*

2. Double-click the first warning in the Error List window to go to the Application Designer for EffortTrackingWeb. The Settings and Constraints window is opened to the AuthenticationSection, where the mode is set to Forms (which is inconsistent with the IIS server), as shown in Figure 10-29. If you click the EffortTrackingService application profile in the application diagram, you will notice that the web application has the Mode value set to Forms as well, which corresponds to the second warning message.

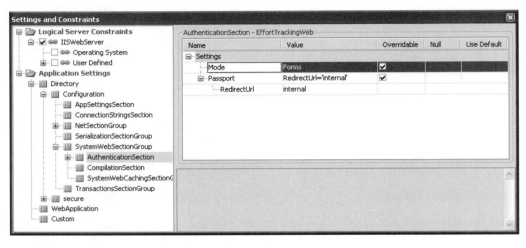

Figure 10-29. *The Settings and Constraints window for EffortTrackingWeb*

3. Switch to EffortTracking.ldd and open the Settings and Constraints window for EffortTrackingWebServer. Within the Logical Server Settings ➤ WebSites ➤ Authentication, notice that AuthFlags is set to Ntlm. Therefore, the Forms authentication in the application needs to support Anonymous, and the IIS server is configured to support only Integrated Windows via Ntlm. You can solve this conflict in two ways: you could change both the web and service applications to use Windows authentication, or you could add Anonymous to the Authentication AuthFlags on the IIS server to allow the support for Forms authentication. Since we want to use our own login in the sample application, you should take the second approach, and change the settings on the IIS server as shown in Figure 10-30.

4. Close the Settings and Constraints window. Select DefaultSystem1.dd from the Window menu, and then select Diagram ➤ Validate Diagram. You will see that the warnings have been resolved, as shown in Figure 10-31.

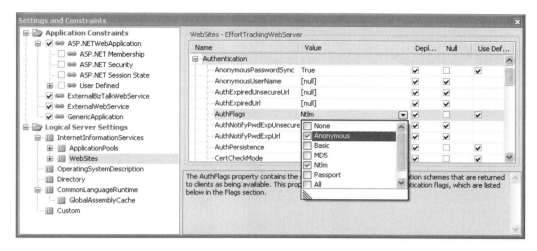

Figure 10-30. *The Settings and Constraints window for EffortTrackingWebServer*

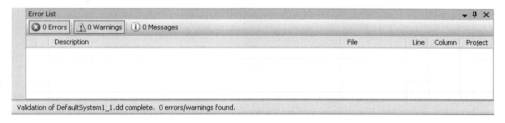

Figure 10-31. *The Error List window with prior warnings resolved*

Setting Deployment Properties

As noted earlier in the chapter, the goal of the Deployment Report is to assist you in creating installation scripts from the XML-based information in the report. A key prerequisite is to set the deployment properties in the Deployment Designer, which you'll do now.

1. Right-click the design surface and select Properties, or press F4, to open the Properties window.

2. Set the Destination Path property to C:\MyDeployments, as shown in Figure 10-32. Set all the Include properties to True. Leave the remaining properties set to their defaults.

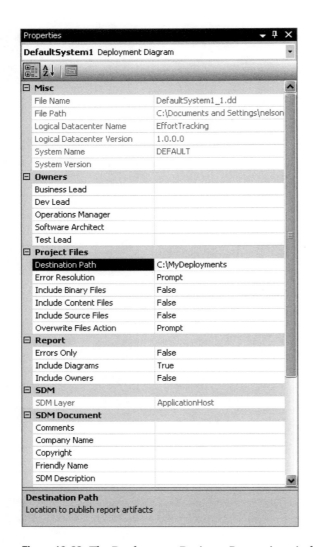

Figure 10-32. *The Deployment Designer Properties window*

Table 10-1 describes the key properties for the Deployment Designer.

Table 10-1. *Key Properties for the Deployment Designer*

Property	Description
Destination Path	This property specifies a path (on disk or a UNC path) to copy source, content, or binary files associated with your applications. By default, this property is blank. If you do not set this property, no files will be copied.
Include Binary Files, Include Content Files, Include Diagrams, Include Owners, and Include Source Files	By default, only diagrams will be included in the Deployment Report. To copy source, content, and binary files to the destination path location, set the corresponding properties to True.
Overwrite Files Action	By default, this property will display a prompt when overwriting files. This can be set to Yes to automatically overwrite files.
Error Resolution	By default, this property will display a prompt when an error occurs. It can be set to Ignore to facilitate automation, or you can also choose to abort Deployment Report creation if an error occurs.
Errors Only	By default, this property is set to False. If set to True, the Deployment Report will contain only the list of validation errors and warnings.

Generating the Deployment Report

Now you're ready to generate the Effort Tracking application Deployment Report. Just right-click the design surface and select Generate Deployment Report. Alternatively, you can select Diagram ➤ Generate Deployment Report. In the status bar at the bottom of the Visual Studio IDE, you will see the Deployment Report generation in progress:

```
Publishing EffortTrackingService: Copying Files...(EffortTrackingService.sdm)
Publishing compiled SDM files: Copying Files...EffortTracking.sdmDocument)
Publishing deployment report: Copying Files...(DefaultSystem1.html)
Deployment report generated.
```

The final report contains detailed information about the bindings, deployment diagram, logical servers, logical datacenter diagram, systems, system diagram, resource settings by type, and endpoints. The Deployment Report for your simple application will be well over 1,000 lines of source HTML. Sample output is shown in Figure 10-33.

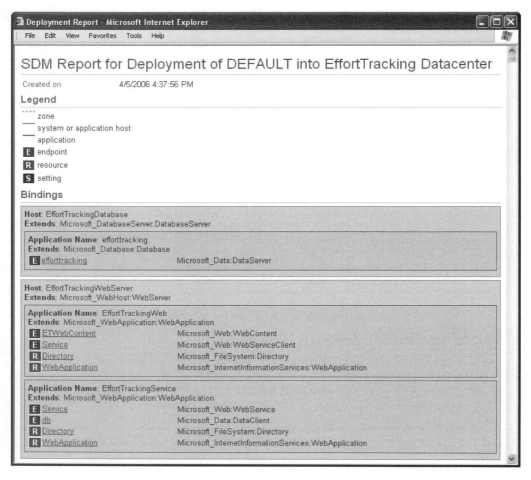

Figure 10-33. *Sample Deployment Report output*

Browse the Deployment Report and search for some of the items we worked on throughout the chapter. Search the document for your favorite endpoint, application, or that elusive AuthFlags setting. Open the File Explorer and see what was deposited in the destination path at `C:\MyDeployments`, as shown in Figure 10-34.

Figure 10-34. *Sample deployment project files*

Summary

In this chapter, you learned how to take your application diagrams or, preferably, your predefined systems and deploy them into target logical datacenters. You've had a wonderful time dropping applications onto the Deployment Designer surface, validating the deployment as you go. Finally, you created a Deployment Report (HTML), including deployable files copied to your selected deployment path.

PART 3

Team Edition for Software Developers

CHAPTER 11

Class Designer

The Class Designer is both an architect's tool and a developer's tool. Architects can use it to communicate ideas about an application's structure to the development team. Developers can use it to build a skeleton of the classes before they dive in to the coding of those types.

In this chapter, you will learn how to use the Class Designer, and then see what happens under the hood. We'll begin by looking at what the Class Designer was designed to do.

Design Goals

The VSTS team set out to accomplish four specific goals when they created the Class Designer:

- Help the developer understand existing code.
- Provide a jump-start on creating the initial class design.
- Review and refactor application structure and code easily.
- Provide diagrams and documentation that are relevant throughout the life of the application and aid in its maintenance.

The VSTS team wanted the class diagrams to be relevant when looking at the code. The code generation and synchronization is first-class and seamless in the IDE.

Let's take a look at each of these goals and see how they benefit you.

Understanding Existing Code

Oftentimes you, as a developer, architect, or tester, are called on to review the code of applications that you have not worked on directly. But where do you start when you perform a code review of another application? Typically, this might involve reviewing the UML diagrams, user requirements, and functional specifications, and then diving into the code. But frequently, the UML diagram turns out to be out-of-date, and the requirements have changed, so these are not very helpful.

Being able to generate an entire class diagram directly from the code means that it is accurate and up-to-date. This functionality will save you hours and hours of headaches. On top of this, you have the ability to reverse-engineer any class from any assembly, including .NET Framework classes.

Initial Class Design

Designing classes and their relationships is the first thing that architects or development leads do once the overall requirements and high-level architecture are understood. Many times during this process, the views on how objects relate to each other, what objects should be created, and what properties and methods they should have change. The Class Designer is meant to be a simple tool to quickly and easily generate and change class and application structure. On this front, it succeeds admirably. Creating classes is as simple as drag-and-drop, and relating classes is as simple as three clicks of a mouse button. This will most likely become your primary class design tool because of its simplicity and power.

Reviewing and Refactoring

One of the key things that architects and developers do is to create an object model and examine it. During that examination, they are likely to discover changes that need to be implemented. In some cases, these changes are discovered after the code is implemented. Typically, this is a problem, since you need to rework the diagram, and then rework the code. Many diagramming tools do not give you the ability to refactor models directly from the user interface.

The VSTS team went the extra length to allow you review and change your application structure directly from the design surface of the Class Designer. These steps can range from creating interfaces based on already existing methods to encapsulating a private field as a public property without having to write any additional code.

Note VB and C# support many of the same operations on the Class Designer, but some of the operations are available only when using a particular language. These will be pointed out throughout the chapter.

Relevant Diagrams and Documentation

How many projects have you been involved with that started out by creating a class diagram, only to discover about two weeks into the actual coding that the classes no longer looked like the diagram? Even tools like Rational, which let you forward-engineer your diagrams and synchronize the diagram and code later, have some problems. They require you to manually start a sync process and fix any issues that come up. The VSTS team devised the Class Designer so that there is an instant update between a change in the class diagram and the code and vice versa. Yes, you read that right. If you change the code, the diagram is immediately updated to reflect the change.

Caution If you have a method with code in it, and you delete the method from the class diagram, your code is lost. Anything contained within the method body is deleted along with the method. However, you also have the option to hide a class member, which will cause that member to not be displayed in the Class Designer but to remain in the code.

The advantage to this is that your code and diagrams are always synchronized. The developers and architects can really see the class structure. Additionally, it makes maintenance far easier because the documentation will always be accurate.

> **Note** Almost all code generators/reverse-engineering tools put GUIDs and other identifiers in the code. Microsoft's implementation does not do that, so you get the added benefit of clean code.

Microsoft, UML, and Visio

Microsoft has begun shifting from a purely UML view of the world. The introduction of the domain-specific designers and Class Designer are a first step in that direction. The Class Designer departs from a standard UML model in numerous small ways, but overall, it maintains the type of structure you would find in a typical UML static model. Microsoft has taken this step away from UML for several reasons.

The first is that UML is outdated, especially in terms of .NET. Have you seen how UML represents a read-write property in .NET? It creates two methods: get*MethodName* and set*MethodName*. But if you ever try to forward-engineer a .NET class from this UML notation, it literally creates two different methods to match the diagram. UML also does not understand events. This is a critical point because application development is now (for the most part) *event-driven*.

Another reason for the move away from UML is that it makes diagramming too difficult when dealing with certain types of relationships. A perfect example is object aggregation. What is the difference between an open diamond, closed diamond, and an arrow in a UML diagram? An open diamond is a loose aggregation, a closed diamond is a strong aggregation, and an arrow indicates a dependency. But what is the difference between these three options? What's the point of fooling around with these subtleties? They are so close in actual practice that spending time on the theory is wasteful, and in many cases, their use is incorrect anyway.

Finally, Microsoft wanted to bring the power of structured application development to people who are not experts in UML. The Object Technology Series of books published by Addison-Wesley is the gold standard in explaining UML. The core set of books were written by Ivar Jacobson, Grady Booch, and James Rumbaugh—the fathers of UML. These books cover several thousand pages in total! To use UML effectively, you need a trained team of experts. To read the UML diagrams in such a way that they are of effective use to you as a developer requires a lot of training (and how the UML diagrams are implemented in code is always language-specific). Most people cannot afford the time or effort it takes to go into this type of detail.

The Class Designer addresses these issues. Microsoft has strived to make this tool simple yet powerful. Rather than an abstract diagram that has general relevancy across all languages, it produces a concrete diagram that has specific relevancy for the language you are using. It ignores the nuances of certain types of relationships because the implementation cannot really be determined by the diagram. And the Class Designer allows anyone to provide a simple and straightforward view of object relationships.

Microsoft will continue to ship Visio with the UML stencils, so that developers and architects can leverage their existing skill set in their current environment.

> ## UNIFIED MODELING LANGUAGE TODAY
>
> Of course, UML still has its place in modern development. We are not advocating that you do not learn UML. However, we are questioning the need for such a rigorous standard that provides only abstract definitions of objects and applications. In addition, UML has nine different types of diagrams. Most applications typically use only a few of these types of diagrams: the use case, class (static), sequence, activity, and deployment diagrams. You have already seen in the previous chapters how Microsoft has created concrete instances of the deployment diagram with the logical designers and that these logical designers do a much better job in terms of documenting the correct deployment of an application (as well as allowing you to configure the deployment nodes).
>
> At many of the meetings we attended at Microsoft, the Microsoft developers said that they were going to include some more of the UML model types in later version of VSTS, but that they could not specify which types (we would argue that the only other model types that are very important are the use case and sequence diagrams). However, they also pointed out that Microsoft will continue to distribute Visio and the UML modeling tools included with Visio. This will allow developers and architects to continue to choose how they model their applications.
>
> You will have to make your own choice in terms of the benefit of an investment in learning UML to the degree needed to create robust diagrams. To learn more about UML, read *UML Distilled (Third Edition)* by Martin Fowler (Addison-Wesley, 2003). This is an excellent introduction to the main diagrams in UML and the correct usage of those diagrams.

Using the Class Designer

As an example of using the Class Designer, we will go through the steps of building the `EffortTracking` web service diagram. Your completed diagram will look like the one shown in Figure 11-1.

Note The VB version will not have the `ITaskService` interface since it does not support interface refactoring.

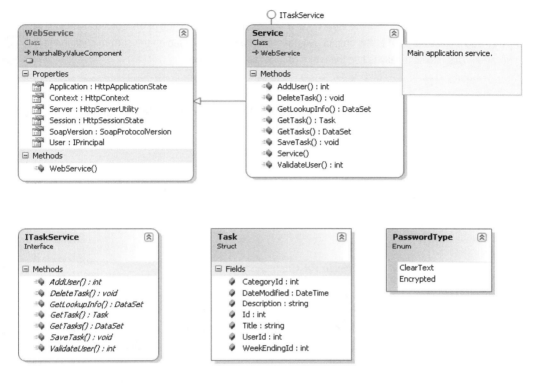

Figure 11-1. *The completed EffortTracking web service*

Note You can create this as a file-based solution or an HTTP-based solution. The sample code distributed with this book is HTTP-based.

To start the diagram, follow these steps:

1. Create a blank solution called EffortTracking.

2. Right-click the EffortTracking solution and select Add ➤ New Website.

3. Select ASP.NET Web Service. Select HTTP (or File) for the location and either C# or VB (whichever you are comfortable with) for the language. Enter the name as http://localhost/EffortTrackingService (or the file location if you selected File). Then click OK. This creates a new web service with a single class called Service.

4. Delete the HelloWorld example from the Service class.

5. Right-click the project, select Add New Item, and then select the Class Designer from the New Item dialog box. Click OK.

Tip Alternatively, you can click the View Class Diagram button from the top of the Solution Explorer, which will also add a class diagram to the project and generate the diagram based on the current code in the application. This makes it easy to see the entire project laid out at once.

6. Drag the `Service.cs` file from the Solution Explorer to the Class Designer surface. This creates the `Service` class, as shown in Figure 11-2.

Figure 11-2. *The Service class in the Class Designer*

Tip You can add existing classes to the diagram by dragging and dropping classes from the Class View window (or right-clicking a class and selecting View Class Diagram) and from the Object Browser, in addition to adding them from the Solution Explorer.

Now, let's look at this single class and some of the options you have for manipulating it.

Exploring a Class

The class name (`Service`) is shown in bold at the top of the class representation. You can edit the name simply by clicking it in the class and changing it. The chevron button in the upper-right corner expands or collapses the class.

Caution Changing the name of the class once you have created it will *not* change the name of the file in which the class is contained. Microsoft is aware of this and hopefully will have this functionality in the next release of VSTS.

Below the object name is the type of object. In this case, Service is a class (as opposed to a struct, enum, interface or delegate). This is not editable. Below the object type is the base class from which the current class derives—in this case, the WebService class. (If the base class type is Object, then no base class type will be displayed.)

When building an object model, you often want to know what the properties of the base classes are or what classes derive from a given class. To see this, right-click the Service class and select Show Base Class. This will result in the WebService class being added to the diagram, as shown in Figure 11-3.

Figure 11-3. *The Service class and WebService class relationship*

If you remove the Service class from the diagram (right-click the Service class and select Remove from Diagram), and then select Show Derived Classes from the WebService class, the Service class would be readded to the diagram. This makes it easy to adjust the depth of information you want to display on the class diagram.

Viewing Properties

The Properties window shows specific property information for the object (or method) that is selected in the Class Designer window, as shown in Figure 11-4.

Figure 11-4. *The Class Designer portion of the IDE*

Table 11-1 describes the class and structure properties that are available. We'll introduce the properties for the other objects in the upcoming sections about those object types.

Table 11-1. *Class/Structure Properties*

Property	Description
Access	Access modifier (public, private, etc.)
Custom Attributes	Any custom attributes that are applied to the class
File Name	Read-only property containing the name of the file in which the class is located
Full Name	Read-only property that gives the full, namespace-qualified name of the class
Generic	Read-only property that indicates if the class is a generic class (for more information, see Generics in the MSDN documentation)
Implements	Read-only property that lists all of the interfaces implemented by this class

Property	Description
Inheritance Modifier	Indicates how (if) this class can be inherited: None, Abstract (MustInherit in VB), Sealed (NotInheritable in VB), or Static (no equivalent in VB) (does not apply to structures)
Inherits	Read-only property indicating the base class of this class (does not apply to structures)
Name	The name of this class
New Member Location	The name of the class file in which new members are added, for use with partial classes (for more information, see Partial Classes in the MSDN documentation)
Remarks	General comments about the class
Summary	A summary of the class's purpose/functionality

Note All of the read-only attributes can be modified by choices made in code. They are just not modifiable via the Properties window.

Working with Class Designer Tools and Options

The Class Designer Toolbox (on the left side of Figure 11-4) shows a list of all of the items that can be added to your applications. Table 11-2 describes the available tools.

Table 11-2. *Class Diagram Toolbox Options*

Shape	Description
Class	Represents a concrete class (i.e., a class that can be instantiated directly)
Enum	Represents an enumeration
Interface	Represents an interface
Abstract Class	Represents a class that cannot be instantiated
Struct (Structure in VB)	Represents a structure
Delegate	Represents a delegate
Inheritance	Represents an inheritance relationship between two classes
Association	Represents an association relationship (aggregation or dependency between two classes)
Comment	A comment regarding the class diagram
Module	A VB code module (not available in C#)

Table 11-3 lists other Class Designer options. These options are accessed either by right-clicking the designer surface or via the Class Diagram menu.

Table 11-3. *Class Designer Menu Options*

Option	Description
Zoom	Allows you to zoom in and out on the diagram
Layout Diagram	Arranges the shapes in a "logical" way (fortunately, this can be undone)
Display Member Types	Displays the field types and the method return types
Adjust Shape Widths	Resizes all shapes on the drawing surface to be as wide as the widest entry in each shape
Group Members ➤ By Kind	Groups each shape by fields, properties, methods, events, etc.
Group Members ➤ By Access	Groups members by access type (public, private, protected, etc.)
Group Members ➤ Sort Alphabetically	Groups all members together alphabetically
Add	Allows you to create types from the design surface without dragging and dropping type shapes from the Toolbox
Export Diagram As Image	Allows you to export any or all of the diagrams in a project to a graphics file (.gif, .jpg, .tif, .png, .emf, and .bmp)

Adding Items to the Class Diagram

When you add items to your diagram, you use the Class Details window, shown in Figure 11-5, to set its attributes. To see this window, right-click an object and select Class Details. It appears at the bottom of the IDE (as shown earlier in Figure 11-4).

Figure 11-5. *The Class Details window*

The title of this window indicates which class you're viewing. All of the methods, properties, fields, and events of a class are listed in this window. The top icon on the left side of this window gives you the option of entering any new item for the class. The four icons below that are used to navigate to different sections of the Class Details window.

The layout will vary depending on the type of object selected on the design surface. The Class Details window for a class includes the Type column, which provides IntelliSense functionality as you enter the member types; the Modifier column, which is a drop-down list of scope options; and the Summary column. To add a summary, click the ellipsis in the Summary column to open the Description dialog box, as shown in Figure 11-6.

Tip By placing a `using` statement (or an `Imports` statement in VB) at the top of the code module, you can avoid having to enter the complete namespace of the type you are trying to add.

Figure 11-6. *The Description dialog box*

Adding Enumerations

You will start the class diagramming process by creating the basic building blocks of the service. The first task is to add a simple enumeration, which will allow the consumer of the service to specify whether the password that is being passed in the `ValidateUser` method (which you will create shortly) is encrypted or in plain text.

Caution Obviously, you would never send a password in clear text in a real application, but this provides a simple example for adding enumerations in the Class Designer.

1. Drag an Enum from the Toolbox onto the design surface. This will bring up the New Enum dialog box.

2. For this enumeration, set the name to PasswordType. Notice that a code file named PasswordType.cs (or PasswordType.vb, depending on the language) is also added to the solution, as shown in Figure 11-7. Click OK to add the enumeration.

Figure 11-7. *The New Enum dialog box*

3. The Class Details window switches to have only four columns: Name, Value, Summary, and Hide. Enter the information in Table 11-4 into the Class Details window.

Table 11-4. *PasswordType Enumeration Details*

Name	Value	Summary
ClearText	0	Indicates the password is unencrypted
Encrypted	1	Indicates the password is encrypted

Tip It is not necessary to enter a value for an enumeration, because the default is to have them sequentially numbered. In many cases, however, it is desirable to be able to perform bitwise operations on an enumeration, so you will want to add specific values.

Now that the information has been entered, you can look at the Properties window for both the enumeration and each class. (The properties are different for almost every item that you can select in the Class Designer.) Table 11-5 describes all of the enumeration properties.

Table 11-5. *Enumeration Properties*

Property	Description
Access	The scope of the enumeration
Base Type	The type of values used for the enumeration (a valid numeric type)
Custom Attributes	Any custom attributes that apply to the enumeration
File Name	Read-only attribute containing the name of the file in which the class is located
Full Name	Read-only attribute that gives the full, namespace-qualified name of the class
Name	The name of this enumeration
Remarks	General comments about the enumeration
Summary	A summary of the enumeration's purpose

Adding Structures

Next, you need to add a `Task` structure to the class diagram. This structure holds a single task item that is used to pass the task from the web service to the web application for use in editing, viewing, and adding information.

1. Drag a Struct (Structure in VB) from the Toolbox to the designer surface.

2. In the New Struct dialog box, enter the name as `Task` and click OK.

3. In the Class Details window, enter each of the items shown in Table 11-6 for the `Task` structure under the Fields node.

Table 11-6. *Task Structure Details*

Name	Type	Modifier	Summary
Id	int (Integer in VB)	public	ID of the task
Title	string	public	Brief description of the task
Description	string	public	Complete description of the task
DateModified	DateTime (Date in VB)	public	Date the task was last updated
WeekEndingId	int (Integer in VB)	public	ID of the week in which the task was performed
CategoryId	int (Integer in VB)	public	ID of the category under which the task falls
UserId	int (Integer in VB)	public	ID of the user who created and owns the task

Note that because a structure is almost identical to a class, all of the options available to you for a regular class are available to you for a structure, except for base classes and derived classes, since structures don't have these. Table 11-1 earlier in the chapter describes the structure properties.

Adding Methods

Now that you have the underlying enumeration and structure, you can start creating methods in the `Service` class. Since the `Service` class is already on the class diagram, you can just start adding methods to it.

1. Select the `Service` class on the design surface. If the Class Details window is not already open, right-click the `Service` class and select Class Details.

2. Click the <add method> entry under the Methods node in the Class Details window and enter `ValidateUser`.

3. Enter `int` (`Integer` in VB) for the Type.

4. Click the ellipsis in the Summary column.

5. Enter **Validates that the user is in the system** for the Summary.

6. Enter **0 if the user is not found, otherwise the ID of the user** for the Returns value.

7. Expand the `ValidateUser` node to expose the method's parameters.

8. Click the <add parameter> entry under the `ValidateUser` method (or press the (key on the keyboard) and enter `userName`. The type defaults to `string`.

9. Enter **The user's name** for the Summary.

10. Click the <add parameter> entry under the `userName` parameter and enter `password`.

11. Enter **The user's password**.

12. Enter a last parameter called `PassType` with a type of `PasswordType`.

13. Enter **Indicates if the user's password is in clear text or plain text** for the Summary.

14. Repeat steps 2–13 for each of the other six methods listed in Table 11-7.

Table 11-7. *Service Class Methods*

Method	Return Type	Parameters	Description
GetLookupInfo	DataSet	N/A	Returns a dataset containing week and category information for use as lookups
ValidateUser	int	string userName, string password, PasswordType type	Validates that the user is in the system

Method	Return Type	Parameters	Description
AddUser	int	string userName, string password	Adds a new user to the system
DeleteTask	void*	int taskID	Deletes a single task item
GetTask	Task	int taskID	Returns a single task
GetTasks	DataSet	int weekID, int userID	Returns an array of Task objects for the given week and user
SaveTask	void*	Task taskToSave	Saves or updates a task in the database

*Void indicates a Sub rather than a Function in VB. When entering these methods in VB, leave the return type blank.

Now that you have all of the methods and descriptions added, switch to the code view for the Service class by double-clicking the class in the diagram (or by right-clicking the class and selecting View Code). Listing 11-1 shows the ValidateUser method.

Note To switch back to the class diagram from the code view, double-click the diagram in the Solution Explorer or select the Class Diagram tab in the main window.

Listing 11-1. *The ValidateUser Method*

C#
```
/// <summary>
/// Validates that the user is in the system.
/// </summary>
/// <param name="userName">The user's name</param>
/// <param name="password">The user's password</param>
/// <param name="passType">Indicates if the user's password is in
/// clear text or plain text.</param>
/// <returns>0 if the user is not found, otherwise the ID of the user</returns>
public int ValidateUser(string userName, string password, PasswordType passType)
    {
        throw new System.NotImplementedException();
    }
```

VB
```
''' <summary>
''' Validates that the user is in the system.
''' </summary>
''' <param name="userName">The user's name.</param>
''' <param name="password">The user's password</param>
```

```
''' <param name="passType">Indicates if the user's password is in clear text or
''' plain text.</param>
''' <returns>0 if the user is not found, otherwise the ID of the user</returns>
Public Function ValidateUser(ByVal userName As String, ByVal password As String, _
ByVal passType As PasswordType) As Integer

End Function
```

All of the information you entered via the Class Details window shows up here in XML comments or in the method signature. All methods created via the Class Details window are created with `NotImplementedException` thrown as the single line of code in the method. Any changes made to either the XML comments or the method signature are automatically updated in the Class Designer. Similarly, if you delete a method from the class in code, it is removed from the designer.

Caution It is critical that you understand that deleting a method in the Class Designer causes the method and *all* of the code in that method to be deleted—nothing will be saved. It is a good idea to ensure that everything is under source code control before you start deleting items from the Class Designer if you have already started writing code. The good news is that you can undo a change to the class diagram.

You also have the option to reorder the parameters of a method. This is available only in C# (in VB you need to do it manually). To do this, right-click the `GetTasks` method in the `Service` class in the diagram and select Refactor ➤ Reorder Parameters. This will bring up the Reorder Parameters dialog box, as shown in Figure 11-8.

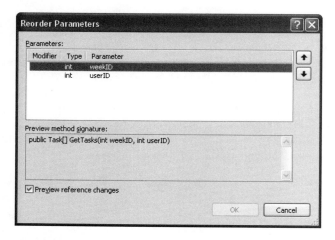

Figure 11-8. *The Reorder Parameters dialog box*

Using this dialog box, you can shift the parameters and view the signature of the method while you are shifting them. This is also the same dialog box that is displayed if you choose to delete a parameter, except that a large warning is displayed at the bottom.

Table 11-8 lists all the method properties, as well as the property, field, and event properties.

Table 11-8. *Method/Property/Event/Field Properties*

Property	Description
Access	The scope of the item (does not apply to destructors)
Accessors	Indicates if the property is read, write, or read-write (applies only to properties)
Constant Kind	Allows you to specify that a field is a constant or read-only field (applies only to fields)
Custom Attributes	Any custom attributes that apply to the item
File Name	Read-only attribute containing the name of the file in which the item is located
Inheritance Modifier	Indicates how (if) this class can be inherited: None, Abstract (MustInherit in VB), Sealed (NotInheritable in VB), and Static (no equivalent in VB) (does not apply to constructors)
Name	The name of this item
New	Indicates if this item overrides or shadows an item with the same name or signature in the base class (applies only to C#) (applies only to properties or methods)
Property Signature	Read-only attribute showing the signature of the property (applies only to properties)
Remarks	General comments about the item
Returns	Description of the value returned (applies only to methods)
Static (Shared in VB)	Indicates if the item is static
Summary	A summary of the item's purpose/functionality
Type	The type the item deals with—the type of the value or the returned value type
Value	The definition of the value supplied to the property (applies only to properties)

Working with Interfaces

While an interface supports essentially all of the same things that a class supports, there are a couple of differences. First, interface methods can only be public—otherwise, why have an interface? And second, there is no implementation in an interface—it is just a set of method signatures. Aside from these two differences, interfaces behave the same as classes in the Class Designer.

Refactoring Interfaces

Refactoring is a fancy term for reorganizing code to make improvements in the architecture of an application. In some cases, it refers to going back and altering code to make it more efficient, but for the purposes of the Class Designer, the first definition applies. (Refactoring is available from a variety of locations, not just the Class Designer.)

> **Note** Refactoring is available only in C#. However, a VB Powertoy is available from www.gotdotnet.com, which provides roughly the same functionality.

To demonstrate how this works, you will extract all of the methods in the Service class in order to create an interface (the interface will not affect the application in any way; it is for demonstration purposes only). To refactor the Service class and create an interface, switch to the designer view (double-click the diagram in the Solution Explorer) and follow these steps:

1. Right-click the Service class, and select Refactor ➤ Extract Interface. This will bring up the Extract Interface dialog box, shown in Figure 11-9.

Figure 11-9. *The Extract Interface dialog box*

2. Name the interface ITaskService and click Select All to include all of the methods as part of the interface. Then click OK.

Extracting the interface does several things:

- Copies the methods to a new interface called ITaskService
- Adds a new code file to the project with the same name as the interface
- Implements the interface on the Service class (represented as a lollipop attached to the Service class)

It will *not* do the following:

- Copy over the XML comments.
- Enclose the `ITaskService` methods in the `Service` class in a region.
- Add the `ITaskService` interface to the Class Designer.

Displaying Interfaces

On the designer, an interface can be represented in a couple of different ways. As you saw when you refactored the `ITaskService` methods, an interface can be represented as a lollipop attached to the class that implements the interface. When the interface is displayed as a lollipop, you can drag it around the outside the class that implements it to any position you want.

You can display an interface on the design surface just as you would any other type of object. To see the refactored `ITaskService` interface, right-click the `ITaskService` lollipop attached to the `Service` class and select Show Interface, or double-click the `ITaskService` text. You can then expand the interface implemented by the class by right-clicking the interface icon and selecting Expand. Figure 11-10 shows the expanded `ITaskService` interface. To collapse the interface display to just the lollipop, right-click and select Collapse.

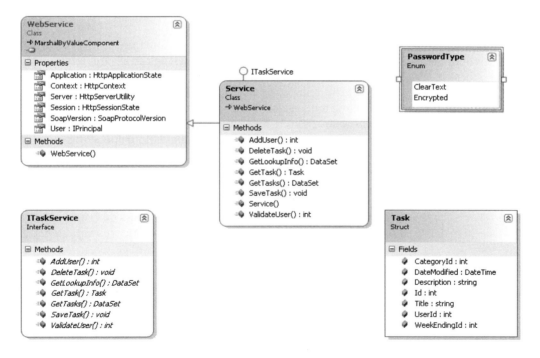

Figure 11-10. *The ITaskService interface*

Deleting Interfaces

You can delete an interface from a class by selecting the interface name and pressing Delete. While the class will no longer implement the interface, the methods are *not* deleted; they are just no longer accessible via the interface definition. To demonstrate how this works, delete the `ITaskService` interface from the `Service` class. You'll see that nothing else is deleted. To reimplement an interface, undo the deletion.

Implementing the Interface

Right-clicking the `ITaskService` lollipop attached to the `Service` class gives you two different options: implement the `ITaskService` interface implicitly or explicitly. Selecting Implicitly (the default) will not make any change to the methods of the implemented interface. Electing to implement the interface explicitly will cause the fully qualified name of the method to be used (while this is an option, it is not recommended).

Showing Object Relationships

With the Class Designer, you can show inheritance and association relationships. Typically, you would do this to identify relationships between classes so that they are explicitly understood.

Displaying Inheritance

Object inheritance is the "classic" relationship shown in diagrams, and the Class Designer will show this automatically between a base class and a derived class. You can see this relationship between the `WebService` class and the `Service` class you created. You can create an inheritance structure manually by clicking the Inheritance tool in the toolbox, selecting the class that you want to subclass, and then selecting the superclass.

You can delete the relationship by deleting the connecting line, or you can hide the inheritance line to help improve the readability of a complicated diagram. Both operations are available by right-clicking the inheritance line.

If you have a generic base class and a superclass of this class, the inheritance Properties window allows you to edit the type arguments that are then displayed in the subclass. To see an example of this, you can create a generic class with the method signature of `public class Class1<T>` (in VB, `Public Class Class1(of T)`), and then have another class inherit from it. Right-clicking the inheritance line will allow you to manipulate the generic type arguments.

Displaying Associations

You can show fields and properties as *associations*. Associations can simply be connections between a field or property and a class or a collection association for an array.

For this section, you will add a field to the Service class for demonstration purposes only. You can delete it at the end of the chapter (again, it does not affect the application in any way).

1. In the Service class, add a field with the name _task of type Task with a private modifier.

2. Right-click the _task field in the Service class (in the class diagram) and select Show As Association. The results are shown in Figure 11-11. This is an alternate way to represent the _task field on the class diagram; it does not alter your class in any way.

Figure 11-11. *The _task field shown as an association*

Note Typically, you will have many connections between items in your diagram and it is impractical to show all of them with an association line. It is best to limit how many of the fields and properties you show like this.

---

3. To convert _task back to the standard type of design, right-click the connection line and select Show As Field.

4. In either the Class Details window or the code, change the _task field to an array of tasks:

```
private Task[] _tasks;
```

5. In the diagram, right-click the _task field again. This time, select the Show As Collection Association option. The results are shown in Figure 11-12. The _task field is now shown as an array with a double arrow. This is yet another way of representing a relationship between two types.

Figure 11-12. *The _task field shown as a collection association*

Using the Association Tool

The Association tool in the Toolbox facilitates the creation of properties that are properties of a given type. For example, if you clicked the Association tool, then the Service class, and then the Task class, the results would be as shown in Figure 11-13. Behind the scenes, a read-write property called Task of type Task was created, with no implementation in either the get or set method (in the next section, you will see how to automate this by refactoring the _task field). This relationship can be converted into a property of the Service class (on the diagram) by right-clicking the association and selecting Show As Property. (Delete the Task property if you added it to experiment.)

Figure 11-13. *The Task property*

Note Unfortunately, in the first release of VSTS, you cannot draw association lines from one type to another that do not have a semantic meaning. Microsoft knows that this is a feature developers and architects want, and realizes that the purpose of the designer is to visualize object relationships, so it is a good bet that you can look forward to this feature in the next release.

Adding Fields and Properties

Properties and fields share similar functionality in the Class Designer. The main difference is that properties have a read-write property. One other difference is the refactoring options. Take a common example: You add a bunch of private fields for which you need to create properties. It is something that we all have to do and we all hate. Microsoft has reduced this effort to zero by allowing you to refactor fields into properties (this is available only in C#).

Tip Many free add-ons duplicate the refactoring options in VB. The VSTS team has noted that this is one of the single most requested features for VB, so it will probably show up in the next version. Until then, any of the add-ons that are available will provide good refactoring support. A web search will return a list of available products (both free and commercial).

Let's see how this works.

1. Select the _task field in the Service class, right-click it, and select Refactor ➤ Encapsulate Field. This will display the Encapsulate Field dialog box, shown in Figure 11-14. Table 11-9 describes all of the fields in the Encapsulate Field dialog box.

Figure 11-14. *The Encapsulate Field dialog box*

2. Select the Preview Reference Changes check box and click OK. This displays the dialog box shown in Figure 11-15.

Figure 11-15. *The Preview Reference Changes dialog box*

3. Select Apply. This generates the following code.

```
C# (Only)
public Task TaskItem
{
    get { return _task; }
    set { _task = value; }
}
```

As you can see, this will be a tremendous time-saver for developers in that they need to code only the fields that persist the data.

■Note The preview screen displays the signature of the new item as it will be seen by other objects and does not necessarily represent the actual format of the final generated code.

Table 11-9. *Encapsulate Field Dialog Box Options*

Option	Definition
Field name	The name of the field to be encapsulated as a property
Property name	The name of the property that will encapsulate the field
Update references	Updates code external to the class that references the field and switches it to use the property
Preview reference changes	Shows a dialog box that previews the code changes (see Figure 11-15)
Search in comments	Performs a search and replace for the field name in comments as well (useful for fixing comments in external classes where the references will be updated)
Search in strings	Performs a search and replace in strings used in code for the field name

Adding Comments

The Class Designer also allows you to add comments. To insert a comment, simply drag-and-drop it from the Toolbox to the designer and enter a note, as shown in Figure 11-16.

Figure 11-16. *A Class Designer comment*

You can add comments anywhere on the diagram, but unfortunately, you cannot link a note to a particular object.

Looking Under the Hood

This section explains how the Class Designer works behind the scenes. To see how the Class Designer generated your diagram, close the Class Designer window, right-click ClassDiagram1.cd, select Open With, and then select the XML Editor. Figure 11-17 shows the XML for the class diagram you created in this chapter. The header information is the standard XML header. Each node of the XML schema is described in Table 11-10.

```xml
 1  <?xml version="1.0" encoding="utf-8"?>
 2  <ClassDiagram MajorVersion="1" MinorVersion="1" DisplayMemberTypes="true">
 3    <Font Name="Tahoma" Size="8.25" />
 4    <Comment CommentText="Main application service.">
 5      <Position X="5.177" Y="1.302" Height="0.75" Width="1.7" />
 6    </Comment>
 7    <Class Name="Service">
 8      <Position X="3.75" Y="1.75" Width="2.25" />
 9      <TypeIdentifier>
10        <FileName>App_Code\Service.cs</FileName>
11        <HashCode>AAAAQAAAAAAAAAAgAAAAAAAgBAAAAgiAAAAAAAAAA=</HashCode>
12      </TypeIdentifier>
13      <Lollipop Position="0.302" />
14    </Class>
15    <Class Name="System.Web.Services.WebService">
16      <Position X="0.5" Y="0.5" Width="2.5" />
17      <TypeIdentifier />
18    </Class>
19    <Struct Name="Task">
20      <Position X="7" Y="1.75" Width="2" />
21      <TypeIdentifier>
22        <FileName>App_Code\Task.cs</FileName>
23        <HashCode>AAAAAAACAAAggEAAAAAAAAwAAAAAIAAAAAAAAAAAAAA=</HashCode>
24      </TypeIdentifier>
25    </Struct>
```

Figure 11-17. *XML view of the Class Designer*

■**Note** All of the XML generated by Microsoft for use throughout Visual Studio conforms to the XML standard.

Table 11-10. *Class Designer Schema Description*

Node	Description
Font	The font family and size used on the Class Designer
Class	The fully qualified name of the class (this node will be the object type—note Struct for the Task object)
Position	The X and Y position and the width of the class
TypeIdentifier	Contains the specification for the class type
FileName	The name of the file in which the type is contained
HashCode	A hash of all of the properties, methods, fields, and events of the type

> **Caution** Microsoft is not, at this time, publishing an "official" XML schema for the Class Designer. Any code that you create to work directly against the schema (there is no good reason for doing this) is created at your own risk because it may not be compatible with the next version.

When we first looked at this, we had only two questions: How does the designer know what is contained within the class if it is not held in the XML, and what the heck is the `HashCode` for? It turns out that both are excellent questions, although the answer to the first question was obvious after it was explained to us.

All of the information displayed on the design surface is gathered from the class itself. It is not stored as metadata specifically for the Class Designer. This is how Microsoft ensures that the data displayed on the designer is identical to the information in the code.

The `HashCode`'s purpose turns out to be a lot more complicated. As noted in Table 11-10, the `HashCode` is a hash of everything found in the type. But what is it used for? It is used to match the object on the designer to the type in the code. It allows the Class Designer to know what object to find and interrogate in order to populate the class details. The explanation makes sense, but then you may have yet another question: What if you change the name of the file that your type is stored in, change the name of the type, change the method names, add or a delete a few methods or properties, and so on? Another good question. The Class Designer uses a fuzzy logic search algorithm to try to match up the type of the Class Designer with the type in your solution. If it cannot do this, the type shape will still appear in the designer, though it will be red. You will need to manually attach it to the correct type in the solution or delete it and readd it. To readd the type, just drag-and-drop it from the Solution Explorer or Class View window.

> **Note** It is unfortunate to note that for this release of VSTS, the Class Designer is not designed to be extensible. We hope this will be a feature added in the next version.

Summary

This chapter has presented an in-depth view of the Class Designer. Throughout the chapter, you have seen how each of the features of the Class Designer supports the four user scenarios that were the guiding factors in the design of the Class Designer. The Class Designer gives you the opportunity to reverse-engineer existing code and visualize existing code in order to better understand it. It allows you to refactor code through the designer without diving into the code itself. The key feature of the Class Designer is that it ensures that your object model and documentation remain accurate and helpful from the first day of the application to the last day of an application, and into the maintenance cycle.

CHAPTER 12

Unit Testing and Code Coverage

Unit testing is a repeatable, automated process of testing specific methods in code to make sure that they do what they are supposed to do. By testing the smallest unit of code for defects, you can be sure that when you are finished, you have a stable base on which to build. The automated nature of unit tests also allows for *regression testing*, which is the process of retesting previously tested units of code after a modification is made.

Unit testing is an area of testing that for many years was performed in a nonrepeatable and haphazard way. Typically, developers would, in addition to having to write the application, also need to write a test harness to run tests. With the introduction of tools such as JUnit for Java and NUnit for .NET, unit testing has become much easier.

This chapter explains how to perform unit tests with VSTS, ranging from simple one-method tests to data-driven tests based on data stored in a testing database. In addition, we will look at code coverage results from the unit tests. *Code coverage* describes the amount of code covered by the unit tests (including manual unit tests).

We've included this chapter in the Developers section of this book because developers are responsible for their code. While testers also may create unit tests, they generally test larger pieces of functionality. However, some items covered in this chapter relate to all types of testing, so it is worthwhile for testers to read through this chapter as well.

Planning Unit Tests

Before you can start performing unit tests, you need a plan. It is not enough to just sit down and write some unit tests without having thought through all of the possible scenarios (or at least all of the common scenarios). You need to start by drawing up a set of unit testing rules that can be used by everyone on your team.

Take a look at this sample method:

C#
```
//Method returns true if the person is over age 18, otherwise false
public bool AgeCheck(DateTime dayOfBirth)
{
//Some processing code here…
}
```
VB

```
'Method returns true if the person is over age 18, otherwise false
Public Function AgeCheck(dob as Date) as Boolean
     'Some processing code here…
End Function
```

The premise of this code is fairly straightforward. It accepts a date of birth and validates the age. At first glance, you may think that you simply need to run a test that provides a date of birth prior to 18 years ago and a date of birth later than 18 years ago. And that works great for 80% of the dates that someone is likely to provide, but that only scratches the surface of what needs to be tested here. The following are some of the tests you may need to run for the AgeCheck method:

- Check a date from exactly 18 years ago to the day.
- Check a date from further back in time than 18 years.
- Check a date from fewer than 18 years ago.
- Check for a null value.
- Check for the results based on the very minimum date that can be entered.
- Check for the results based on the very maximum date that can be entered.
- Check for an invalid date format being passed to the method.
- Check two year dates (such as 05/05/49) to determine what century the two-year format is being treated as.
- Check the time (if that matters) of the date.
- Check for graceful failure.
- If the age to check against is provided via a configuration file, check that the correct age to check against is being set/read.

As you can see, based on just a simple method declaration, you can determine at least 5 and maybe as many as 11 valid unit tests (not all tests may be required). Dates are, in general, one of the most difficult things to handle in development (right behind strings). Therefore, you will almost always have more rules for date testing than any other type of tests.

Here are the basic unit testing areas:

Boundary values: Test the minimum and maximum values allowed for a given parameter. An example here is when dealing with strings. What happens if you are passed an empty string? Is it valid? On the other hand, what if someone passes a string value of 100,000 characters and you try to convert the length of the string to a short?

Equality: Test a value that you are looking for. In the case of the age check example used here, what if the date passed also includes the time? An equality check will always fail in that case, but in every other case, the results would come out correctly.

Format: Never trust data passed to your application. This is particularly applicable to any boundary methods, where you can get malicious hackers looking to crack your system. But poorly formatted data from any source can cause problems if you do not check it.

Culture: Various tests need to be performed to ensure that cultural information is taken into account. In general, you can skip these tests if the application is written for a single culture only (although, even this is not a good indicator, because you can write a test for a U.S. English system but have it installed by someone in the U.K.). Otherwise, string, date, currency, and other types of values that can be localized should always be checked (for example, if you are expecting a date in the U.S. format but get it in the European format, then some values will work, but some will not). An example is the date 02/01/2000. In the U.S. format, this is February 1, 2000; in the European format, it is January 2, 2000. While this test would pass (most of the time), changing the U.S. format to 01/23/2000 would fail in the European format.

Exception paths: Make sure that the application handles exceptions—both expected and unexpected—in the correct manner and in a secure fashion. Frequently, developers test the normal path and forget to test the exception path. VSTS includes a special process for testing the exception paths. Additionally, this will test how data is logged during a failure.

Tip Not *everything* needs to be tested. In most cases, you want to test the most used paths of the application for the most common scenarios. An example of wasted time would be writing tests for simple property assignments. While this may be needed in specific situations, you cannot possibly write every test for every scenario—it takes too long even with VSTS!

These five areas cover the majority of the situations you will run into when performing unit tests. Any plan should take into account tests that cover these areas of potential failure. Of course, this is by no means a comprehensive set of rules for unit testing. You will undoubtedly discover others related to your specific applications.

Note The unit testing areas listed here apply to the .NET platform. We have not included basic testing rules regarding languages such as C and unmanaged C++. Tools like PREfast are designed to catch those areas of potential failure that are outside the realm of unit testing. PREfast (discussed in Chapter 13) catches typical unmanaged code errors, such as buffer overflow errors.

> **TEST-DRIVEN DEVELOPMENT**
>
> In the past several years, Agile Development methodologies have risen in popularity. Extreme Programming (XP) is probably the best known Agile Development methodology, and a core tenet of XP is that unit tests are written before the code is written. One of the key benefits of writing unit tests first is that you know, without a doubt, when a piece of functionality has been completed, because that's when the test succeeds. Because XP is a short-release cycle methodology, coding must often be done as quickly and as accurately as possible. The practice of writing unit tests first supports this goal.
>
> The process of creating tests first (at the construction stage) to validate your application is called *test-driven development*. The methodology of test-driven development follows this path: Write the unit test, write enough code for the test to succeed, and then refactor the code to make it more efficient. Another way of saying this in the test-driven development terminology is "red/green/refactor." Red is the test fail stage, green is the test pass stage, and refactoring is altering the code to make it more efficient. While VSTS does not, per se, support this specific process, since it is a process and not a technology, you can use VSTS to support the test-driven development methodology.
>
> The problem with test-driven development is that it still relies on developers to plan the unit tests, write them, and execute them. While tools like JUnit, NUnit, and VSTS make this process a lot easier, it is still a process that needs to be followed by all. Most developers (and we are speaking from experience here) cannot stand to do testing. VSTS helps eliminate that problem by providing policies, which you can enable to say that unit tests must have been performed before code can be checked in (refer to Chapter 3).
>
> Then there is the problem of how to come up with a comprehensive set of criteria on which the individual unit tests should be based. The list of tests must be developed by the developer in conjunction with a functional or business analyst. The analyst alone will not supply you with all of the possible combinations of issues that could arise, simply because analysts do not think like developers. Likewise, a developer cannot necessarily come up with all of the valid tests because some of those tests may be predicated on business situations. In the list of unit tests shown earlier for the sample AgeCheck method, an analyst might supply you with the first three items in the list. All of the other tests in the list are generally language-specific tests and input validation tests, so they are not tests that a business user would consider.
>
> You can find a lot more information about test-driven development on the Web. An excellent book on unit testing is *Test Driven Development: By Example* by Kent Beck (Addison-Wesley, 2002).

Creating Unit Tests

Now that you have seen some of the thought that goes into planning for unit testing, it is time to look at how to create unit tests. In this section, you will learn how to generate unit tests.

Note For the examples in this chapter, use the downloadable code available from the Source Code section of the Apress website (www.apress.com).

To create your first test, follow these steps:

1. Open the `Service` class.

2. Right-click within the `Service` class (but not within a specific method) and select Create Tests.

3. In the Generate Unit Tests dialog box, ensure that the `AddUser` method is checked and that the output project is set as Create a New Visual [*Language Choice*] Test Project, as shown in Figure 12-1.

Figure 12-1. *The Generate Unit Tests dialog box*

4. Optionally, click the Settings button to configure how the tests are generated. This displays the dialog box shown in Figure 12-2. Table 12-1 describes the settings available in this dialog box. For this example, we will use the defaults, so you don't need to change any of these settings. Click Cancel to close the dialog box.

5. Click OK in the Generate Unit Tests dialog box.

6. Enter the project name as `EffortTrackingServiceTests`, and then click OK. A new project called `EffortTrackingServiceTests` will be added to the `EffortTracking` solution.

Figure 12-2. *The Test Generation Settings dialog box*

Tip While you do not have to add tests to specific testing projects, it is a good idea. This way, you can keep your tests separate from the code that you are testing, and more important, separate from those you are releasing.

Table 12-1. *Test Code Generation Configuration Options*

Item	Description
File Name	The name of the file in which the tests will be created. The [File] in front of the name indicates that the generated test file will be prefixed with the name of the file in which the class you are testing resides.
Class Name	The name of the class given to the test class. The [Class] in front of the name indicates that the generated class will be prefixed with the name of the class being tested.
Method Name	The name of the generated test method. The [Method] in front of the name indicates that the generated method will be prefixed with the name of the method that you are testing.
Mark all test results Inconclusive by default	The Assert statement will identify this method as being inconclusive. Checking this adds the following line to the end of each test method: Assert.Inconclusive("Verify the correctness of this test method.").
Enable generation warnings	Reports any warnings during the test code generation process.

Item	Description
Globally qualify all types	Adds the root namespace to all type declarations. This is important if you have classes with the same names in multiple namespaces. If you do not select this, the compiler makes a best guess, which frequently can be wrong.
Generate tests for items that already have tests	Creates additional tests for the same method by appending an incremented number to the end of the test method name. If you don't select it, a test method will not be generated.
Enable doc comments	Generates XML comments with each test. Turning this off simply removes the comments.

You can also start the Unit Test Wizard from the main menu. Just select Test ➤ New Test to open the dialog box shown in Figure 12-3. Select Unit Test Wizard and click OK. This will take you to the dialog box shown in Figure 12-1.

Figure 12-3. *The Add New Test dialog box*

As you can see, the Add New Text dialog box offers several other test types. Selecting the Unit Test icon from the Add New Test dialog box will create a blank testing class in the test project of your choice. The Manual Test and Ordered Test types are covered later in this chapter. The other test types are covered in Chapters 15 and 16.

■**Note** Generic Tests are not covered in this book. The reason for this is that the Generic test is a wrapper for use with simple, existing test tools. More information on this "test type" can be found in the MSDN documentation.

Understanding Unit Tests

VSTS creates several files in your testing solution. In reality, VSTS can only do so much work for you. It generates the skeleton, which you will need to complete. Here, we'll look at the key parts of the unit test. In the "Completing the Test Methods" section later in this chapter, you'll see how to add the other necessary pieces.

The primary file in the testing solution is the `ServiceTest` file. (The naming convention for this file is customizable, but in general it is best to leave it in the *ClassName*Test form.) First, we'll look at a method in this file, and then we'll look at the test class.

Exploring a Test Method

Open the `ServiceTest` file and scroll down to the `AddUserTest` method, which is shown in Listing 12-1.

Listing 12-1. *The AddUserTest Method*

C#
```
[TestMethod()]
public void AddUserTest()
{
    Service target = new Service();
    string userName = null; // TODO: Initialize to an appropriate value
    string password = null; // TODO: Initialize to an appropriate value
    int expected = 0;
    int actual;
    actual = target.AddUser(userName, password);
    Assert.AreEqual(expected, actual,
    "EffortTrackingServiceTests.localhost.Service.AddUser did "
    + "not return the expected value.");
    Assert.Inconclusive("Verify the correctness of this test method.");
}
```
VB
```
<TestMethod()>
Public Sub AddUserTest()
    Dim target As Service = new Service()
    Dim userName As String = nothing ' TODO: Initialize to an appropriate value
    Dim password As String = nothing ' TODO: Initialize to an appropriate value
    Dim expected As Integer
    Dim actual as Integer
     Actual = target.AddUser(userName, password)
    Assert.AreEqual(expected, actual, _
    "EffortTrackingServiceTests.localhost.Service.AddUser did " _
    & "not return the expected value.")
    Assert.Inconclusive("Verify the correctness of this test method.")
End Sub
```

The first line is the `TestMethod` attribute, which denotes that this is a test method. This allows this method to be displayed in the various test management dialog boxes. The `TestMethod` attribute takes no arguments; it is simply an identifier.

Each test method is created based on the settings in the Test Generation Settings dialog box (Figure 12-2). The default setting creates the test method in the format of the name of the method being tested followed by `Test`.

Tip Because you can have more than one test method that targets a given application method, you want to make sure you develop a standard naming convention. A good naming convention is the method being tested, plus the type of test, followed by `Test`. For example, if you were testing a null username value in the `AddUser` tests, you might name the test `AddUserNullUsernameTest`.

Each test method that is set up for you will provide a variable for each of the parameters requested by the method being tested and an instantiated reference to the object being tested—in this case, a web service. The call to the method being tested is created for you. All you need to do is initialize the variables for the call to work (unless you are testing null values).

Notice the last two lines of the method, which contain the `Assert` statements. These are the most important statements in the method because they report the status to the testing infrastructure to enable the infrastructure to mark the test as a success or failure. If the `Assert` statement is true, then no exceptions are thrown and the method is marked as "passed." If the `Assert` statement is false, an exception is thrown and the test is marked as "failed."

In the case of a generated test where the method being tested returns a value, two calls to `Assert` are made. The first one is the standard comparison statement, which will throw an exception if the values are not equal. The second statement is placed in all generated tests to indicate that no one has yet looked at the method and initialized the values used in the method call or the expected value.

Caution Never catch an `AssertFailedException`, as this exception is used by the testing infrastructure to mark a test as failed.

When generating a unit test for a method that does not return a value, the `Assert` statement reads, "A method that does not return a value cannot be verified." For these types of methods, a different process must be followed in order to verify the outcome of a test, depending on the purpose of the method being tested. For methods that write to a database, for example, you could write a statement that reads from the database to verify that the method succeeded.

Exploring a Test Class

The ServiceTest class is a test class because it is tagged with the TestClass attribute, which makes the ServiceTest class visible in the various test management windows. The TestClass attribute takes no arguments. Several attributes are provided for you automatically upon the creation of a test class.

The method tagged with the TestInitialize attribute will be called before each and every run of a test in the given test class. This is important to note because it limits when and how you should use this method. The TestCleanup attribute is used to denote the method that will be called after each and every test is run in a given class. For example, suppose you are running a test that changes or adds data, but you need to run the test several times to test various aspects of a change. You could use a method tagged with the TestInitialize attribute to start a transaction that can be rolled back in the TestCleanup method, or you might perform some other action to reset test conditions for the next run.

■**Caution** If more than one method is tagged with the TestInitialize attribute, an exception will be thrown.

The TestContext class is used in data-driven tests and to gather information for a *specific* test that is currently running. You will see how this works in the "Data-Driven Testing" section later in this chapter.

Other attributes are listed in Table 12-2. Several of these attributes will be demonstrated later in this chapter.

Table 12-2. *Additional Testing Attributes*

Attribute	Description
AssemblyInitialize	Runs before any other classes in an assembly are run.
AssemblyCleanup	Runs after all other classes in an assembly are run.
ClassInitialize	Runs before any tests in a class are run. See the "Preparing the Production Database" section later in this chapter.
ClassCleanup	Runs after all tests in a class are run. See the "Preparing the Production Database" section later in this chapter.
DataSourceAttribute	Specifies the data source for a data-driven test. See the "Data-Driven Testing" section later in the chapter.
DeploymentItemAttribute	Specifies specific items (typically files), which must be deployed to the test directory (which is different from the debug folder) before a test is run.
DescriptionAttribute	Describes the test in the test management screens.
PriorityAttribute	Sets the priority of the test. This is more of a notational attribute as it has no actual effect on the order in which tests are run.

Attribute	Description
OwnerAttribute	Indicates who owns the test.
TestPropertyAttribute	Allows you to specify custom properties for a test. See the "Adding Test Properties" section later in this chapter.
AspNetDevelopmentServerAttribute	Specifies that the given test is hosted by either the ASP.NET Development Server or IIS if this is an ASP.NET test.
UrlToTestAttribute	The URL that contains the website that will be tested.
AspNetDevelopmentServerHostAttribute	Provides various settings to point the test to the correct web server host.

Managing Unit Tests

VSTS gives developers and testers the ability to manage tests in many different ways. It provides ways to view both high-level and detailed information. You can view test results or code coverage results from within the IDE, and test management is intuitive, so you do not need to learn how to use a new and complex tool.

The two main starting places for test management are the Test View window and the Test Manager window.

Using the Test View Window

To open the Test View window, select Test ➤ View and Author Tests from the main menu.

Figure 12-4. *The Test View window*

As shown in Figure 12-4, the Test View window displays the list of tests and the type of test. The options at the top of the window allow you to run the tests, edit the test configuration, and apply a filter in order to be able to find specific tests. You can start a test run in debug mode. This allows you to run the test and debug the unit test code and the code in the method being tested.

Double-clicking the test will open the code module where the test is contained. Right-clicking a test will allow you to perform various actions such as running a specific test, creating a new test, and viewing the properties of a test. The properties of the tests are described in Table 12-3.

Note Manual tests, such as `manualtest1` in Figure 12-4, are treated somewhat differently in the IDE. When you double-click a manual test, VSTS will open the manual test in a Word or another text editor, so it can be edited. Manual tests are covered in the "Manual Testing" section later in this chapter.

Table 12-3. *Test Properties*

Property	Description
Associated Work Items	Work items associated with the specific test in the Team Foundation work item database (applicable only if Team Explorer is installed)
Class Name	The name of the class in which the test method resides
Data Access Method	For use by data-driven testing; specifies sequential or random access
Data Connection String	The connection string to the database providing the data to drive tests
Data Provider	The database connection provider
Data Table Name	The table from which the data to drive the test is pulled
Deployment Items	List of all items to be deployed (see the `DeploymentItemAttribute` in Table 12-2)
Description	A description of the purpose of the test
Full Class Name	The fully qualified name of the class
ID	Unique test name
Iteration	The iteration in the life cycle with which this test is associated
Namespace	The namespace in which the test resides
Non-runnable	Error
Owner	The name of the individual who owns the test
Priority	Indicates the importance of the test but has no effect on the order in which the test is run
Project	The project in which the test resides
Project Area	The area (in the Team System methodology being used) where the test resides (active only when using Team Explorer and when the test is associated with a team project)
Project Relative Path	The path to the file in which the test class resides relative to the project

Property	Description
Solution	The solution in which the test resides
Test Enabled	Indicates if the test will be executed during a test run
Test Name	The name of the test
Test Storage	The assembly that contains the compiled test
Test Type	Unit or manual test

With the Test View window, you can look at, categorize, and view test properties. The Test Manager window offers other options for managing your tests.

Using the Test Manager Window

The main window for managing tests is the Test Manager window, shown in Figure 12-5.

Figure 12-5. *The Test Manager window*

■**Note** The Test Manager window is available only in the Team Edition for Software Testers edition, not the Developers edition. To manage tests in the Developers edition, you must use the Test View window.

As you can see, there are a few more options for managing and categorizing your tests in this window than in the Test View window. You can view lists of tests, tests that are not in a list, and all loaded tests. In addition, you can load additional tests that are not part of the current solution by selecting the Load Tests into Test Manager option from the list of available tasks in the lower-left side of the Test Manager window.

Note To view the different tests in each grouping, just select the text in the tree view. Do not check the box next to the test. Checking the box will mark the test as enabled for the next test run.

Creating Test Lists

Test lists allow you to organize tests into distinct groupings to make them easier to manage. In the example you have been using so far, a logical breakdown might be to group the tests in Tasks, Users, Build Verification, and Miscellaneous lists.

To create a new test list, click Organize Tests in the lower-left corner of the Test Manager window. This will display the dialog box shown in Figure 12-6.

Figure 12-6. *The Create New Test List dialog box*

Enter the name and description for your new test list and select where you want it to show up in the list of existing test lists (note that there is no existing hierarchy when you create your first list).

Note You can nest the lists as deep as you like, but in general, they should not be listed too deep. As a best practice, do not nest tests any more than two deep to keep the test order and dependencies understandable and maintainable.

To organize the tests into the test lists, simply drag tests from the Tests Not in a List view to the appropriate lists. A test can also be associated with more than one list. To do this, hold down the Ctrl key and drag the test to the additional list. This will cause the test to be displayed twice in the full list of tests—once for each list it is in.

As you add items to the lists, they will disappear from the Tests Not in a List view. You can select to view all the loaded tests to see all of your tests at once, or you can view a specific list to see only the tests associated with that list.

Tip In the Test Manager window, you can select the Add/Remove columns option and add the Test List column, which will allow you to see which list each test is associated with when you have all of the loaded tests displayed.

Adding Test Properties

The `TestProperty` attribute is a special attribute that allows you to define one or more additional properties for any specific test. The `TestProperty` attribute accepts a property name and a description. This is useful as a way to further describe tests with information that is displayed in the Properties window.

To see how this works, switch to the code view for the `ServiceTest` class and select the `ValidateUserTest` method. Add the following attribute to the method:

C#
```
[TestProperty("My Property", "A new attribute")]
```
VB
```
<TestProperty("My Property", "A new attribute")>
```

Next, switch to the Test Manager window and select the `ValidateUserTest`. Right-click it and select Properties. In the Properties window, you will see a new property called My Property with the accompanying description. These properties are accessible from within the tests through the use of reflection. See the MSDN `TestPropertyAttribute` topic for more information.

Creating Ordered Tests

Another step you can take to manage your tests is to specify the order in which they run. For example, you might be testing that a user can be added to the system, and then that this new user can log on to the system successfully. This means that you need to execute the `AddUser` method and then the `ValidateUser` method. If you execute the second test first, then both methods will fail. To make sure the methods are executed in the correct order, you can create an *ordered test*.

> **Note** It is considered a best practice to write tests that are independent of one another (again, the goal of a unit test is to test the smallest unit of code available and not a whole chain of events if possible). To do this, you can run scripts that set the database up before each test run. However, in real-world practice, circumstances may prevent this. In those cases, an ordered test run is the best solution to the problem.

To create an ordered test, follow these steps:

1. Select Test ➤ New Test from the main menu.

2. Select Ordered Test. Name it NewUserLogonTest, and make sure it is set to be added to the EffortTrackingServiceTest project. Then click OK

3. In the Ordered Test window, shown in Figure 12-7, select AddUserTest and then ValidateUserTest.

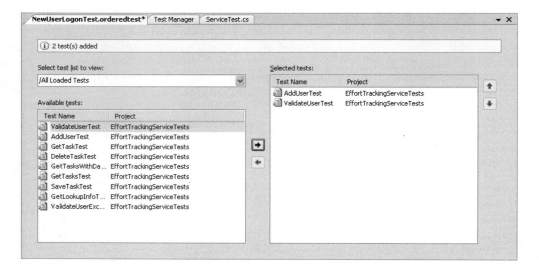

Figure 12-7. *The Ordered Test window*

4. Save your changes.

In the Test Manager window, you will now see an additional test called NewUserLogonTest. Double-clicking this test will reopen the Ordered Test window. When you run this test, both the AddUserTest and the ValidateUserTest will run in the correct order.

> **Note** While you can nest ordered tests inside each other (that is, create one ordered test and then a second ordered test that contains one or more other ordered tests), a best practice is not to nest them any more than two tests deep. This will help make it easier to determine which tests you are going to run and will keep the interdependencies to a minimum.

Setting Up Tests

Up to now, you have seen how to create and manage tests. But you're still not ready to run your tests. Before you run a test, you should configure it so that it runs the way you want it to run. You also need to complete the test methods so the tests run correctly. You need to go through the setup process for each group of tests only once.

Configuring Test Runs

Under the Solution Items folder in your solution is a file called `localtestrun.testrunconfig`. This file contains all of the test configuration information for your solution. Double-click this file to open the dialog box shown in Figure 12-8.

Tip Your solution can have multiple test run configuration files associated with it and you can specify, for each test run, which configuration file will be used.

Figure 12-8. *The Test Run Configuration dialog box*

The Test Run Configuration dialog box allows you to configure properties that apply to any tests associated with this test configuration. To associate a configuration file with a test run, select Test ➤ Select Active Test Run Configuration from the main menu and choose the appropriate configuration file.

The Test Run Configuration dialog box includes eight sections, which are described in the following sections.

General

The General section allows you to specify a configuration name and optionally a configuration description. The naming scheme section is used for the report of results for the given test run. The default naming scheme uses the currently logged-on user logon name and the name of the machine on which the tests are run, followed by the date and time of the test run. You can also create a user-defined naming scheme and choose whether to append the date and time.

Controller and Agent

In the Controller and Agent section, you can specify whether to run the tests locally or on a remote machine. Change this setting with care, however, because you cannot debug the test code or the code being tested if you choose to run the test on a remote machine. Controllers and agents are discussed in more detail in Chapter 16.

Code Coverage

Code coverage is an important companion to unit testing. For example, suppose you have an application that is 1,000 lines long scattered in several classes, and it seems to work fine. Now say that you run unit tests (which all pass) and look at the coverage results, and find that only 790 lines of code were actually run (also described as *exercised*) by your tests. This would indicate that even though all of your unit tests passed, you are not testing everything! It may indicate that you have 210 lines of code that cannot be reached by the current application structure or that the unit tests are not complete. In some cases (especially in reference to regression tests), the code may be "dead," which is a situation that occurs when code is no longer needed. In these cases, the code should be removed. Issues like these cannot be discovered simply by unit testing alone.

In the Code Coverage section of the Test Run Configuration dialog box, you can specify that you want to enable or disable code coverage statistics during a test run by selecting the assemblies or web pages for which you want to enable the coverage. By default, all of the web pages and assemblies that your current solution knows about are displayed. You can add other assemblies to this list by clicking the Add Artifacts button and selecting the assemblies to instrument.

Caution When you select the Add Artifacts option, the resulting assemblies are copied and altered by Visual Studio in order to insert the correct code to instrument them for this procedure.

When you select the option to use code coverage, you have two additional options:

- Instrument the Assembly in Place, which specifies that the assemblies are altered and placed in the same deployment area as your project would normally place them. If the assemblies are not instrumented in place, they are placed in a separate test directory, which contains all of the binaries for the given test.

- Re-sign the Assembly, which allows Visual Studio to re-sign the assemblies after they have been altered.

■**Caution** Code coverage and performance testing do not play well together. In general, if you have code coverage enabled, your performance sessions will not run correctly.

Deployment

In order to isolate tests from any other environment, Visual Studio runs the test in a location different from the one where the code is compiled. The Deployment section of the Test Run Configuration dialog box allows you to specify where that code is copied (a local folder or a remote folder). In addition, you can specify other files (such as database files, configuration files, or graphics files that are not directly part of your project) or folders to be deployed to the temporary testing folder.

Hosts

The Hosts section allows you to specify the host for your code. There are two options: Default and ASP.NET. The Default setting is used for non-ASP.NET unit tests. There are no configuration options for the Default setting.

Selecting ASP.NET allows you to specify some additional settings. You will need to supply the URL to test, and then specify if the tests will be run in a virtual web server or an IIS web server. If you specify a virtual web server (ASP.NET Development Server), you will need to provide the path to the website (the physical location of the files, not a URL) and the application root name. For ASP.NET applications, if you select Default, everything will be configured according to the project settings.

■**Note** The Hosts section properties correspond directly with the attributes listed in Table 12-2 earlier in this chapter. Entering these properties causes the information to be added in the form of attributes to the test class.

Setup and Cleanup Scripts

The Setup and Cleanup Scripts section allows you to specify a script that will run at the beginning of an entire test run and another script that runs at the end. This is different from the initialize and cleanup methods in an actual test class, because those are run at the beginning and end of tests that reside in the given test class. The scripts themselves can be batch files, executables, or virtually any other type of script that can be executed. Additionally, these scripts are independent of the test itself so they will run before and after any test associated with the configuration file.

Test Timeouts

The Test Timeouts section allows you to specify that a test will be either aborted after a given period of time or marked as failed after a given period of time.

Web Test

The Web Test section allows you to specify properties specific to web applications, including the following:

- The number of times a test is run
- Whether that run count is specified by you or by the data available in a database
- The type of web browser that the test requests will come from
- The connection speed of those requests
- Specify think times (delays between actions) for the requests to provide a more realistic simulation of how your website will be used

---

Caution The Web Test settings do not take the place of true load tests. See Chapter 16 for details about performing load tests.

Completing the Test Methods

For your test to run correctly, you need to complete the test methods. Listing 12-2 shows the changes necessary for the `ValidateUserTest` method. The database included with the code for this chapter has two entries in the `Owners` table, `TestUser1` and `TestUser2`, both with a password of `password`.

Listing 12-2. *The Finished ValidateUserTest Method*

C#

```
[TestMethod()]
public void ValidateUserTest()
{
    Service target = new Service();
    target.Credentials = System.Net.CredentialCache.DefaultCredentials;
    string userName = "TestUser";
    string password = "password";
    PasswordType type = PasswordType.ClearText;

    int expected = 1;
    int actual;

    actual = target.ValidateUser(userName, password, type);

    Assert.AreEqual(expected, actual,
        EffortTrackingServiceTests.localhost.Service.ValidateUser did not " +
           "return the expected value.");
}
```

VB
```vb
    <TestMethod()>
Public Sub ValidateUserTest()
    Dim target As Service = New Service()
    target.Credentials = System.Net.CredentialCache.DefaultCredentials
    Dim userName  As String = "TestUser"
    Dim password  As String = "password"
    Dim type As PasswordType = PasswordType.ClearText

    Dim expected  As Integer = 1
    Dim actual  As Integer

    actual = target.ValidateUser(userName, password, type)

    Assert.AreEqual(expected, actual, _
        EffortTrackingServiceTests.localhost.Service.ValidateUser did not " _
        & "return the expected value.")
End Sub
```

These changes must be made for each of the tests in your solution.

Setting Other Configuration Options

Visual Studio provides some default options for testing that you can change via the IDE. To edit these values, select Tools ➤ Options from the main menu and expand the Test Tools node. You'll see three sections of options:

- The Default Dialog Box Action section allows you to specify the prompt settings that Visual Studio will display to you based on certain actions.

- The Test Execution section allows you to specify the defaults for code coverage coloring, in-place instrumentation, and the web root for all web-based tests.

- The Test Project section allows you to specify the default type of test project created (the language that it is created will appear as the default in the Add New Test dialog box, shown earlier in Figure 12-3) and the files that are automatically added to the new test project.

Running Tests

You are finally ready to run a test. Go to the Test Manager window and check the `ValidateUserTest` method and the `DeleteTaskTest` (without making any changes to the `DeleteTaskTest` code). Make sure that you have selected the Code Coverage option in your configuration file.

■**Caution** Because selecting the Code Coverage option modifies your assemblies, make sure that if the class files are under configuration control, they are checked out. Otherwise, the debugging and instrumentation will not work!

From the Test Manager window, click the Run icon and select the Run Checked Tests option. Alternatively, you can select the Debug Checked Tests option, which allows you to add breakpoints in the test class. With breakpoints, you can trace through setup and teardown and into the actual code being tested.

After you select to run a test, you will see the Test Results window, as shown in Figure 12-9. While the test is running, you can pause or cancel the test run as a whole by clicking the Pause or Stop button in the Test Results window.

Figure 12-9. *The Test Results window*

During the test run, the status of the test is shown on the yellow status bar of the Test Results window, and each test is shown in the list below with its status (Pending, Running, Passed, Aborted or Failed). If a test fails, the error message for the failure is also shown, as you can see for the `DeleteTaskTest` in Figure 12-9. Also notice the Rerun link in the Test Results window, which allows you to rerun tests that failed (note that the one failed test was left checked).

■**Note** To delete a specific run (or all of the runs), right-click in the Test Results window and selecting Delete Test Run.

Viewing the Test Run Information

Through the Test Results window, you can get more information about specific tests as well as the test run as a whole. Let's begin with the Test Run Failed link in the yellow bar of the Test Results window. Clicking this link displays the window shown in Figure 12-10.

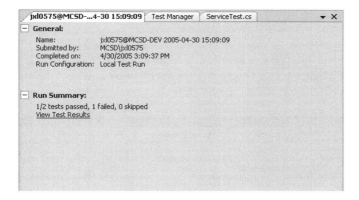

Figure 12-10. *The test run details window*

The test run details window contains general information about the test run, such as the name of the test run, who submitted it, when it was completed (notice that the run took 28 seconds, which is derived by subtracting the timestamp at the end of the test run name by the timestamp on the Completed On line), and which configuration was used for it. The run summary contains either details of the test run (as shown in Figure 12-10) or exception information (a complete stack trace) if there was a catastrophic failure with the tests and none of the tests were able to run. Clicking the View Test Results link returns you to the Test Results window.

Double-clicking any of the tests in the Test Results window displays the detailed test results window, as shown in Figure 12-11.

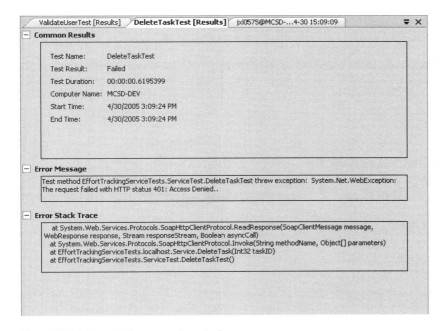

Figure 12-11. *Detailed test results window*

As you can see, the reason for this test failure is obvious and easily fixed. Because you did not modify the `DeleteTaskTest` method to pass the credential cache to the web service, your access was denied.

If you have a large number of tests that you need to examine, you can view the list based on your task list entries, as shown in Figure 12-12. This makes the list of tests easier to manage. To do this, select the second icon from the left at the top of the Test Results window.

Figure 12-12. *Test Results displayed by result list*

From the Test Results window, you can also export the test results to a test results file (with a `.trx` extension) for later review. Another option is to import previously saved test results for a nicely formatted view in the Test Results window.

Viewing Code Coverage Results

To view your code coverage results, click the Code Coverage Results icon on the far right of the Test Results window toolbar or select Test ➤ Measure Test Effectiveness from the main menu. The Code Coverage Results window is shown in Figure 12-13.

Figure 12-13. *The Code Coverage Results window*

Earlier in the chapter, we mentioned that having test results without knowing how much code was exercised (that is, how much code actually ran) is useless. For example, with the `ValidateUser` method, you might assume, based on the test results, that this method works fine and that there is nothing more to test. But looking at the code coverage, you can see that this is not true at all. Table 12-4 contains a complete list of the code coverage statistics for the ValidateUser method.

Table 12-4. *Code Coverage Statistics for the ValidateUser Method*

Item	Value
Not Covered (Blocks)	3
Not Covered (% Blocks)	14.29%
Covered (Blocks)	18
Covered (% Blocks)	85.71%
Not Covered (Lines)	2
Not Covered (% Lines)	11.76%
Covered (Lines)	14
Covered (% Lines)	82.35%
Partially Covered (Lines)	1
Partially Covered (% Lines)	5.88%

The numbers themselves may be somewhat confusing, because they indicate how many lines of code were covered but not which lines of code were covered. But the VSTS testing tools allow you to put it in perspective by graphically showing the code coverage directly over the code, as shown in Figure 12-14. To see this display, in the Code Coverage Results window, double-click the ValidateUser method line or right-click the ValidateUser result and select Go to Source Code.

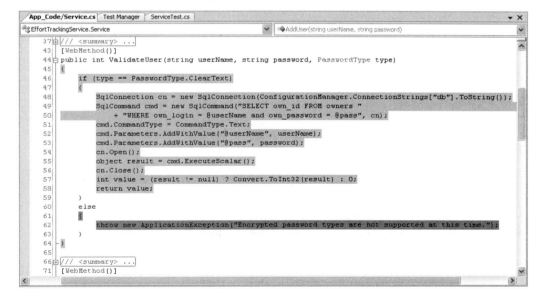

Figure 12-14. *The ValidateUser method code coverage display*

In the graphic display, the green lines were executed, the blue lines were partially executed, and the red lines were not executed at all. The method signature is not covered because it is not an executable line of code and so is not included in the code coverage statistics.

Note For VB developers, the partially executed line is a conditional `if` statement, which is almost identical to the `iif` statement. In this case, the result was not null, so only the first part of the conditional statement ran. The last part (0) did not run.

Now the numbers in Table 12-4 should make more sense. The lines indicated by the Not Covered (Blocks) number refer to the closing brace of the `if` block, the `else` line, and the closing brace of the `else` block. You might think that because the first part of the `if` block executed that the closing bracket was executed, but you will notice that the `return` statement occurs above this brace. Also note that the method's closing brace was executed because the `return` statement caused a jump to the end of the method (in VB, the `End Function` would be highlighted).

Note Another item you might notice is that in VB there are no braces in an `if` block. Therefore, the percentage of code coverage, and indeed even the number of lines executed, would be different.

Because the password type was Clear, the `else` statement was never evaluated. You might be wondering why it was not marked as a line not tested. The reason is that, as with the method signature, this line of code is not executable. One big issue here is that the closing brace can never be evaluated because it is unreachable in code, since there is a `throw` statement immediately above it.

Tip You can configure the colors in which the code coverage is rendered. To change the colors, select Tools ➤ Options from the main menu, expand the Environment node, and select Fonts and Colors. The values for code coverage are Coverage Not Touched Area, Coverage Partially Touched Area, and Coverage Touched Area.

Testing for Exceptions

One of the tests that you still need to perform is the test that passes the password type as encrypted. This should trigger an application exception. If the exception is triggered, you know the test passed. However, if you use the standard test method with no modifications, any time your method throws an exception, the test will immediately fail. Any method that throws an exception that you need to test for *must* be tested with a separate method.

> **Tip** While testing for the success path is always a good idea, because you want to know if your code actually works, an exception path is just as valid a path. Too often, the issues that cause exceptions are not tested for at all and when they do occur, the code cannot handle them.

To demonstrate how this works, add the method shown in Listing 12-3 to the `ServiceTest` class.

Listing 12-3. *The Exception Test for ValidateUser*

C#
```
    /// <summary>
    ///An exception test case for ValidateUser (string, string, PasswordType)
    ///</summary>
     [TestMethod()]
     [ExpectedException(typeof(System.Web.Services.Protocols.SoapException),
         + "An encrypted password type was allowed which is not supported.")]
    public void ValidateUserExceptionTest()
    {
        Service target = new Service();
        target.Credentials = System.Net.CredentialCache.DefaultCredentials;
        string userName = "TestUser";
        string password = "password";
        PasswordType type = PasswordType.Encrypted;
        int actual;

        actual = target.ValidateUser(userName, password, type);
    }
```
VB
```
    ''' <summary>
    '''An exception test case for ValidateUser (string, string, PasswordType)
    '''</summary>
     <TestMethod()> _
     <ExpectedException(GetType(System.Web.Services.Protocols.SoapException), _
           "An encrypted password type was allowed which is not supported.")> _
    Public Sub ValidateUserExceptionTest()
        Dim target As Service = new Service()
        target.Credentials = System.Net.CredentialCache.DefaultCredentials
        Dim userName As string = "TestUser"
        Dim password  As string = "password"
        Dim type As PasswordType = PasswordType.Encrypted
        Dim actual As integer

        actual = target.ValidateUser(userName, password, type)
    End Sub
```

The key to this type of test is the `ExpectedException` attribute. Notice that the `Assert` method is not even called here because it is not needed. The `ExpectedException` attribute ensures that .NET will wait for a `SoapException` to be thrown, and if it is, the test will be marked as successful. If it is not thrown, the message included with the `ExpectedException` attribute will be displayed as the failure message.

Caution You will notice that something appears to be wrong with what you are testing here. Your application throws an `ApplicationException`, yet you are testing for a `SoapException`. The reason is that when an exception is thrown during the invocation of a web service, the service throws its own exception and includes the message from any other exceptions as part of its message.

Once you have made this change, run this test plus the original `ValidateUser` test. Your test results will show that both tests pass. Your code coverage results will be 100% because the two lines in the `else` statement have been reached.

Now, the problem with this is that you still do not know if the right exception was thrown, but there is a way to solve this. Modify the code in the `ValidateUserExceptionTest` method to match that shown in Listing 12-4 (note that this is a partial listing only) and *remove* the `ExpectedException` attribute.

Listing 12-4. *Modified ValidateUserTestException Method*

C#
```
    int actual;

    try
    {
        actual = target.ValidateUser(userName, password, type);
    }
    catch (Exception ex)
    {
        if (ex.Message.IndexOf("ApplicationException") > 0)
            Assert.Equals(1, 1);
        else
            Assert.Fail();
    }
```
VB
```
    Dim actual As integer

    Try
        actual = target.ValidateUser(userName, password, type)
    Catch (Exception ex)
        If (ex.Message.IndexOf("ApplicationException") > 0
            Assert.Equals(1, 1)
        Else
            Assert.Fail()
    End Try
```

This simple modification allows you to check to see if a specific exception was thrown when throwing an exception from a web service.

Data-Driven Testing

As you've seen in this chapter, you might need to create an enormous number of tests in order to test your entire application. As you saw earlier, if a parameter is a date or there is an intensive amount of processing occurring in a method, you might have to create in the vicinity of 20 tests for just one method, just to test different method arguments. This not only does not make a lot of sense, but it is extremely time-consuming. This is where *data-driven testing* comes in.

Data-driven testing is not only helpful in keeping down the number of tests that you need to write, but it also makes it easier to change tests later on without having to change the test code itself. Data-driven testing is the process of feeding data to test your methods from a database instead of coding values directly into the test code. The `TestContext` object, which you looked at briefly earlier in the chapter, makes this task extremely easy. The basic principle is that you create a separate test database with one table per test method, which will supply the values for that test to use.

Note The SQL Express components make data-driven testing incredibly easy, as they can handle a fairly high volume of data and the test data can remain with the testing solution. However, if you are performing load testing or other very high-volume tests, you will probably want to create a separate SQL Server 2005 database to store the test data.

Building a Test Database

Before you start constructing the test table, you need to determine what it should contain. Each test will have a different number of columns because the columns will always relate to the number and type of parameters that need to be passed to the method. However, you should always have a primary key, which is an identifier column, and you will always need a column that holds the expected value.

For this demonstration, you will build the table shown in Table 12-5 to hold the information to test the `ValidateUser` method.

Table 12-5. *ValidateUser Test Table*

Column	Type	Nullable	Purpose
vu_id	int (Identity)	No	Primary Key
vu_username	varchar(50)	No	Holds the username
vu_password	varchar(50)	No	Holds the password
vu_pw_type	int	No	Indicates clear text or encrypted
vu_expected	int	No	Indicates the value that should be returned

Now that you know what the test table is going to contain, you need to build the database and create the table, as follows:

1. In the Solution Explorer, right-click the `EffortTrackingServiceTests` project and select Add New Item.

2. Select the SQL Database and name it `ServiceTestDB.mdf`.

3. In the Server Explorer, select Add a New Data Connection, and then browse to the `ServiceTestDB.mdf` file and select it.

4. Expand the `ServiceTestDB.mdf` file, right-click the Tables node, and select Add New Table.

5. Enter the information shown in Table 12-5.

6. Name the table `ValidateUserTest`.

7. In the `ValidateUserTest` table, enter the information shown in Table 12-6. These values will be used by the test method to pass values to the `ValidateUser` method in the service.

Table 12-6. *The ValidateUserTest Table Values*

vu_id	vu_username	vu_password	vu_pw_type*	vu_expected
1	TestUser1	password	1	1
2	TestUser1	pass	1	0
3	TestUser5	password	1	0

* The `vu_pw_type` value corresponds with the `PasswordType` enumeration.

This is everything you will need to perform the tests for this method. Note that we are *not* testing for the exception condition by passing a password type of 2. Exception tests must be carried out as separate tests. Theoretically, you could create exception handling as you did in the previous section on testing for exceptions and handle it appropriately, but it is usually easier to keep those tests separate.

Preparing the Production Database

The tests that we have come up with so far are perfectly acceptable (although you could quite easily come up with some tests that are not listed in Table 12-6), but they will not work every time. This is because the `Owners` table in the `EffortTracking` database uses an Identity column and you are looking for very explicit values to be returned (listed in the `vu_expected` column). In order for these tests to work correctly every time, the data you are testing against must be the same every time. To do this, you need to load the production database with the correct information before a test run. This is where the `Initialize` method is very helpful.

Table 12-2 earlier in the chapter includes the `ClassInitialize` and `ClassCleanup` attributes. Whereas the `TestInitialize` and `TestCleanup` methods are executed at the beginning and end of each and every test, the `ClassInitialize` and `ClassCleanup` methods are executed before any test in a class is run and after all of the tests in a class are run. This means that each method is guaranteed to execute only once during the course of a test run, regardless of how many tests are in the class. In this example, you will use the `ClassInitialize` attribute to tag a method, which will set up the production database for testing. No cleanup will be necessary for this set of tests.

Based on the information in Table 12-6, only one row of data needs to be created in the `Owners` table of the production database. The information is listed in Table 12-7.

Table 12-7. *The Owers Table Entry*

Column	Value
own_id	1
own_login	TestUser1
own_password	password

Before doing anything else, add a reference to the `System.Configuration` assembly in the `EffortTrackingTests` project and import the `System.Data.SqlClient` and `System.Configuration` namespaces. In order to set up the database, add the code shown in Listing 12-5 to the `ServiceTests` class.

Listing 12-5. *The TestClassInitialize Method*

C#

```csharp
[ClassInitialize()]
public static void TestClassInitialize(TestContext context)
{
    SqlConnection cn = new SqlConnection(
        ConfigurationManager.AppSettings["db"].ToString());
    SqlCommand cmd1 = new SqlCommand("SET IDENTITY_INSERT owners ON", cn);
    SqlCommand cmd2 = new SqlCommand("DELETE FROM work_items", cn);
    SqlCommand cmd3 = new SqlCommand("DELETE FROM owners", cn);
    SqlCommand cmd4 = new SqlCommand("INSERT INTO owners (own_id, "
        + "own_login, own_password) VALUES (1, 'TestUser1', 'password')",
        cn);
    SqlCommand cmd5 = new SqlCommand("SET IDENTITY_INSERT owners OFF",
        cn);

    cmd1.CommandType = CommandType.Text;
    cmd2.CommandType = CommandType.Text;
    cmd3.CommandType = CommandType.Text;
    cmd4.CommandType = CommandType.Text;
    cmd5.CommandType = CommandType.Text;

    cn.Open();
    cmd1.ExecuteNonQuery();
    cmd2.ExecuteNonQuery();
    cmd3.ExecuteNonQuery();
    cmd4.ExecuteNonQuery();
    cmd5.ExecuteNonQuery();
```

```
            cn.Close();
    }
```
VB
```
    <ClassInitialize()>
    Public Shard Sub TestClassInitialize(TestContext context)
        Dim cn As SqlConnection = new SqlConnection( _
            ConfigurationManager.AppSettings("db").ToString)
        Dim cmd1 As SqlCommand = new SqlCommand( _
            "SET IDENTITY_INSERT owners ON", cn)
        Dim cmd2 As SqlCommand = new SqlCommand("DELETE FROM work_items", cn)
        Dim cmd3 As SqlCommand = new SqlCommand("DELETE FROM owners", cn)
        Dim cmd4 As SqlCommand = new SqlCommand("INSERT INTO owners (own_id, " _
            & "own_login, own_password) VALUES (1, 'TestUser1', 'password')", cn)
        Dim cmd5 As SqlCommand = new SqlCommand( _
            "SET IDENTITY_INSERT owners OFF", cn)

        cmd1.CommandType = CommandType.Text
        cmd2.CommandType = CommandType.Text
        cmd3.CommandType = CommandType.Text
        cmd4.CommandType = CommandType.Text
        cmd5.CommandType = CommandType.Text

        cn.Open()
        cmd1.ExecuteNonQuery()
        cmd2.ExecuteNonQuery()
        cmd3.ExecuteNonQuery()
        cmd4.ExecuteNonQuery()
        cmd5.ExecuteNonQuery()
        cn.Close()
    End Sub
```

Now that the `ClassInitialize` method is set up to re-create the database for each of the tests necessary for the data-driven tests, you can move on to actually setting up the test to use data from the database.

Setting Up the Test

In the Test Manager window, select the `ValidateUserTest` and view its properties. Select the ellipsis for the Data Connection String property, and then browse to the `ServiceTestDB.mdf` file and select it. Leave the Data Access property as Sequential. Next, select the `ValidateUserTest` table from the Data Table Name property. This will add the `DataSource` attribute to the `ValidateUserTest` method in the `ServiceTests` class (it is much easier to do it this way than typing the attribute in manually).

Now that everything is hooked up, you need to be able to read the information from the `ValidateUserTest` table. To access the information in the row, you use the `TestContext.DataRow` property and access the data as you normally would from a database, as shown in Listing 12-6.

Listing 12-6. *Data-Driven Test Method*

C#
```csharp
/// <summary>
///A test case for AddUser (string, string)
///</summary>
 [TestMethod()]
 [DataSource("System.Data.SqlClient", "Data Source=.\\SQLEXPRESS;
AttachDbFilename=\"C:\\ServiceTestDB.mdf\";Integrated Security=True;
User Instance=True",
"AddUserTest", DataAccessMethod.Sequential)]
public void AddUserTest()
{
    Service target = new Service();
    string userName = testContextInstance.DataRow["au_username"].ToString();
    string password = testContextInstance.DataRow["au_password"].ToString();
    PasswordType type =
    (PasswordType)testContextInstance.DataRow["au_password_type"];

    int expected = Convert.ToInt32(testContextInstance.DataRow["au_expected"]);
    int actual;

    actual = target.AddUser(userName, password);

    if (userName == "Test User 2")
        _newUserId = actual;

    Assert.AreEqual(expected, actual,
        "EffortTrackingServiceTests.localhost.Service.AddUser did "
            + "not return the expected value.");
}
```

VB
```vb
''' <summary>
'''A test case for AddUser (string, string)
'''</summary>
 <TestMethod()> _
 <DataSource("System.Data.SqlClient", "Data Source=.\\SQLEXPRESS; " & _
"AttachDbFilename=\"C:\\ServiceTestDB.mdf\";Integrated Security=True; _
    User Instance=True", _
"AddUserTest", DataAccessMethod.Sequential)>
Public Sub AddUserTest()
    Dim target As Service = New Service()
    Dim userName As String = testContextInstance.DataRow("au_username").ToString()
    Dim password As String = testContextInstance.DataRow("au_password").ToString()
    Dim type As PasswordType = _
        CType(PasswordType, testContextInstance.DataRow("au_password_type"))
```

```vb
        Dim expected As Integer = _
        Convert.ToInt32(testContextInstance.DataRow("au_expected"))
        Dim actual As Integer

        actual = target.AddUser(userName, password)

        If userName = "Test User 2" Then
            _newUserId = actual
        End If

        Assert.AreEqual(expected, actual, _
        "EffortTrackingServiceTests.localhost.Service.AddUser did " _
            & "not return the expected value.")
End Sub
```

The `DataSource` attribute indicates to VSTS that an external data source is being used to drive this particular test method. The syntax for the `DataSource` constructor is *Connection String, Table, Access Method*. The connection string is a standard database connection string. The table is the table in the database that contains your test data, and the access method is how the test should access the data.

Note The access method has no effect on a unit test. The test will always be run using the sequential access method. This setting has an effect for load testing, which is covered in Chapter 16.

The test will be run once for every row of data in the table. The `DataRow` property of the `testContextInstance` changes for every method according to the `DataSource` attribute for the method.

Note You cannot artificially change the row that is currently being used in the test.

The test results from a data-driven test look slightly different than those you've seen so far, as shown in Figure 12-15.

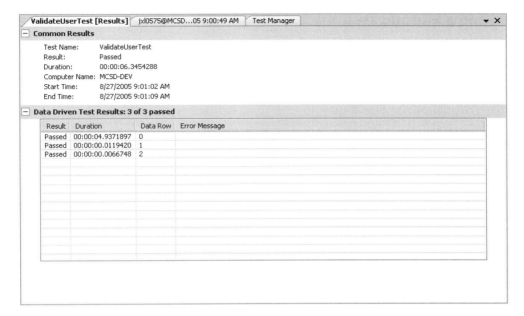

Figure 12-15. *Data-driven test results*

For each row in the test, the result and the amount of time the test took are displayed. If there were any errors, those messages will be displayed here as well.

Tip As a best practice, and to make the results of this test more valuable, the error message should also come from the test database. This allows you to more easily tie a failure to a specific entry, since it is difficult to do that with the data displayed. You could also provide the supplied values in the error message. To do this, simply add a description column to each test table and use it to supply the exception message. Now your tests will be self-documenting.

Manual Testing

Some tests just cannot be run in an automated fashion. These tests may require some external actions to prepare certain aspects of a server. An example of this may be testing an IIS failure in which the manual step of stopping the World Wide Web service may be required. Or if you are using VSTS, which does not currently support Windows Forms testing, and you want to test the user interface, then manual testing would be the way to go.

Creating a Manual Test

Manual tests consist of a series of written instructions that the user follows to complete the test. At the end of the manual test, the tester marks whether the test passed or failed.

To set the test steps, double-click the `ManualTest1.mht` file in the testing solution. This will open the test in Microsoft Word for editing.

Note You can add a text version of the `ManualTest` file by selecting it from the Add Test Wizard, which allows you to edit the test in Notepad or another text editor.

Here, you enter the test title, details, steps, and revision history of the test. An example is shown in Figure 12-16.

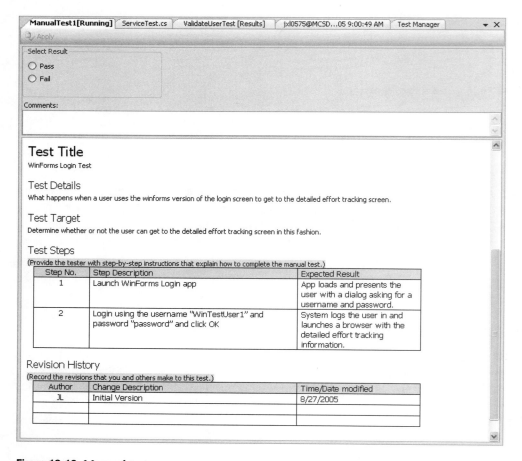

Figure 12-16. *Manual test run*

> **Note** Figure 12-16 shows the file during an actual manual test run so it is not displayed in the Word environment here. This test is not a test you will be running, but is for example purposes only.

The test steps are the key to this test. The tester simply walks through the steps of the test performing the actions noted in the step description. The result of each step should be documented in the far-right column. If the expected result is not the actual result at any point in the set of steps, the test should be marked as failed and a comment explaining which step failed and the actual result that was displayed. The version history should also be maintained so you know who made changes, if any, to the test script.

Running a Manual Test

When a test run reaches a manual test, it will pause and wait for you to complete the manual test. When you have finished with the manual test, you mark it as Pass or Fail using the options at the top of the manual test window, and then click Apply. Once the test is marked as Pass or Fail, the rest of the tests in the test run will continue.

> **Caution** Do not include manual tests in automated test runs as a rule. If, for example, you set up a series of tests for the nightly build and you include a manual test, the nightly set of tests will *not* run. The test will be paused at the first manual test in the list of tests.

Manual testing gives you the ability to perform virtually any test in Visual Studio and have those tests recorded just as it would with any automated tests.

> **Tip** One added benefit of running manual tests this way is that code coverage results are recorded for these tests.

Testing Using MSTest

VSTS includes a command-line tool called MSTest. The executable is located in the C:\Program Files\Microsoft Visual Studio 8\Common7\IDE folder. This tool provides a simple way to automate the tests. Team Foundation Build invokes this tool when performing automated builds, but you can include it in batch files or invoke it manually for whatever purposes you may need.

For example, to invoke MSTest in order to run the tests included with the sample Effort Tracking application, open a Visual Studio command-line prompt and navigate to the folder that contains the `EffortTrackingServiceTests.dll`. Then enter the following at the command prompt:

`Mstest /testcontainer:efforttrackingservicetests.dll /test:orderedTest1`

The results will be displayed in the command window. There are numerous options for customizing the output, choosing the configuration file, columns to display, and so on. You can also publish tests to Team Foundation Server using this tool. See the MSDN documentation for more information.

Summary

As you've seen in this chapter, unit testing is an integral part of any development process. Without unit tests, you cannot be assured that the code works as planned at the method level.

In this chapter, you learned how to plan the unit tests and create them. This includes being able to prepare the development database so that tests are repeatable using the various methods of the test class. You learned how to manage and group test runs, as well as how to order test runs so that dependent tests run in the correct order. You have seen how to configure a test run to accomplish specific goals and the benefits of using code coverage and understanding what that coverage means. Then you learned how to run data-driven tests, which allow you to create a test database to supply values to your tests without having to create a myriad of different test methods for each method to be tested. Next, you learned about manual testing. Finally, we briefly covered the MSTest command-line tool.

In short, this chapter has provided you with a new set of tools that you can use to make your code more stable than it has ever been before. This leads to fewer bugs, a shorter time to fix discovered bugs, and fewer regression bugs.

CHAPTER 13

Static Code Analysis

Static code analysis is the process of examining your code, while it is not in a running state, for defects. These defects can range from naming conventions not being followed to potential security holes, which can lead to buffer overrun attacks and many other problems. (Performance analysis, which occurs while the code is running, is covered in the next chapter.)

VSTS provides two tools for static code analysis: PREfast and FxCop. PREfast is a tool for checking for potential issues when dealing with C/C++ code bases. It was originally developed as an internal tool for use by Microsoft developers to check their own code. FxCop is a tool developed for .NET in order to check code for proper formatting, correct usage of the language, potential security holes, and other issues.

In this chapter, you will examine both of these tools. You will see how to use them and where they fit into an automated build process (particularly the FxCop tool). You will also learn how to extend and customize the FxCop tool so that you can check that the code meets your organization's standards as well as the predefined rules.

Note that pointer issues are only a problem in C++; they do not occur in C# or VB .NET code. If you do not program in C or C++, you may want to skip the section on PREfast. If you are a development manager, you will probably want to at least be aware of what PREfast does.

Static Code Analysis vs. Code Reviews

You may have never performed a static code analysis before except via code reviews. Code reviews are great tools, and you should in no way discount them because VSTS has provided tools to help with the analysis. But what's the first thing to go when you hit crunch time on a project? It's the meetings—*all* of the meetings, including code reviews.

The static code analysis tools are another example of VSTS working to help ensure that you produce the highest quality code base with the fewest number of defects. The static code analysis tools provide a way to automate some of the process of code reviews. The tools can be run manually or via an automated build process using Team Foundation Build. At the very least, they provide a backup in case your code review process gets cut because of project deadlines (which, of course, causes more problems than it solves). At best, they provide a more robust set of checks for you and your development team.

> ## THE VALUE OF CODE REVIEWS
>
> Code reviews are often the first things to get the axe when push comes to shove and deadlines start looming over a development team. When this happens, bugs are not spotted during development time when they are easier to fix. Typically, the product is just about ready for shipping when a tester discovers a bug while performing functional tests, or worse yet, during user tests. The code goes back for review, where it takes a team of people some work to find and fix it, and then the product goes through the testing process all over again. At this point, the release date has slipped, and the entire development team is in trouble. Instead, a fraction of the time could have been spent on code reviews, and the problem could have been captured and fixed in about five minutes.
>
> Have you had this experience? We have seen many projects start off with lofty goals regarding code reviews, only to have those plans sacrificed because of budget and time constraints. VSTS, by integrating these analysis tools, has given developers a huge hand in exposing potential problems. But the results of these tools should always be checked by others in code reviews.
>
> There is a common misconception that a developer with his head down coding is more effective than one who takes the time to review his code with others. This has given rise to many of the Agile Development methodologies, which have the advantage of code reviews during coding.
>
> Steve McConnell, in his book *Code Complete, Second Edition* (Microsoft Press, 2004) takes a great deal of time to examine the cost of fixing bugs at various points in the development process. It has been proven that the costs of fixing bugs found during testing or after release are orders of magnitude higher than catching and fixing them during development. We recommend that developers read this book.

Using PREfast

PREfast was originally developed by Microsoft Research and has been employed for several years within the company to check for coding defects in Microsoft products. At this time, running these checks is seen as an essential part of getting a product ready for shipping. If you are shipping a product written in C or C++, you will certainly want to make sure that these checks are run on your code. PREfast is designed to detect some of the most serious coding errors that a normal compilation alone will not detect, including buffer overruns, dereferencing null pointers, using uninitialized variables, and so on.

Enabling PREfast Checking

PREfast was integrated into the VSTS version of the Visual C++ 2005 compiler, so it is available to you when using any release of the Visual C++ 2005 C/C++ compiler, cl.exe. Unlike FxCop, PREfast does all its checking at compile time, so it makes sense as an add-on to the compiler. In fact, all you need to do to enable the PREfast code analysis is to set the /analyze compiler option, which you can also do from a Visual Studio project. In the Project Properties dialog box, under C/C++, look under Advanced and set the Enable Code Analysis for C/C++ option to Yes.

You can enable the PREfast checking when compiling C or C++ code. Regardless of whether C or C++ code is being checked, the effect of setting the option is to enable specific diagnostics (compiler warnings) that are not generated in a compilation without the `/analyze` option.

The PREfast diagnostics are normally issued as warnings. Often, code projects have the `/WX` compiler option set, which changes warnings to errors. However, you probably won't want all the PREfast warnings to be issued as errors, since you may not be able to fix these immediately. To tell the compiler to report PREfast diagnostics as warnings even when the `/WX` option is set, use the `/analyze:WX-` version of the `/analyze` option.

Reviewing PREfast Results

The PREfast diagnostics can be distinguished from other compiler warnings by the range of the codes. PREfast warnings have codes between 6000 and 6999. Table 13-1 lists the PREfast checks and their associated warning codes.

Table 13-1. *PREfast Checks*

Category	Warning Codes	Items Checked
Bad memory use	C6001, C6011, C6200, C6278, C6279, C6280, C6283	Use of uninitialized memory, dereferencing a null pointer, using out-of-range array indices, new and delete mismatches
Buffer overruns	C6029, C6057, C6201, C6202, C6203, C6204, C6327, C6383, C6385, C6386	Code that could allow writing past the end of a buffer, which is a serious security vulnerability
Unchecked return values	C6031	Failure to check for error codes returned from functions
Null termination	C6053, C6054	Strings that are not null-terminated passed to functions that expect it
Incorrect arguments	C6059, C6066, C6067, C6270, C6271, C6272, C6273, C6274, C6284, C6298, C6306, C6309, C6328, C6331, C6332, C6333, C6381, C6387, C6388	Various invalid or incorrect arguments
Format string errors	C6063, C6064	Using the incorrect or wrong number of conversion characters in a formatting string
Wide/narrow character and character vs. byte count issues	C6209, C6260, C6303	Using `sizeof` with a wide character string as the length, passing a wide character string to a function that requires a narrow character string, using `sizeof * sizeof`

Continued

Table 13-1. *Continued*

Category	Warning Codes	Items Checked
Memory leaks	C6211, C6308	Leaking memory due to an exception
Questionable casts	C6214, C6215, C6216, C6217, C6218, C6219, C6220, C6221, C6225, C6226, C6230, C6276	Various dangerous casts and conversions
Questionable expressions	C6235, C6236, C6237, C6239, C6240, C6268, C6269, C6281, C6282, C6285, C6286, C6287, C6288, C6289, C6290, C6291, C6299, C6302, C6313, C6314, C6315, C6316, C6317, C6323, C6326, C6336	Operator precedence errors, Boolean expressions that are always true or always false, confusion between bitwise operators and relational operators, incorrect use of bit fields, confusion between equality and assignment operators, and so on
Questionable `Case` statements	C6259	Case statements that have values that are not reachable
Questionable looping constructs	C6292, C6293, C6294, C6295, C6296	Loops that count down from the minimum or up from the maximum, loops that never execute, loops that execute only once
Variable hiding	C6244, C6246	Hiding a variable at a larger scope with one at a smaller scope
Incorrect use of `sizeof` or `countof`	C6305, C6334, C6384	Potential mismatch between `sizeof` and `countof` quantities, `sizeof` applied to an expression with an operator, dividing `sizeof` a pointer by another value
Exception handling problems	C6242, C6310, C6312, C6318, C6319, C6320, C6322	Actions that trigger a local unwind, improper use of __try/__except blocks and exception filters, and so on
Stack corruption	C6255, C6262, C6263	Using _alloca instead of _alloca_s, calling _alloca in a loop, using a stack greater than specified stack size set with /analyze:stacksize*nnnn* (where *nnnn* is the stack size above which the warning will be issued)
Security risks	C6248, C6277	Improper use of access control lists (ACLs)
Resource leaks	C6250, C6335	Failing to release various Windows resources

Category	Warning Codes	Items Checked
Thread termination	C6258	Terminating a thread without proper cleanup
Case-insensitive comparisons	C6400, C6401	Comparison functions used in a way that doesn't work on non-English locales
Integer overflow error	C6297	32-bit value shifted and cast to a 64-bit value
Possible wrong function call	C6324	Using a string copy function (such as `strcpy`) where a string comparison function (such as `strcmp`) should have been used

To see PREfast in action, try compiling the code in Listing 13-1 with the `/analyze` option. Also specify `_CRT_SECURE_NO_DEPRECATE` so that you can use `strcpy` without getting a warning that it is deprecated in favor of the more secure `strcpy_s` version, new with Visual C++ 2005. If you used the `strcpy_s` version, you won't get the warning we are demonstrating in this example: a potential buffer overrun.

Listing 13-1. *Buffer Overrun Example*

```cpp
// buffer_overrun.cpp
// compile with /D_CRT_SECURE_NO_DEPRECATE /analyze
#include <string.h>
#include <malloc.h>
#include <stdio.h>

void f(char* str)
{
   char* x = (char*) malloc(10 * sizeof(char));

   if (x != NULL)
   {
      strcpy(x, str);
   }
}

int main()
{
  f("A random string of arbitrary length");
}
```

The output is as follows:

```
Microsoft (R) 32-bit C/C++ Optimizing Compiler Version 14.00.50727.42 for 80x86
Copyright (C) Microsoft Corporation.  All rights reserved.

buffer_overrun.cpp
c:\nutshell\PREfast_code\buffer_overrun.cpp(12) : warning C6204:
Possible buffer overrun in call to 'strcpy': use of unchecked parameter 'str'
```

As you can see, warning 6204 is generated, letting you know of a potentially serious error. To address this, you might modify the code as shown in Listing 13-2.

Listing 13-2. *Buffer Overrun Correction*

```
// buffer_overrun.cpp
// compile with /D_CRT_SECURE_NO_DEPRECATE /analyze
#include <string.h>
#include <malloc.h>
#include <stdio.h>

void f(char* str)
{
   char* x = (char*) malloc(10 * sizeof(char));

   if (x != NULL)
   {
      if (strlen(str) < sizeof x)
      {
         strcpy(x, str);
      }
      else
      {
         printf("The string passed in was too long.");
      }
   }
}

int main()
{
  f("A random string of arbitrary length");
}
```

You, the developer, may already be certain that there cannot be any input that would actually cause an overrun. PREfast does not look beyond the individual function scope to try to analyze what input might be passed to a function. However, you can extend PREfast's reach by using attributes to annotate your code. This lets you specify in metadata which constraints PREfast should check. You'll learn how to use such annotations shortly, after we explain how to turn off the undesired warnings, since there are often quite a few of them.

Enabling, Disabling, and Suppressing PREfast Warnings

Some PREfast warnings are more serious than others, and you will probably want to enable some of them and disable others, depending on the goals for a particular project and the risks associated with the particular type of error. For example, if you are shipping consumer software, you may have more stringent requirements than if you are working on a research project.

For a large body of existing code that has not been checked with PREfast or a similar source analysis tool before, the number of warnings generated may be quite large. You will need to make a business decision that balances the risks of not detecting certain types of errors versus the risks of changing code that has been stable and tested, as well as taking into account the time it will take to make the code changes to eliminate the warnings.

Another factor to consider is who will be addressing the errors with the code. Are these developers familiar with that code? If you have a stable code base, you certainly don't want to allow code changes that eliminate the warnings but introduce semantic errors that might be hard to detect.

Another issue you are likely to encounter is PREfast warnings in header files from third parties or from libraries that you have no direct control over. You may want to disable some of these warnings.

Development teams may want to agree on the set of warnings that will be enforced and those that will be disabled, with an understanding of the risks and costs associated with each warning. Once these are agreed upon, it is a simple matter to set up an include file with the appropriate pragma directives to disable or enable the desired warnings.

The easiest way to add a consistent level of checking to your existing build process is to add an include file to the compilation using the /FI (Force Include) compiler option. Listing 13-3 shows an example of an include file with pragma directives.

Listing 13-3. *PREfast pragma File*

```
// PREfast.h -- add /FIPREfast.h to your compilation command line
#pragma once

#pragma warning(disable: \
        6001 6002 6003 6004 6005 6006 6007 6008 6009 \
    6010 6011 6012 6013 6014 6015 6016 6017 6018 6019 \
    6020 6021 6022 6023 6024 6025 6026 6027 6028 6030 \
    6031 6032 6033 6034 6035 6036 6037 6038 6039 6040 \
    // etc...
    )
```

```
/* It's a good idea to explicitly list those PREfast warnings
 * you do enable.  This is a list of PREfast
 * warnings that are considered a minimum bar for a shipping
 * product.
 *
 * 6029;6053;6056;6057;6059;6063;6067;6200;6201;6202;6203;6204;
 * 6205;6207;6241;6243;6248;6252;6259;6260;6268;6276;6277;6281;
 * 6282;6287;6288;6289;6290;6291;6296;6298;6299;6305;6306;6308;
 * 6334;6383
 */
```

You may also want to disable specific occurrences of a given warning on a case-by-case basis. To do this, surround the code with #pragma warning (suppress: C6*xxx*) with the specific warning number. You could also use #pragma warning (disable: C*xxx*), as with any other warning, but this has the effect of suppressing the warning throughout the remainder of that file. The suppress version of this pragma affects only the line of code immediately following the pragma, so it is preferable since it avoids the risk of missing other errors in the file. An example of suppressing a warning is shown in Listing 13-4.

Listing 13-4. *PREfast Warning Suppression Example*

```
// suppress_warning.cpp
// compile with /D_CRT_SECURE_NO_DEPRECATE /analyze
#include <string.h>
#include <stdio.h>

int p;

void f()
{
   // char * p hides the global p, but we know this is safe and simply
   // want to suppress the warning.
   #pragma warning (suppress: 6244)
   char* p = new char[10];

   strcpy(p, "xyz");
   printf("%s\n", p);
}

void g()
{
   // the same error here triggers the warning
   char* p = new char[10];

   strcpy(p, "xyz");
   printf("%s\n", p);
}
```

```
int main()
{
   f();
   g();
}
```

Annotating Code for PREfast Checks

In addition to the warnings that are generated simply by turning on the /analyze compiler option, you can achieve further testing with PREfast by annotating your code with specific attributes. For example, you can annotate a function call with an attribute that tells PREfast that the return value of this function must be checked. Then when that function is used, PREfast will report a warning whenever that function is used without checking the return value.

To enable the use of the attributes from C code, simply include the following include directive:

`#include <CodeAnalysis/SourceAnnotations.h>`

When compiling C++ code, add the preceding include directive, but also add the following using namespace statement:

`using namespace vc_attributes;`

To annotate your code, you add PREfast attributes to parameters and return values. Attributes appear in square brackets and have various properties you can set to signal PREfast to perform a check.

You use two attributes with PREfast:

- The Pre attribute is used with function parameters only and is designed to tell PREfast to check for various conditions whenever parameters are passed to the function whose parameter is attributed.

- The Post attribute is used on the function's return values and on out parameters, such as pointers that are intended to be set or filled in during the function call.

For example, you might use the Pre attribute to enforce that a pointer parameter is a valid non-null pointer. If this attribute is set, then PREfast will check any pointers used when calling this function to ensure that they can be verified to be valid, as demonstrated by the code in Listing 13-5.

Listing 13-5. *Using the Pre Attribute*

```
#include <CodeAnalysis\SourceAnnotations.h>
using namespace vc_attributes;

void f ([Pre(NullTerminated=Yes)] char* str);
```

```
int main ( )
{
   char x[100];
   f(x); // error C6054 - x is not null-terminated
}
```

Listing 13-6 shows an example of using the Post attribute to specify conditions on how the function handles the return value. The attribute contains a tag that specifies that this attribute applies to the return value, not the function as a whole.

Listing 13-6. *Using the Post Attribute*

```
// checkreturn.cpp
#include <stdio.h>
#include <codeanalysis\sourceannotations.h>
using namespace vc_attributes;
[returnvalue:Post(MustCheck=Yes)]
int f()
{
   FILE* fp;
   fopen_s(&fp, "file1.txt", "rw+");
   if (fp == NULL)
       return -1;
   fprintf_s(fp, "add some text");
   fclose(fp);
   return 0;
}

int main()
{
   f();  // triggers an error, C6031 since the return value is not checked
}
```

In this case, the output is as follows:

```
Microsoft (R) 32-bit C/C++ Optimizing Compiler Version 14.00.50727.42 for 80x86
Copyright (C) Microsoft Corporation.  All rights reserved.

checkreturn.cpp
c:\PREfast_code\checkreturn.cpp(19) : warning C6031:
 Return value ignored: 'f'
Microsoft (R) Incremental Linker Version 8.00.50727.42
Copyright (C) Microsoft Corporation.  All rights reserved.

/out:checkreturn.exe
checkreturn.obj
```

Remember that using the /analyze option is not a guarantee that there are no potential problems with the code. It is actually rather easy to fool PREfast, as the example in Listing 13-7 demonstrates.

Listing 13-7. *Missed PREfast Check*

```cpp
// annotated_function.cpp

#include <iostream>
#include <CodeAnalysis/SourceAnnotations.h>
using namespace std;
using namespace vc_attributes;

void f( [Pre(NullTerminated = Yes)] char* str)
{
   cout << str << endl;
}

int main()
{
   // create a string that is not null-terminated
   char test[5] = { 'a', 'b', 'c', 'd' };
   f( test ); // error not flagged

   char* s = (char*) malloc(10 * sizeof (char));
   f(s); // error not flagged

   char s1[10] = "abcdefgh";
   char* s2 = (char*) malloc(5 * sizeof (char));
   if (s2 != NULL)
      s2 = strncpy(s2, s1, 5);
   f(s2); // error not flagged
}
```

If you run this example with the Visual C++ 2005 compiler with the /analyze option, the use of non-null terminated strings is not detected. The bottom line is that you should run PREfast to catch errors, but you cannot use it as a substitute for any other testing or validation.

Using FxCop

FxCop has been offered as a stand-alone tool since the release of Visual Studio 2002 and .NET Framework version 1.0. It was originally written as a tool to check the work of the Microsoft .NET development teams because it was the only way to ensure consistency in naming conventions, implementation, and overall structure. You will want to use it to perform these checks on your own code.

> **Tip** FxCop is still offered in a stand-alone format. It is available for download from www.gotdotnet.com.

Enabling FxCop

Up until now, whenever you have done a build, the compiler has gone through and compiled the code, checking for compile errors and nothing else. FxCop is not enabled by default.

To enable FxCop, right-click the project in the Solution Explorer, select Properties, select the Code Analysis node, and check Enable Code Analysis. Alternatively, for a web application, you can select Website ➤ Code Analysis Configuration from the main menu, and then check Enable Code Analysis. After you have enabled code analysis, build the solution. No other steps are necessary to run the code analysis.

> **Note** Depending on the size of your code base, it can take considerably longer to build a project with FxCop enabled. Rather than enabling FxCop on every build, you should consider running the code analyzer only after you have added a lot of working code that you do not intend to change.

You can also analyze code without performing a build by selecting Build ➤ Run Code Analysis on [*project name*] from the main menu.

Examining FxCop Results

To demonstrate how FxCop works, enable it for the project you created in Chapter 12 (right-click the `EffortTrackingServiceTests` project in the Solution Explorer, select Properties, select the Code Analysis node, and check Enable Code Analysis), and then build the solution. The results of the build should look those in Figure 13-1.

> **Note** For the examples in this chapter, you can also use the downloadable code available from the Source Code section of the Apress website (www.apress.com). The code for this chapter contains only methods with no implementation of those methods.

Realize that all of the information reported by the code analysis is reported as a warning; the results are not errors. (Although you can configure them to be errors, as described in the upcoming "Configuring FxCop Rules" section.) Nothing shown here will stop your code from running. Everything is a suggestion based on the code analyzer rules. When running automated builds using Team Foundation Build, these warnings can be logged to the Team Foundation Server, and they can show up in a report later.

CHAPTER 13 ■ STATIC CODE ANALYSIS

Figure 13-1. *FxCop code analysis warnings*

■**Tip** You can sort the results of an FxCop run, just as can sort any other pieces of information that are displayed in the Error List window. Sorting the list by description will sort the warnings by category.

Let's take a look at the warning highlighted in Figure 13-1:

```
CA1008: Microsoft.Design: Add a member to 'PasswordType' that has a value of zero
with a suggested name of 'None'.
```

The first part of the line, CA1008, is the rule number (also called CheckID). Microsoft.Design is the category under which the warning is classified. The last part of the line is the rule that was broken and a suggested way of fixing it. To get further information about the rule, right-click the rule and select Show Error Help. This opens a web page (for built-in rules, this page is displayed in the online help window) with detailed information about the warning, including why it is a warning and how to fix it. Now, in this case, do you want follow this suggestion? Yes and no. The first value in an enum should always be zero, but the name should not be None. (This particular issue is fixed in the downloadable code for other chapters.)

You'll find that many of the FxCop rules are not applicable to a given circumstance. One of the advantages of FxCop is that it is fully customizable. You can suppress rules and configure rules, as described in the following sections.

Scan through the rest of the list to determine if there are any items that really should be fixed (also, this is a good overview of the types of issues that FxCop can help you catch). The four items that should jump out at you are the naming conventions regarding the term ID. FxCop correctly notifies you that ID is an abbreviation and not an acronym, and therefore it should be correctly cased as Id. Fix each of these four items in the Task structure. Rebuilding the solution will remove each of these warning from the list. In addition, each object in C# should be declared in a namespace, so this is also a valid warning you would want to fix.

> **Tip** If you recognize that a warning is an issue that needs to be fixed, you can also create a work item by right-clicking the warning and selecting Create Work Item. Then choose to log the issue as a Bug, Task, or Quality of Service item. Work items are discussed in Chapter 5.

How you handle other warnings will be governed by the standards for your particular project. Issues such as `CategoryID` being made a private member with a public accessor rather than just a public field are project-specific. In this case, you are just using the Task structure to serialize your data, so these rules do not apply here. The key benefit is that FxCop provides guidelines, and you can apply them as appropriate.

Suppressing Messages

If you do not want a rule that you see in the results applied in a particular case, say to the `PasswordType` enum in our example, you can remove it from the list of checked rules by right-clicking it and selecting Suppress Message(s). At this point, the rule is not removed, but is changed to a strike-through font to indicate it is no longer checked. In addition, the `SuppressMessage` attribute is added to the type, as shown here:

`[System.Diagnostics.CodeAnalysis.SuppressMessage("Microsoft.Design", "CA1008: EnumsShouldHaveZeroValue")]`

This is called an In Source Suppression (ISS). The `SuppressMessage` attribute has a number of options; this is just the default. The constructor parameters for the `SuppressMessage` attribute are shown in Table 13-2.

Table 13-2. *SuppressMessage Attribute Constructor Parameters*

Parameter	Description
Category	Category under which the rule is classified
CheckId	The identifier for the rule
Justification	Should be used to indicate why a rule has not been followed (it is often important to note why a developer is not following a particular coding convention)
MessageId	The name of the method to which the suppression applies
Scope	Identifies where the scope of the suppression; valid values are Module, Namespace, Resource, Type, Member, and Parameter
Target	Indicates the full namespace of the target method or namespace.

Messages can be suppressed at various levels of the application. To insert a suppression line at the module level, use the `SuppressMessage` attribute in the following way:

`[module: SuppressMessage(. . .)]`

To unsuppress a message, just delete the attribute from the code file.

Configuring FxCop Rules

To view the list of rules that are available in FxCop (and any custom rules) select Website (or Project if you are creating a Windows Forms application) ➤ Code Analysis Configuration. This will bring up the dialog box shown in Figure 13-2. Notice that this dialog box also contains an Enable Code Analysis check box, which you can check to enable FxCop scanning during the build process.

Figure 13-2. *The Code Analysis Configuration dialog box*

The predefined rules are divided into nine categories, as described in Table 13-3.

Table 13-3. *FxCop Rule Categories*

Category	No. of Rules	Description
Design	63	Rules related to the application architecture, such as when to use certain pieces of functionality and rules regarding generics
Globalization	6	Rules regarding the globalization of an application
Interoperability	15	COM and platform invoke rules to help ensure compatibility across systems
Maintainability	3	Rules designed to make application maintenance easier
Naming	25	Rules relating to the naming of methods, parameters, variables, and classes
Performance	20	Rules that can help improve performance such as when boxing becomes an issue
Reliability	7	Rules that help prevent memory leaks
Security	26	Rules to help prevent potential security issues such as SQL injection attacks
Usage	41	Rules to help in proper usage of classes, attributes, parameters, and various other pieces of code

Notice that, by default, all of the rules have a status of Warning. You can change the status to Error simply by double-clicking the status for the rule (and double-click Error to change it back to Warning). This allows you to mark rules as errors, which will prevent your code from running after a build if certain rules are violated. Again, this will depend on the specific requirements of your project or organization.

You can disable rule checking on certain rules or on all rules by unchecking the box next to the specific rules or categories.

Note If you have used the FxCop tool in beta versions of VSTS, you probably noticed that there were checks for correct spelling. This functionality was removed from the release because of the lack of time for building in the management of additional words, acronyms, and so on. This functionality is expected to be included in an upcoming release.

Running FxCop from the Command Line

You can run FxCop from the command line to validate compiled assemblies outside Visual Studio. The executable is `FxCopCmd.exe`, located by default in `C:\Program Files\Microsoft Visual Studio 8\Team Tools\Static Analysis Tools\FxCop`.

You can use various command-line options to customize how FxCop is run. For information about these rules, run the following command:

`FxCopCmd /?`

Creating Custom FxCop Rules

You can extend the capabilities of FxCop by creating your own rules. These rules can be placed in any category or a custom category you create.

Note In VSTS version 1, rules cannot be pulled from a central area. You need to deploy the custom FxCop rules on each machine that has the VSTS client on it in order for everyone to be able to use those rules.

Before you create custom rules, it helps to know where FxCop lives and where you will eventually need to deploy your custom rules. FxCop is located in `C:\Program Files\Microsoft Visual Studio 8\Team Tools\Static Analysis Tools\FxCop`. The `Engines` folder contains any rules processing engines (in this case, only `IntrospectionAnalysisEngine.dll`). The `Rules` folder contains all of the default rules that ship with VSTS. The `XML` folder contains XSL transformations for use in displaying the output from the FxCop tool.

> **Note** FxCop used to have two different engines to process rules: the Reflection engine and the Introspection engine. The Reflection engine was phased out starting with version 1.30 of FxCop. The version of FxCop that comes with VSTS processes rules exclusively through the Introspection engine. Any rules that you have from the Reflection engine will need to be migrated. See the MSDN documentation for guidelines for migrating rules.

As an example, you will create a rule to check to see that any privately declared fields that have a class scope are prefixed with an underscore (_). While this is not an official naming convention, it has become very common and is an easy way to help differentiate class-scoped private fields.

> **Note** In VB, the common naming convention is to use an m_ or just an m to prefix a module- or class-scoped variable. You are certainly welcome to change the example here to check for that, but the underscore is becoming the standard prefix for these types of fields.

A rule is composed of the rule class that validates a rule and a rule file (XML) that contains details and guidance concerning the rule (displayed to the user if the rule is broken). First, you'll create the project for the custom rule, and then you'll create the rule class and the rule file.

Creating the Custom Rule Project

You can have more than one rule in an assembly, so a good naming practice (and the practice that Microsoft uses) is to create one assembly per category of rule and include all of the rules for that category in the assembly. The naming convention should be something like [Company][Category]Rules.dll, where Company is the company the rules are being created for and Category is the category to which the rules in the assembly belong.

Follow these steps to start a new project for the rule and add a reference to FxCopSdk.dll and Microsoft.Cci.dll.

1. Create a new project called OrgNamingRules.

2. Right-click the References node and select Add Reference.

3. Select the Browse tab and browse to C:\Program Files\Microsoft Visual Studio 8\Team Tools\Static Analysis Tools\FxCop. Select FxCopSdk.dll and Microsoft.Cci.dll, and then click OK.

Caution The Introspection SDK has not been released. The information contained in this chapter comes largely from the FxCop team and a reverse-engineering of the FxCop SDK and IntrospectionAnalysisEngine assembly. Visit the GotDotNet website (www.gotdotnet.com) to check for a release of the Introspection SDK. Microsoft has said that this will likely be released after VSTS ships. At this point, it is an entirely unsupported feature and is not guaranteed to remain the same for VSTS version 2.

Creating the Rule Class

Microsoft's convention is to create one base rule per rule category, which is what you will do here. This way, the constructor is a little simpler and the type of each rule is clear.

All of your custom rules should inherit from the BaseIntrospectionRule class.

Delete the Class1 class, which is created by default, and create a new class called BaseOrgNamingRule. Import the Microsoft.Tools.FxCop.Sdk.Introspection namespace into this new class file. As shown in Listing 13-8, set the class as abstract and so it inherits from the BaseIntrospectionRule, and then create the two constructors for the class. The default constructor will call the second constructor. The second constructor (the one that takes the name argument) will be used by all of the classes that inherit from the BaseOrgNamingRule class.

Listing 13-8. *OrgNamingRule Base Rule*

C#
```
public abstract class OrgNamingRule:BaseIntrospectionRule
{
    protected BaseOrgNamingRule() : this("BaseOrgNamingRule") { }
    protected BaseOrgNamingRule (string name) :
           base(name, "OrgNamingRules.Rules", typeof(BaseOrgNamingRule).Assembly) { }
}
```
VB
```
Public MustInherit Class BaseOrgNamingRule : Inherits BaseIntrospectionRule
    Protected Sub New()
        Me.New("BaseOrgNamingRule")
    End Sub
    Protected Sub New(ByVal name As String)
        MyBase.New(name, "OrgNamingRules.Rules", _
        GetType(BaseOrgNamingRule).Assembly)
    End Sub
End Class
```

You now have a custom, base FxCop rule from which all of your other rules can inherit.

To create the actual rule, add a new class to your project called UnderscorePrefixRule. Add the following lines (replace using with Imports in VB):

```
using Microsoft.FxCop.Sdk.Introspection;
using Microsoft.FxCop.Sdk;
```

Set the class to inherit from the BaseOrgNamingRule class and add a constructor and the Check method, as shown in Listing 13-9.

Listing 13-9. *UnderscorePrefixRule FxCop Custom Rule*

C#
```
    public class UnderscorePrefixRule:BaseOrgNamingRule
    {
        public UnderscorePrefixRule() : base("UnderscorePrefixRule") { }

        public override ProblemCollection Check(Microsoft.Cci.Member member)
        {
            if (member == null || member.IsPublic)
            {
                return null;
            }

            if (member.NodeType == Microsoft.Cci.NodeType.Field)
            {
                if (!member.Name.Name.StartsWith("_"))
                {
                    string[] textArray1 =
                        new string[1] { RuleUtilities.Format(member) };
                    Resolution resolution1 =
                        this.GetNamedResolution("Member", textArray1);
                    Problem problem1 = new Problem(resolution1, "Member");
                    base.Problems.Add(problem1);
                    return base.Problems;
                }
                else
                {
                    return null;
                }
            }
            else
            {
                return null;
            }
        }
    }
```
VB
```
Public Class UnderscorePrefixRule : Inherits BaseOrgNamingRule
    Public Sub New()
        MyBase.New("UnderscorePrefixRule")
    End Sub

    Public Overrides Function Check(ByVal member As Microsoft.Cci.Member) As _
        ProblemCollection
```

```
            If member is Nothing OrElse member.IsPublic Then
                Return Nothing
            End If

    If member.NodeType = Microsoft.Cci.NodeType.Field Then
                If Not member.Name.Name.StartsWith("_") Then
                    Dim textArray1 As String() = _
                        New String(0) {RuleUtilities.Format(member)}
                    Dim resolution1 As Resolution = _
                        Me.GetNamedResolution("Member", textArray1)
                    Dim problem1 As Problem = New Problem(resolution1)
                    Me.Problems.Add(problem1)
                    Return Me.Problems
                Else
                    Return Nothing
                End If
            Else
                Return Nothing
            End If
        End Function
End Class
```

In order to create your own rule, you must override the `Check` method. This method is overloaded to accept various types as arguments. The member type passes any members of a class—that is, fields, events, delegates, properties, methods, and so on. There are five overloaded methods of `Check` that can be used to gather information from your project or assembly. The member overload will probably be the most used method.

In the `UnderscorePrefixRule`, the `Check` method does the following:

- Check to see if the member being examined is a public member. If it is, the rule is skipped because we want to check only private fields.

- If the type of the member is a field, continue with the check; otherwise, skip the rule.

- If the member name does not start with an underscore, continue with the check; otherwise, skip the rule.

- If the rule was broken, format the member name for display (`RuleUtilities` is a method in the FxCop SDK for formatting output) and set any values that are needed by the resolution string.

- Get the resolution text from the rule information file and pass it any parameters (in this case, the name of the rule). (Resolutions are discussed in the next section.)

- Create a new `Problem` object and pass it the resolution of the problem.

- Add the `Problem` to the `Problem` collection and exit the method.

This is a fairly straightforward example, but these rules can become extremely complicated and detailed.

Creating the XML Rule File

The rule file contains all of the details regarding the rule that was broken. By default, the rule file is named `Rules.xml` and is an embedded resource file within the project. Typically, there is one rule file per assembly, and all of the rule information goes in this file. The schema for this file is shown in Listing 13-10.

Note The schema in Listing 13-10 is not complete. Microsoft has yet to release documentation for the Introspection engine. Here, we show the result of research using the Reflection tool from Lutz Roeder (www.aisto.com/roeder/dotnet/). The FxCop team will be releasing detailed documentation of the Introspection engine as soon as possible.

Listing 13-10. *Rule File XML Schema*

```
<?xml version="1.0" encoding="utf-8"?>
<xs:schema attributeFormDefault="unqualified" elementFormDefault="qualified"
xmlns:xs="http://www.w3.org/2001/XMLSchema">
  <xs:element name="Rules">
    <xs:complexType>
      <xs:sequence>
        <xs:element name="Rule">
          <xs:complexType>
            <xs:sequence>
              <xs:element name="Name" type="xs:string" />
              <xs:element name="Description" type="xs:string" />
              <xs:element name="LongDescription" type="xs:string" />
              <xs:element name="GroupOwner" type="xs:string" />
              <xs:element name="DevOwner" type="xs:string" />
              <xs:element name="Owner" type="xs:string" />
              <xs:element name="Url" type="xs:string" />
              <xs:element maxOccurs="unbounded" name="Resolution">
                <xs:complexType>
                  <xs:simpleContent>
                    <xs:extension base="xs:string">
                      <xs:attribute name="Name" type="xs:string" use="required" />
                    </xs:extension>
                  </xs:simpleContent>
                </xs:complexType>
              </xs:element>
              <xs:element name="Email" type="xs:string" />
              <xs:element name="MessageLevel">
                <xs:complexType>
                  <xs:simpleContent>
                    <xs:extension base="xs:string">
                      <xs:attribute name="Certainty" type="xs:unsignedByte"
```

```
                        use="required" />
                  </xs:extension>
                </xs:simpleContent>
              </xs:complexType>
            </xs:element>
            <xs:element name="FixCategories" type="xs:string" />
          </xs:sequence>
          <xs:attribute name="TypeName" type="xs:string" use="required" />
          <xs:attribute name="Category" type="xs:string" use="required" />
          <xs:attribute name="CheckId" type="xs:string" use="required" />
        </xs:complexType>
      </xs:element>
    </xs:sequence>
    <xs:attribute name="FriendlyName" type="xs:string" use="required" />
  </xs:complexType>
</xs:element>
</xs:schema>
```

For this example, add an XML file named Rules.xml to your project. The complete text of this file is shown in Listing 13-11.

Caution The rule filename must match the fully qualified name of the rule as specified in the base rule constructor (in this case, it is OrgNamingRules.Rules, without the xml). While the filename is Rules, the root namespace for the project is OrgNamingRules, so this must prefix the filename in the constructor.

Listing 13-11. *The Rules.xml File for the UnderscorePrefixRule*

```
<Rules FriendlyName="Organization Naming Rules">
<Rule TypeName="UnderscorePrefixRule" Category="Organization.Naming"
CheckId="OR5555">
    <Name>
      UnderscorePrefixRule: Prefix private class scoped variables (fields)
          with an underscore "_").
    </Name>
    <Description>
      The [organization name]'s naming standards require an underscore
          to be prefixed to private fields in all cases.
    </Description>
    <LongDescription>
      The underscore is a visual indication that a variable is a private,
          class scoped field and is used for ease of reading and to
          differentiate between class fields and local variables within methods.
    </LongDescription>
    <GroupOwner>
      [organization] Developer Standards Group
```

```
      </GroupOwner>
      <DevOwner>
        John Smith
      </DevOwner>
      <Owner>
        [organization] Developer Standards Group
      </Owner>
      <Url>
        http://localhost/organizationrules/default.aspx
      </Url>
      <Resolution Name="Member">Add an underscore in front of the field {0}.
            </Resolution>
      <Email>
        OrganizationStandards@organization.com
      </Email>
      <MessageLevel Certainty="80">
        Error
      </MessageLevel>
      <FixCategories>
        NonBreaking
      </FixCategories>
    </Rule>
</Rules>
```

Table 13-4 describes each of the nodes in Listing 13-11.

Table 13-4. *Rules.xsd Nodes*

Node Name/Attribute	Description
Rules	Root node. It contains a collection of `Rule` elements.
FriendlyName	The name displayed in the Code Analysis Configuration dialog box.
Rule	Describes an individual rule.
TypeName	The name of the .NET type that contains the rule.
Category	Displayed when the rule is broken to help categorize the broken rule.
CheckId	Unique identifier for the rule. The ID is two characters followed by four digits.
Name	The name of the rule followed by a very brief description.
Description	A short description of the rule.
LongDescription	A detailed description of the rule.
GroupOwner	The group that developed the rule. In an organization, this would typically be the group in charge of development standards.
DevOwner	The developer who wrote the rule.
Owner	The person or group who owns the rule.
Url	The URL of the web page that contains detailed information about the rule, including code examples and where to go for more information.

Continued

Table 13-4. *Continued*

Node Name/Attribute	Description
Resolution	A series of named resolutions. The resolution names should correspond with the types with which a problem can be associated. For example, a certain type of resolution may exist for members in general, or one resolution may refer to a field problem or another with a property problem for the same rule. There can be multiple named resolutions.
Name	The name of the resolution. This is used to specify which resolution to take to solve a given problem.
Email	The e-mail address where queries regarding the rule can be sent.
MessageLevel	Describes the type of level. This can be Error, Warning, or Information and corresponds with the ability to filter messages in the Error List window.
Certainty	The level of certainty that the rule really has been broken or really is a problem.
FixCategories	This is either `Breaking` or `NonBreaking`. A breaking rule indicates that the functionality will not be consistent from one version to the next if this rule is not fixed.

When you have added the `Rules.xml` file shown in Listing 13-11, you can then compile the project. Copy the resulting assembly to the FxCop Rules folder (`C:\Program Files\Microsoft Visual Studio 8\Team Tools\Static Analysis Tools\FxCop\Rules`).

Note If you examine the list of rules, you will note that the new rule you created is listed there, but there is no `CheckId`. This is a known issue but does not affect how FxCop runs or checks rules.

Close all instances of Visual Studio and then reopen Visual Studio. Create any type of project and add a class field without the underscore in front of the name. Run the code analysis on the project. Your Error List window should show the rule violation, as in Figure 13-3.

	Description	File	Line	Column	Project
⚠ 1	CA2209 : Microsoft.Usage : No valid permission requests were found for assembly 'ConsoleApplication1'. You should always specify the minimum security permissions using SecurityAction.RequestMinimum.				ConsoleApplication1
⚠ 2	CA2210 : Microsoft.Design : Sign 'ConsoleApplication1' with a strong name key.				ConsoleApplication1
⚠ 3	OR5555 : Organization.Naming : Add an underscore in front of the field Person.last.	Person.cs	10		ConsoleApplication1
⚠ 4	CA1801 : Microsoft.Usage : Parameter 'args' of Program.Main(String[]):Void is never used. Remove the parameter or use it in the method body.	Program.cs	10		ConsoleApplication1

Figure 13-3. *The UnderscorePrefixRule custom FxCop rule implemented*

Pressing F1 on a violated rule will take you to the web page (or the part of the help file) specified by the Url value. Microsoft includes the following on the help pages to aid in fixing the problem:

- *Cause:* Why the rule was broken.
- *Rule Description:* What the rule means.
- *How to Fix Violations:* The changes to make.
- *When to Exclude Warnings:* If it is permissible to exclude this type of warning, this explains when you can exclude it.
- *Example Code:* An example of the incorrect and correct versions of code.

If you open the Code Analysis Configuration dialog box, you'll see your custom rule listed under the Organization Naming Rules node.

Summary

In this chapter, you learned how to perform static code analysis to identify potential problem areas and known defects. Using the PREfast tool, you can eliminate a majority of the problems that may cause your code to have potential security holes and other instabilities. You can suppress messages and ensure that some messages are treated as warnings and others are treated as errors. On the whole, this makes working with C/C++ code much safer.

With the FxCop tool, you can ensure that your code is compliant with the latest Microsoft specifications for writing .NET code. This provides a well-structured, robust code base, which you can expand easily. In addition, as an organization using this tool to enforce coding standards specific to your needs, you can provide custom rules or more advanced rule checking than the defaults provided by FxCop. Combined with the check-in policy feature of VSTS (discussed in Chapter 3), FxCop can ensure that code created with VSTS conforms to your organization's standards.

CHAPTER 14

Performance Analysis

Testing application performance has always been one of the most difficult things to do. The reasons for this are varied, but mostly it is because performance is just plain difficult to effectively test. For example, how do you know from one test to another which one is accurate? What are you actually performing the test on? Is it the method level or the application level? How do you modify the application to test for performance? Once you are done with the test, how do you interpret the results? How do you know, when you think you are measuring something, that it is all you are measuring (in other words, that you are measuring the subject of the test and not collateral processes)? These and many other questions have, in the past, been very difficult to answer.

Visual Studio Team System aims to help solve these problems and make sense of application performance so you can do the following:

- Assess your application performance before deployment.
- Fix those areas that are performing poorly.
- Verify that the performance quality attributes have been met.
- Monitor production application performance as needed.

In addition, VSTS allows you to understand the results of a performance test. The results of the test are very clearly displayed and easily understood and traced. By traced, we mean that the call stack can be followed to determine the performance of each call made in a chain of calls.

Note The performance tool in VSTS can be used to monitor your applications' performance without logging items to the performance monitor built into Windows. Though this was easier with previous versions of .NET, it was still not "easy" if you wanted to get information that matters to you.

With previous versions of Visual Studio, running performance tests (without the use of very expensive tools) consisted of outputting data to log files or to the Windows Performance Monitor and trying to make sense of these values. In the case of the Performance Monitor, sometimes it is difficult to figure out if you are logging valid information. Performance monitoring in VSTS does away with all of those issues.

This chapter focuses on how to profile an application using the VSTS performance tools, understanding the results of a profile, and identifying performance bottlenecks in an application. In addition, this chapter covers how to profile a production application, which is useful if end users are having performance issues but cannot articulate them well to the development team.

Note Users, when they experience performance problems, are typically unable to provide details on where and when the problems occur in an application. In addition, how do you determine if the problem is your application or another process running on the same system? Because of this, monitoring the performance of a production application is invaluable.

Performance Profiling Terms

Before you get into actually using the performance tools, a few terms need to be explained. This section is intended for those who have not worked with performance profiling and analysis tools before.

Note There is a great deal more to performance profiling and analysis, in an overall sense, than is indicated in this chapter. This chapter focuses on how VSTS performance tools work, rather than on an overall review of how performance analysis is done.

Table 14-1 defines the terms that will help you understand what is presented in this chapter.

Table 14-1. *Performance Terms*

Term	Definition
Sampling	The process of taking periodic "samples" of application processes. This includes incrementing a counter for the currently executing function and recording the call stack leading to this function.
Instrumentation	The process of taking detailed measurements of all aspects of code execution. The code, during compilation, is altered to allow the performance tool to monitor entry and exit times of each and every function in the application.
Application time	A measure of the time the application code is executing. This does not include OS calls or any time spent waiting for threads to execute.
Elapsed time	A total measure of system time spent during a functions time. In other words, the elapsed time is the "clock" time (absolute time) and includes all system and other events.
Exclusive	Information gathered from the executing function, and does not include any subfunctions.

Term	Definition
Inclusive	Information gathered from the executing function and all of the subfunctions.
Exclusive allocations	The allocation of type instances (or memory) that occur only within the given function.
Inclusive allocations	The allocation of type instances (or memory) that occur within the function and in all subfunctions called by the given function.
Instrumenting	The process of inserting probes into the code to record data.
Probes	Code placed within the source code to monitor function start/stop times and other relevant information.
Transition events	Events that occur outside of the application time. The application time + transition events time = elapsed time.
Trace	Another way of saying the application was profiled using instrumentation.
Exclusive bytes allocated	The number of bytes allocated during the execution of a given function, excluding any subfunctions.
Inclusive bytes allocated	The number of bytes allocated during the execution of a given function and any subfunctions.

Instrumentation

As defined previously, *instrumentation* is a process that results in the gathering of comprehensive data relating to the performance of an application. To show you how this works, Listing 14-1 shows a simple console application in C# that writes a line to the console and waits for the user to press a key to end the application.

Listing 14-1. *C# Console Application*

```
static void Main(string[] args)
{
    Console.WriteLine("This is a test.");
    Console.ReadLine();
}
```

Listing 14-2 shows the exact same application after it has been instrumented by the performance tool.

Listing 14-2. *C# Instrumented Console Application*

```
private static void Main(string[] args)
{
    1 _CAP_Enter_Function_Managed((int)   Microsoft.VisualStudio.Instrumentation.
        g_fldMMID_2D71B909-C28E-4fd9-A0E7-ED05264B707A, 0x6000005);
    2 _CAP_StartProfiling_Managed((int) Microsoft.VisualStudio.Instrumentation.
        g_fldMMID_2D71B909-C28E-4fd9-A0E7-ED05264B707A, 0x6000005, 0xa000010);
    3 Console.WriteLine("This is a test.");
```

```
    4 _CAP_StopProfiling_Managed((int) Microsoft.VisualStudio.Instrumentation.
        g_fldMMID_2D71B909-C28E-4fd9-A0E7-ED05264B707A, 0x6000005);
    5 _CAP_StartProfiling_Managed((int) Microsoft.VisualStudio.Instrumentation.
        g_fldMMID_2D71B909-C28E-4fd9-A0E7-ED05264B707A, 0x6000005, 0xa000011);
    6 _CAP_StopProfiling_Managed((int) Microsoft.VisualStudio.Instrumentation.
        g_fldMMID_2D71B909-C28E-4fd9-A0E7-ED05264B707A, 0x6000005);
    7 Console.ReadLine();
    8 _CAP_Exit_Function_Managed((int) Microsoft.VisualStudio.Instrumentation.
        g_fldMMID_2D71B909-C28E-4fd9-A0E7-ED05264B707A, 0x6000005);
}
```

■Note The line breaks are for formatting purposes. There are really only eight lines of code here as denoted by the line numbers for clarity.

This illustrates how instrumentation alters the code to gather data. The key thing to note in this example is that instrumentation does add overhead to an application. Is it such a large amount of overhead that you could not do this in production? No. It is not recommended that you instrument a production application—but you can do it. The real issue is that, compared to a noninstrumented application, the performance is slower.

■Caution Instrumenting production applications as a matter of course should not be done. It is best done when you know there is a problem with the application and you need to pinpoint it using the performance tools. For day-to-day monitoring of applications, sampling provides better performance and over the longer term will help you narrow down the area of performance problems.

With this implementation, the performance tool can tell how long a function takes to execute, how long subfunctions take to execute, how many times a function is called, and other detailed information. This is the real power of instrumentation: the ability to know everything about an application while it is running. However, there is a drawback to this. Instrumentation uses averages and totals. It does not display information about single calls.

■Tip To get information about specific calls, you can instrument an application and run it through one set test at a time; however it can be somewhat tedious.

Sampling

Sampling, as defined in Table 14-1, takes periodic "snapshots" of your application as it is running. It gathers the current function information and the call stack and stores it for later analysis. It does not alter the code output from a build. Instead, the performance tool "interrupts" a running application to gather data at a user-defined interval.

The information provided by sampling is not a complete picture of the application. It does not include information such as the amount of time spent in a function, or the time spent in anything, for that matter. It simply provides information on the number of times a method is invoked, and how many other types are allocated during the invocation. This provides indirect evidence of how an application is performing. A method being called too many times may indicate a problem with how the code is structured.

On the other hand, sampling does not provide information on all the functions in your application. Since it takes only periodic readings, you may not see the allocation information for a method you are curious about. This is one of the drawbacks of using sampling.

Running a Performance Test

Now that you understand the differences between instrumentation and sampling it is time to actually run a performance test and examine the results.

Note For comparison purposes later on, this exact test was run twice: once with instrumentation selected and once with sampling selected.

1. Open the sample application.

2. Select Tools ➤ Performance Tools ➤ Performance Wizard.

3. Select the default profile by clicking Next (see Figure 14-1).

4. Select the Instrumentation test and click Next.

5. Click the Finish button.

6. Next, the Performance Explorer will open (see Figure 14-2).

7. Right-click the root node in the Performance Explorer (EffortTrackingWeb.psess) and select Properties.

8. On the General tab of the properties dialog check the "Collect .NET object allocation information" and the "Also collection .NET object lifetime information" options and click OK (this dialog will be covered in detail in the section "Performance Session Options" later in this chapter).

CHAPTER 14 ■ PERFORMANCE ANALYSIS

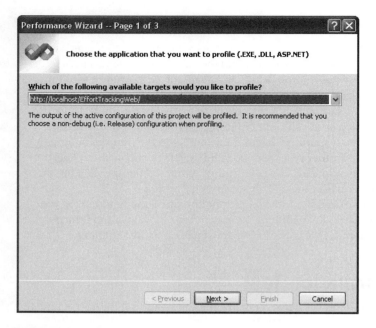

Figure 14-1. *Performance Wizard page 1*

The Performance Explorer window opens with one test that is set to be run on the EffortTrackingWeb and there are no reports. Before running the test, build the application using the Release configuration. To launch the application, click the Launch button on the Performance Tools toolbar and not the regular Run button.

For this first test, keep things simple and perform the following steps:

1. Enter new user login information (username = **PerformanceUser**, password = **password**, Verify Password= **password**) and click New User.

2. Click the Add button.

3. Enter **Chapter 1** for the title, **Read it** for the description.

4. Leave all of the other drop-downs as they are and click Save.

5. After the default screen reloads, select the entry you just added by clicking the Edit link.

6. Change the title to "Test" and click Save.

7. Exit the application.

As you can see, running a performance test is straightforward and simple. There are no additional steps. You just need to remember to launch the test from the Performance Explorer.

> **Tip** When running an instrumented performance test, the probes are inserted during compile, but after the test is run, binaries are reverted. This means that the probes are removed! The code used for a performance test cannot be instrumented for deployment using this process. This is discussed later in the section "Profiling Production Applications."

Understanding the Performance Report

Figure 14-2 shows the results of your first test of the performance analysis tool, and the Performance Explorer (if the report does not show up, double-click the report in the Performance Explorer). In this section you will examine each of the parts of the performance report and learn how to understand the information presented. Each page of the report provides information about your application with a different view into the data. Later you will see how to use the information to improve your application performance.

Figure 14-2. *Performance Report Summary (Instrumentation) and Explorer*

Summary Tab

The summary page contains general statistics about your application. Some of the properties (such as the number of most called functions) can be changed via the options dialog, which you will see later in this chapter. Also, each of the tabs displays different information, depending on whether you ran a sampled or instrumented performance test. The differences for each will be discussed in the following sections.

The summary for a performance test using sampling displays other information. The information presented is summarized and described in Table 14-2.

Table 14-2. *Summary Tab Description*

Type	Measurement	Description
Instrumentation	Most Called Functions	List of functions that were called the most.
Instrumentation	Functions With Most Individual Work	List of functions that, exclusively, took the longest time to execute.
Instrumentation	Functions Taking Longest	List of functions that, exclusively, but including application time, took the longest to execute.
Sampling	Functions Allocating Most Memory	List of functions that allocated the most bytes.
Sampling	Types With Most Allocated Memory	List of types and how many bytes were allocated to instances of that type.
Sampling	Types With Most Instances	List of types that were instantiated the most.

For comparison purposes, the summary page of the sampled performance session is shown in Figure 14-3.

Figure 14-3. *Performance Report Summary (Sampling)*

Double-clicking any item on this page will take you to that item on the Functions view. Optionally you can right-click the item and select one of the following three choices: View Source Code (for non-Framework functions), the Function View for that method, and the Caller/Callee graph for that function (either the functions called by the function or the function that called the functions).

If you look through both reports (included with the downloaded code) you will note that some functions are just not listed in the sampled performance data. Those functions that are listed in both have a lower instance count in the sampled data vs. the instrumented data.

Functions Tab

The function page reports on each individual function (or just the sampled functions) called during the course of the testing run. Figure 14-4 shows one view of the Function tab of the performance report.

Function Name	Number of Calls	Elapsed Exclusive Time
App_Web_xv0gd3w4.DLL	29	11.026238
ASP.login_aspx.ProcessRequest(class System.Web.HttpContext)	2	0.001266
Login.btnNew_Click(object,class System.EventArgs)	1	0.006313
ASP.login_aspx.__BuildControlContent1(class System.Web.UI.Contr	2	7.041892
ASP.login_aspx.__BuildControltxtUserName()	2	0.001624
__ASP.FastObjectFactory_app_web_xv0gd3w4.Create_ASP_login_	2	2.069308
ASP.login_aspx..ctor()	2	0.423075
ASP.login_aspx.FrameworkInitialize()	2	1.318431
Login..ctor()	2	0.153604
ASP.login_aspx.__BuildControltxtPassword()	2	0.001818
ASP.login_aspx.__BuildControlbtnNew()	2	0.001729
ASP.login_aspx.__BuildControlTree(class ASP.login_aspx)	2	0.001669
ASP.login_aspx.__BuildControllblErrors()	2	0.001808
ASP.login_aspx.__BuildControlbtnLogin()	2	0.001343
ASP.login_aspx.__BuildControltxtVerifyPassword()	2	0.001544
ASP.login_aspx.GetTypeHashCode()	2	0.000812
App_Web_i6fdp_mn.DLL	304	45.122230
App_Code.rw1-jqzn.DLL	28	3.540814
CommonProcess.LoadWeekEndingCombo(class System.Web.UI.We	10	2.086287
CommonProcess.LoadWeekEndingCombo(class System.Web.UI.We	10	0.198520
CommonProcess.LoadCategoryCombo(class System.Web.UI.WebC	4	1.249314
CommonProcess.LoadCategoryCombo(class System.Web.UI.WebC	4	0.006693
App_Web_zppzylgg.DLL	60	4.345506
ASP.secure_edit_aspx.ProcessRequest(class System.Web.HttpCont	6	0.004354
ASP.secure_edit_aspx.__BuildControlContent1(class System.Web.L	6	1.071082
ASP.secure_edit_aspx.__BuildControlDetails1()	6	0.004021
ASP.FastObjectFactory_app_web_zppzylgg.Create_ASP_secure_	6	1.100895

Figure 14-4. *Function tab of the Performance Report (Instrumentation)*

The columns on each of the tabs (with the exception of the Summary tab) are customizable. You can add or remove or change the order the columns are displayed in. To do this, right-click anywhere in the report window and select Add/Remove Columns. The list of columns for both types of performance tests is extensive and allows you to see every bit of data collected about each function. The following two lists show the complete data available for the Functions tab. Other windows contain other columns of data specific to those windows.

This list shows the column names for the instrumentation data:

- Function Name
- Number of Calls
- Elapsed Exclusive Time
- Function Address
- Line Number
- Percentage of Calls
- Source File Name
- Process Name
- Module Name
- Module Path
- Module Identifier
- Application Exclusive Time
- Elapsed Inclusive Time
- Application Inclusive Time
- MAX Elapsed Exclusive Time
- MAX Application Exclusive Time
- MAX Elapsed Inclusive Time
- MAX Application Inclusive Time
- MIN Elapsed Exclusive Time
- MIN Application Exclusive Time
- MIN Elapsed Inclusive Time
- MIN Application Inclusive Time
- AVG Elapsed Exclusive Time
- AVG Application Exclusive Time
- AVG Elapsed Inclusive Time
- AVG Application Inclusive Time
- % Elapsed Exclusive Time
- % Application Exclusive Time
- % Elapsed Inclusive Time
- % Application Inclusive Time

- Exclusive Transitions
- Inclusive Transitions
- Process ID
- Unique Process ID
- Unique ID
- Exclusive Transitions Percentage
- Inclusive Transitions Percentage
- Root Node Recursion
- Time Exclusive Probe Overhead
- Time Inclusive Probe Overhead

The following is a list of column names available in the sampling data:

- Function Name
- Exclusive Allocations
- Inclusive Allocations
- Exclusive Bytes Allocated
- Inclusive Bytes Allocated
- Line Number
- Source File Name
- Module Name
- Module Path
- Process Name
- Exclusive Allocations Percent
- Inclusive Allocations Percent
- Exclusive Bytes Percent
- Inclusive Bytes Percent
- Process ID
- Unique Process ID
- Unique ID
- Module Identifier
- Function Address

Note The MSDN documentation on this subject is very complete. Refer to the Functions View in the MSDN documentation to see the definition of each column available for the report.

One thing you may have noticed while looking at the performance results is that it is not at all obvious where the application code is located. This is because with web applications, which use the shadow copy mechanism, the actual website is not instrumented or sampled, the shadow copy is. The way .NET 2.0 works (at least as far as it relates to being able to find code for a website in the performance report) is that the shadow-copied code is prefixed with the folder it resides in for the website. Looking at the report results in Figure 14-4 you can see that App_Web contains code in the root website folder. Code contained in lower branches are prefixed with the folder name. So the edit.aspx page is noted in the App_Web\secure folder and indicated by ASP.secure_edit_aspx. Anything that refers to the actual web page ends with _aspx and any code residing in those pages is noted by the page name, a period, and the method name (for example the Login_aspx.ctor()).

Caller/Callee Tab

This tab displays information about specific calls and the (partially sorted) order in which they are made (explained later on). The function that is being examined is displayed on the Current function line (see Figure 14-5). The function that called that function (the caller) is listed above it and the functions called by it (the callees) are listed below it. The reason the list is only partially ordered is because many different functions can call one function and one function can call many different functions (for example, if you are using many else statements). Therefore, this list of calls is not always accurate.

Function Name	Number of Calls	Elapsed Exclusive Time	Application Exclusive Time
Functions that called Login.btnNew_Click			
System.Web.UI.Page.ProcessRequest(class System.Web.HttpC...	1	0.006313	0.006313
Current function:			
Login.btnNew_Click(object,class System.EventArgs)	1	0.006313	0.006313
Functions that were called by Login.btnNew_Click			
localhost.Service.AddUser(string,string)	1	0.657870	0.001354
localhost.Service..ctor()	1	1.196706	0.001640
System.Web.HttpResponse.Redirect(string)	1	37.625266	0.000000
System.Web.Security.FormsAuthentication.SetAuthCookie(strin...	1	1.055977	0.000000
System.Web.HttpRequest.get_Item(string)	1	0.491402	0.000000
System.Web.SessionState.HttpSessionState.Add(string,object)	1	0.064657	0.064657
System.Web.UI.Page.get_Session()	1	0.034941	0.000000
System.Web.UI.WebControls.TextBox.get_Text()	5	0.019129	0.019129
System.Web.UI.Control.get_Page()	3	0.001569	0.001569
System.String.op_Equality(string,string)	1	0.000651	0.000651
System.Web.UI.Page.get_Request()	1	0.000370	0.000370
System.Web.UI.Page.get_Response()	1	0.000079	0.000079

Figure 14-5. *Caller/Callee tab of the Performance Report (Login.btnNew_Click)*

To understand this information, examine the data in Figure 14-5. This information tells us that the call to the btnNew_Click function triggered a call to the AddUser function of the web service and that the constructor was called next. You might be telling yourself right now that something looks wrong with this. You would be right. This is out of order, as you will see in the next section, "Calltree Tab."

Caution Because in many cases only a partially sorted order of function invocations is listed, it is not always practical or advisable to use this list to determine the order of the call stack at any given time except in a very general sense. Keep this in mind when looking at the following set of points. Being able to view this list and easily understand it only works because the application was run once through a very specific set of steps so it would be easily understandable by the reader.

To help you understand, line by line, this display is telling you

- The New User button was clicked.
- The Service object (web service) was instantiated.
- The AddUser method was called.
- The authorization cookie was set.
- The user was redirected to another page (the default page).

These types of low-level details concerning your applications call stack can be invaluable in solving performance-related issues. One additional piece of very-nice-to-have functionality is that you can double-click any function in the Caller/Callee view and that function will become the Current function.

Caution It is extremely important to note, when looking at the Caller/Callee view, that it is an aggregation of all the calls leading up to and called by a function. This detail is broken down into specific information on the Calltree tab, discussed next.

Calltree Tab

The Calltree tab is used to display all levels of a given call tree, whereas the Caller/Callee tab displays aggregate information and only three levels of the call tree. The Calltree tab gets into the details whereas the Caller/Callee tab really contains the overview information. The call tree helps you trace a call from the beginning to the end of the call sequence and allows you to determine if there are calls that you did not intend to make that may be wasting time unnecessarily.

As was pointed out in the previous section, the call order is incorrect for the invocation of the AddUser function. To see the actual call tree, switch to the Calltree tab. Then expand the Login.btnNew_Click node and all of the other children nodes underneath that node. Your view should look like that in Figure 14-6.

Function Name	Number of C...	Elapsed Excl...
ASP.login_aspx.ProcessRequest(class System.Web.HttpContext)	2	0.001266
System.Web.UI.Page.ProcessRequest(class System.Web.HttpContext)	2	352.945350
__ASP.FastObjectFactory_app_web_t22vta7o.Create_ASP_masterpage_maste	2	1.177882
ASP.login_aspx.FrameworkInitialize()	2	1.318431
ASP.login_aspx.GetTypeHashCode()	2	0.000812
ASP.masterpage_master.FrameworkInitialize()	2	1.257208
Login.btnNew_Click(object,class System.EventArgs)	1	0.006313
localhost.Service..ctor()	1	1.196706
localhost.Service..ctor()	1	0.119868
System.Collections.Specialized.NameValueCollection.get_Item(string	1	0.011475
System.Configuration.ConfigurationManager.get_AppSettings()	1	0.008620
System.Web.Services.Protocols.SoapHttpClientProtocol..ctor()	1	414.530867
System.Web.Services.Protocols.WebClientProtocol.set_Url(string)	1	0.011060
localhost.Service.AddUser(string,string)	1	0.657870
localhost.Service.AddUser(string,string)	1	0.010238
System.Web.Services.Protocols.SoapHttpClientProtocol.Invoke(strir	1	1438.010720
System.String.op_Equality(string,string)	1	0.000651
System.Web.HttpRequest.get_Item(string)	1	0.491402
System.Web.HttpResponse.Redirect(string)	1	37.625266
System.Web.Security.FormsAuthentication.SetAuthCookie(string,bool)	1	1.055977
System.Web.SessionState.HttpSessionState.Add(string,object)	1	0.064657

Figure 14-6. *The Calltree tab*

The call tree for the AddUser service call involves invoking the service constructor (the service then runs through its startup processes) and then invoking the AddUser function. This is the actual order of calls made for a given set of calls. You can switch to several other views by right-clicking the function in the list and selecting the appropriate view.

Allocation

When you set up the test at the beginning of this chapter, you elected to collect the .NET object allocation information. If you had not selected this option, this tab would be empty. By default, the allocation and lifetime information is not collected as part of a performance session.

This information is extremely useful for determining how much memory objects consumed and how many times they were instantiated (allocated) during the course of an application. This provides a detailed breakdown. Note also that this information can be seen on the Functions tab by selecting the appropriate columns. Figure 14-7 shows the object allocation information (partially) for the performance session.

Expanding the instantiated object type will show you the method that instantiated the object. As you can see in Figure 14-7 the localhost.Service class was instantiated by several different methods, including the LoadCategory method, the LoadRecord method, and the btnNew_Click method.

Figure 14-7. *Application allocation information*

Objects Lifetime

Object lifetime information is displayed in the last tab of the performance report. This tab gives you details on the garbage collection patterns related to a given object. Figure 14-8 shows the Objects Lifetime tab. However, as a preview of improving performance, this view shows how many objects were collected in Gen2. Objects collected in Gen2 cause performance problems because they require a complete stack walk to collect them. This essentially pauses the application.

Figure 14-8. *Objects Lifetime tab*

The columns on this tab are described in Table 14-3.

Table 14-3. *Objects Lifetime Tab Columns*

Column	Description
Class Name	The name of the class being described.
Instances	The number of instances of the class created during the session.
Total Bytes Allocated	The number of bytes allocated for all instances of the object that were created.
% of Total Bytes	Percentage of the number of bytes allocated during the performance session.
Gen 0 Instances Collected	Number of instances collected in generation 0.
Gen 1 Instances Collected	Number of instances collected in generation 1.
Gen 2 Instances Collected	Number of instances collected in generation 2.
Large Object Heap Instances Collected	Number of instances collected from the heap.

> **Note** Garbage collection is beyond the scope of this book. For a detailed discussion of garbage collection in .NET, see Jeffrey Richter's excellent MSDN article from December 2000 available on MSDN: http://msdn.microsoft.com/msdnmag/issues/1200/GCI2/default.aspx.

Performance Session Options

Now that you have run a performance session and reviewed a performance session report it is time to dive into the options available to you and learn when to use them. To get to a performance session's options, open the Performance Explorer window (if it is not already open, you can access it by selecting View ➤ Performance Explorer from the main menu). The performance session nodes are bold and contain the Targets and Reports folders. Right-click the root node (from the previous examples this would be EffortTrackingWeb.psess) and select Properties. Table 14-4 covers the available options.

> **Tip** There are two sets of property pages for the performance tools: the one that you just opened and a node in the Options for Visual Studio. Those options are covered later in this section.

Table 14-4. *Performance Session Options*

Tab	Option	Description
General	Profiling collection	Allows you to choose between instrumentation and sampling types of performance monitoring.
	.NET memory profiling collection	Indicates whether the performance session should include statistics about the .NET Framework and its memory usage.
	Report	Allows you to specify the location for the reports, the name, the naming convention, and whether the reports are added to the project.
Launch	Binary selection	Allows you to select the order in which the binaries are launched. The binaries that are identified here are those in the Target folder of the performance session. See the "Target Options" section of this chapter.
Sampling	Sample Event	Allows you to specify what type of event you are sampling. The options are Clock Cycles, Page Faults, System Calls, and Performance Counter.
	Interval	Sets the length of time or number of operations before the data is sampled. This is Sample Event–specific.
	Available performance counters	Shows the performance counters you can choose to sample. This only applies to the Performance Counter sampling event.
Binary	Relocate instrumented binaries	Allows the binaries to be profiled and to be compiled and run from a different location.
Instrumentation	Pre/post instrumentation events	Allows you to specify commands to run either before or after the instrumentation session occurs. These activities can be instrumented or not, depending on your needs.
Advanced	Additional instrumentation options	Allows you to supply command-line arguments to the performance application (discussed in the section "Profiling Production Applications" later in this chapter).
Counters	Collect on-chip counter performance data	Allows you to collect performance information as it relates to the actual CPU. This information is more useful for understanding the processes occurring on the system while your application is being profiled.

Continued

Table 14-4. *Continued*

Tab	Option	Description
Events	Event trace providers	Allows you to specify that you will collect performance trace data from a number of providers. This is information that typically goes directly to the Performance Monitor in Windows.
General*	General settings	Allows you to choose to display the performance information by number of clock cycles or in milliseconds. You can also change the number of functions displayed in the summary view on the first page of the performance report.

*The General settings are in the Tools ➤ Options ➤ Performance Tools dialog; they are not part of the Other performance options dialog.

Target Options

Right-clicking the Target folder in the Performance Explorer will allow you to specify the binary, project, or existing website you want to profile. In general, you will be targeting projects you are currently working on, but there will be many instances where you will want to profile an existing application. How many times has a customer come to you and said that the website was acting slow or that certain pages were taking a long time? In such a case, there is no way to go in and diagnose specific problems on the pages except by looking at general server logs and hoping it is the server causing the problems. By using the profiler, you will gain a great deal more information about the application and its performance issues.

Note In order to be able to profile production applications, Visual Studio can be installed on the system where the binaries you want to profile are located. Since the overhead of having Visual Studio installed can have its own effect on the performance of a production application, you can profile applications using the command-line tools, which do not require Visual Studio to be on the target system. This is described in the section "Profiling Production Applications" later in this chapter.

Once you have added a target to the Target folder you can set certain options for just that target (right-clicking the target brings up target-specific options). You may choose to launch a different assembly or website and thereby override the settings of the target you are currently pointing to. Additionally, because multiple targets may be run during a performance session, you can elect to specify code (or command-line applications) to run pre- and post-target activation during the performance session.

Profiling Unit Tests

Yes, exactly what the title says; you can profile a unit test! This allows you to create performance sessions that do not require you to walk through your application each time, and allows you to pinpoint specific functionality for testing. This is an invaluable ability but a little limited in this release.

To profile a unit test (note that this is singular because you can only profile one unit test at a time) you need to run the test first (without profiling it). When the test results are displayed, right-click the test you want to profile and select Create Performance Session.

Note This will not work for Ordered Tests, only for individual tests.

This will bring up the Performance Wizard in which you can select Sampling or Instrumentation for the test. Once you have finished with the wizard, a new Performance Session in the Performance Explorer is displayed. Simply select the correct session and launch the performance test.

Tip Because you can profile only one test, it is a good idea to create a data-driven test to profile—one that will be run many times—in order to get the most valuable results.

When the test is complete, the performance results for the code tested will be displayed. Viewing a performance result in this format is extremely helpful because it does not contain an overwhelming amount of information and you can comfortably digest the information. This will allow you to discover issues in individual methods (or processes, depending on how complicated your unit test is) and fix them easily (well, hopefully).

Profiling Web/Load Tests

After all of this, you have to be asking yourself if it is possible to run performance profiles for existing tests. The answer is yes, you can, but it is not quite an automated process. It is not built into VSTS, per se, but there is a simple workaround for it. To profile a web or load test, do the following:

1. Create a performance test.
2. Create a Web or Load test.
3. Launch the performance session from the Performance Explorer.
4. Minimize the browser (this is the key part here).
5. Run the Web or Load test.

6. Click OK when the message saying the process is already being profiled appears. The test will begin after this.

7. Close the minimized browser window.

Caution You *must* disable code coverage by unselecting all assemblies marked for code coverage in the configuration file used by the Web or Load test.

This will provide you with a set of performance data you can use to consistently compare performance for the same test run again and again. You can either sample or instrument these tests, but we would recommend you instrument them to be able to perform more accurate comparisons between one run and another.

Profiling Production Applications

Now that you have seen how to profile applications in the development environment, it is time to understand how to do it in a production environment. Before you begin profiling a production application you should have a good reason for doing so. Any of the standard answers will work: the application runs slowly; the application is using a huge amount of CPU time or memory; the system the application is running on is starting to slow down; etc. So now that you have your good reason for profiling a production application, you need to know how to profile it.

Tip For non-ASP.NET applications, the best practice is to run a sampled performance profile first in order to help pin down possible problem areas. For ASP.NET applications, however, an instrumented performance profile should be run first. The reason for this is that an instrumented profile will target only the application code. A sampled profile will target not only the application, but the entire ASP.NET/IIS system.

Before you begin profiling a production application you must install the performance tools redistributable on the machine that houses the application you want to profile. You can install Visual Studio on the production box, but it is not recommended because it may cause other problems. When you install the performance tools, you are installing the assemblies you need to run performance tests, and the command-line tools, which allow you to run the tests. These tools are detailed in the next section.

Command-Line Performance Tools

VSTS includes five command-line tools that are available to run performance profiles and report the results. These tools and their purpose are listed in Table 14-5.

Table 14-5. *Command-Line Performance Tools*

Application	Description
VSInstr	Performs the instrumentation of the binaries, which can then be deployed to a production machine.
VSPerfCmd	Starts and stops the performance profiling.
VSPerfMon	Can also be used to start and stop performance profiling, but contains different options than the VSPerfCmd application (discussed briefly below).
VSPerfClrEnv	Sets CLR environment options so the performance tools can be properly loaded.
VSPerfReport	Creates the performance reports (or a subset of those reports that you see in the IDE).

Because the MSDN documentation contains detailed information about each of these applications the information will not be re-presented here.

■**Tip** To find information about these applications in the MSDN documentation, go to its table of contents, navigate to Visual Studio Team System ➤ Team Edition for Developers ➤ Analyzing Application Performance ➤ Command-Line Tools.

The next sections focus on how to profile applications using these tools.

Profiling Windows Applications and Windows Services

By Windows applications, we mean any application deployed to a machine. This can be one part of an application (i.e., the front end of a distributed application, a console application, or a custom server) or the complete application. It does not include Windows services or ASP.NET applications. Windows services are discussed at the end of this section because the steps are only slightly different for a Windows service than for a Windows application. For this example, the application being instrumented is the console application presented in Listing 14-1. It was compiled using the Release configuration. The application name is Performance-InstrumentationExample and it is located in the root of drive C (C:\). To profile this application using instrumentation, take the following steps (sampling is described afterward):

1. Open the Visual Studio Command Prompt.

2. Navigate to the Performance Tools location (the default installation is C:\Program Files\Microsoft Visual Studio 8\Team Tools\Performance Tools).

3. Run the following (use /globalsampleon to run sampling performance tests):

   vsperfclrenv /globaltraceon

   This sets up the CLR to enable the loading and running of performance tools.

CHAPTER 14 ■ PERFORMANCE ANALYSIS

4. Reboot the machine.

5. Restart the Visual Studio Command Prompt and navigate back to the Performance Tools folder (you can avoid this step by adding the location to your path environment variable—see Windows help for how to do this).

6. Run the following:

   `vsinstr C:\PerformanceInstrumentationExample.exe`

   This instruments the binary and renames the original file to `PerformanceInstrumentationExample.exe.orig` and creates a symbol file called `PerformanceInstrumentationExample.exe.pdb`.

7. Run the following (use /sample instead of /trace for a sampled performance test) which starts the profiling:

   `vsperfmon /trace /output:c:\PerformanceInstrumentationResults.vsp`

8. Launch the application and once the message is displayed press any key to end the PerformanceInstrumentationExample application.

9. Start a new Visual Studio Command Prompt and navigate to the Performance Tools folder. (This is necessary because the first command prompt contains the running VSPerfmon application and nothing else can be entered in that window.)

10. Run the following:

    `vsperfcmd -shutdown`

11. Run the following:

    `vsperfreport C:\PerformanceInstrumentationResults.vsp /packsymbols`

    This compiles the report with whatever options you choose. Packsymbols stores the symbols so the report can be viewed on another machine.

12. Run the following:

    `vsperfclrenv /globaloff`

    This removes the ability to load profile information and can be a performance issue if not done.

13. Reboot the machine.

The test report can now be viewed in Visual Studio.

■**Tip** If you are running multiple performance tests (i.e., one after another), then do not re-run the vsperfclrenv /globaloff command until after you are done with all of the tests. However, Microsoft notes that not running this once you are done profiling an application can have an adverse effect on the application.

This is the basic process for using the command-line tools to instrument and run performance tests on production applications. This process is essentially the same for ASP.NET applications and for Windows Services applications although there are some differences. These differences are described in the following sections.

Tip Remember that when you are sampling an application you never have to instrument the assemblies; so that step is always skipped. In addition, remember that the options for the CLR environment are /globaltrace (on or off) for instrumentation performance tests, and /globalsample (on or off) for sampling performance tests.

To profile an application using sampling, you would start the application (which in the case of the sample application is not particularly useful since everything occurs on startup) and attach to the process using the vsperfmon /attach [PID]. Then you would use the application; when it is complete you would use the vsperfmon /detach command.

To profile a service, using either sampling or instrumentation, the only changes you would make would be to start the monitor (include the /user parameter option of the vsperfcmd application with the username the service is running under); start the service; attach to the executable the service is running; run the tests; and detach afterward. The setup and shutdown steps are the same as listed above.

Profiling ASP.NET Applications

ASP.NET applications contain their own bit of complexity in that they run under a separate process and can be precompiled or dynamically compiled. On top of this, the process for sampling an ASP.NET application is slightly different than that of instrumenting the same application. ASP.NET applications come in a couple of different flavors with version 2 in .NET. Assemblies in a web application can be precompiled or contain dynamically built assemblies (built at runtime). Precompiled assemblies are those assemblies that are copied to the bin folder of the virtual directory. Everything else is dynamically compiled (this consists of web pages, code behind pages, and code located in the App_Code folder). Either of these can be instrumented.

Instrumenting Precompiled ASP.NET Applications

To instrument precompiled assemblies in ASP.NET, do the following:

1. Open the Visual Studio Command Prompt.

2. Navigate to the Performance Tools location.

3. Run the following:

    vsperfclrenv /globaltraceon

4. Reboot the machine.

5. Restart the Visual Studio Command Prompt and navigate back to the performance tools folder.

6. Run the following:

    vsinstr [*path to assembly*]

7. Run the following:

    vsperfmon /trace /output:[*File Name*].vsp /user:"[*ASP.NET worker process user*]"

8. Run the tests against the web application.

9. Start a new Visual Studio Command Prompt.

10. Run the following (the iisreset.exe program is located in the %windir%\sytem32 folder):

    iisreset /stop

    Note that this will stop IIS, so be aware of everything running under IIS at the time, or just stop the IIS process by using the Services window or the IIS Administrator Console.

11. Run the following:

    vsperfcmd -shutdown

12. Run the following:

    vsperfreport [*File Name*].vsp /packsymbols

13. If you are going to perform more testing, run the following (or restart it from the Services window or the IIS Administration Console):

    iisrestart /start

14. Run the following:

    vsperfclrenv /globaloff

15. Reboot the machine.

Instrumenting Dynamically Built ASP.NET Applications

To instrument dynamically built assemblies in ASP.NET, do the following:

1. Open the Visual Studio Command Prompt.

2. Navigate to the Performance Tools location.

3. Run the following:

    vsperfclrenv /globaltraceon

4. Reboot the machine.

5. Back up the application's web.config file.

6. Update (or alter) the web.config file for the website with the information presented in Listing 14-3.

Listing 14-3. *Web.Config Changes for Dynamic Code Instrumentation*

```
<!-- Add or modify the compilation tag -->
<system.web>
<compilation assemblyPostProcessorType=
"Microsoft.VisualStudio.Enterprise.Common.AspPerformanceInstrumenter,
 Microsoft.VisualStudio.Enterprise.ASPNetHelper, Version=8.0.0.0,
 Culture=neutral, PublicKeyToken=b03f5f7f11d50a3a" />
</system.web>

<!--Add or modify the runtime tag
Note there are no spaces in the href - this is a formatting
 consideration for the book. -->
<runtime>
  <assemblyBinding xmlns="urn:schemas-microsoft-com:asm.v1">
    <dependentAssembly>
      <assemblyIdentity name="Microsoft.VisualStudio.Enterprise.ASPNetHelper"
                        publicKeyToken="b03f5f7f11d50a3a" culture="neutral" />
      <codeBase version="8.0.0.0"
          href="file:///C:/Program%20Files/Microsoft%20Visual%20Studio%208
          /Common7/IDE/PrivateAssemblies
          /Microsoft.VisualStudio.Enterprise.ASPNetHelper.DLL" />
    </dependentAssembly>
  </assemblyBinding>
</runtime>

<!-- Add or modify the appSettings tag to include the following two tags
Note, there are no spaces in the value - this is a formatting
 consideration for the book -->
<appSettings>
   <add key="Microsoft.VisualStudio.Enterprise.AspNetHelper.VsInstrLocation"
value="C:\Program Files\Microsoft Visual Studio 8\Team Tools\Performance
Tools\vsinstr.exe" />
   <add key="Microsoft.VisualStudio.Enterprise.AspNetHelper.VsInstrTools"
value="C:\Program Files\Microsoft Visual Studio 8\Team Tools\Performance Tools\" />
</appSettings>
```

7. Run the following:

   vsinstr [*path to assembly*]

8. Run the following:

   vsperfmon /trace /output:[*File Name*].vsp /user:"[*ASP.NET worker process user*]"

9. Run the tests against the web application.

10. Start a new Visual Studio Command Prompt.

11. Run the following:

    iisreset /stop

    The iisreset.exe program is located in the %windir%\sytem32 folder. (Note that this will stop IIS, so be aware of everything running under IIS at the time, or just stop the IIS process by using the Services window or the IIS Administrator Console.)

12. Run the following:

    vsperfcmd -shutdown

13. Run the following:

    vsperfreport [File Name].vsp /packsymbols

14. Restore the web.config file (unless you are going to do more testing).

15. Run the following (or restart it from the Services window or the IIS Administration Console):

    iisrestart /start

16. Run the following:

    vsperfclrenv /globaloff

17. Reboot the machine.

Here are a couple of notes related to what shows up in the changes to the web.config file:

- The public key token for the ASPNetHelper assembly must match the entry here.
- The HREF for the code base must be a file URL and not a path name.
- To determine the username of the ASP.NET worker process, open the Process Manager, display the username and PID columns, and look for either aspnet_wp.exe (usually on Win2k or WinXP machines) or w3wp.exe (on Win2k3).

Sampling an ASP.NET Application

The process for sampling an ASP.NET application is slightly different because the generated code (whether it is the dynamic or precompiled assemblies) is not altered. To sample an ASP.NET application, take the following steps:

1. Open the Visual Studio Command Prompt.
2. Navigate to the Performance Tools location.
3. Run the following:

    vsperfclrenv /globaltraceon

4. Reboot the machine.
5. Run the following:

    vsinstr [path to assembly]

6. Run the following:

    vsperfmon /sample /output:[File Name].vsp /user:"[ASP.NET worker process user]"

7. Run the following:

    vsperfcmd /attach:[ASP.NET Worker Process PID (Process ID)]

8. Run the tests against the web application.
9. Start a new Visual Studio Command Prompt.
10. Run the following:

    vsperfcmd /detach

11. Run the following:

    vsperfcmd /shutdown

12. Run the following:

    vsperfreport [File Name].vsp /packsymbols

13. Run the following:

    vsperfclrenv /globaloff

14. Reboot the machine.

As you can see, this process is much simpler, since the profiler is only attaching to an existing process.

Tip The VSTS profiling team recommends that you get the CPU running 100% for several minutes during the test to get usable results.

Summary

This chapter has introduced to you what may be a whole set of new concepts regarding performance profiling of an application. You have learned why you need a performance testing/profiling tool and how it can be used by a development team to improve application performance. In addition, you can now read the performance report and understand what the various terms and results mean, and you can put these in perspective to solve a performance problem. This ability will only help developers and development teams write better, more efficient code in the short and long term.

With these tools you can now profile unit tests, web tests, and load tests in order to find problems with an application at various stages in the development life cycle. This allows you to catch problems at an earlier (and less costly) stage. In addition, once you move out of the development phase and into production you also have ways to monitor applications.

Because VSTS allows you to monitor production applications, you can discover why they may not be running correctly. Too often production systems have performance problems that don't occur during testing and become large problems in production. With the ability to monitor production applications, you can quickly and easily diagnose a problem—whether it is in the application itself or in the machine it is running on. This leads to lower maintenance costs, because less time is needed to fix any given problem.

PART 4

Team Edition for Software Testers

CHAPTER 15

Web Testing

Up to this point you have seen various testing tools within Visual Studio Team System. This chapter brings you the one tool that will probably get the most amount of use in today's environment—the web testing tool. Web testing tools allow you to test an application in the same way that a user would actually use your application—that is, by filling in entries on a web page, submitting those entries, navigating web pages, and so forth. This chapter will introduce you to the new (and improved) tools in Visual Studio Team System to help you get the most out of your web applications. You will also learn how to use the web testing tool to test web services by creating SOAP calls.

> **Note** Microsoft has yet to incorporate functional test tools for Windows forms-based applications.

While the next chapter covers load testing, every load test must start with a web test. For this reason, it is almost guaranteed that you will have different versions of various web tests—some that test for specific conditions, to ensure the application responds appropriately, and some that perform a task or a series of tasks correctly every time. The latter tests will be used to test "happy" path functionality, and the former will be used to test happy, alternate, and exception-path functionality. The happy-path functional tests will serve as the basis for running your load tests.

Web testing in previous versions of Visual Studio is accomplished with Application Center Test (ACT). ACT is a decent tool that allows you to script actions and play those scripted actions in order to test functionality. In general, though, ACT is designed as a load-testing tool and does not perform much in the way of functional testing. This lack of functionality is one of the key reasons why the web test tools were created.

Another reason for this flexible and powerful testing tool is the continuing shift toward web-based applications. While web-based applications are not suitable for all applications, there are a large number that can be used in a web environment with little extra work. Web applications also provide the advantage of a simple deployment and maintenance process, since no desktop installations are required. Because many new applications today are web-based, this tool will prove of use to almost anyone writing new applications for the web.

Web tests come in two different flavors—recorded tests and coded tests. Recorded tests, which you launch in a browser, record the session while you run through the functionality in your application. Coded tests are those where you code each step, one at a time. The playback is the same for both except that there is no user interface for a coded test. In general, you will always record a test first and then convert it into code so that you have a good starting point and do not have to do some of the mundane work.

Recording Web Tests

To begin, select Test ➤ New Test from the main menu and then select Web Test. Change the test name to CreateNewUser.webtest and create a new C# or Visual Basic (VB) project to contain the test.

Tip Typically, developers will create unit test projects, and the quality assurance testers will create functional test projects (those projects containing web and load tests).

Call the new project "EffortTrackingWebTests." The first thing that occurs after you create your new test project is that the test recording pane will be displayed in your browser as shown in Figure 15-1.

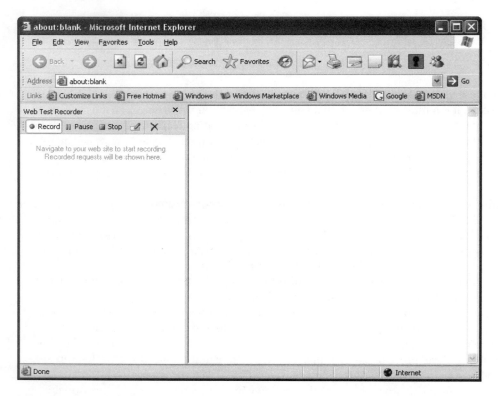

Figure 15-1. *The web test recording pane*

Navigate to the EffortTrackingWeb website (if you used IIS, your website will be at `http://localhost/EffortTrackingWeb/secure/Default.aspx`) to begin recording the web test. This will bring up the Login page. Do the following:

1. In the User Name textbox enter **WebTestUser1**.

2. In the Password textbox enter **password**.

3. In the Verify Password textbox enter **password**.

4. Click Add User.

Once you have done this, the browser window should look like the one in Figure 15-2.

Figure 15-2. *Recorded web test*

Click the Stop button in the Web Test Recorder Pane.

Tip At any point during the test you can pause it in order to take other actions with the browser. An example of this might be when you come to a page that should not have a record on it and you want to delete it before continuing the test. You may pause the test, delete the record, and then continue recording the test.

When you are finished you will see the WebTest1.webtest window in the IDE as shown in Figure 15-3.

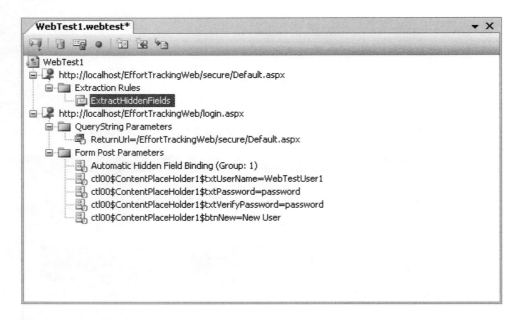

Figure 15-3. *The Web Test window*

You have now recorded your first web test—and it was simple. The first and most obvious thing you will note by looking at this window is that it contains almost the same information as the recording window, in that it records the pages you visit and the order you visit them. It also captures query string content, hidden field content, and form field content. All of this is configurable. There is no more to recording a web test than this.

Note This test as a stand-alone test is not very useful because it can only be run once. The second time it is run an exception will be thrown since the username cannot be duplicated. Therefore, a test preparation script must be run in order to allow this test to be used over and over again with the same results.

To make these demonstrations easier, record a second test that uses the WebTestUser1 user that you just created by doing the following:

1. Select Test ➤ New Test from the main menu.

2. Select Web Test and call it **AddItem** and click OK.

3. When the recording window opens, navigate to `http://localhost/EffortTrackingWeb/secure/Default.aspx`.

4. On the login page enter the username as **WebTestUser1** and the password as **password** and click Login.

5. Click the Add button.

6. For the Title enter **Test Entry**.

7. For the Description enter **Description of Test Entry**.

8. Click Save.

9. Stop the test.

Now you have a test that can be easily worked with and requires no setup script to run. There are no constraints on the names of the items entered into the effort tracking system, so they can all be identical if you choose (although you will see how to programmatically change this as you progress through the chapter).

Test Steps Explained

The test steps are fairly straightforward, in that they comprise an ordered list of URLs visited during the recording of the test. For each URL, a number of pieces of information are recorded (as explained in the next section "Test Detail Properties") and stored. Since you will be using the AddItem test for the majority of this chapter, it is worthwhile to examine the steps shown. There are four steps listed for this test:

- *Step 1*: This is the initial request for the default page in the secure folder.

- *Step 2*: The user is redirected to the login page where the ReturnUrl parameter notes the page the user is trying to go to so it can redirect the user there after the user has been authenticated. The user enters the username and password and then clicks the btnLogin button.

- *Step 3*: The user is successfully redirected to the default page where they select the week ending with an ID of 1 and click the Add button.

- *Step 4*: The user is directed to the edit page, which received three parameters (id, mode, and we_id). The user then enters various values in the different fields on this page and clicks the btnOK button.

Note that the last page the user is directed to, the default page, is not displayed because the user did not do anything on this page when recording the test (i.e., nothing was tested on this page). All of the information presented in the previous list was taken directly from the request tree, which contains all of the information for a given test.

Test Detail Properties

For a recorded web test, not only does the test itself have properties, but every step in the list of tests also has properties. The list of steps is referred to as the request tree. To begin with, examine the properties for the test itself by right-clicking the AddItem node in the request tree and selecting Properties. The properties for the test are described in Table 15-1.

Table 15-1. *Recorded Web Test Properties*

Property	Description
Description	This describes the test that appears in the Test Manager window.
Name	This is the name of the test.
Password	This is the password required when logging onto a website with Integrated Authentication.
PreAuthenticate	This ensures that the username and password are automatically supplied to websites protected with Integrated Authentication.
Proxy	This notes the server name for connection purposes in case the test has to run through a proxy server. This field can also be bound to a data source.
Request Plug-in	This contains the location of the assembly, which contains the custom request (if you are using one).
User Name	This is the username required when logging onto a website with Integrated Authentication.
Web Test Plug-in	This is the name of the plugin for the entire web test.

Note The Request Plugin and the Web Test Plugin are discussed later in this chapter.

The Password and User Name properties can be bound to a data source. In this case, the web test will use the usernames and passwords from this data source when authenticating against a website protected by Integrated or Basic Authentication. Note that these credentials are used to authenticate you against the web server, not the application you're testing (unless they use the same mechanism).

Next, select the node that reads http://localhost/EffortTrackingWeb/login.aspx. The properties for a request node are shown in Table 15-2.

Table 15-2. *Request Node Properties*

Property	Description
Cache Control	Indicates True/False if the request is cached or not.
Follow Redirects	Indicates True/False if a page redirect will be followed when that line of code is run.
Method	Post/Get: Determines how information will be passed to the website.
Parse Dependent Requests	Indicates with True/False whether other URLs within the requested web page are processed (such as images that are loaded from another URL).

Property	Description
Record Results	Indicates True/False if performance data is gathered for use when this test is run as part of a Load Test.
Response Time Goal	Indicates the response time you want to get from a page. It is used as a threshold to mark how many times the page meets or exceeds the set goal.
Think Time (seconds)	Indicates the amount of time that should be used to simulate a think time before moving on to the next step in the request tree. A think time is the amount of time an average user might spend reading a page rather than clicking something on the page.
Timeout (seconds)	Indicates the maximum amount of time to wait before a timeout is declared. This is great for testing what happens when a user session times out, for example, as on an e-commerce site.
URL	Indicates the URL of the requested page. This can be bound to a data source, which allows for dynamic site navigation during a test.
Version	Indicates the HTTP version to use for this request—1.1 is the default, although you can select 1.0.

Each folder beneath the request node contains a different set of properties. Select the first node under the QueryString Parameters node. These properties are shown in Table 15-3.

Table 15-3. *QueryString Parameter Properties*

Property	Description
Name	Indicates the name of the query string parameter
Show Separate Request	Indicates True/False if the specific value should be shown separately in reports, or grouped with the rest of the information about the request
Value	Indicates the value passed for the given query string parameter

The Form Post Parameters have only two properties—name and value of the parameter posted to the form.

Test Options

Once you have recorded a test, you have various options for configuring, altering, or making comments on specific tests or requests. The options range from altering requests and inserting requests to specifying data sources. To access these options, right-click the root test node (AddItem in this example) or any of the request nodes in the request tree. The options are described in Table 15-4.

Table 15-4. *Test/Test Step Options*

Option	Description
Add/Insert Request	Adds a request that was not included in the recorded test.
Add/Insert Web Service Request	Adds a web service request that was not included in the recorded test.
Add/Insert Transaction	Groups a set of web requests into a single transaction. All requests must pass or they all fail.
Add/Insert Comment	Allows the addition of one or more comments associated with the entire test or with single steps.
Add/Insert Recording	Allows additional web test recordings to be made and inserted into the current web test.
Add Data Source	Allows the addition of a data source that is used to bind various parameters to an external set of data.
Add Context Parameter	Holds any value—this can be the result of an extraction, for instance, that can be used as an argument to another call further in the test script.
Add Dependent Request	Is run in parallel (with the other dependent requests) after the current page is finished processing.
Add Header	Allows the addition of custom headers in order to test various scenarios.
Add URL QueryString Parameter	Allows additional parameters.
Add Form Post Parameter	Allows additional parameters.
Add File Upload Parameter	Indicates the path to a file and the context the value should be stored in. This will cause the specified file to be uploaded during the test.
Add Validation Rule	Validates that certain conditions are true on a response page.
Add Extraction Rule	Extracts data from the response page.

Some of these options are available at the root test level and others are only available from a request node.

Running Recorded Web Tests

Now that you have recorded a test, you need to be able to play it back for actual use in a test. There are various ways to replay a test depending on the type of test you are setting up (for example a load test does not work via a user interface so what follows does not apply to this type of playback).

Tip It is a best practice that once you record your test you play it back to ensure that it will work correctly and that nothing unwanted was recorded.

To run a recorded test you can either open the recorded test (the file with the .webtest extension) and click the Run button from the top of the window or select the test from the Test Manager window and click the Run Checked Tests button. Open the recorded test file and click Run to begin this test. This will bring up the Web Test window shown in Figure 15-4.

Figure 15-4. *The Web Test window (test completed)*

You have the option of running the test in an automated or interactive fashion in which you can step through each part of the test.

Tip Turn off your firewall for these tests because unless you have previously recognized the program, it will prompt you to allow the application to interact with the web application (if you are using HTTP as opposed to Cassini, the built-in web server).

Clicking the Run button will run through all steps without stopping. You must click the Step button after each step has been completed in order to move to the next step. As you move through the test, the website is displayed in the lower window. Either during the test run (if you are using the Step method) or after the test run you can examine the Request details (header and body), the Response details (header and body), and the test Details (rules, context, and exceptions).

Tip After the test has been run, you will see the test details in the same window as shown in Figure 15-4. You can then click each individual node, which will show the web page as it looked during a particular step of the test.

To change the settings for a specific run, you can select the Edit Run Settings button from the top of the window. This will display the dialog box shown in Figure 15-5.

Figure 15-5. *Web Test Run Settings dialog box*

The number of iterations allows you either to set a fixed number of runs or to bind the count of runs against a data source (you will see this later in this chapter in the section "Data-Driven Web Testing"). The browser type allows you to choose the type of browser that will be "making" and "consuming" the requests and responses. Currently you can choose from five types of browsers but you could also add your own browser types if the one you want to test against is not listed here (for example, Netscape 6.0 is listed, but not Mozilla or Opera). The network type allows you to configure your connection speed. The values range from a 56.6K connection to a T1 line.

Note Customizing these values is discussed in Chapter 16.

The simulated think times allow the automated tests (this doesn't apply to the Step test) to take into account the think times you set for the individual test steps (if any). For a single test run these think times are not very useful, though, so you will most likely find yourself only using these during a load test. You can also turn the think times on and off by selecting the Think Times button on the toolbar in the test window.

Passing or Failing Tests

A test passing or failing is entirely up to whether an error occurs or a specific validation fails. When a web test is first recorded and played back, it is assumed to have passed if no errors occur during the run on the test. However, you can add specific validations to occur at various points of the test, which will throw exceptions if they fail (and fail the test).

To demonstrate how this works, you are going to record a test that validates the Login form via the user interface (this is similar to the initial test recorded previously, but this is explicitly to test a login failure). Start recording a new web test called "LoginFailure" and in the recording window navigate to the EffortTrackingWeb website (if you used IIS your website will be at http://localhost/EffortTrackingWeb/secure/Default.aspx) to begin recording the web test. This will bring up the Login page. Do the following:

1. In the User Name textbox enter **Test User 1** (note that this user does not exist).
2. In the Password textbox enter **password**.
3. Click Login.
4. Stop recording the web test.

What should occur is that the login does not succeed and an error message is shown. Now, if this test is run as it is, the test will succeed because no "exceptions" occurred. However, that does not really help you. In many cases you need to ensure that when an expected failure occurs (which is not triggered by throwing an exception), the correct actions are taken. In order to do this you can add a Validation Rule.

To change this test to something more meaningful, the test will check to see if the words "Invalid username or password" (part of the error message if a login fails) are displayed in the resulting web page. Open the LoginFailure.webtest file and right-click the Login.aspx node (the last node in the node list) and select Add Validation Rule (validation rules are discussed in more detail later in this chapter in the section "Validation Rules"). Click the Find Test validation rule and enter **Invalid username or password** for the Find Text property and click OK. When it is run, the test will search for this text within the resulting HTML body. If it finds the text, the test will pass; if it does not, it will fail. This ensures that you are checking for a specific type of failure.

Data-Driven Web Testing

Data binding allows a database to provide parameters to the test at various steps instead of having to change multiple tests of the same type by hand. Data binding can be used for individual data-driven web tests or for load testing (discussed in Chapter 16). For data-driven web tests (as with unit tests) the test will cycle through a table in the database and run the test once for each row in the table. Each column can supply a value to various parts of the web test. Because of this, there is no set structure to a table used for data-driven testing.

Tip It is a best practice to add a comment field in the table supplying data to the test so the exact purpose of the provided data can be noted. In other words, let everyone know what is being tested by the data provided—do not make the tests cryptic. This makes it easy for all developers and testers to understand the purpose for a set of test data.

For this example, you will use the previously created AddItem test with data from a SQL Server database to drive the test. To add a data source to the web test you first need to create a table to hold the information to be used for the test. The included testing database (efforttrackingtests) contains a table called save_task_test with the structure shown in Table 15-5.

Table 15-5. *The save_task_test Table Structure*

Column	Description
st_id	Unique identifier
st_wi_title	Title of the item being added
st_wi_description	Description of the item being added
st_cat_id	ID of the category
st_own_id	ID of the owner
st_we_id	ID of the week ending

Once the data source has been created in the database, click the Add Data Source button in the Web Test window (shown in Figure 15-6).

Figure 15-6. *Web Test window*

The data source and the selected table(s) are listed under the Data Sources node in the Web Test window. Now that a data source has been selected, the individual parameters of the form fields can be hooked up to specific columns in the data source. To do this, right-click a form parameter field (the highlighted line in Figure 15-7 is a form parameter field) and select Properties. Select the Value Property and click the drop-down button. Select the data source, table, and column to bind to the parameter field value. In Figure 15-7, the txtTitle field is bound to the `efforttrackingtests1.save_task_test.st_wi_title` column. Do the same for the txtDescription, cboCategory, and cboWeekEnding fields.

Tip Another great feature is the ability to bind to a validation rule or an extraction rule. While not part of this test, in order to do the binding, just select a rule, view the properties for the rule and where you need to bind to a data field, enter the name of the data field in double braces. As an example, if you were to bind a Find Text validation rule to a data source, you would enter `{{efforttrackingtests1.save_task_test.st_wi_title}}` in the Find Text parameter. There is currently no drop-down available for this.

Once the data source has been chosen, the method of access to the database should be chosen (it does not matter what order you take these steps in). To select an access method, right-click a table in the Web Test window (under the Tables node) and select Properties. The Access Method property allows you to choose from three options: Sequential, Random, or Unique. The descriptions are noted in Table 15-6.

Table 15-6. *Data-Driven Access Options*

Option	Description
Sequential	For a load test, this method reads through every row in the table from top to bottom and continues to loop for the duration of the load test.
Random	For a load test, this method reads through every row in the table in a random order and continues to loop for the duration of the load test.
Unique	For a load test, this method reads through every row in the table from top to bottom and runs the test once for each row.

Note that these options only apply to load tests. They have no effect on non–load tests.

The final step before the data-driven test can be run is to change the test configuration settings. As noted in Chapter 12, the `localtestrun` file contains the Web Test configuration settings (shown in Figure 15-7).

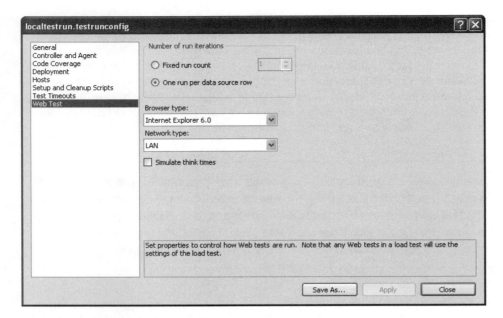

Figure 15-7. *Web Test configuration settings*

The number of run iterations must be switched from "Fixed run count" to "One run per data source row."

Caution If you decide to use the fixed run count instead, it will use the data from the rows in the data source sequentially, looping through them until the test has reached the number of iterations specified.

Apply the changes, switch back to the Web Test window, and run the test. To see the details of the test, double-click the test in the Test Results pane (shown in Figure 15-8).

The most obvious difference between this and the test results in Figure 15-4 is that there is one run for every row in the data source table. You will examine the web test results in more detail in the "Test Results" section of this chapter.

Note The reason the test failed is because there were no checks for invalid values. The test table contained several tests that were designed to fail, but the web test did not reflect that. In the real world, the test should be updated to validate that an error did in fact occur.

Figure 15-8. *AddItem test results*

Using the web testing tool in a data-driven fashion allows you to create one test and then change the values being tested simply by altering the database. In the past, this would have required a change in the test itself or manually changing parameters. The savings in time from using simple methods like these will be enormous.

Coded Web Tests

Coded web tests are written entirely in code. For the most part, coded web tests are required only when you have to create a loop in the test or dynamically navigate the list of URLs called during the test. Whatever your purpose in creating a coded web test, you will almost always begin from a recorded web test, which will provide the basic outline for your code.

Since the AddItem test has already been created, convert the test into a coded test by following these steps:

CHAPTER 15 ■ WEB TESTING

1. Open the AddItem request tree by double-clicking the AddItem test in the Solution Explorer.

2. Select the AddItem root node.

3. Click the Generate Code button from the toolbar.

4. Leave the default name of AddItemCoded in the Generate Coded Web Test dialog box that is displayed, and click OK.

5. The `AddItemCoded.cs` file (or .vb file if you are using VB.NET) is added to the EffortTrackingWebTests project.

These are all the steps required to create a coded web test. The class file contains a single class called AddItemCoded, which inherits from the WebTest class. Within this class there are only two methods (you are free to add as many methods as you like, but you are required to have at least these two methods): the constructor, and the GetRequestEnumerator method, which is part of the IEnumerator interface. The constructor contains information (if there is any) needed to initialize the web test. The IEnumerator implementation, while fairly straightforward, is helpful to walk through.

The generic implementation of the IEnumerator interface returns a WebTestRequest type. Looking at the method body (partially shown in Listing 15-1) you can see a straightforward list of requests is being returned by the test.

Listing 15-1. *The GetRequestEnumerator/Run Method (partial)*

C#
```
// (GetRequestEnumerator Method)
    WebTestRequest request1 = new WebTestRequest(
    "http://localhost/EffortTrackingWeb/secure/Default.aspx");
    request1.ThinkTime = 5;
    ExtractHiddenFields rule1 = new ExtractHiddenFields();
    rule1.ContextParameterName = "1";
    request1.ExtractValues += new EventHandler<ExtractionEventArgs>(rule1.Extract);
    yield return request1;

    WebTestRequest request2 = new
    . . .
    yield return request2;
```

VB
```
' (Run Method)
  Dim request1 As WebTestRequest = New WebTestRequest( _
  "http://localhost/EffortTrackingWeb/secure/Default.aspx")
  request1.ThinkTime = 10
  Dim rule1 As ExtractHiddenFields = New ExtractHiddenFields
  rule1.ContextParameterName = "1"
  AddHandler request1.ExtractValues, AddressOf rule1.Extract
  MyBase.Send(request1)
```

```
Dim request2 As WebTestRequest = New
    WebTestRequest("http://localhost/EffortTrackingWeb/login.aspx")
. . .
MyBase.Send(request2)
```

Looking at the generated code, you can see that it is pretty simple in terms of what is going on. Each request in the request tree is generated with all of the properties for the previously set request. The extraction rules and any other rules (validation rules, etc.) are also generated. One of the key advantages of coding your own test is that you can respond to specific events. As you can see here, there is an event handler for the ExtractValues event and there are other events (PostRequest, PreRequest, ValidateResponse) you can respond to as well. You can read more about these events in the MSDN documentation.

Note The yield statement (MyBase.Send in VB calls the GetRequestEnumerator in the base class) essentially puts a break in the code and allows the enumerator to iterate over the collection of requests. This is a new statement in C# and VB in the .NET 2.0 Framework. There are differences in how these work which is reflected in the base class that the coded web tests inherit from. C# inherits from WebTest and VB inherits from ThreadedWebTest. For more information, see the MSDN documentation.

Coded web tests can only be run via the Test Manager window, as there is no interface to this type of test.

Coded Data-Driven Tests

The coded data-driven test has a different structure to it. To create this type of test, do the following:

- Record a web test.
- Add a data source.
- Hook up the data source columns to form parameters.
- Select the Generate Coded Test button from the Web Test window for the specific test.

The AddItem test is a good starting point to demonstrate this type of test. Simply generate the coded test from the AddItem test window. A partial view of the coded, data-driven test is shown in Listing 15-2 (please note that the line breaks are due to formatting and do not exist in the generated code). This listing shows the class header and the fourth step of the test so you can see how data binding works in a coded web test.

Listing 15-2. *Coded Data-Driven Web Test*

```
C#
[DataSource("efforttrackingtests1", "Provider=SQLNCLI.1;
Data Source=localhost;Integrated Security=SSPI;
Initial Catalog=efforttrackingtests",
```

```csharp
Microsoft.VisualStudio.TestTools.WebTesting.DataBindingAccessMethod.Sequential,
"save_task_test")]
[DataBinding("efforttrackingtests1", "save_task_test", "st_wi_title",
"efforttrackingtests1.save_task_test.st_wi_title")]
[DataBinding("efforttrackingtests1", "save_task_test", "st_wi_description",
"efforttrackingtests1.save_task_test.st_wi_description")]
[DataBinding("efforttrackingtests1", "save_task_test", "st_cat_id",
"efforttrackingtests1.save_task_test.st_cat_id")]
[DataBinding("efforttrackingtests1", "save_task_test", "st_we_id",
"efforttrackingtests1.save_task_test.st_we_id")]
public class AddItemCoded : WebTest
{
    public AddItemCoded()
    {
        this.PreAuthenticate = true;
    }

    public override IEnumerator<WebTestRequest> GetRequestEnumerator()
    {
        WebTestRequest request1 = new WebTestRequest(
"http://localhost/EffortTrackingWeb/secure/Default.aspx");
        . . .
        . . .
        WebTestRequest request4 = new
           WebTestRequest("http://localhost/EffortTrackingWeb/secure/Edit.aspx");
        request4.Method = "POST";
        request4.QueryStringParameters.Add("id", "0", false, false);
        request4.QueryStringParameters.Add("mode", "add", false, false);
        request4.QueryStringParameters.Add("we_id", "1", false, false);
        FormPostHttpBody request4Body = new FormPostHttpBody();
        request4Body.FormPostParameters.Add("__VIEWSTATE",
          this.Context["$HIDDEN1.__VIEWSTATE"].ToString());
        request4Body.FormPostParameters.Add
            ("ctl00$ContentPlaceHolder1$Details1$txtTitle",
            this.Context["efforttrackingtests1.save_task_test.st_wi_title"]
  .ToString());
        request4Body.FormPostParameters.Add(
            "ctl00$ContentPlaceHolder1$Details1$fldID",
            this.Context["$HIDDEN1.ctl00$ContentPlaceHolder1$Details1$fldID"]
  .ToString());
        request4Body.FormPostParameters.Add(
            "ctl00$ContentPlaceHolder1$Details1$fldWE",
            this.Context["$HIDDEN1.ctl00$ContentPlaceHolder1$Details1$fldWE"]
  .ToString());
        request4Body.FormPostParameters.Add(
            "ctl00$ContentPlaceHolder1$Details1$txtDescription",
            this.Context["efforttrackingtests1.save_task_test.st_wi_description"]
```

```csharp
            .ToString());
        request4Body.FormPostParameters.Add(
            "ctl00$ContentPlaceHolder1$Details1$cboCategory",
            this.Context["efforttrackingtests1.save_task_test.st_cat_id"]
    .ToString());
        request4Body.FormPostParameters.Add(
            "ctl00$ContentPlaceHolder1$Details1$cboWeekEnding",
            this.Context["efforttrackingtests1.save_task_test.st_we_id"].ToString());
        request4Body.FormPostParameters.Add(
            "ctl00$ContentPlaceHolder1$Details1$btnOK", "Save");
        request4Body.FormPostParameters.Add("__EVENTVALIDATION",
            this.Context["$HIDDEN1.__EVENTVALIDATION"].ToString());
        request4.Body = request4Body;
        yield return request4;
    }
}
```

VB
```vb
<DataSource("efforttrackingtests1", "Provider=SQLNCLI.1;Data Source=localhost;
Integrated Security=SSPI;Initial Catalog=efforttrackingtests",
Microsoft.VisualStudio.TestTools.WebTesting.DataBindingAccessMethod.Sequential,
"save_task_test"), _
DataBinding("efforttrackingtests1", "save_task_test", "st_wi_title",
"efforttrackingtests1.save_task_test.st_wi_title"), _
DataBinding("efforttrackingtests1", "save_task_test", "st_wi_description",
"efforttrackingtests1.save_task_test.st_wi_description"), _
DataBinding("efforttrackingtests1", "save_task_test", "st_cat_id", _
 "efforttrackingtests1.save_task_test.st_cat_id"), _
DataBinding("efforttrackingtests1", "save_task_test", "st_we_id", _
 "efforttrackingtests1.save_task_test.st_we_id")> _
Public Class AddItemCoded
    Inherits ThreadedWebTest

    Public Sub New()
        MyBase.New()
        Me.PreAuthenticate = True
    End Sub

    Public Overrides Sub Run()
        Dim request1 As WebTestRequest = New
            WebTestRequest("http://localhost/EffortTrackingWeb/secure/Default.aspx")
        . . .
        . . .
        Dim request4 As WebTestRequest = New _
            WebTestRequest("http://localhost/EffortTrackingWeb/secure/Edit.aspx")
        request4.Method = "POST"
        request4.QueryStringParameters.Add("id", "0", False, False)
        request4.QueryStringParameters.Add("mode", "add", False, False)
        request4.QueryStringParameters.Add("we_id", "1", False, False)
```

```vbnet
        Dim request4Body As FormPostHttpBody = New FormPostHttpBody
        request4Body.FormPostParameters.Add("__VIEWSTATE", _
            Me.Context("$HIDDEN1.__VIEWSTATE").ToString)
        request4Body.FormPostParameters.Add( _
            "ctl00$ContentPlaceHolder1$Details1$txtTitle", _
            Me.Context("efforttrackingtests1.save_task_test.st_wi_title").ToString)
        request4Body.FormPostParameters.Add( _
            "ctl00$ContentPlaceHolder1$Details1$fldID", _
            Me.Context( _
"$HIDDEN1.ctl00$ContentPlaceHolder1$Details1$fldID").ToString)
        request4Body.FormPostParameters.Add( _
            "ctl00$ContentPlaceHolder1$Details1$fldWE", _
            Me.Context("$HIDDEN1.ctl00$ContentPlaceHolder1$Details1$fldWE").ToString)
        request4Body.FormPostParameters.Add( _
            "ctl00$ContentPlaceHolder1$Details1$txtDescription", _
            Me.Context( _
"efforttrackingtests1.save_task_test.st_wi_description").ToString)
        request4Body.FormPostParameters.Add( _
            "ctl00$ContentPlaceHolder1$Details1$cboCategory", _
            Me.Context("efforttrackingtests1.save_task_test.st_cat_id").ToString)
        request4Body.FormPostParameters.Add( _
            "ctl00$ContentPlaceHolder1$Details1$cboWeekEnding", _
            Me.Context("efforttrackingtests1.save_task_test.st_we_id").ToString)
        request4Body.FormPostParameters.Add( _
            "ctl00$ContentPlaceHolder1$Details1$btnOK", "Save")
        request4Body.FormPostParameters.Add("__EVENTVALIDATION", _
            Me.Context("$HIDDEN1.__EVENTVALIDATION").ToString)
        request4.Body = request4Body
        MyBase.Send(request4)
    End Sub
```

The key to this scenario is the Attributes added to the class (at the top of the code listing). The DataSource attribute specifies the database in which the table to be used for testing is located. There can be as many data sources as necessary to complete a test. The last part of the data source contains the table (or tables) the test is specifically bound to. This controls how many iterations of the test will be performed. The DataBinding attribute maps table columns to form fields and is a simple and straight mapping. To assign the bound fields to the form parameters, use the same syntax as is shown in the Web Test window:

```
request4Body.FormPostParameters.Add("ctl00$ContentPlaceHolder1$Details1$fldID",
    this.Context["$HIDDEN1.ctl00$ContentPlaceHolder1$Details1$fldID"].ToString());
```

Aside from these differences, a data-driven coded web test and a non-data-driven web test are identical.

Now that you have seen how to record, run, and convert a web test into code you can examine how to create plugins and custom extraction and validation rules.

Extraction Rules

Extraction rules are used to extract parts of either the header or the body of a request for whatever purpose you need the extracted information. There are several prebuilt extraction rules that should cover many, it not all, the situations you will run in to. These extraction rules are described in Table 15-7.

Table 15-7. *Built-in Extraction Rules*

Rule	Description
Extract Attribute Value	Extracts the value of a given HTML attribute.
Extract Form Field	Extracts the value of a given form field.
Extract HTTP Header	Extracts the value of a given header.
Extract Regular Expression	Extracts any text that matches the given regular expression.
Extract Text	Extracts any text based on a beginning and ending set of criteria. Regular expressions can be used for this extraction rule also.
Extract Hidden Fields	Extracts all hidden fields from a response.

Based on these rules, there are very few reasons you would want to code a custom extraction rule. One reason is that you have a very complex regular expression and want to code it into an extraction rule or for some other reason such as to encourage reuse when dealing with web tests.

To add an existing extraction rule to a test, right-click a request node and select Add Extraction Rule. This will display the dialog box shown in Figure 15-9.

Figure 15-9. *Add Extraction Rule dialog box*

As with the validation rule demonstrated in the "Data-Driven Web Testing" section of this chapter, any field available here can be bound to a data source.

Each extraction rule has various different properties. One of the properties that you will find most useful is the Required property (if the rule has this property). Setting it to True indicates that the information the rule is trying to extract must exist or else the test will fail.

The Context Parameter Name value is a value available to all extraction rule tests. Providing a value here requires that you have previously created a context parameter.

Tip To create a Context Parameter field, right-click the name of the test in the Web Test window (the root node) or the Context Parameters folder, if it exists, and select Add Context Parameter. This creates a variable you can pass values to and read values from during the test.

Creating Custom Extraction Rules

Custom extraction rules allow you to encapsulate logic and complex extraction processes. Take an example where a regular expression contains recursive groups. This can be a very complex regular expression to write. Or maybe your organization routinely performs a certain type of security test and you want to encapsulate the rules so they do not have to be rewritten for every application. These are good reasons to create a custom extraction rule.

For this example, you will create a simple Extraction Rule that finds all of the telephone numbers, in the North American format (with variations) on a web page. Follow these steps to create the custom extraction rule:

1. Create a new code library called CustomExtractionRules (with either VB or CS appended to it for the example).

2. Add a reference to the Microsoft.VisualStudio.QualityTools.WebTestFramework.dll assembly. This assembly is located in the `C:\Program Files\Microsoft Visual Studio 8\Common 7\IDE\Public Assemblies` folder.

3. Change the generated class (Class1) to TelephoneExtractionRule (rename the code file as well).

4. Add the following using or Imports statement to the top of the code file:
   using Microsoft.VisualStudio.TestTools.WebTesting.Rules; or, in VB, Imports Microsoft.VisualStudio.TestTools.WebTesting.Rules.

5. Change the class to inherit from the ExtractRegularExpression Rule class.

6. Implement (override) the RuleName and Extract methods (if needed) (see the code in Listing 15-3).

7. Build the solution.

Listing 15-3. *The Telephone Extraction Rule*

C#
```csharp
using System;
using Microsoft.VisualStudio.TestTools.WebTesting.Rules;

namespace CustomExtractionRulesCS
{
    public class ExtractTelephoneRule : ExtractRegularExpression
    {
        public ExtractTelephoneRule():base()
        {
            this.RegularExpression = @"\(?[0-9]{3}\)?[-. ]?[0-9]{3}[-. ]?[0-9]{4}";
        }

        public override string RuleName
        {
            get { return "Extract Telephone Numbers"; }
        }

        public override string RuleDescription
        {
            get { return "Extracts all telephone numbers which match "
                + "the North American convention."; }
        }
    }
}
```
VB
```vb
Option Explicit On
Option Strict On

Imports Microsoft.VisualStudio.TestTools.WebTesting.Rules

Public Class ExtractTelephoneRule : Inherits ExtractRegularExpression

    Public Sub New()
        MyBase.New()

        Me.RegularExpression = "\(?[0-9]{3}\)?[-. ]?[0-9]{3}[-. ]?[0-9]{4}"
    End Sub

    Public Overrides ReadOnly Property RuleName() As String
        Get
            Return "Extract Telephone Numbers"
        End Get
    End Property
```

```vb
    Public Overrides ReadOnly Property RuleDescription() As String
        Get
            Return "Extracts all telephone numbers which match " _
                & "the North American convention."
        End Get
    End Property
End Class
```

As you can see, creating your own custom rule is extremely simple. The regular expression here will return all phone numbers that match the following formats: 1234567890, 123.456.7890, 123-456-7890, 123 456 7890, (123) 456 7890. The rule is also clearly documented by the description. Also note that because the rule simply uses a specific regular expression, the Extract method does not have to be overridden. In other circumstances you may want to override this method (and if you inherit from the base ExtractionRule you have to override this method).

Extract Method

If you were to inherit from the base ExtractionRule you would override the Extract method. This method's signature provides you with the access to both the Request and the Response objects to allow you to not only extract information but to compare the objects to each other. More information on the ExtractEventArgs can be found in the MSDN. It is important to note one particular class exposed by the ExtractEventArgs—the WebTest object. This object provides yet another object—the Context object. The Context object contains information about the running test. With these two objects you can dynamically change a number of values relating to the currently running tests and examine various pieces of information to put the extracted values into a proper context.

As you can see, overriding the Extract method provides a lot of options that are available to you. These same options are available when you create a custom validation rule (see the section below on "Creating Custom Validation Rules").

Implementing Custom Extraction Rules

Once the rule has been created, you need to actually incorporate it into the testing project. In the EffortTrackingWebTests project add a reference to the CustomExtractionRules assembly you just created. Right-click a request node in the Web Test window and select Add Extraction Rule. You should see the same dialog box as shown in Figure 15-10.

There cannot be a whole lot that is simpler than this. What you can do with this, in terms of extracting values, is limited only by what you can dream up. Since this is a standard property dialog you can create enumerations that fill the value lists, connect to databases to grab extraction rules (although this is certainly not recommended), or even provide configuration files that are user changeable to make configurable rules.

Figure 15-10. *The Extract Telephone Numbers extraction rule implemented*

■**Tip** One possible solution to this problem is to have a variety of regular expressions (a library, as it were) that could be added to a configuration file and read by the rule so they would be easily extensible by the end user.

Validation Rules

Validation rules, as you have previously seen, can be used to test whether certain conditions on a web page are true once a response to a request has been made. In the previous example in the "Data-Driven Web Testing" section, the test validated that the system did return an error notification when a login failed. Likewise, it also validated that no error message was returned when a valid login occurred.

To add a validation rule to a request, right-click the request in the Web Test window and select Insert Validation Rule. This brings up the dialog box shown in Figure 15-11.

Figure 15-11. *Add Validation Rule dialog box*

The predefined validation rules are described in Table 15-8.

Table 15-8. *Predefined Validation Rules*

Rule	Description
Form Field	Verifies that a field exists on the form and what the value in that field is
Find Text	Verifies that certain text appears somewhere in the response page
Maximum Request Time	Verifies that a request finishes in a given amount of time
Required Attribute Value	Verifies that a specified HTML tag exists in the response and contains an attribute with a given value
Required Tag	Verifies that a specified HTML tag exists in the response

Caution The validation rules operate on the response, not the request, even though they are associated with the request in the Web Test window. They are processed after the response has been returned.

The level option indicates the threshold the validation rule will be tested at during a load test. For example, if the validation rule level is set to Low and the load test validation level is set to Medium or High, then the validation rule will not be checked (this is discussed in a little more detail in Chapter 16).

Creating Custom Validation Rules

Creating a custom validation rule is almost identical to creating a custom extraction rule. To do this, you follow the same steps outlined previously in the "Creating Custom Extraction Rules" section except that instead of inheriting from the base ExtractionRule or one of its derivatives, you inherit from the base ValidationRule class or one of its derivatives. In this case, you would override, in addition to the RuleName property, the Validate method.

Web Test Request Plugins

Request plugins are plugins that allow you to perform external code execution when each request in the web test is executed. This can be used for a variety of reasons, but you will see in the next section that the Web Test Plugin is a more valuable alternative. The problem with the Web Test Request Plugin is that you cannot determine the start and stop of the test.

Web Test Plugins

A web test plugin is an application that can be executed in response to any event that occurs during a web test run. While the Web Test Request Plugin could only respond to individual requests, the Web Test Plugin encompasses all of the functionality of the request plugin plus more. There are various reasons why you might want to create your own test plugin. You may need to log specific details, or log those details in such a way that you can easily compare them from one test to another. Other reasons may include the fact that you need to change aspects of the tests during the test run. This could be something like having to change the URL the test is navigating to based on variables that can't be anticipated in a data-bound test. Whatever the reasons, the ability to dynamically change a test shows just how flexible the web testing tool is in VSTS.

In the example presented in Listing 15-4 you will see how to write a web test plugin that lets you perform custom logging of the test steps. To create a web test plugin, do the following:

1. Create a new project called "WebTestLogger."

2. Add a reference to the Microsoft.VisualStudio.QualityTools.WebTestFramework.dll.

3. Change the generated Class1 file to Logger (.cs or .vb depending on the language) and add the code shown in Listing 15-4.

Listing 15-4. *Logger Web Test Plugin*

```
C#
using System;
using System.Collections.Generic;
using System.Text;
using Microsoft.VisualStudio.TestTools.WebTesting;
using System.IO;
```

```csharp
namespace LoggingRequest
{
    public class Logger: WebTestPlugin
    {
        private FileStream _logStream = null;
        private StreamWriter _logWriter = null;

        public Logger() { }

        public override void PreWebTest(object sender, PreWebTestEventArgs e)
        {
            _logStream = new FileStream("c:\\logfile.txt", FileMode.Append);
            _logWriter = new StreamWriter(_logStream);
            _logWriter.AutoFlush = true;
            _logWriter.WriteLine("Beginning Test (" +
              DateTime.Now.ToString() + ")");
            e.WebTest.PostRequest += new
                EventHandler<PostRequestEventArgs>(WebTest_PostRequest);
        }

        void WebTest_PostRequest(object sender, PostRequestEventArgs e)
        {
            _logWriter.WriteLine(e.Request.Url.ToString());
        }

        public override void PostWebTest(object sender, PostWebTestEventArgs e)
        {
            _logWriter.WriteLine("Ending Test (" + DateTime.Now.ToString() + ")");
            _logWriter.Close();
            e.WebTest.PostRequest -= new
                EventHandler<PostRequestEventArgs>(WebTest_PostRequest);
        }
    }
}
```

VB
```vb
Option Explicit On
Option Strict On

Imports Microsoft.VisualStudio.TestTools.WebTesting
Imports System.IO
```

```vb
Public Class Logger : Inherits WebTestPlugin
    Private _logStream As FileStream = Nothing
    Private _logWriter As StreamWriter = Nothing
    Private WithEvents _test As WebTest = Nothing

    Public Overrides Sub PreWebTest(ByVal sender As Object, ByVal e As _
        Microsoft.VisualStudio.TestTools.WebTesting.PreWebTestEventArgs)
        _logStream = New FileStream("c:\logfile.txt", FileMode.Append)
        _logWriter = New StreamWriter(_logStream)
        _logWriter.AutoFlush = True
        _logWriter.WriteLine("Beginning Test (" + Now.ToString() + ")")
        _test = e.WebTest
    End Sub

    Public Sub Webtest_PostRequest(ByVal sender As Object, ByVal e As _
        Microsoft.VisualStudio.TestTools.WebTesting.PostRequestEventArgs) Handles _
        _test.PostRequest
        _logWriter.WriteLine(e.Request.Url.ToString())
    End Sub

    Public Overrides Sub PostWebTest(ByVal sender As Object, ByVal e As _
        Microsoft.VisualStudio.TestTools.WebTesting.PostWebTestEventArgs)
        _logWriter.WriteLine("Ending Test (" + Now.ToString() + ")")
        _logWriter.Close()
    End Sub
End Class
```

The Logger class is pretty straightforward. It inherits from the WebTestPlugin class and overrides the PreWebTest and PostWebTest methods. These methods are called at the beginning and end of the test respectively. The additional step taken here is that the PostRequest event of the WebTest is being handled so the URL for each event can be logged to the log file. Aside from that, there are no especially difficult steps for creating your own plugin.

One key thing to note is that the PreWebTest and PostWebTest are called once for *each* data row in a data-driven test. Because of this, the test explicitly closes and opens the file stream for each row in the test. So the constructor should be used for global test initialization and the PreWebTest should be used for individual run initialization.

To implement the plugin, open the EffortTracking Solution. Add a reference to the assembly, which contains the Logger class. Double-click the AddItem web test so it is displayed in the Web Test window. Click the Set Web Test Plugin button at the top of the window. Select the Logger class and click OK.

Note Only one Web Test Plugin and Web Test Request Plugin can be used for each test.

Run the web test as normal. The results will be a log file in the root C drive, which is partially shown in Listing 15-5.

Listing 15-5. *Log File Results*

```
Beginning Test (1/22/2006 2:07:12 PM)
http://localhost/EffortTrackingWeb/secure/Default.aspx
http://localhost/EffortTrackingWeb/login.aspx?
    ReturnUrl=/EffortTrackingWeb/secure/Default.aspx
http://localhost/EffortTrackingWeb/login.aspx
http://localhost/EffortTrackingWeb/secure/Default.aspx
http://localhost/EffortTrackingWeb/secure/Default.aspx
http://localhost/EffortTrackingWeb/secure/Edit.aspx?id=0&mode=add&we_id=1
http://localhost/EffortTrackingWeb/secure/Edit.aspx
http://localhost/EffortTrackingWeb/secure/Default.aspx?we_id=3&last=29
Ending Test (Sunday, January 22, 2006)
Beginning Test (1/22/2006 2:09:52 PM)
http://localhost/EffortTrackingWeb/secure/Default.aspx
http://localhost/EffortTrackingWeb/login.aspx?
    ReturnUrl=/EffortTrackingWeb/secure/Default.aspx
http://localhost/EffortTrackingWeb/login.aspx
http://localhost/EffortTrackingWeb/secure/Default.aspx
http://localhost/EffortTrackingWeb/secure/Default.aspx
http://localhost/EffortTrackingWeb/secure/Edit.aspx?id=0&mode=add&we_id=1
http://localhost/EffortTrackingWeb/secure/Edit.aspx
http://localhost/EffortTrackingWeb/secure/Default.aspx?we_id=3&last=32
Ending Test (Sunday, January 22, 2006)
Beginning Test (1/22/2006 2:10:01 PM)
. . .
```

As you can see from the file, each individual run is recorded separately.

Testing Web Services

Web services are the new "cool" way to implement a service-oriented architecture (SOA). While there are pluses and minuses to this approach, it is fast catching on as the new way to integrate systems. With that in mind, Microsoft built the Web Test tool so that it could also test web services.

■Note The main purpose of the Web Test tool is to test websites, not web services. Therefore, while it can be used to test web services, it is not necessarily the best tool, depending on the situation. If you are testing web services that are not very complicated, the Web Test tool is a simple solution. For more complex situations, software from AmberPoint (www.amberpoint.com) may be better suited to your needs.

Since there are some web services in the solution, you will use the EffortTrackingService. To set up the basic test, do the following:

1. Right-click the EffortTrackingWebTests solution in the Solution Explorer and select New Web Test.

2. When the recording window is displayed, click Stop (you do not want to record anything).

3. Rename the `webtest1.webtest` file to `ServiceTest.webtest`.

Now you have a blank test you can use to write the web service test. The best way to write these tests is to use the built-in help that ASP.NET provides you when browsing a web service. To begin with, open Internet Explorer and browse to `http://localhost/EffortTrackingService/Service.asmx`. Select the GetLookupInfo link from the list of available services. This will bring up the page shown in Figure 15-12.

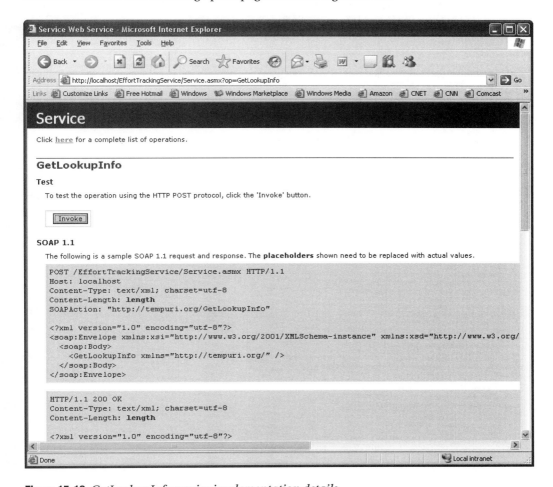

Figure 15-12. *GetLookupInfo service implementation details*

The beauty of this page is that it provides you the text necessary to make the SOAP or HTTP calls. Leaving this alone for the moment, switch back to the IDE browser and right-click the ServiceTest node (the root and only node) in the Web Test window. Select Add Web Service Request. This will add a blank node with a stub URL. Enter the following URL in the URL property of the request node: http://localhost/EffortTrackingService/Service.asmx/GetLookupInfo.

Note The Transport Method at this time is only available as a Post call. The body of the request may be in the format of either a SOAP request or an HTTP request.

Next, click the String Body node beneath the request node. Set the Context Type to text/xml (the only option available at this time) and paste the entire SOAP 1.1 request (shown in Figure 15-12) from the browser into the String Body property.

Tip Remember that when calling a service that requires values you need to put those values into the body of the request.

Run the test. The results should look like those in Figure 15-13.

Figure 15-13. *Web service test result*

As you can see, it is virtually identical to the result of a regular web test except there is no graphical interface, just the service result.

Note In general, the only way to validate the results is to use a regular expression validation rule or a custom validation rule that parses XML looking for specific values.

You can also run data-driven web service tests. To do this, hook up a data source (as described in the "Data-Driven Web Testing" section in this chapter) as usual. However, to place values in the actual SOAP body, use the data field syntax: {{database.table.field}}. Replace any text in the body with this syntax (specific to your data source of course) and the value will be replaced during the test.

Test Results

When viewing the Test Results window (shown in Figure 15-14) you have several options, one of which is exporting the results file to a Test Results XML file (.trx file).

Figure 15-14. *Test Results window*

To export the results, select the Export button from the Test Results window. All of the test results can be exported or just selected test results. The .trx file can be reloaded into the Visual Studio environment at a later date by selecting the Import Test Results button and selecting the .trx file from the browser (this can be from a local computer or a remote computer).

The .trx file is a well-formed XML document you can use in any way you see fit. Transforms can be applied against the XML for either viewing or extracting data.

Note The full description of the XML Schema (XSD) for this file is beyond the scope of this book (it is more than 2,000 lines long). Microsoft is set to release the XML Schemas for most of the documents contained in Visual Studio 2005.

Test Results Schema

The XML Schema, which backs this file, is fairly large so this section only touches on some of the highlights. This schema is very hierarchical in nature with almost every node allowing for an unbounded number of sub-elements. This is because of the nature of the tests it is recording. Take for example the data-driven test run results, which contain four separate tests that went through three or four URL navigations. Representing this data is a fairly complex task, which is why the resulting XSD file is so complex.

Figure 15-15 represents the high-level structure of the XSD file. Figures 15-16 and 15-17 represent the TestRun and the WebTestResults nodes.

Note The following graphics were taken from the XML development tool Altova XMLSpy 2005. If you work with XML a lot, this is the single best tool available. In addition, if you want to create your own style sheets to view the results in a custom format, use Altova's StyleVision 2005. This is an incredible tool for creating style sheets and transformations with drag-and-drop simplicity.

Figure 15-15. *Root node of the test results schema*

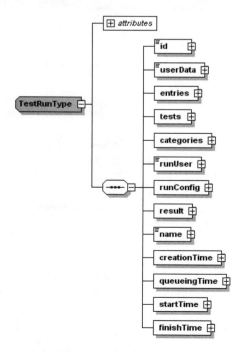

Figure 15-16. *TestRun node of the test results schema*

The TestRun node contains information about each run of the test. It contains information such as who ran a test, what computer a test was run for, when a test started, when it stopped, etc. Specific nodes in the TestRun type are listed in Table 15-9.

Table 15-9. *Notable TestRun Nodes*

Node	Description
Tests	Contains the test name, test file (.webtest) location, associated work item IDs, the project the test is contained in, and various other pieces of information
categories	Contains information related to how the test (or tests) is categorized in the Test Manager
runConfig	Contains all the configuration information from the run configuration associated with the test(s) in general
result	Contains the test result—summed if there was more than one test

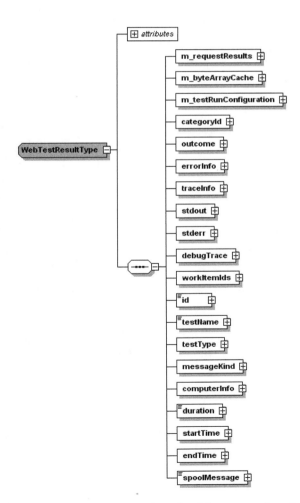

Figure 15-17. *WebTestResult node of the test results schema*

The WebTestResult node contains information specific to each test run. This information includes the request page, the response page, and all the information about each of them and their state for every step of the test (they include the headers but not the body). This is the largest portion of the XSD because of the detailed information contained about each test.

Specific nodes in the WebTestResult type are listed in Table 15-10.

Table 15-10. *WebTestResult Nodes*

Node	Description
m_requestResults	Contains all of the information about specific steps in a test. A simple XSLT applied to a portion of this node can be seen in Figure 15-16.
m_testRunConfiguration	Contains information specific to the configuration as it relates to the specific test run.
errorInfo	Contains any error messages generated by the test step.
computerInfo	Identifies the computer on which each was run.

Microsoft also provides one XML transformation file with VSTS which is used to format the results of the .trx file for display in a web page. This display is used in conjunction with the Builds report.

Tip This file is only available if you have access to a Team Foundation Server.

On the Team Foundation Server, navigate to the `C:\Program Files\Microsoft Visual Studio 2005 Team Foundation Server\Web Services\Build\Test Tools\v1.0\Transforms\ testresult.xsl` file. This file can be used to transform the .trx file for display or it can be used as a starting point for creating your own transform.

Publishing Test Results

The option to publish a test result is only available if you have Team Explorer (the client portion of the Team Foundation Server) installed. Load the test result you want to publish (or use the existing one if you just ran a test) and click the Publish button (located in the middle of the Test Results pane). This will display the Publish Test Results dialog box shown in Figure 15-18.

Select the test run(s) you want to publish, then select the associated build and the build flavor and click OK.

Figure 15-18. *Publish Test Results dialog box*

Note You must do a build with TFSBuild for there to be a build number to associate this test result to. If there are no existing build numbers, then the test result cannot be published. For more information, see Chapter 7.

Multiple test results can be associated with a build/build-flavor combination.

Summary

This chapter has been a whirlwind tour of web testing using Microsoft's new web testing tools. You have seen how to record a web test and dissect all of the steps in order to determine what the test is doing. The various options available to you for the web test have also been covered as well as, more importantly, how to customize the functionality for particular problems you are trying to solve.

You can now convert recorded web tests to coded web tests and implement data binding in either scenario. This gives you a more powerful and controlled way to test different conditions without writing hundreds of individual tests. And, finally, you have seen how to view the test results, publish them, and examine the resulting XML file, so you can create your own transformations to extract the data you feel is the most important.

You have also seen how web services can be tested in a way that exercises the service interface rather than using a unit test. This is especially useful if you are using custom handlers that might inject custom SOAP into the response.

All of this shows the flexibility of the web testing tool. The tool lends itself to being used in almost any situation—from the mundane to the complex. While it is better suited to some tasks than others, as a base testing tool it should cover about 95% of your web testing needs.

CHAPTER 16

Load Testing

Up to this point you have seen how to run web tests from a single machine and run performance testing on discrete pieces of code or on the application as a whole. The last step in testing a system is load testing. Load testing can be defined as "the act of determining whether an application will continue to perform at a defined level, given a set number of connections and requests." While this is our definition (and there are many different definitions for load testing), it does give you one important piece of information: It is measurable.

Often the terms scalability testing, stress testing, and performance testing are used interchangeably. And while they are all definitely linked—and in some cases use the exact same type of tests—the goal is different. You have seen that in performance testing the goal is to discover bottlenecks. To do this, the performance tests can use the exact same testing methodology as load tests. In other words, you can instrument your assemblies and run a load test on them. However, you would not look at the load test results when trying to determine if there are bottlenecks in the application—you would examine the performance results at the method or system level. See? Same test but the information you are looking at is completely different. The question now is what would you look at if you were running a load test?

A load test looks at the performance of the application in relationship to the environment that the application is running in. It looks for external causes for application failure. To illustrate, if you navigate to a website and get an internal server error or a "site unavailable" message, does this mean the website (the application) itself failed? Or does it mean that it is taking so many requests (as in a denial of service attack) that it cannot respond to more requests? This is probably not a result of the application failing (although it could be) but of how the environment is handling the requests. Load testing can also be used to determine database connectivity issues under high load as well. It is quite possible that the application can handle 10,000 requests up front but the act of creating 10,000 connections to the database causes it to fail. Why did it fail? It could be the number of allowed users was exceeded or the back-end network failed to meet the demand placed on it. These are all questions that load testing seeks to answer.

Stress testing, which can be a component of load testing, is designed to cause an application to fail. It does this by placing the system under such a high load that it has no choice but to fail. This high load may be because of the number of connections to the application as in a regular stress test or it may be because other variables were introduced into the environment. These variables range from simulating a hard drive failure to a network card failure or a power supply failure. It tells the tester exactly how many things can go wrong with an environment before the application itself no longer performs. Fortunately this chapter does not cover those issues.

> **▇Note** No application is infinitely scalable or can handle an infinite amount of demand. For one thing, there just is not enough money or need to make that type of system a reality. The types of tests explained here are all determined to help ensure that the application performs as it has been specified to and if it fails the reasons for the failure are known. Then, intelligent decisions can be made concerning how to handle the projected number of users or limitations in the environment.

With the gain in popularity of web services as a sort of "universal" medium through which various applications can communicate, and the increase of web applications, the use of web servers (be it IIS, Apache, or any of a dozen others) is on the rise. This increased usage has ancillary effects on a network environment. If the application is hosted on a machine with other applications, will it negatively affect those applications? Will other applications that happen to use the same network segments as your application be affected? The answers to these questions can help you tune the configuration of both specific machines and the network environment as a whole. And as you will see, Visual Studio Team System provides enough information to allow an organization to make the right decisions.

This chapter will round out your understanding of running tests using VSTS. Many of the previous chapters deferred some of the testing information until this chapter. Load testing is really built on top of web testing. That is, you need to have a web test before you can have a load test. Load testing works by either running the same tests from different machines (using agents) or simulating different machines (through the use of Virtual Machines) even though there may in reality be only one machine.

Controllers and Agents

Before working on actually running a load test, you need to understand how the tests are run (and should be run) and how to deploy the various components of a test. A controller is a service that, conveniently enough, controls a set of agents when performing a specific test. An agent performs the actual work of sending instructions to an application. This set of computers (the controller and all agent computers) is called a rig. For a given load test there can be only one controller, and each agent can belong to only one controller. The physical topography of this setup is shown in Figure 16-1.

Figure 16-1 shows the optimal configuration for a controller/agent deployment, but it is not the only configuration. Essentially any configuration will work provided that a controller and at least one agent are deployed to a machine (this can be the same machine Visual Studio is installed on or the same machine the application is installed on).

> **▇Note** For the load tests performed in this chapter, the deployment consisted of a laptop with Visual Studio on it and a Win2k3 server with the application, the controller, and one agent installed.

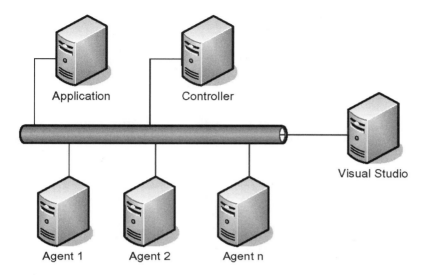

Figure 16-1. *Controller/agent load testing deployment*

Only one agent can be deployed to a given computer, and the controller must be installed first (the controller location information is necessary for the agent installation). Aside from this, there are no limitations on the topography of the test setup.

■**Tip** For this application, a separate controller and agent were installed to perform the load tests. Team Test Load Agent contains the load test agent and controller and needs to be purchased separately. Visual Studio Team System can be used as both the controller and the agent for small load tests (up to about 500 simulated users per processor), but it is best to use a separate controller and agents.

Whenever possible, load testing should be done in an environment that is as close to the real-world environment as possible. This will provide you the most accurate results on which to base decisions.

Once you have the controller and agents set up, you can create and run a load test.

Administering a Controller

Assuming at this point that you have actually set up a controller (or more than one), you can configure it through the Administer Test Controller dialog box shown in Figure 16-2.

Figure 16-2. *Administer Test Controller dialog box*

■Tip SQL Express is installed during the install of the controller.

To add a new controller, you can just type the name of the computer into the controller drop-down. The load test result store holds a copy of the load tests. By default, it is automatically set up on the controller computer.

■Caution You can select <local>, which is the machine on which VSTS is installed, as the controller. Agents *cannot* be assigned to the <local> controller (there is a default local agent, but only one when using <local> as the controller).

The agents assigned to each controller are shown in the Agents list. In this case, the controller and the agent are installed on the same machine. Various options are available for each agent and for the controller. An agent can be removed from a particular controller by selecting the Remove button. To re-add the agent, simply select the Add button and enter the name of the agent in the Agent Properties dialog box when it is displayed (shown in Figure 16-3). Specific agents can also be taken offline, in which case it will not be a part of a test run (the status will change to Offline). Restart can be used to bring an offline agent back online, and Refresh will refresh the statuses of the agents.

Note The status can also be shown as running (if it is currently running a test) or disconnected if VSTS cannot find the agent on the network.

Figure 16-3. *Agent Properties dialog box*

The Delete Temp Files option deletes all files deployed to the agents and controllers. The Restart Rig option restarts the controller and all agents.

Note Several of these options are available even if a test is in progress. If there is a test currently running, you will be notified and given the option to cancel the operation.

In the Agent Properties dialog box you can change the weight of the tests run by that agent. This weight number determines the amount of tests sent from the agent to the test system. This number is independent of the other agents (i.e., you can have three agents with a weight of 50%).

Enable IP Switching allows an agent to send requests over a range of IP addresses to the application to be tested, instead of just a single static IP address. You can also specify the network interface card (NIC) that the requests should be sent from, if there is more than one network card installed on the agent machine.

The Attributes section allows you to add a series of name/value pairs that allow you to constrain which agents are used in a given test. This filter is set in the Test Run Configuration dialog box shown in Figure 16-4.

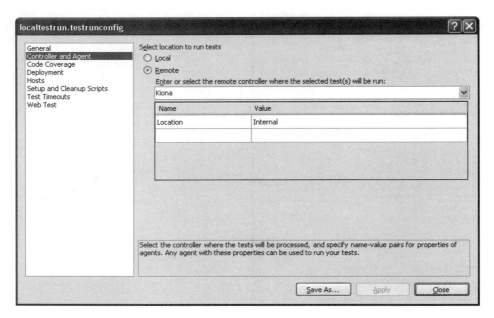

Figure 16-4. *The Controller and Agent configuration tab*

Configuring the Test Run

The solution configuration file has been covered in various chapters (an overview of the entire configuration file was presented in Chapter 12). There is one tab in the configuration file that applies to load testing: the Controller and Agent tab shown in Figure 16-4.

This tab allows you to configure where the tests are run from and allows you to filter the agents used in the run. The tests can be run either from the local machine (if no controller is installed) or from a remote machine (if you have previously installed a controller). When selecting Remote, you have the option of constraining which agents are used as part of the test by specifying the Attribute name you assigned to the agents and the value of that attribute. An example of this may be the network configuration between the agent and the test machine. The situation may be such that several computers are set up as internal to the enterprise and several are external and go through a proxy and a firewall. For this scenario you may add an attribute name to each agent with a value of Location and a value of either Internal or External. Then, when running the test, you can elect to only use some of the agents by entering **Location** in the name and **External** in the value if you want to simulate connections coming in from outside of the firewall.

Tip A best practice is to add the same attribute name to each of the agents. By doing this you are explicitly including an agent with a given value. If you do not add an attribute name and value to a given agent but specify it in the test configuration dialog, the agent without that attribute will not run. By adding the same name to each agent you will not accidentally exclude an agent.

Load Test Wizard

Now that you have seen how to configure the controller and agents, you can create a load test. The easiest way to create a load test is to use the Load Test Wizard. To do this, select Test ➤ New Test from the main menu. Select the Load Test icon and click OK (select the EffortTrackingWebTests as the project in which the test should be located). The first page of the load test is an introduction to the wizard. Click Next on the Introduction screen to move to the Scenario screen (shown in Figure 16-5).

Figure 16-5. *Scenario settings wizard dialog box*

Scenario

This dialog box allows you to set the name for the test and specify think times. The think times control how real the scenario is. The think time is the amount of time a user spends looking at a web page or reading a web page without actually doing anything. A perfect example is a news site. You might browse to a site and read an article. It may take you up to five minutes to read that page, during which time you are not actually hitting the web server at all.

The three think time options are described in Table 16-1. Think times are discussed in more detail in the sidebar.

Table 16-1. *Think Time Options*

Profile	Description
Recorded think times	The test will use the think times you entered for each page of the web test (one of the properties of the Request Node of a web test).
Normal distribution	The test uses a statistical distribution of think times based on the time entered for each page. For example, if you set the think time property of a page to 8 seconds, the test may use times between 5 and 11 seconds as the think time.
No think times	The test executes as fast as it possibly can for the specified number of iterations.

THINK TIMES

Think times allow you to more accurately profile your website under a realistic load. Part of the problem with the testing tool, Application Center Test, is that you cannot simulate think times. Often the think times will give you a much different view of the load that your website can accurately handle. Selecting the normal distribution, which is the default, provides the most realistic load test.

A perfect example of why think times make a difference occurs with a news website. When you visit www.msnbc.com or www.cnn.com you do not click through all the pages as quickly as you can; you read the stories. Often these stories are broken up into multiple pages. Consider how you might design your website to handle this situation. Maybe when a user selects a news story that is three pages long, you automatically cache (or check the cache) on a separate thread to ensure that pages two and three of the story are loaded. You do this because you have a good idea based on logical reasoning that the user will want to read the whole story.

Now if you do not use think times when testing the website, you might discover that the site has a high rate of database access, or a high cache miss rate (the rate at which the cache is accessed but the page is not found in the cache). In reality, the site may be perfectly capable of handling the load, but you would not be aware of that based on the test results.

Similarly, a static set of think times allows the testing of a website under a constant load; but this load is not very realistic. The chance that ten users will access the site at the same time, spend eight seconds on each page, and move through the site in parallel is not realistic either. But by using a normal distribution you can be guaranteed that the page access times will become varied, and it will simulate people accessing the website at various times on each page.

This is not to say that static think times and no think times do not have a place—they do. They allow the testing of a website under a constant but reasonable load and with the worst case scenario. A perfect example of why you would want to test with no think times is a denial of service attack, in which packets requesting pages are constantly sent against one page or many. This provides a great test to see how your website will respond in such a circumstance.

The think time between test iterations allows you to specify how quickly the test will repeat after it has completed.

Load Pattern

The load pattern allows for the specification of how many simulated users will access the website and in what distribution. You can specify a constant load or a step load (shown in Figure 16-6).

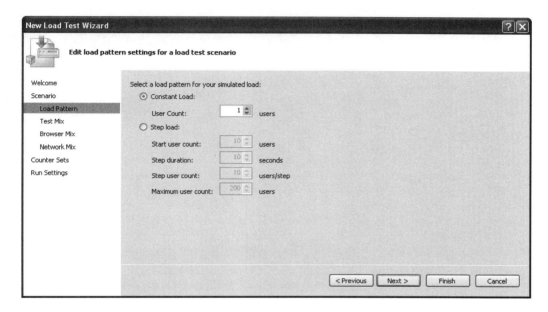

Figure 16-6. *Load Pattern dialog box*

A constant load means that the number of users specified will start accessing the website immediately upon activation of the test. A step load test allows you to specify how the user count will "ramp up" (see Table 16-2).

Table 16-2. *Step Load Values*

Values	Description
Start user count	Number of simulated users who will access the website as soon as the test run is started.
Step duration	Amount of time each step will last.
Step user count	Number of simulated users who will be added to the user count at each step.
Maximum user count	Maximum number of simulated users who will access the website.

CHAPTER 16 ■ LOAD TESTING

It is not necessary to run the step load in order to get an accurate assessment of your website. In the run settings (see the "Run Settings" section later in this chapter) you can specify a warm-up time for the test, which will allow the site time to compile and cache pages before the "real" test starts.

Test Mix

The next part of the wizard is to add the tests you want to load test your site with. The dialog box for this is shown in Figure 16-7.

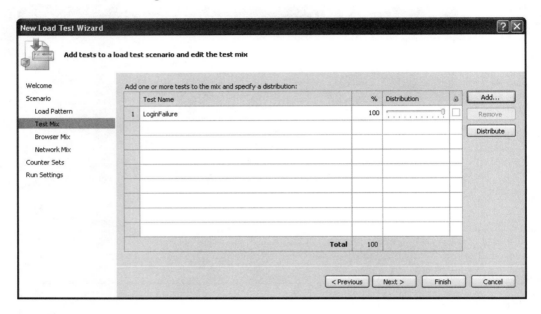

Figure 16-7. *Select Tests dialog box*

To add a test, select the Add button and select each of the tests from the Add Tests dialog box shown in Figure 16-8.

From here you can add any previously created tests.

The distribution value is an indicator of the likelihood of a user actually running through the sequence of events described in the web test. For example, in the effort tracking application there is a higher probability that a user will log on to the application and add a task rather than logging on, selecting a different week, and deleting a task. The distribution must equal 100%.

■**Caution** Nothing prevents you from adding unit tests or manual tests to this list. Do not do this! The load test will run but no usable information will be returned (and it will pause the load test if you specify a manual test).

The check box to the right of the distribution allows you to lock a particular test's distribution so it does not change dynamically as you change the distributions on other tests.

Figure 16-8. *Add Tests dialog box*

Browser Mix

The load test allows you to specify the types of browsers that will be accessing the website and allows you to specify the distribution of those requests (shown in Figure 16-9).

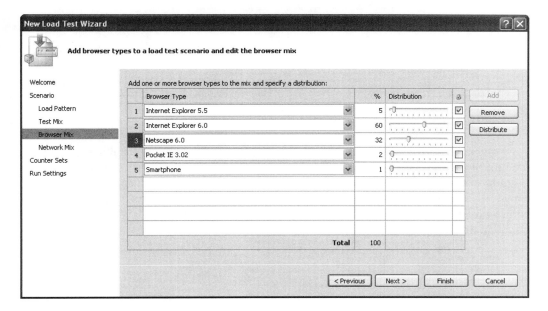

Figure 16-9. *Browser Mix dialog box*

Figure 16-9 shows the list of built-in browsers that are supported by load testing. This list is extensible, although undocumented, so you can create additional browser types such as Opera and Firefox (this is described in the section "Extending Load Test Settings" later in this chapter). The distribution here is identical to that of the tests. It allows you to specify the portion of browsers of a given type accessing your system. This allows you to exercise any code you have that targets specific browsers (for example, if your website is accessible via Pocket Internet Explorer or a Smartphone, you typically send a page that has been formatted differently).

Network Mix

The Network Mix dialog box allows you to specify the types of connections that will access the website (shown in Figure 16-10).

Figure 16-10. *Network Mix dialog box*

This is useful for accurately describing the types of connections and for allowing you to monitor the time it takes to generate pages for different types of connections. An example of this might be a brokerage website. The site may have quality requirements that specify that results are returned to the user in less than three seconds regardless of the type of network connection they are using. This selection allows for the verification of this type of quality requirement.

Counter Sets

Counter sets are literally the set of counters you want to use to monitor information about various computers during the test (shown in Figure 16-11).

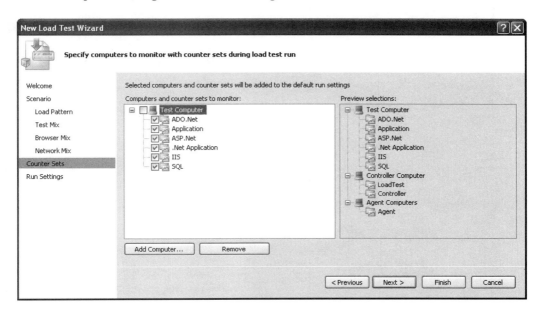

Figure 16-11. *Counter Sets dialog box*

By default, the controller computer and all agent computers are monitored. However, you can elect to monitor additional computers on the network for performance during the testing. A common example of this might be a proxy server. Since some of the requests are going to go through this computer, knowing how it is performing during the test is crucial. Another example would be a load balancing server, a database server, or a failover server. This will tell you if the hardware and network connections on the external systems your application has a dependency on are capable of handling the load.

Note For this chapter, the controller, agent, and website are all located on the same computer, so there is no separate test computer as shown in Figure 16-11. That is an example only.

Run Settings

Run settings allow you to specify the warm-up time (the amount of time the website is "exercised" before the real test begins), the run duration, the frequency of sample collection, a test description, the number of details that should be captured for each error, and the validation level (Figure 16-12).

Figure 16-12. *Run Settings dialog box*

The only item that really needs to be described on this dialog box is the validation level; everything else is self-explanatory. The validation level describes what validation rules the load test will ignore or process (see the section "Validation Rules" in Chapter 15 for more details). During a regular web test you most likely want to know when a value violates a rule. During a load test this information is not necessarily important unless you need to know how the site reacts to these violations under load.

Extending Load Test Settings

For a load test you can extend or alter three of the settings for a load test—browser types, network types, and counter sets—using a ridiculously simple feature that is currently undocumented.

Extending the Browsers

The list of browsers included with the out-of-the-box package is pretty small. It does not include such popular browsers as Firefox or Opera and there are numerous other browsers that, while not all that common, are definitely in use by a large number of users (for example, the browsers that work on non-Windows phones). So adding to this list is a fairly logical step. To add a new browser you will create a browser file. The default browser files are located in C:\Program Files\Microsoft Visual Studio 8\Common7\IDE\Templates\LoadTest\Browsers. If you open the IE6.browser file you will see the XML shown in Listing 16-1.

Listing 16-1. *The IE6 Browser File*

```
<Browser Name="Internet Explorer 6.0">
  <Headers>
    <Header Name="User-Agent" Value="Mozilla/4.0 (compatible; MSIE 6.0; Windows NT 5.1)" />
    <Header Name="Accept" Value="*/*" />
    <Header Name="Accept-Language" Value="{{$IEAcceptLanguage}}" />
    <Header Name="Accept-Encoding" Value="GZIP" />
  </Headers>
</Browser>
```

If you are not familiar with how browsers work, here's a one-sentence introduction (although, hopefully, if you are reading this chapter you know how a browser header works): when the client browser sends a request to the server it includes various pieces of information about itself so the server can take appropriate action. To see this in action, try visiting www.ranks.nl/tools/envtest.html to see what is sent to a server. With this information, understanding what is included here is pretty simple.

■Tip More information on header field values can be found at www.w3.org/Protocols/rfc2616/rfc2616-sec14.html (W3C specification).

In Listing 16-1 the User-Agent value indicates the capabilities of the agent (the browser in this case) accessing the server. As you can see, IE is Mozilla 4.0 compliant and compatible with Microsoft Internet Explorer 6 and is running on the Windows NT 5.1 platform (Windows XP).

The Accept header indicates what extensions will be honored in the response. */* indicates that all extensions are acceptable to the client. If, for example, you only want to accept images, you would see image/*, which indicates the type and what subtypes to accept (* indicates all).

The Accept-Language value is the language the browser can understand. The $IEAccept-Language is replaced with the culture in use on the local machine. Some of the actual values (i.e., the values that are actually transmitted) are "en" or "en-us" for English or U.S. English, "hu" for Hungarian, "zh" for Chinese, etc.

Tip More information about the language codes can be found in any book on application globalization or localization. A shorter list can be found here: www.hashemian.com/tools/browser-simulator.htm.

The Accept-Encoding header indicates the type of encoding of the data that can be understood by the browser. In this case, GZIP indicates that IE6 can understand the data transmitted to the client if it is compressed in a gzip format (a compression format that is in standard use by web servers to minimize the size of the data stream sent to the client).

Now that you understand the contents of this file, add a new Opera browser by creating a new browser file called `Opera.browser` and enter the information contained in Listing 16-2.

Listing 16-2. *The Opera Browser File*

```
<Browser Name="Opera 8.0">
  <Headers>
    <Header Name="User-Agent" Value="Opera/8.00+(Windows+NT+5.1;+U;+en)" />
    <Header Name="Accept" Value="text/html, image/jpeg, image/gif,
      image/x-xbitmap, */*" />
    <Header Name="Accept-Language" Value="en" />
    <Header Name="Accept-Encoding" Value="GZIP" />
  </Headers>
</Browser>
```

Once you save the file, if you edit the Browser Mix you will see Opera 8.0 as an option.

Extending the Network Types

Creating a new network type or altering an existing network type is even easier than adding or changing a browser type. The network types are located in the folder `C:\Program Files\Microsoft Visual Studio 8\Common7\IDE\Templates\LoadTest\Networks` and have the extension .network. The 56.6 dial-up type is shown in Listing 16-3.

Listing 16-3. *Dial-up 56.6K Network Type*

```
<Network Name="Dial-up 56k" BandwidthInKbps="53.3">
</Network>
```

The bandwidth controller is the BandwidthInKbps attribute. 53.3 represents the number of kilobytes/second. The T1 network is represented by 1544 Kbps. The LAN network is represented by a value of 0, which indicates maximum throughput. To create a new network type just add the code from Listing 16-3 to a file with the extension .network and customize it as you need. This is handy for when more advanced connections are developed or special network needs require nonstandard throughput.

Extending the Counter Sets

The counter sets allow you to preconfigure frequently used counters for performance monitoring. A good use of this might be to create a standard counter configuration file to be used by all of your applications, or a configuration file for any other standards-based testing where you have to ensure that the same counters are captured for different tests. The counter sets are located in `C:\Program Files\Microsoft Visual Studio 8\Common7\IDE\Templates\LoadTest\ CounterSets` and have the extension .CounterSets. The ADO.NET counter set is shown in Listing 16-4.

Listing 16-4. *The ADO.NET Counter Set*

```
<CounterSet Name="ADO.Net" CounterSetType="ADO.Net">
    <CounterCategories>
        <CounterCategory Name=".NET CLR Data">
            <Counters>
                <Counter Name="SqlClient: Current # connection pools" />
                <Counter Name="SqlClient: Current # pooled and
 nonpooled connections" />
                <Counter Name="SqlClient: Current # pooled connections" />
                <Counter Name="SqlClient: Peak # pooled connections" />
                <Counter Name="SqlClient: Total # failed commands" />
                <Counter Name="SqlClient: Total # failed connects" />
            </Counters>
            <Instances>
                <Instance Name="*" />
            </Instances>
        </CounterCategory>
    </CounterCategories>
</CounterSet>
```

The category name is what shows up in the list, and in the list of counters are the names of the specific counters (you can get these values from the Windows Performance Monitor (perfmon). The Instance name specifies the machine from which the counters are to be collected. The star (*) indicates that these counters will be collected from all of the machines involved in the test.

Load Test Window

After the Load Test Wizard has completed, the settings can be viewed in the Load Test window shown in Figure 16-13.

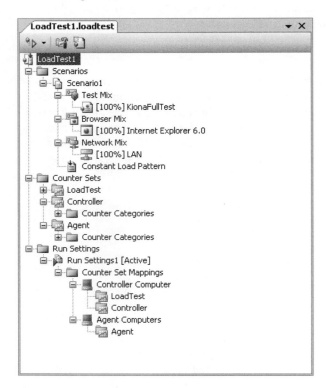

Figure 16-13. *Load Test window*

From the Load Test window you can configure several additional options (shown in Table 16-3) and add additional run settings.

Note While only one run setting can be active at a given time, by being able to configure multiple settings, the same load test can be reused in order to focus given tests on various aspects of the systems under load.

Table 16-3. *Additional Load Test Options*

Option	How To	Description
Add Custom Counters	Right-click the Counter Sets node.	Allows you to add any counters available in the system at a very fine-grained level (Figure 16-14).
Add Threshold Rule	Expand the Counter Sets until you find the counter you want to set a threshold rule for, right-click, and select Add Threshold Rule.	Allows you to add a warning that informs you of when a counter has exceeded a given threshold (Figure 16-15).
Add Run Settings	Right-click the Run Settings node.	Allows you to add additional run settings.

Note When additional run settings are added, make sure you have selected the correct run setting for a test either by right-clicking the settings and selecting Set as Active, or by selecting the load test root node and setting it in the properties dialog box.

Figure 16-14. *Pick Performance Counters dialog box*

In Figure 16-14 the computer Januik (which contains the SQL Server 2005 database) is selected and the SQL Server Statistics counters are displayed. You can select either specific counters or all of the counters from a category.

Figure 16-15. *Add Threshold Rule dialog box*

A threshold rule can be set for any counter. It generates either a warning or a critical warning message during the load test run if the counter exceeds a given value. There are two ways of setting a threshold rule: either it can be a constant value or it can be based on the value of another counter. For a constant value you simply enter the values for the warning and critical levels and indicate when an alert should be generated. Do not be fooled by the title "Alert If Over." If this value is set to False, an alert is generated if it is under the stated value. Otherwise it generates an alert if it is over the stated value.

When electing to set threshold rules based on another counter, you select the Compare Counters rule. This rule throws an exception if one counter performs faster than another counter or vice versa. This allows you some degree of dynamic performance monitoring based on the environment.

Tip To see what threshold rules have been set for a test, you need to drill down into the Load Test tree view. Select Counter Sets ➤ [Computer Name] ➤ Counter Categories ➤ [Category] ➤ Counters ➤ [Counter Name] and you will get to the threshold rules. If there is no plus (+) next to the counter name then there is no threshold rule set for that counter.

Once you have set the test run settings and configured the load test you can either run or debug the load test. The reason there is no section called "Running a Load Test" is because it is entirely automatic. You can view various results from the load test while the test is running but once you start the test you can grab a cup of coffee.

Analyzing Load Test Results

There is so much information collected from a load test that you need to be able to understand it effectively in order to be able to use it to improve the performance of your website. Because of this, the various test results are discussed in general terms. There are several hundred counters available to you, which all indicate various things and this book is not about performance counters. Instead, this section discusses what results are found where and the various ways of diving into the data to get answers concerning the load test results.

Figure 16-16 shows the load test results from the FullTest load test.

Figure 16-16. *Load test results*

The four panes represented in the load test results window are (clockwise from upper left) Counters, Graphs/Tables, Points, and Summary. Each of the panes is described in the following sections.

Tip You can switch to full-screen mode by selecting View ➤ Full Screen from the main menu or pressing Shift + Alt + Enter (this will also revert the screen to normal mode).

Counters Pane

The Counters pane contains a list of all the counters on all the computers recorded during the test. During the actual test run, only a subset of these counters is shown; but once the test is completed the full set of counters can be found. Figure 16-17 shows a more detailed view of the Counters pane.

Figure 16-17. *Counters pane*

The first node in the list, Overall, displays (as its name suggests) a list of counters that covers the overall set of counters. These are counters that have been summed and placed into this node.

As you can see in Figure 16-17, the details related to the Scenario (the second node) are shown. One node for each test is displayed here. Drilling into the FullTest (the name of the web test) shows all of the collected data relating to a specific test. Double-clicking on any of the counters in this pane (or dragging and dropping the counter on the graph) will add that item to the graph (and it will be displayed in the legend beneath the graph).

The Computers node shows all of the counters recorded for each computer that you elected to record data from. In this example, data was recorded only from the KIONA computer.

The last node, Errors, records the total number of errors grouped by type.

Graphs/Tables Pane

The pane containing the graphs in Figure 16-16 can be switched to a table view by selecting the Table button from the top of the window. Figure 16-18 shows the table view.

Table:	Pages						
Page	Scenario	Test	Total	Page Time	Page Time Goal	% Meeting
Default.aspx	Scenario1	KionaFullTest	707	0.36	-	100
edit.aspx	Scenario1	KionaFullTest	202	0.18	-	100
Edit.aspx	Scenario1	KionaFullTest	404	0.18	-	100
login.aspx	Scenario1	KionaFullTest	202	0.54	-	100

Figure 16-18. *Table view of data*

This view provides access to various tables of data and detail about that data. For example, if there were errors, the Errors table could be selected and you would see details about the types of errors and be able to drill down into the stack trace, depending on the errors.

■**Note** If the web test runs without problems there should not be any errors in the load test caused by the test itself. However, because this is a load test and the system or application may not be able to handle it, you will very likely see errors such as "500 – Internal Server Error."

■**Caution** When you first create a load test, one of the default counters that is set is the Threshold counter. This sets a specified period of time for the page to respond, and if it does not respond in time an exception is thrown. When the exception is thrown, it is recorded, but part of the test ends up being skipped. Because of this, all sorts of weird errors start appearing (though this is partially based on how your test is set up). Our suggestion would be to disable this threshold check if you are running the test on your local machine and manually determine how many pages did not respond in a set period of time (using Excel or some other tool to sort and analyze the data). This will stop the problem of the application throwing unrelated and hard-to-trace exceptions that are not actually occurring.

The graph itself has various options for displaying data. The data displayed on the graph is located below the graph in the legend. To highlight a specific metric, select it from the legend and it will become bolded in the graph.

At the top of the graph there is a drop-down menu containing a list of computers for which counter information was collected, and a Default option. The Default option displays data for all computers. In addition, you can create additional graphs. The purpose of this is to be able to create graphs that display various counters. For example, one graph may show the processor time of all the computers involved in the load test so a comparison can be made (this type of comparison is useful, for example, when your application is deployed to a web farm) and another may show entirely different, unrelated information.

Options for the graph can be set by right-clicking the graph and selecting Graph Options or by selecting the Graph Options button from the top of the graph. The options you can set are the following:

- Select Graph
- Show Legend
- Show Plot Points
- Show Horizontal Grid Lines
- Show Min/Max Lines
- Show Threshold Violations
- Display data for the entire run or recent data only (available while the run is in progress)

Just below the graph but above the legend is a bar (shown in Figure 16-16) which allows you to zoom in on a portion of the graph. You can also zoom in by clicking in the graph and dragging your mouse until the portion you want to zoom in on is highlighted.

Below the graph is the legend. Selecting a counter in the legend will bold it on the graph. A counter can be deleted from the graph by right-clicking it and selecting Delete, or selecting the counter and pressing the Delete key. To temporarily remove the counter from the graph, simply uncheck the box next to the counter. For each counter you can set three options in the Plot Options dialog box shown in Figure 16-19.

Figure 16-19. *Plot Options dialog box*

As you can see from Figure 16-19, you can change the color of the counter line, the style of the line, and the range of display for the counter. The default is to allow VSTS to automatically control the range, which takes into account other values on the graph.

The columns in the legend give you detailed information on the counter itself: which computer it was recording information from, what counter category it is part of, and the min, max, average, and last values it recorded.

Points Pane

The graph points are actually part of the Graph pane and can be hidden by selecting the Show/Hide Graph Points option of the graph. This pane always displays data in the form of time (in the left column) and the value (in the right column). The time displayed is based on the polling interval selected during the Load Test setup. The value is dependent on the counter selected.

Summary Pane

The Summary pane simply provides a summary of all of the data collected during the test run.

Publishing Test Results

As with web tests, load test results can be published to a Team Foundation Server. For the steps to publish a load test, see the "Publishing Test Results" section in Chapter 15.

Summary

In this chapter you have seen how and why you run a load test and what information you expect to get out of it. Running a load test based on an existing web test (or a set of web tests) in order to validate system performance under high demand is the key focus of this chapter. The setup of the controller and associated agent(s) was covered, which gives you a solid starting place for creating your own load test lab. Setting options for the load test and, finally, being able to view and analyze the load test results was presented.

This chapter used steps from previous chapters, combined with the abilities of the VSTS load testing tool to provide you detailed information about an application's environment. This information will help you build better, more reliable applications by allowing you to configure the environment in which the application runs, with the foreknowledge of how it will perform. While this tool may not solve all of the problems with an environment, it will help you prepare by giving you information about any weaknesses in the environment and allowing you to plan for the future.

APPENDIX

Command-Line Tools Reference

Various command-line tools are available for performing Visual Studio Team System operations. In many cases, the functionality provided by these tools is also available from the IDE. When possible, it is best to use the functionality presented by the IDE because of the complexity of the command-line tools. For example, the TFSSecurity server command-line tool allows you to control security, but the command-line options can be overwhelming and difficult to use. It's much more straightforward to use the IDE tools for controlling security, as described in Chapter 2 of this book.

Also be aware that the use of the command-line tools is not recommended by Microsoft in most cases. This is especially true of the server tools. Certain tools can cause a lot of problems when used incorrectly (for example, accidentally deleting items, erasing all permissions, ruining existing assemblies, and so on). These tools should be used with caution, and you should test their usage in a nonproduction environment first, so you understand all of their nuances. While many of these tools are well documented, some are not.

That said, this appendix presents brief lists of the server and client command-line tools. More information about each tool can be found in the MSDN documentation, and some are discussed in more detail in this book.

Server Command-Line Tools

Table A-1 describes each of the server command-line tools. All of the server tools are located in `C:\Program Files\Microsoft Visual Studio 2005 Team Foundation Server\Tools`.

Table A-1. *Server Command-Line Tools*

Tool	Description
CreateDS	Used to create a data source for reporting services.
InstanceInfo	Used to return a GUID for the specified Team Foundation Server (TFS) database(s). It works for most TFS databases, but not the data warehouse.
ProcessTemplateManager	Used to upload a new process template.

Continued

Table A-1. *Continued*

Tool	Description
SetupWarehouse	TFS Server Warehouse Setup tool, used to set up a new instance of the TFS data warehouse. It can also be used to repopulate an existing data warehouse.
TFRSConfig	TFS Reporting Server Configuration tool.
TFSAdminUtil	TFS Administration Utility, used to change passwords, accounts, machine locations, and connections between the application tier and the data tier.
TFSReg	TFS Registration tool.
TFSSecurity	TFS Server Security tool, used to control security of projects, users, and groups (Windows and TFS groups). It can also be used to report on that information.

Client Command-Line Tools

The client command-line tools that you have available depend on the version of Visual Studio Team System that is installed. The majority of these tools are available from within the IDE. Table A-2 describes these tools and notes their location.

Table A-2. *Client Command-Line Tools*

Tool	Description	Location
VSInstr	Used to perform the instrumentation of binaries, which can then be deployed to a production machine.	C:\Program Files\Microsoft Visual Studio 8\Team Tools\Performance Tools
VSPerfCmd	Used to start and stop performance profiling.	C:\Program Files\Microsoft Visual Studio 8\Team Tools\Performance Tools
VSPerfMon	Used to start and stop performance profiling, but contains different options than the VSPerfCmd application.	C:\Program Files\Microsoft Visual Studio 8\Team Tools\Performance Tools
VSPerfClrEnv	Used to set Common Language Runtime (CLR) environment options so the performance tools can be properly loaded.	C:\Program Files\Microsoft Visual Studio 8\Team Tools\Performance Tools
VSPerfReport	Used to create performance reports (or a subset of those reports that you see in the IDE).	C:\Program Files\Microsoft Visual Studio 8\Team Tools\Performance Tools
FxCopCmd	Used to run managed static code analysis.	C:\Program Files\Microsoft Visual Studio 8\Team Tools\Static Analysis Tools\FxCop

Tool	Description	Location
WitExport	Used to export work items from TFS.	C:\Program Files\Microsoft Visual Studio 8\Common7\IDE
TFSBuild	Used to perform command-line builds, with the results published to TFS.	C:\Program Files\Microsoft Visual Studio 8\Common7\IDE
TFSDeleteProject	Used to delete a project from TFS. This can be done only via the command line.	C:\Program Files\Microsoft Visual Studio 8\Common7\IDE
TFSFieldMapping	Used to change the mappings from the server fields to local fields and to add or remove mappings for Microsoft Project and Excel integration.	C:\Program Files\Microsoft Visual Studio 8\Common7\IDE
MSTest	Used to run tests from the command line. It can publish the test results to TFS, if TFS is installed.	C:\Program Files\Microsoft Visual Studio 8\Common7\IDE
MSBuild	Used to build a solution and optionally run tests associated with the solution.	C:\%winnt%\Microsoft.NET\Framework\v2.0.50727

Index

A

Access property (classes), 318
Access property (items), 327
Accessors property, 327
ACT (Application Center Test), 9, 433
Activate policy, 99
Active Directory (AD), security and, 46
Actual Quality vs. Planned Velocity report, 163, 165
AD (Active Directory), security groups and, 46
AD. *See* Application Designer
.ad (application diagrams), 221, 223
   system diagrams and, 259, 261
add command, 102
AddItemCoded class, 448
AddUser method, 325
AddUserTest method, 346, 354
Administer labels permission, 65
adminpak.msi tool, 46
.adprototype files, 224
agents, 471–477
Agile Development methodologies, 342
Agile method, 26
Agile process template, 25
   predefined queries and, 125
   predefined reports and, 163
   reports and, 30
   work item types and, 29, 131
alert states, 253
alerts, 32, 141
allocation information, 416
Altova tools, 466
AmberPoint, 462
analyzing load test results, 491–495
Application Center Test (ACT), 9, 433

application definitions (.sdm), 271, 286
Application Designer (AD), 6, 219–253
   Toolbox objects for, 224
application diagrams (.ad), 221, 223
   system diagrams and, 259, 261
application endpoints, 260
application prototypes, 224, 256
application systems, 221
application time, 404
applications, 221
   comments, adding to, 244
   defined, 256
   implementing, 233–240
   reverse-engineering for, 251
   servers bound to
      explicit model, 289
      implicit model, 299
   troubleshooting, 253
   vs. systems, 256
   web applications, adding to, 240–244
architects, benefits of VSTS for, 2, 5
   Class Designer and, 311
   distributed designers and, 221
architecture, 2
   process templates and, 37
areas, 32, 112
   security for, 54
ASP.NET applications
   operations for, defining, 232
   performance profiles for, 425–429
Assert statements, 347
AssertFailedException, 347
Assigned To field, modifying, 145–149
Associated Work Items property, 350
association relationships, displaying, 330
Association tool, 332
atomic systems, 220

attachments, adding to work items
    in Microsoft Project, 109
    in Team Explorer, 125
Atwood, Jeff, 95
authoring tools, 161
automated builds, 197–215

B

base work item type, 153
BaseIntrospectionRule class, 394
BI (Business Intelligence), 159
BIDS (Business Intelligence Development Studio), 166
Block operation, 181
Booch, Grady, 222
boundary values testing, 340
branch command, 102
branches command, 102
branching, 80
browser mix, load testing and, 481, 486
Bug Rates report, 163, 165
Bug work items, 133, 142–144
Bugs by Priority report, 163, 165
Bugs Found Without Corresponding Tests report, 163, 165
Build Detail Report, 204–208
build details, 209
build history, viewing, 208
build quality, 209
build results, viewing, 203–208
Build Services group, 52
build steps (Build Detail Report), 205
build summary (Build Detail Report), 205
build type configuration file, 211
build types
    creating, 198–203
    deleting, 203
build verification tests (BVTs), 197
builds
    automated, 197–215
    customizing, 211
    deleting, 214
    history of, displaying, 208
    running, 203–208
    starting/stopping, 213
Builds report, 163, 165
Business Intelligence (BI), 159
Business Intelligence Development Studio (BIDS), 166
Business Intelligence Platform, 159
BVTs (build verification tests), 197

C

C#, Class Designer and, 312
call trees, 415
callers/callees, performance reports and, 414
Capability Maturity Model Integrated (CMMI), 4
change requests (CRs), 136
changesets, 72–75
ChangeSetting operation, 181
check-in notes, 71, 93
Check in other users' changes permission, 65
Check-in permission, 65
check-in policies, 91
    creating, 95–100
    installing, 99
    Team Foundation Build and, 198
Check method, 396
Check-out permission, 65
check-out settings, 90
checkin command, 102
checkout command, 102
CIZs (corporate intranet zones), 270, 272
Class Designer, 7, 311–337
    design goals of, 311–314
    menu options for, 319
    Toolbox options for, 319
    XML view of, 336
class diagrams
    creating, 315
    fields/properties, adding to, 333–335
    items, adding to, 320–327
    XML view of, 336
Class Name property, 350
Class node, 336

class properties, 318
ClassCleanup method, 368
ClassInitialize method, 368
classes
    adding to diagrams, 316
    exploring, 316
    renaming, 316
cleanup scripts, 357
client command-line tools, 497
cloaking folders, 68
CMMI (Capability Maturity Model Integrated), 4
CMMI process template, 25
    predefined queries and, 125
    predefined reports and, 163
    reports and, 30
    work item types and, 29, 131
code analysis policy, 92
code analysis tools, 7, 377–401
code coverage, 339, 356
    performance testing and, 357
code coverage results, viewing, 206, 362–364
code reviews, 377
coded web tests, 447–452
colors, for code coverage information, 364
column mappings, viewing in Microsoft Project, 112–115
command-line access, for TFVC, 101
command-line tools, 422, 497
comments
    check-in policies and, 95–98
    for class diagrams, 335
    for applications, 244
    for attachments/links, 112
communication tools, Project Portal and, 5, 26, 32–36
composite systems, 221
configuration files
    localtestrun.testrunconfig, 355
    manifest.xml, 28
    build type, 211
    web.config, 427–428

configure command, 102
configuring
    application designs, 249
    controllers, 473
    deployment properties, 303
    FxCop, 391–401
    lists, in Excel, 117
    load tests, 476–486
    project alerts, for work item tracking, 141
    projects, 90, 93
    recorded tests, 439
    servers, 276
    test runs, 355–359
    TFVC, 89–95
    zones, 271
conflicts, resolving, 85
connected systems, 219
connections, rules/guidelines for, 246
Constant Kind property, 327
constant loads, 479
constraints
    for application designs, 249
    overriding, 265
    for servers, 276
    setting for zones, 270, 273
    viewing in System Designer, 264
consumer endpoints, 245
Context class, 456
continuous integration testing, 214
contract-first approach, 219, 232
Contributors group, 52
controllers, 472–477
Cook, Steve, 223
corporate intranet zones (CIZs), 270, 272
cost considerations
    automated builds and, 197
    VSTS and, 2
count measures, 187
counter sets, 483, 487
counters, 492
    deleting, 494
CRs (change requests), 136

creating
- build types, 198–203
- check-in policies, 91
- class diagrams, 315
- deployment diagrams, 287, 297
- global lists, 150
- groups, 145
- interfaces, 328
- lists, in Excel, 116
- load tests, 477–487
- logical datacenter diagrams, 267–283
- manual tests, 374
- namespaces, 157
- ordered tests, 353
- policies, 95–100
- product schedules, in Microsoft Project, 106
- projects, 20
- queries, 126
- reports, 166–170, 187, 195
- solutions, 68
- system diagrams, 256–262
- test database, 367
- tests lists, 352
- unit tests, 342–345
- user interfaces, 242
- work item types, 152–156
- work items, 122
- workspaces, 67

culture testing, 341
Custom Attributes property (classes), 318
Custom Attributes property (items), 327
customizing
- builds, 211
- extraction rules, 454
- process guidance, 43
- process templates, 36–43
- Project Portal, 32–36
- reports, 166–172
- Team Foundation Build, 211
- validation rules, 459

D

Data Access Method property, 350
data binding
- coded web tests and, 449
- data-driven web testing and, 443

Data Connection String property, 350
data-driven access options, 445
data-driven testing, 367–373
data-driven web testing, 443
- coded, 449

data mining, 182–189
Data Provider property, 350
data sources, reporting and, 169
Data Table Name property, 350
Data Warehouse (Team Foundation), 172–189
- adding elements to, 182
- managing, 181

data warehouse schema, 174–180
database endpoints, 259
databases
- connecting to web services, 228
- database component, for sample application, 226
- production, 368
- test, 367

DD (Deployment Designer), 220
.dd (deployment diagrams), 221, 287–307
- validating implementation of, 291, 301

delegation, 260
delete command, 102
DeleteTask method, 325
DeleteTaskTest method, 359–362
deleting
- build types, 203
- builds, 214
- counters, from graphs, 494
- inheritance relationships, 330
- interfaces, 330
- work items from projects, 145

demilitarized zones (DMZs), 269, 272
Deployment Designer (DD), 6, 220, 285–307

deployment diagrams (.dd), 221, 287–307
    validating implementation of, 291, 301
Deployment Items property, 350
deployment methods, 285–307
Deployment Reports, 295, 303, 305
Description policy, 99
Description property, 350
designers, 6, 219–223
Destination Path property, 305
developers, benefits of VSTS for, 2, 7
    Class Designer and, 311
development, 2
DiffDoc.exe tool, 95
dimensions (data warehouse schema), 177
dir command, 102
DisplayHelp policy, 99
distributed system designers, 219, 220–223
    benefits of, 221
    locating, 224
.dll files, 28
DMZs (demilitarized zones), 269, 272
document libraries, 28
documents, 29
DSL (Domain-Specific Language), 6, 221
.dwp files, 28

E

e-mailing
    project alert messages, 141
    queries, 127
Edit policy, 99
Effort Tracking (sample application), 10, 20
    deployment diagram for, 297
    Deployment Report for, 305
    Logical Datacenter diagram for, 281
    reverse-engineering applications and, 251
    web service diagram and, 314
elapsed time, 404
endpoint notation, 245
endpoint prototypes, 224, 268
endpoints, 259, 268
    constraints on, 277
enumeration properties, 322
enumerations, adding to class diagrams, 321

equality testing, 340
Error Resolution property, 305
errors
    application diagrams and, 253
    data source binding and, 172
    viewing in Build Detail Report, 206
Errors Only property, 305
Errors table, 493
Evaluate policy, 99
event properties, 327
Evolutionary Prototyping method, 26
Excel (Microsoft)
    data mining and, 182–189
    project management and, 115–118
exception path testing, 341
exception tests, 364–367
exclusive allocations, 405
exclusive bytes allocated, 405
exclusive information, 404
ExpectedException attribute, 366
explicit deployment method, 285–296
exporting work item types, 146
Extract method, 456
extraction rules, 445, 449, 453–458
Extreme Programming (XP), 342

F

fact tables (data warehouse schema), 175
FactLinks (data warehouse schema), 179
failing tests, 443
field properties, 327
field reference names, 156
fields
    Bug work items and, 133
    Change request work items and, 136
    class diagrams and, 333–335
    Issue work items and, 140
    in reports, moving, 169
    Requirement work items and, 138
    Review work items and, 137
    Risk work items and, 134
    Task work items and, 131
    work item types and, 151
File Name property (classes), 318

File Name property (items), 327
File properties (Source Control Explorer), 62–66
FileName node, 336
files
    labeling versions and, 76
    merging, 83–89
    Pending Changes window and, 70
    version comparisons and, 74
Firefox browser, 485
flow behavior, setting, 276
Folder properties (Source Control Explorer), 62–66
folders
    cloaking, 68
    labeling versions and, 76
Font node, 336
forking, 80
form view, 123
format testing, 341
Full Class Name property, 350
Full Name property, 318
functions, performance reports and, 411–414
FxCop code analysis tool, 7, 377, 387–401
    customizing, 391–401
    running from command line, 392
    warnings and, 388
FxCop rules, 391–401

G

garbage collection, 417
Generic property, 318
get command, 102
GetLookupInfo method, 324
GetNextInterval operation, 181
GetRequestEnumerator method (IEnumerator), 448
GetTask method, 325
GetTasks method, 325
GetWarehouseStatus operation, 181
.gif files, 28
glexport tool, 144
glimport tool, 144

global groups, Team Foundation Server and, 47
global lists, 149–152
graph points, 495
graphs, 493
group permissions, 48
    for projects, 52
groups
    creating, 145
    managing, 50

H

HashCode node, 336
history command, 102
history of file changes, 73
.htm files, 28

I

ID property, 350
IDE version control configuration, 93
IEnumerator interface, 448
IIS (Internet Information Services), importing settings from, 277
images, adding to
    Project Portal, 34
    reports, 170
implementing applications, 233–240
Implements property, 318
implicit constraints, 250, 277
implicit deployment method, 296
importing work item types, 148
Include Binary Files property, 305
Include Content Files property, 305
Include Diagrams property, 305
Include Owners property, 305
Include Source Files property, 305
inclusive allocations, 405
inclusive bytes allocated, 405
inclusive information, 405
infrastructure support, benefits of VSTS for, 2
Inheritance Modifier property (classes), 319
Inheritance Modifier property (items), 327
inheritance relationships, displaying, 330
Inherits property, 319

InstallationInstruction policy, 99
instrumentation, 404, 405, 410
    for ASP.NET applications, 425–428
instrumenting code, 405
integration, 2
Integration services operational data store, 173
interfaces, 327–330
    deleting, 330
Internet Information Services (IIS), importing settings from, 277
Introspection SDK, 394
Issue work items, 140
Issues and Blocked Work Items report, 164
ITaskService interface, 328
items. *See* work items
Iteration property, 350
iterations, 32, 112
IWarehouseAdapter interface, 174

K

Kelly, Kevinch, 121

L

label command, 102
Label permission, 65
labeling versions, 76
language codes, 486
languages
    Report Definition Language, 161
    Work Item Query Language, 125, 128
    Work Item Type Definition, 142
LaPlante, Rick, 222
LDD (Logical Datacenter Designer), 255, 266–283
.ldd (logical datacenter diagrams), 221, 285
    creating, 267–283
.lddprototype files, 268
life cycle, distributed system designers and, 221
lifetime information, 417
links, adding to items, 109, 124

lists, 28
    configuring, in Excel, 117
    creating in Excel, 116
    working with, 36
load pattern, 479
Load Test Detail report, 164
Load Test Summary report, 164
Load Test window, 488
Load Test wizard, 477–487
load tests, 9, 471–495
    analyzing results, 491–495
    creating/configuring, 477–487
    naming, 477
    performance profiles for, 421
localtestrun.testrunconfig file, 355
lock command, 102
Lock permission, 65
locking error, 253
Logical Datacenter Designer (LDD), 6, 220, 255, 266–283
    Toolbox object for, 268
logical datacenter diagrams (.ldd), 285
    creating, 267–283
logical server prototypes, 268

M

Macroscope template, 25
manifes.xml file, 28
Manipulate security settings permission, 65
Manning, James, 95
manual testing, 9, 373
    Test View window and, 350
McConnell, Steve, 378
MDA (Model Driven Architecture), 6, 221
@Me query macro, 128
merge command, 102
Merge Tool, 86
merges command, 102
merging files, 83–89
    configuring, 89
message-centric approach, 219
method properties, 327

methods
    adding to class diagrams, 324–327
    deleted in Class Designer, 326
    policies and, 99
    reordering parameters of, 326
Microsoft
    Class Designer and, 313
    Excel, 115–118, 182–189
Microsoft namespace, 156
Microsoft Project, 105–115
Model Driven Architecture (MDA), 6, 221
MSBuild, 214
MSF for Agile Software Development.
        See Agile process template
MSF for CMMI Process Improvement.
        See CMMI process template
MSFAgile.stp, 27
MSFFormal.stp, 27
MSTest, 375
MyDatabase sample database, 226–231, 239
MyWebApp sample web application, 241
MyWebService sample web service, 227–241

N

Name property (classes), 319
Name property (items), 327
Namespace property, 350
namespaces, predefined, 156
naming conventions
    for field reference names, 157
        FxCop and, 391, 393
    for test files, 346
    for test methods, 347
nesting systems, 262
network mix, load testing and, 482, 486
New Member Location property, 319
New property, 327
nightly builds, benefits of, 197
Non-runnable property, 350
notifications (alerts), 28
Notify operation, 181
NotImplementedException, 326

O

object allocation information, 416
object lifetime information, 417
object relationships, displaying, 330
OLAP databases, 172
Opera browser, 485
operational data stores, 173, 180
operations, viewing in System Designer, 264
ordered tests, 353
Overwrite Files Action property, 305
Owner property, 350

P

parameters, reordering, 326
passing tests, 443
passwords, enumerations and, 322
Pending Changes window, 70
performance analysis, 8, 403–430
Performance Explorer, 409, 418
Performance Monitor (Windows), 403
performance reports, 409–418
performance testing, code coverage and, 357
Performance Wizard, 407, 421
perimeter network, 269
permission command, 102
permissions
    for areas, 54
    for files/folders, 65
    for groups, 48
    for projects, 52
picture libraries, 28
plugins, 94, 459
policies
    creating, 95–100
    Pending Changes window and, 71
Position node, 336
Post attribute, 385
pragma directives, 383
Pre attribute, 385
predefined constraints, 250, 277
predefined queries, 125
PREfast checks, list of, 379

PREfast code analysis tool, 8, 341 377, 378–387
   annotating code and, 385
   warnings and, 379–385
Priority property, 350
probes, 405
process guidance, 23
   customizing, 43
process templates, 25, 125, 131. *See also* Agile process template; CMMI process template
   architecture of, 37
   customizing, 36–43
   project planning and, 18
ProcessTemplate.xml, 38–41
production applications, performance profiles for, 422–429
production database, 368
profiling, 421–429
Project Administrators group, 52
project alerts, 32, 141
Project Area property, 350
project management, 103–120
project managers, benefits of VSTS for, 2
Project Portal, 5, 26
   customizing, 32–36
Project property, 350
@Project query macro, 128
Project Relative Path property, 350
project schedules, creating in Microsoft Project, 106
Project Velocity report, 164
projects, 17–57
   configuring, 90–93
   creating, 20
   managing security for, 52
   planning, 17–19
   project management for, 103–120
properties
   adding to class diagrams, 333–335
   QueryString parameter, 439
   recorded web test, 438
   request node, 438
   viewing, 317

properties command, 102
property properties, 327
Property Signature property, 327
provider endpoints, 245
proxy endpoints, 260
publishing work items, 108, 115
PublishOnly setting, 115

Q

Quality Indicators report, 164
queries, 125–129
   creating, 126
   predefined, 125
query macros, 128
query view, 123, 125–129
QueryString parameter properties, 439

R

Reactivations report, 164
Read permission, 65
Readers group, 53
recorded web test properties, 438
recorded web tests, 434–447
.rdl filename extension, 161, 168
refactoring interfaces, 328
regression testing, 339
Regressions report, 164
Reinitialize operation, 182
Related Work Items report, 164
relational data warehouses, 172
release.txt file, 206
Remaining Work report, 164
Remarks property (classes), 319
Remarks property (items), 327
rename command, 102
renaming work item types, 146
Report Builder, 161
report definition
   extracting/adding to projects, 168
   modified, saving, 170
Report Definition Language, 161
Report Designer, 161, 166
reportable option, 182

reporting (Team Foundation), 5, 30, 159–196
    adding reports to Project Portal, 35
    customizing reports and, 166–172
    deploying/viewing reports and, 171
    life cycle of, 161
    predefined reports and, 162, 165
    project planning and, 19
reports, about deployments, 295, 303, 305
request node properties, 438
Required property, 454
Requirement work items, 138
Requirements Detail report, 164
Requirements Test History and Overview
        report, 164
Rerun link, 360
resolve command, 102
resolving conflicts, 85
resources for further reading, 100
    application diagram troubleshooting, 253
    code, costs and, 378
    configuring tools, 95
    default system, 296
    garbage collection, 418
    header field values, 485
    language codes, 486
    MSTest, 376
    project alerts, 32
    test properties, 353
    test-driven development, 342
    tf.exe tool, 101
    UML, 313
    VSTS command-line tools, 423
    yield statement, 449
results details (Build Detail Report), 206
results view, 123, 129
retrieving versions, 78
return on investment (ROI), VSTS and, 3
Returns property, 327
reverse-engineering, for applications, 251
Review work items, 137
Revise other users' changes permission, 65
Richter, Jeffrey, 418
Risk work items, 134
ROI (return on investment), VSTS and, 3

roles, project planning and, 18
rule file, 397–401
Run icon, 360
Run operation, 182
run settings, 484
running unit tests, 359–367
RUP template, 25

S

sample applications
    Effort Tracking. *See* Effort Tracking
    MyDatabase sample database and,
        226–231, 239
    MyWebApp, 241
    MyWebService sample web service and,
        227–241
    weather-reporting web service, 232, 242
sampling, 404, 407, 410
    for ASP.NET applications, 428
SaveTask method, 325
SCE (Source Control Explorer), 31, 61–66
    displaying deleted items in, 95
Scenario Detail report, 165
scripts, setup/cleanup for, 357
Scrum template, 25
SD (System Designer), 220
.sd (system diagrams), 221, 255–263, 285
.sdm (application definitions), 221, 271, 286
SDLC (Software Development Lifecycle), 26
SDM (System Definition Model), 6, 220, 256,
        286
security
    managing for Team Foundation Server,
        45–56
    project planning and, 18
    TFVC and, 64
Seemann, Jochen, 222
SEI (Software Engineering Institute), 4
servers
    binding applications to
        explicit model, 289
        implicit model, 299
    command-line tools for, 497
    constraints/settings for, 276

Logical Datacenter Designer for, 266–283
zones and, 272
Service Accounts global group, 47
Service class, 315
    adding methods to, 324
service-oriented architecture (SOA), 462
ServiceTest class, 348
ServiceTest file, 346
settings
    for application designs, 249
    for deployments, 303
    importing from IIS, 277
    overriding, 265
    for servers, 276
    viewing in System Designer, 264
    for zones, 271
setup/cleanup scripts, 357
SharePoint custom template files, 27
shelve command, 102
shelvesets/shelving changes, 82
    branching and, 80
SOA (service-oriented architecture), 462
Software Development Lifecycle (SDLC), 26
Software Engineering Institute (SEI), 4
software engineering methodologies, 26
Software Factories, 222
Solution property, 351
solutions, creating, 68
Source Control Explorer (SCE), 31, 61–66
    displaying deleted items in, 95
source control providers, list of available, 94
Spiral method, 26
SQL Server Analysis Services (SSAS), 160
SQL Server Business Intelligence platform, 159
SQL Server Integration Services (SSIS), 160
SQL Server Reporting Services. *See* SSRS
SSAS (SQL Server Analysis Services), 160
SSIS (SQL Server Integration Services), 160
SSRS (SQL Server Reporting Services), 5, 159
    predefined reports and, 162–165
SSRS reports, 30
SSRS security, 46, 56

stakeholders, benefits of VSTS for, 2
star schemas, 174
static code analysis, 377–401
Static property, 327
status command, 102
step loads, 479
strcpy function, 381
strcpy_s function, 381
stress testing, 471
structure properties, 318
structures, adding to class diagrams, 323
StyleVision 2005 (Altova), 466
Summary property (classes), 319
Summary property (items), 327
SuppressMessage attribute, 390
synchronization alert, 253, 258
System Definition Model (SDM), 6, 220, 256, 286
System Designer (SD), 6, 220, 255–266
    Toolbox objects for, 260
system diagrams (.sd), 255–263, 285
    nesting systems and, 262
system endpoints, 260
System namespace, 156
systems, defined, 255, 256

■T

tables of data, 493
Target folder, 420
target options, 420
Task structure, 323
Task work items, 131
tasks. *See* work items
Team Build Browser, 208
Team Build operational data store, 173, 180
Team Edition for Software Architects, 5
Team Edition for Software Developers, 7
Team Edition for Software Testers, 8
Team Explorer, 24
Team Explorer window, work items and, 121
Team Foundation, 4
Team Foundation Administrators global group, 47
Team Foundation Administrators group, 53

Team Foundation Build, 5, 30, 197–215
    customizing, 211
Team Foundation Data Warehouse. *See* Data
        Warehouse
Team Foundation Licensed Users global
        group, 48
Team Foundation Proxy Server (TFPS),
        version control configuration and, 94
Team Foundation Server
    build details published to, 209
    connecting to, 19
    data warehouse schema and, 174, 180
    deleting work items and, 145
    global groups and, 47
    managing security for, 45–56
    version control configuration and, 94
Team Foundation Valid Users global
        group, 47
Team Foundation Valid Users group, 53
Team Foundation version control. *See* TFVC
team members
    adding to groups, 145
    modifying Assign To field and, 145–149
team projects. *See* projects
team reporting. *See* reporting (Team
        Foundation)
test classes, 348
test code generation configuration options,
        344
test database, building, 367
Test Enabled property, 351
Test Manager, 8, 351–353
    data-driven testing and, 370
test methods, 346, 358
test mix, load testing and, 478
Test Name property, 351
test options, 439
test properties, 350, 353
Test Results window, 360
test results, 465–469
Test Run Failed link, 360

test runs, 355–367
    configuring, 355–359, 476
    deleting, 360
    viewing information about, 360
Test Storage property, 351
test timeouts, 357
Test Type property, 351
Test View window, 349
    vs. Test Manager window, 351
test-driven development, 342
TestContext class, 348, 367
testers, benefits of VSTS for, 2, 8
testing, 2, 8
    application performance, 403–430
        options for, 418
        running tests, 407
        understanding reports, 409–418
    continuous integration, 214
    load, 471–495
    unit. *See* unit testing
    web. *See* web testing
testing attributes, 348, 357
testing policy, 92
TestProperty attribute, 353
TestRun node, 466
Tests Failing With Active Bugs report, 165
Tests Failing Without Active Bugs report, 164
tests lists, creating, 352
Tests Passing with Active Bugs report, 164
tests results, viewing in Build Detail Report,
        206
tf.exe tool, 101
TFPS (Team Foundation Proxy Server),
        version control configuration and, 94
tfsbuild.exe tool, 213
TFSFieldMapping tool, 112
TfsOlapReportDs data source, 169
TfsReportDS data source, 169
TFVC (Team Foundation Version Control), 4,
        31, 59–102
    command-line access for, 101
    configuring, 89–95

labeling versions and, 76
migrations from Visual SourceSafe and, 100
project management and, 103
project planning and, 18
retrieving versions and, 78
think times, 477
Threshold counter, 493
@Today query macro, 128
@Today-1 query macro, 128
@Today-30 query macro, 128
@Today-7 query macro, 128
Tool Artifact Display Url table (data warehouse schema), 180
tools
   adminpak.msi, 46
   Association, 332
   authoring, 161
   code analysis, 377–401
   command-line, 422, 497
   integrating with VSTS, 3
   MSBuild, 214
   MSTest, 375
   performance, 403–430
   permissions management and, 50
   Project Portal. *See* Project Portal
   specifying your own, 95
   tfsbuild.exe, 213
   TFSFieldMapping, 112
   Toolbox objects
      for Application Designer, 224
      for Logical Datacenter Designer, 268
      for System Designer, 260
   Web Test, 462
   web testing, 433–469
   for work item type customization, 144
   XML development, 466
trace, 405
transition events, 405
Triage report, 164
triage view, 123, 129
trial deployment, 296
troubleshooting applications, 253
.trx files, 463

Type policy, 99
Type property, 327
TypeDescription policy, 99
TypeIdentifier node, 336

U

UI (user interface), creating for weather-reporting web service, 242
UML (Unified Modeling Language), 222, 313
Unblock operation, 182
undelete command, 102
undo command, 102
Undo other users' changes permission, 65
Unified Modeling Language (UML), 222, 313
Unit Test Wizard, 345
unit testing, 7, 339–376
   creating tests and, 342–345
   manual, 373
   planning, 339–342
   performance profiles for, 421
   running tests and, 359–367
unlabel command, 102
Unlock other users' changes permission, 65
Unplanned Work report, 164
unshelve command, 102
user interface (UI), creating for weather-reporting web service, 242
user-defined constraints, 250, 277

V

Validate method, 459
ValidateUser method, 324
   code coverage statistics for, 362
   exception test for, 365
   test table for, 367
ValidateUserExceptionTest method, 366
ValidateUserTest method, 353, 358
   running unit tests and, 359
validating
   deployment diagram implementations, 291, 301
   new work item types, 148
validation rules, 443, 445, 449, 457
   run settings and, 484
ValidationRule class, 459

Value property, 327
VB, Class Designer and, 312
VB Powertoy, 328
version comparisons, 74
Version Control operational data store, 173, 180
version control. *See* TFVC
view command, 102
View Results icon, 129
Visio, 6, 313
Visual SourceSafe. *See* VSS
Visual Studio Integration Partners (VSIP), 10
Visual Studio Team System. *See* VSTS
<VALIDUSER /> tag, 145
VSInstr tool, 423
VSIP (Visual Studio Integration Partners), 10
.vsmdi files, 92
VSPerfClrEnv tool, 423
VSPerfCmd tool, 423
VSPerfMon tool, 423
VSPerfReport tool, 423
VSS (Visual SourceSafe), 4, 59
   changesets and, 72
   migrations to TFVC and, 100
VSTS (Visual Studio Team System)
   areas of, 2
   benefits of, 2–9
   components of, 25–36

W

warehouse adapters, 174
warnings, viewing in Build Detail Report, 206
Waterfall method, 26
weather-reporting web service (sample application), 232
   UI for, 242
web applications, adding to applications, 240–244
web pages, UI and, 242
web parts, 28, 33
Web Service Definition Language (WSDL), 219, 225, 247
Web Service Details window, 264
web service diagrams, creating, 315

web service endpoints, 260
web services
   connecting to database, 228
   exceptions and, 366
   operations for, defining, 232
   testing, 238, 462–465
   web service component, for sample application, 227
   web service endpoints, adding to, 247
web sites
   domain-specific framework tools, 6
   gotdotnet, 7
   VSIP, 10
web test plugins, 459–462
web test request plugins, 459
Web Test settings, 358
Web Test tool, 462
web testing, 9, 433–469
   data-driven, 443
   data-driven access options for, 445
   load testing and, 472
   passing/failing tests and, 443
   performance profiles for, 421
   recording/running web tests and, 434–447
   test options for, 439
   web services testing and, 462–465
WebTest class, 456
WebTestResults node, 466
Windows applications, performance profiles for, 423
Windows Forms, testing and, 8
Windows Performance Monitor, 403
Windows Server 2003 Administration Tools Pack, 46
Windows services, performance profiles for, 423
Windows SharePoint custom template files, 27
.wiq files, 128
WIQL (Work Item Query Language), 125
   query macros and, 128
WIT. *See* work item tracking
WITD (Work Item Type Definition), 142
witexport tool, 144

witfields tool, 144
witimport tool, 144
Work Item Query Language (WIQL), 125
    query macros and, 128
work item tracking (Team Foundation), 5, 29, 121–157
Work Item Tracking operational data store, 173, 180
Work Item Type Definition (WITD), 142
work item types, 29, 130–140
    creating, 152–156
    customizing, 144–157
    project planning and, 18
work items, 29, 121–157
    adding to class diagrams, 320–327
    creating/managing, 122
    deleting from projects, 145
    options for working with, 122
    Pending Changes window and, 71
    project alerts for, configuring, 141
    publishing, 108, 115
    PublishOnly setting and, 115
    retrieving versions and, 78
    views of, 123–130
    working with
        in Microsoft Project, 107
        in VSTS, 119
work items policy, 93
Work Items report, 164
Work Items with Tasks report, 164
Work Items with Test Results report, 164
WorkItemsAre table, 144
WorkItemsAreUsed view, 144
WorkItemsWere table, 144
WorkItemsWereUsed view, 144
WorkItemTypeDefinition.xsd, 142
workspace command, 102
workspaces, 66
WSDL (Web Service Definition Language), 219, 225, 247
.wsdl files, 225, 247
WSS security, 46, 55

X

XML Schema (XSD), 466
XMLSpy 2005 (Altova), 466
XP (Extreme Programming), 342
XSD (XML Schema), 466

Y

yield statement, 449

Z

zone endpoints, 273
zones, 28, 269–277
    connecting servers to, 274
    placing servers within, 272

FIND IT FAST
with the Apress SuperIndex™

Quickly Find Out What the Experts Know

Leading by innovation, Apress now offers you its *SuperIndex*™, a turbocharged companion to the fine index in this book. The Apress *SuperIndex*™ is a keyword and phrase-enabled search tool that lets you search through the entire Apress library. Powered by dtSearch™, it delivers results instantly.

Instead of paging through a book or a PDF, you can electronically access the topic of your choice from a vast array of Apress titles. The Apress *SuperIndex*™ is the perfect tool to find critical snippets of code or an obscure reference. The Apress *SuperIndex*™ enables all users to harness essential information and data from the best minds in technology.

No registration is required, and the Apress *SuperIndex*™ is free to use.

- ❶ Thorough and comprehensive searches of over 300 titles
- ❷ No registration required
- ❸ Instantaneous results
- ❹ A single destination to find what you need
- ❺ Engineered for speed and accuracy
- ❻ Will spare your time, application, and anxiety level

Search now: *http://superindex.apress.com*

You Need the Companion eBook

Your purchase of this book entitles you to buy the companion PDF-version eBook for only $10. Take the weightless companion with you anywhere.

We believe this Apress title will prove so indispensable that you'll want to carry it with you everywhere, which is why we are offering the companion eBook (in PDF format) for $10 to customers who purchase this book now. Convenient and fully searchable, the PDF version of any content-rich, page-heavy Apress book makes a valuable addition to your programming library. You can easily find and copy code—or perform examples by quickly toggling between instructions and the application. Even simultaneously tackling a donut, diet soda, and complex code becomes simplified with hands-free eBooks!

Once you purchase your book, getting the $10 companion eBook is simple:

1. Visit **www.apress.com/promo/tendollars/**.

2. Complete a basic registration form to receive a randomly generated question about this title.

3. Answer the question correctly in 60 seconds, and you will receive a promotional code to redeem for the $10.00 eBook.

2560 Ninth Street • Suite 219 • Berkeley, CA 94710

eBookshop

THE EXPERT'S VOICE™

All Apress eBooks subject to copyright protection. No part may be reproduced or transmitted in any form or by any means, electronic or mechanical, including photocopying, recording, or by any information storage or retrieval system, without the prior written permission of the copyright owner and the publisher. The purchaser may print the work in full or in part for their own noncommercial use. The purchaser may place the eBook title on any of their personal computers for their own personal reading and reference.

Offer valid through 11/2006.

forums.apress.com
FOR PROFESSIONALS BY PROFESSIONALS™

JOIN THE APRESS FORUMS AND BE PART OF OUR COMMUNITY. You'll find discussions that cover topics of interest to IT professionals, programmers, and enthusiasts just like you. If you post a query to one of our forums, you can expect that some of the best minds in the business—especially Apress authors, who all write with *The Expert's Voice™*—will chime in to help you. Why not aim to become one of our most valuable participants (MVPs) and win cool stuff? Here's a sampling of what you'll find:

DATABASES
Data drives everything.
Share information, exchange ideas, and discuss any database programming or administration issues.

INTERNET TECHNOLOGIES AND NETWORKING
Try living without plumbing (and eventually IPv6).
Talk about networking topics including protocols, design, administration, wireless, wired, storage, backup, certifications, trends, and new technologies.

JAVA
We've come a long way from the old Oak tree.
Hang out and discuss Java in whatever flavor you choose: J2SE, J2EE, J2ME, Jakarta, and so on.

MAC OS X
All about the Zen of OS X.
OS X is both the present and the future for Mac apps. Make suggestions, offer up ideas, or boast about your new hardware.

OPEN SOURCE
Source code is good; understanding (open) source is better.
Discuss open source technologies and related topics such as PHP, MySQL, Linux, Perl, Apache, Python, and more.

PROGRAMMING/BUSINESS
Unfortunately, it is.
Talk about the Apress line of books that cover software methodology, best practices, and how programmers interact with the "suits."

WEB DEVELOPMENT/DESIGN
Ugly doesn't cut it anymore, and CGI is absurd.
Help is in sight for your site. Find design solutions for your projects and get ideas for building an interactive Web site.

SECURITY
Lots of bad guys out there—the good guys need help.
Discuss computer and network security issues here. Just don't let anyone else know the answers!

TECHNOLOGY IN ACTION
Cool things. Fun things.
It's after hours. It's time to play. Whether you're into LEGO® MINDSTORMS™ or turning an old PC into a DVR, this is where technology turns into fun.

WINDOWS
No defenestration here.
Ask questions about all aspects of Windows programming, get help on Microsoft technologies covered in Apress books, or provide feedback on any Apress Windows book.

HOW TO PARTICIPATE:
Go to the Apress Forums site at **http://forums.apress.com/**.
Click the New User link.